British History in

General Editor: J

201478833

David Powell   *The Edwardian Crisis: Britain, 1901–1914*
Richard Rex   *Henry VIII and the English Reformation (2nd edn)*
Matthew Roberts   *Political Movements in Urban England, 1832–1914*
David Scott   *Politics and War in the Three Stuart Kingdoms, 1637–49*
G. R. Searle   *The Liberal Party: Triumph and Disintegration, 1886–1929 (2nd edn)*
John Stuart Shaw   *The Political History of Eighteenth-Century Scotland*
George Southcombe & Grant Tapsell   *Restoration Politics, Religion and Culture:*
Britain and Ireland, 1600–1714
W. M. Spellman   *John Locke*
William Stafford   *John Stuart Mill*
Robert Stewart   *Party and Politics 1830–1852*
Alan Sykes   *The Radical Right in Britain*
Bruce Webster   *Medieval Scotland*
Ann Williams   *Kingship and Government in Pre-Conquest England*
Ian S. Wood   *Churchill*
John W. Young   *Britain and European Unity, 1945–99 (2nd edn)*
Michael B. Young   *Charles I*
Paul Ziegler   *Palmerston*

Please note that a sister series, Social History in Perspective, is available covering
the key topics in social and cultural history.

British History in Perspective
Series Standing Order
ISBN 978–0–333–71356–3 hardcover
ISBN 978–0–333–69331–5 paperback

You can receive future titles in this series as they are published by placing a
standing order. Please contact your bookseller or, in case of difficulty, write to
the address below with your name and address, the title of the series and
one of the ISBNs quoted above.

Customer Services Department, Macmillan Distribution Ltd,
Houndmills, Basingstoke, Hampshire, RG21 6XS, UK

Britain and the Seventy Years War, 1744–1815

Enlightenment, Revolution and Empire

Anthony Page

First published 2015 by
PALGRAVE

Palgrave in the UK is an imprint of Macmillan Publishers Limited, registered in England, company number 785998, of 4 Crinan Street, London N1 9XW.

Palgrave Macmillan in the US is a division of St Martin's Press LLC, 175 Fifth Avenue, New York, NY 10010.

Palgrave is a global imprint of the above companies and is represented throughout the world.

Palgrave® and Macmillan® are registered trademarks in the United States, the United Kingdom, Europe and other countries

ISBN: 978–0–230–57769–5 hardback
ISBN: 978–0–230–57770–1 paperback

This book is printed on paper suitable for recycling and made from fully managed and sustained forest sources. Logging, pulping and manufacturing processes are expected to conform to the environmental regulations of the country of origin.

A catalogue record for this book is available from the British Library.

A catalog record for this book is available from the Library of Congress.

Printed in China.

For Damian X. Powell

Contents

Preface

This book argues that between the battles of Fontenoy in 1745 and Waterloo in 1815 Britain fought a 'Seventy Years War' with France. In hindsight, many view the British as inevitable imperialists, confidently building toward their global empire of the nineteenth century. In reality, eighteenth-century Britons frequently fretted about the threat of invasion, military weakness, possible financial collapse and potential revolution. Historical developments only look inevitable in hindsight and with the aid of the social sciences. A combination of people, policies and contingent events forged a winding path to the unexpected post-1815 *Pax Britannica*.

This book has been written on Australia's island state, Tasmania, which was once called Van Diemen's Land and was among the most distant of Britain's colonies. As Australia is positioning itself at the start of 'The Asian Century', the nature and consequences of British settlement continue to be a subject of 'culture wars' in our public debate. It is debate, however, that on all sides often reflects limited knowledge of developments in British history. Australians often say 'England' when they mean 'Britain'. Thus, even an excellent essay by David Malouf was titled *Made in England: Australia's British Inheritance* (2003). No modern nation was more 'Made in Britain' than Australia. All around us are names of people and places from across Wales, Scotland and Ireland, as well as England. While this book focuses on developments in Britain, there are a number of nods toward Australian examples in the text. Many Australian historians study the British Empire and Britishness in Australia. Like my teaching at the University of Tasmania, however, this book is written in the conviction that some history of Britain itself should continue to be done in an Australian accent.

Britain and the Seventy Years War aims to present an argument and synthesis that will be of use to fellow academic historians. Yet it also aims to be accessible to students, and so I have tried to avoid assuming knowledge as much as possible and have repeatedly quoted some particular historical figures who, while interesting and important, may be unknown to many in our postmodern world.

Acknowledgements

Warm thanks to fellow historians who have kindly read and commented on sections of this book: Wilfrid Prest, Damian Powell, Luke Badcock, Martin Fitzpatrick, Grayson Ditchfield, Emma Vincent Macleod, the series editor Jeremy Black and Palgrave's two anonymous referees. I met the amazingly productive, enthusiastic and encouraging Jeremy Black when he visited Tasmania, and this book is in part a response to his question 'What are you tackling at the moment?' Thanks to Jeremiah Dancy and Priya Satia for sharing their important research ahead of publication. Thanks to my students, past and present, for continually reminding me of the joy of history, and especially my 2014 honours class who read and discussed the draft of this book in detail: Andrew Koumoukelis, Anna Reddington, Connaire Bellew, David Huf and Thomas McCormack. And special thanks to Gavin Daly: for over a decade we have been having enjoyable and stimulating discussions about our teaching and research at the University of Tasmania. Among other things, the idea for this book grew out of talking about the writing of his brilliant book, *The British Soldier in the Peninsular War: Encounters with Spain and Portugal, 1808–1814* (Palgrave, 2013).

My colleagues in History and staff in the library at the University of Tasmania have been very supportive in a time of institutional restructuring. Sonya Barker, Felicity Noble and Alec McAulay at Palgrave have been a pleasure to work with and generous in granting extensions of both time and word limit. Maney Publishing have kindly allowed me to reproduce in Chapters 1 and 2 parts of 'The Seventy Years War, 1744–1815, and Britain's Fiscal Naval State', *War and Society*, 34:3 (2015).

As ever, friends and family in Victoria and Tasmania have helped to keep life meaningful and entertaining. I could probably have written this book without Carmen, and our daughters Katherine and Maryanne – but would have been more disengaged from the present and much less happy. Most of this book was written in Launceston and finished after moving to our dream home in Taroona, nestled in the bush between Mt Nelson and the beach, where the Truganini Reserve provides a wonderful place to walk and reflect upon the complexity of British history.

This book is dedicated to my old mate Damian X. Powell – whose daughter Nieve is our goddaughter. Not long after arriving in Adelaide to do a PhD in 1993, I decided to quit, given the dire academic job market, among other things. My mind changed after a talk on the banks of the Torrens River in which Damian insisted I would spend the rest of my life wondering whether I had the ability to write a thesis. Along with a lot of effort and luck, this book and many better things have followed from that change of mind.

Map 1 is a modified version of 'Central Europe 1789', in J.G. Bartholomew, *A Literary and Historical Atlas of Europe* (E. P. Dutton & Co., New. York, 1910), pp. 40–41. Map 2 is a modified version of 'North Atlantic Naval War', in A.W. Ward, G.W. Prothero and Stanley Leathes, eds., *The Cambridge Modern History Atlas* (Cambridge University Press, 1912), map 91.

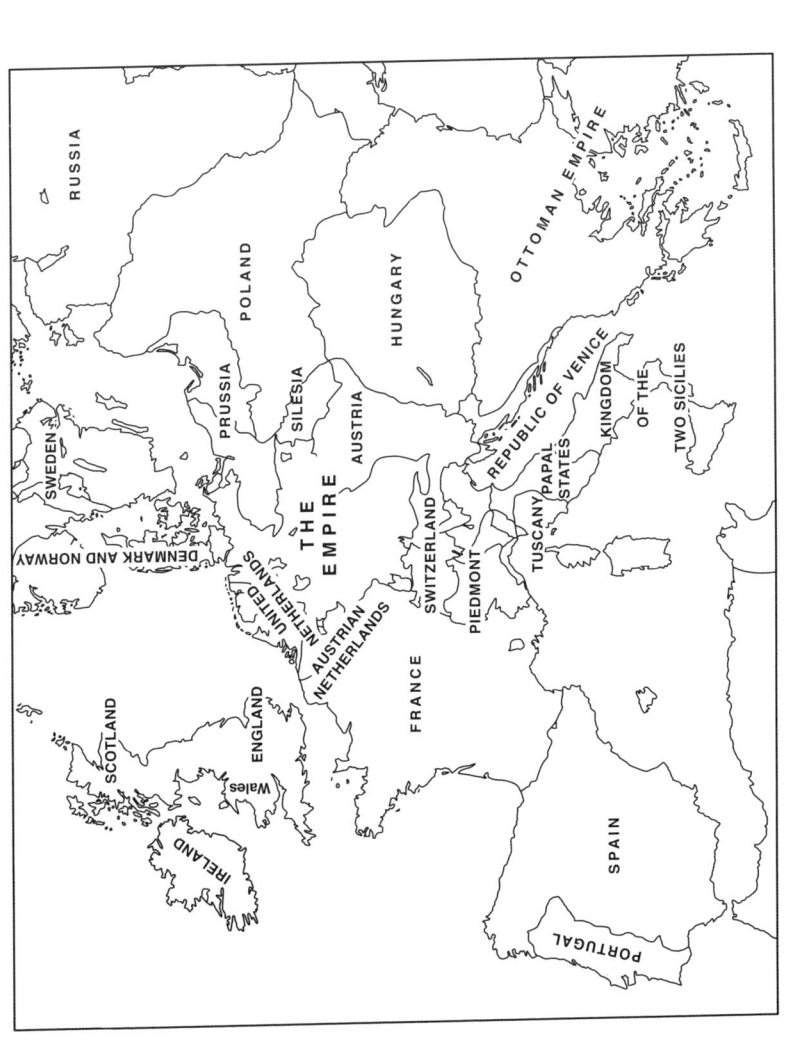

Map 1 Europe 1789

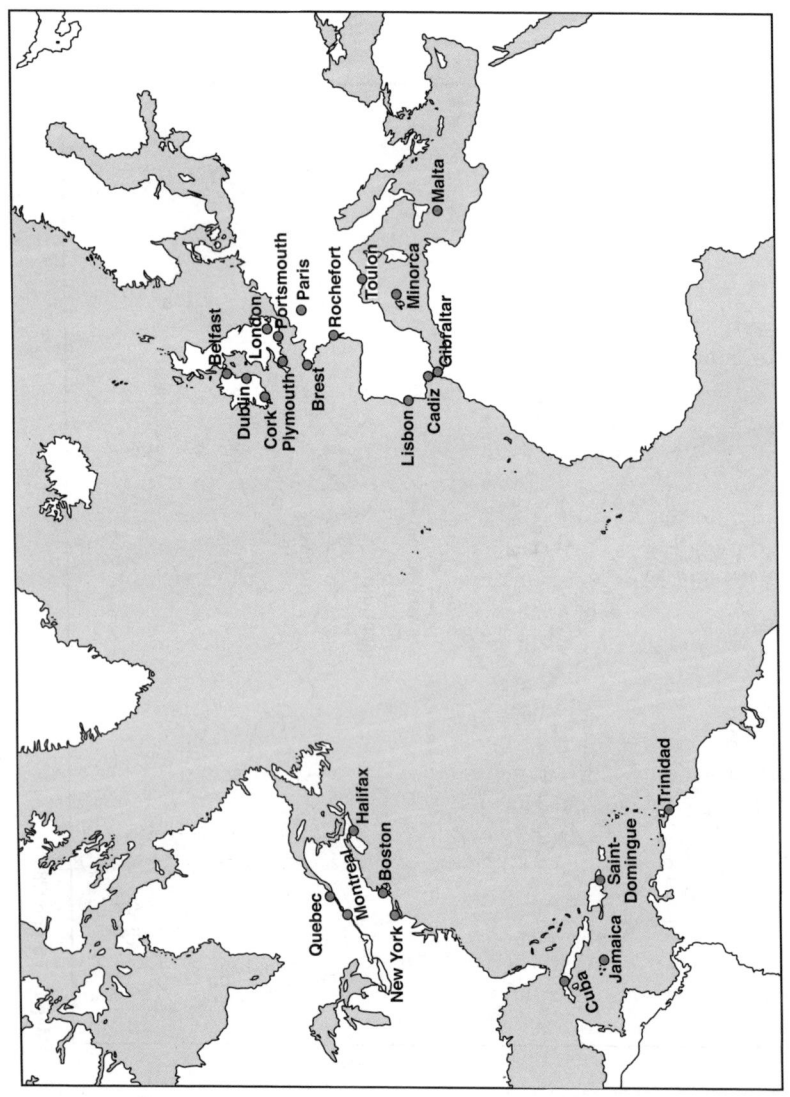

Map 2 North Atlantic

Introduction

In December 1745 Prince Charles Edward Stuart marched into the English town of Derby at the head of an army of Scottish Highlanders. He hoped to restore his family to rule over England, Scotland and Ireland. In 1688 his Catholic grandfather, James II, had fled into exile in the face of a Dutch invasion and Protestant revolution that placed William and Mary on the throne. In 1707 the Scottish elite had abolished their country's own parliament and united with England to form 'Great Britain'. They were encouraged to do this by bribes and the lure of access to English colonial trade, but their main reason had been to strengthen the defence of Britain as a Protestant island in the face of French Catholic aggression.[1] As 'Bonnie Prince Charlie' marched south through Edinburgh and into England he hoped to spark a widespread uprising that, with the aid of a French invasion, would enthrone his Catholic father James III, in place of the Hanoverian George II.

Far from being the 'bare-arsed banditti' of the Hanoverian regime's propaganda, Charles's army of tartan-clad 'Jacobites' appeared fierce, formidable and well-organised – and they were able to raise taxes from the English as they moved south. Only a small government force defended London, 130 miles away, and there were signs that a run on the Bank of England was beginning. Charles wanted to press on and capture the seat of government, but, at a council of war in Derby, Charles's desire to advance on London was overruled by his commanders, who were dismayed by the absence of promised French military support or an English Jacobite uprising. In hindsight, we can see this as the beginning of the end of Jacobitism. Charles and his army retreated into Scotland, harassed by increasingly numerous government forces, and were eventually decimated at the Battle of Culloden in April 1746. This crisis

1

marked the start of seventy years of armed struggle between Britain and France.

Leon Trotsky famously described war as 'a great locomotive of history'. Historians of the twentieth century have subscribed to his view and produced volumes of scholarship on war and society. The situation has been very different in the historiography of eighteenth-century Britain. The field was long dominated by two groups of historians who focused on developments in England: Namierite historians studied the high political machinations of the Whig oligarchy, while Marxist and economic historians debated the nature of the agricultural and industrial revolutions. In the 1980s religion and Enlightenment began to attract some attention.[2] With some notable exceptions, such as Clive Emsley's *British Society and the French Wars, 1793–1815* (1979), the impact of war was neglected. Asa Briggs had to remind his colleagues that 'the way into the nineteenth century led across the battlefield as well as through the cotton mill and the iron foundry'.[3]

War began to attract the attention of eighteenth-century historians in the years around 1990. John Brewer's *The Sinews of Power: War, Money and the English State, 1688–1783* (1988) and Linda Colley's *Britons: Forging the Nation* (1992) were seminal books that raised interest in the economic, political and cultural impact of war in what had come to be called the 'long eighteenth century' 1688–1815. H.V. Bowen's incisive but short *War and Society in Britain 1688–1815* (1998) and a growing number of specialist articles and monographs are highlighting the importance of war in shaping modern Britain. Stephen Conway, in particular, has done much to demonstrate the importance of developments during the mid-century and American wars.[4] Conway's work is an important corrective to the tendency of scholars to focus on the large-scale conflict against the French Revolution and Napoleon.[5] Bigger is not necessarily more important. The unprecedented pressures of the struggle against Napoleon fostered new developments, but these largely extended a process of political, administrative, social and economic evolution that had been occurring in previous decades. The last decades of struggle are now charted in Roger Knight's monumental study *Britain against Napoleon*.[6] Building on such scholarship, *Britain and the Seventy Years War* aims to show the many ways in which Britain was influenced by decades of struggle with a much larger France.

The Jacobite '45 was part of a broader war between Britain and France. A French attempt to invade Britain in February 1744 had been wrecked by a storm in the English Channel. In May 1745 the French king Louis XV won an impressive victory at the Battle of Fontenoy in the Austrian Netherlands. 'The combination of the Jacobite threat and of French success on the Continent in the War of the Austrian Succession', according to Jeremy Black, 'constituted what was truly a mid-eighteenth century crisis'.[7]

This book argues that the '45 occurred at the start of a 'Seventy Years War' between Britain and France. It develops Hamish Scott's suggestion, in *The Birth of a Great Power System, 1740–1815*, that we might best consider the period 1744–1815 'a "Seventy Years War" ... so continuous was the rivalry during these decades and so extensive and frequent the periods of open warfare'.[8] In addition to starting decades of war, the 1740s saw a strengthening of the state and British identity.[9] It is the decade in which 'Rule Britannia' and 'God Save the King' became popular anthems, and a sense of shared Britishness developed in response to the shock Jacobite uprising. The failure of the '45 gave a new sense of security to the Hanoverian regime. While a 'Financial Revolution' occurred during the wars against Louis XIV, the magnitude of its importance in strengthening the British state was not realised until the national debt was refinanced in 1749.[10] With the spread of print culture and reporting of parliamentary debates, heated argument over war fuelled the growth of popular politics. After a long period of stagnation, population growth began to accelerate in the 1740s.[11] And a consumer revolution was under way that would lead to industrial revolution in the latter half of the Seventy Years War.

In the 1740s a united 'British Empire' was seen to have developed. Until mid-century people thought in terms of different 'empires' in different regions, such as 'the British Empire in America', but in 1743 we find reference to 'the British Empire, taking all together as one body'.[12] In contrast to territorial empires of conquest garrisoned by large armies such as those of ancient Rome and modern Russia, Britons saw theirs as an 'empire of the seas' centred on trade – an 'empire of goods' according to one historian.[13] Kathleen Wilson has argued that the emergence of an aggressive popular imperialism was driven by an expanding commercial 'middling sort', who were often involved in colonial trade. Opposition to the perceived corruption, incompetence and Eurocentrism of George II's ministers was a key way in which the growing commercial middling ranks exerted their political voice.[14]

In 1744 the British Empire was scattered and diverse. Ireland was in many ways the first colony. While it was a kingdom under George II with its own parliament, between the Declaratory Act of 1720 and its repeal in 1782 the Irish parliament was wholly subordinate to Westminster. Catholics made up 80% of the population but were subject to severe civil disabilities. On the east coast of North America settler colonies were acting as 'ghost acres' for the British economy in producing food, tobacco, timber and other raw materials. Their rapidly growing populations were becoming important markets for British manufactured goods. At the start of the eighteenth century Britain's colonies in North America had a population of approximately 250,000, of which about 10% were African slaves. By the time they declared independence in 1776 the total figure for the thirteen colonies had risen to around 2.5 million including half a million slaves. Islands in the West Indies such as Jamaica were regarded as the jewels of the empire, with plantations worked by African slaves producing sugar for a growing consumer market in Britain. In the eighteenth century Britain became dominant in the Atlantic slave trade. The triangular trade proved particularly lucrative, with guns and other manufactured goods shipped from Britain to Africa, slaves then carried to the Americas, and ships returning to Britain loaded with plantation produce. Like some other European states, the British had a well-established East India Company, chartered with a monopoly over the growing trade in spices and cloth. The voyage via ship from trading factories in India to ports in Britain was long and dangerous, and this trade remained relatively small scale until the late eighteenth century.

Britain's empire of commerce was regulated by the mercantilist Navigation Acts. Mercantilism was the dominant economic theory in early modern Europe, and dictated that states should capture land and regulate trade in order to increase their wealth. Wealth was seen as rooted in supposedly finite land and population, and so states were locked in competition to acquire more territory at the expense of rivals. Holland was viewed as an economic miracle because the Dutch had pushed back the sea to create land by using dikes and windmills, and had grown rich through maritime trade. In response, from 1651 England passed Navigation Acts that required all trade with its colonies to be carried in English ships. This benefited both English merchants and the state, which could levy duties on trade, including goods re-exported to Europe. While ideas of free trade were advocated in the eighteenth century, they were not fully embraced by the state until the more peaceful nineteenth century when British naval and economic dominance seemed secure.

Pride in the expansion of empire was often linked to anxiety about its nature and impact on Britain. While there was broad enthusiasm for maritime commercial empire, territorial empire was seen as problematic.[15] Educated eighteenth-century Britons were familiar with Roman history and its tale of republican virtue giving way to the rule of emperors over a vast territorial empire, followed by corruption, decline and fall. Britain, the argument ran, must remain an empire of loosely connected trading posts and small settler colonies. Empire was seen as a necessary source of wealth without which Britain could not fund its navy and army.[16] Statesmen, in particular, viewed colonies primarily in terms of their economic and strategic contribution to the defence of Britain. They were usually willing to swap colonies for strategic security concessions in Europe.

The threat of invasion by France loomed during the years 1744–46, 1756–57, 1759, 1779, 1782, 1796–1805, and 1811.[17] This often carried with it the threat of a revolution in the British political system. Down to 1759 French invasion plans were linked to a potential Jacobite uprising. During the French Revolutionary wars there were multiple attempts to organise an invasion of the Atlantic Archipelago, with an expectation of support from British and Irish admirers of French republicanism.[18] On more than one occasion invasion was narrowly prevented by a storm in the English Channel or victory by the Royal Navy.

The twists and turns of the Seventy Years War are charted in Chapter 1. Diplomacy, military effort and the element of good or bad fortune combined to make the final outcome of Anglo-French conflict unpredictable down to the last year. This conflict was rooted in strategic, economic, religious and political differences.

It was widely believed, on both sides of the English Channel, that Britain and France were 'natural and necessary enemies'.[19] Both nations had Atlantic ports, and in the wake of the Spanish, Portuguese and Dutch, both were late to join the competition for colonies. Added to imperial and economic rivalry, they were divided by religion and political systems. Louis XIV (1638–1715) had promoted himself as Europe's leading Catholic monarch and in 1685 tried to forcefully convert France's Protestant Huguenots, causing thousands of refugees to flee, with many bringing their tales of persecution to England and its colonies. Claiming absolute sovereign power, Louis XIV tried to extend his realm into the Netherlands. If the 'Sun King' ultimately failed to dominate Western Europe, he left his heirs a stunning imperial palace at Versailles that encouraged grand visions.

In contrast, Britain was a fiercely Protestant constitutional monarchy whose politics were entwined with international relations. Conflict over religion and the respective rights of crown and parliament had led to civil war and the execution of Charles I in 1649, followed by a decade of parliamentary republican rule. The monarchy was restored in 1660 when the Stuart heir, Charles II, returned to London. Ongoing tensions between crown and parliament saw the formation of two broad political groups: Tories upheld the principle of divine right monarchy and demanded conformity to the Protestant episcopalian Church of England; Whigs championed the rights of parliament and toleration of nonconformist Protestants. After inheriting the throne in 1685, the openly Catholic James II put Tories in an impossible situation – torn between loyalty to the hereditary monarch and their desire to preserve a Protestant Church of England. Matters came to a head in 1688 after the birth of a son who would be raised a Catholic. James fled into exile when his Protestant daughter Mary and her Dutch husband William of Orange invaded England. Parliament declared the throne vacant and crowned William and Mary, who signed a 'Bill of Rights' recognising the powers of parliament and various rights of the subject. In addition to upholding the established Protestant Church of England, an act was passed granting limited religious toleration to nonconformist Protestants. With Protestantism and parliamentary rights secured, the realm proceeded to support its new Dutch king's struggle against Louis XIV.

Yet for decades to come, the gains of the 'Glorious Revolution' of 1688–89 remained vulnerable to a French backed Jacobite restoration. The lack of a surviving heir to William and Mary, or their successor Queen Anne, raised the prospect of a Catholic James III inheriting the throne. To preserve a Protestant monarchy the Act of Settlement (1701) by-passed fifty hereditary claimants to the throne, owing to their Catholicism, and settled on Sophia of Hanover, a Lutheran granddaughter of James I. The Hanoverian succession was reaffirmed by the Act of Union in 1707, which abolished the Scottish parliament and created a Great Britain centred on the Crown and Parliament at Westminster. When Queen Anne died in 1714, Sophia's Protestant German son travelled to London to be crowned King George I. As Hannah Smith has noted, installing a monarch with such a dubious hereditary claim to the throne by act of parliament was 'unprecedented in the history of the British Isles'.[20]

Owing his crown to an act of parliament, the Hanoverian George I soon faced Jacobite uprisings in Scotland and the north of England. Many Tories were sympathetic to the young James Stuart's claim to the throne, while Whigs solidly supported the new German monarch.

The 1715 Jacobite uprising was repressed and the Tories found themselves condemned to the opposition benches. Hence the decades down to 1760 have become known as the 'Whig Ascendancy'. Throughout those years, however, Whigs worried about the possibility of a Jacobite uprising, backed by military aid from France or Spain.

In developing a robust constitutional monarchy the British went against the European trend in a century traditionally called the 'Age of Absolutism'. Measuring themselves against the proclaimed absolute power of the Bourbon kings of France, many monarchs sought to increase their powers at the expense of the traditional rights and liberties of corporate bodies such as churches, representative institutions and aristocracy. Recent scholarship has questioned the extent to which the theory of absolute monarchy became a reality. To a large extent so-called absolute monarchs had to govern via cooperation and conciliation.[21] While the magnificent palace of Versailles was intended to help Louis XIV exert absolute power, to an extent aristocrats turned it into a golden cage for French monarchs in the eighteenth century. In Russia, the coercive westernisation policies of Peter the Great in the early eighteenth century were followed by a long golden age of the Russian nobility. Yet if they had to govern in cooperation with aristocracies, there was nevertheless a growing centralisation of power in monarchs. Down to the eve of the French Revolution absolute monarchy seemed to be on the march as a system of government, with traditional rights and liberties being replaced or eroded by proliferating royal laws and officials. Witness the cases of Prussia under Frederick the Great, Austria under Joseph II and Gustav III's absolutist coup against the Swedish Riksdag in 1772. The British boasted about preserving their religious, legal and parliamentary liberties in an age of absolute monarchy – and were flattered by praise from French Enlightenment thinkers such as Voltaire and Montesquieu.

The British also saw themselves as champions of a balance of power between states. This was depicted as defending the 'liberties of Europe' against the threat of Bourbon 'universal monarchy'. Henry Fielding, the novelist and Whig journalist, declared in 1746 that by fighting France and supporting allies on the continent Britain was resisting a 'scheme of universal monarchy, framed by the house of Bourbon'. According to Colin Jones, a distinguished historian of France, this 'was a familiar British fantasy'.[22] It owed much to memories of the two decades of war against Louis XIV and his efforts to subjugate Western Europe. With the benefit of hindsight, historians can see that, weakened by the wars of the early and mid eighteenth century, France's relative power in Europe declined as new states such as Prussia and Russia emerged in the east. And in the 1740s French strategists began to worry about Britain establishing a 'universal monarchy' of the sea.[23] Aspiring to be like the Roman Empire, the French often equated Britain with Carthage – an unstable, less civilised and aggressive maritime state that threatened the imperial authority, order and advanced civilisation of France. 'England' was described as a home to pirates, assassins, usurpers, perjurers, vultures, brigands, and homicidal monsters.[24]

Contemporary British fears of potential French domination of Western Europe are nevertheless understandable. While some in the early twenty-first century Anglosphere ridicule the French as 'cheese-eating surrender monkeys', this was far from their image in the eighteenth century. France raised large armies led by gallant aristocrats keen for glory. While significantly weakened by Louis XIV's unsuccessful wars, by the 1730s France's economy was recovering. At the end of the eighteenth century the population of France was 30 million – approximately three times that of Britain, and twice that of Austria. The palace of Versailles was designed to overawe foreign ambassadors with the imperial power of French kings. Louis XIV's heirs lacked his ability and determination to become a universal monarch, but still maintained France's pretension to being the dominant kingdom in Western Europe. At the very least, the France of Louis XV aimed, in the words of Cardinal de Bernis, to 'play in Europe that superior role which suits her seniority, dignity and grandeur'.[25] After Louis XVI was overthrown by the revolution that started in 1789, a modern form of universal monarchy was briefly achieved by Napoleon.

Wars were frequent in early modern Europe because it had a relatively high number of competing states and deep religious divisions. A 'military revolution', it has been argued, saw larger states grow at the expense of smaller, and a trend toward bureaucratic centralisation.[26] Growing military needs saw monarchs struggle to extract increasing amounts of tax from their populations. Britain was long neglected by historians of the military revolution because it appeared to have a small state and army constrained by its parliament. Yet this is to underestimate the expense of the Royal Navy and the degree to which parliament acted as an agent of centralisation after the Glorious Revolution of 1688 secured its control over the Crown's finances.

Chapter 2 outlines how Britain developed a fiscal system that could support the world's biggest navy and an imperial army. It is widely assumed that France had a revolution in 1789 because its population was too heavily taxed. In fact the reverse is true, as the French monarchy was brought down by a fiscal crisis caused by inefficient taxation. As France's population was much larger, its government could easily have outspent Britain had it been able to collect the same per capita level of taxation. To be competitive, Britain developed a robust fiscal system that saw rates of taxation and public debt far exceed that of France when measured per head of population. The British state was able to do this because it presided over a relatively unified, dynamic and taxable economy that was linked to a thriving maritime trade. John Brewer described Britain as having developed a 'fiscal-military state' in the decades after the revolution of 1688. Yet given the centrality of the navy to Britain's military performance and expanding empire, it is better to characterise it as having a 'fiscal-naval state'.[27] In addition to defending the island and extending a commercial empire, the fiscal-naval state stimulated the economy in a number of ways that helped foster the world's first industrial revolution.

Chapter 3 shows how British foreign policy was underpinned by the war-fighting capacity of Britain's armed forces. The Royal Navy was central to the defence of Britain, its trade and imperial expansion. In addition to being the biggest navy in the world, it became a relatively efficient organisation, with high-quality manpower and leadership. The creation of a 'Western Squadron' in 1747, tasked with cruising in the approaches to the English Channel, has been described as a revolution in naval strategy.[28] It enabled the Royal Navy to blockade French ports while guarding British merchant ships. Cruising in the stormy Atlantic off the French coast was difficult and dangerous, and only possible at all owing to the high level of skill and logistical support developed by the British navy. The Western Squadron was crucial to Britain gaining naval superiority over France.

Britons had a deep-seated suspicion of soldiers, regarding armies as tools of overbearing monarchs. The demands of the Seventy Years War, however, saw the British army grow in size, professionalism and reputation. Augmented by the increasingly large-scale mobilisation of militia and volunteers, the army proved central to the forging of a British national identity. To a large extent the army was dependent upon the navy for transport and supply, and the two forces had to learn to work together. Amphibious operations were particularly difficult to conduct in the age of wooden sailing ships, but they proved crucial to the success of many British military operations. They were most often successful in periods when the Royal Navy had command of the ocean.

Chapter 4 demonstrates how war was linked with Enlightenment and the rise of evangelical religion. The 'Age of Reason' manifested in different ways in different national contexts.[29] Britain already had many of the goals desired by enlightened reformers on the continent, such as representative government, religious toleration and a free press. A moderate form of Enlightenment was espoused by the British elite as a means of defending the constitution and discouraging religious 'enthusiasm'. To an extent, the British armed forces became agents of moderate Enlightenment values that used reason to bolster social order and promote improvement. The Duke of Wellington, often thought of as a reactionary for his contempt toward the lower classes, was an Enlightenment military officer in the vein of Frederick the Great. Calm, rational and calculating, Wellington employed an Enlightenment approach to war in his fight against the revolutionary forces of France.

The start of the Seventy Years War coincided with the rise of Methodist evangelical Protestantism. While there were obvious tensions between Enlightenment and this new version of religious enthusiasm, there were also points of similarity. Both sought to promote improvements in society and government administration. While a limited number of soldiers and seamen became Methodists, a number of prominent naval officers became evangelicals and vigorously promoted moral and organisational reform. Evangelicalism revitalised and strengthened the identity of Britain as a Protestant nation struggling against a Catholic France that turned revolutionary in the 1790s.

The institutional structure of British politics changed little, but Chapter 5 shows how war fostered the rise of popular politics. In the realm of high politics the cabinet and office of prime minister were strengthened, and the Foxite Whigs pioneered the modern political party. Foreign policy and war were by far the main topics of political discussion, and 'public opinion' played an increasingly important role. Newspapers proliferated and wartime developments were widely debated in press, pamphlet, coffeehouse and tavern. The elder William Pitt returned to power in 1757 in part owing to his wartime popularity. Following this, the increasing organisation of popular politics around 'Wilkes and Liberty', the Association movement of the early 1780s, and in response to the French Revolution were all influenced by the pressures of war. Popular English patriotism was wielded by opponents of government in the mid eighteenth century, but by 1800 a popular British nationalism had become an essential support of the Crown's ministers.

The Battle of Waterloo in 1815 marked the end to any hope that France could dominate the Continent, and the start of one hundred years in which the British consolidated a global empire. With the world's oceans under a *Pax Britannica*, international trade boomed and modern globalisation began. While Europeans visited plenty of violence on other continents as they extended empires around the globe, there was an absence of any 'great war' in Europe until 1914. Britain's first Prime Minister, Robert Walpole, had struggled to preserve peace in the 1720s and 1730s. Had he been resurrected in the nineteenth century he would have been amazed at the change in Anglo-French fortunes.

Chapter 1: The Seventy Years War

Historians have long thought in terms of an eighteenth-century Anglo-French 'Second Hundred Years War' running between 1689 and 1815.[1] Yet there are problems with talking of a Second Hundred Years War that stretches over 125 years. And the conflicts of this period can be better seen in two groups. The Glorious Revolution sparked the Nine Years War/War of English Succession (1689–1697) that was soon followed by the War of Spanish Succession (1702–1713). Britain during these two decades of war with Louis XIV's France continues to attract much scholarly attention.[2] The death of France's Sun King in 1715 was followed by three decades of Anglo-French peace. They were formally allies from 1716 to 1731 – a period in which 'France's navy was practically non-existent'.[3] Indeed, as Jonathan Dull has observed, 'never had Europe seen a period of peace as wide-ranging and long-lasting as that which endured from late 1721 to late 1733'.[4] Thus, in *The Wealth of Nations*, Adam Smith observed that early eighteenth-century 'England had enjoyed a profound peace for about eight-and-twenty years'.[5]

Historians sometimes date one of the periods of warfare 'with France, and allies of France' as 1739–1748, which began with Britain's War of Jenkins' Ear against Spain and merged with the War of the Austrian Succession.[6] Yet direct war between Britain and France was not declared until March 1744. Though the end of the War of the Austrian Succession brought 'a few years of uneasy peace in Europe', in Stephen Conway's words, 'Anglo-French hostilities continued almost unabated elsewhere' until war was again officially declared in 1756.[7] The years following the end of the Seven Years War (1756–1763) saw ongoing rivalry in the Caribbean, India and exploration of the Pacific. Rebellion in Britain's 13 North American Colonies provided France with an opportunity for revenge by providing military assistance to the insurgents. The War of American Independence (1775–83) transformed into another round of open war between France and Britain, with significant consequences for both states. The 1780s proved a decade of tension in which Britain and France backed opposing sides in the Dutch Revolt. In 1789, revolution ended absolute monarchy in France, and the republican regime declared war on Britain in early 1793. There followed more than two decades of intense warfare that ended with defeat of Napoleon at Waterloo in 1815.

From 1744 to 1815 Britain was officially at war with France in 42 of 71 years. If we include the years from 1749–55, when Britain and France were clashing in India and North America, then it was 49 years, or nearly 70% of the period. In addition there were moments of mobilisation such as the gunboat diplomacy over the Bahamas and Gambia 1764–65, the near-war over the Falkland Islands in 1771 and the Dutch Revolt in 1787. And before France entered the American conflict in 1778, it encouraged the Patriots in their War of Independence. Talk of a Second Hundred Years War obscures the intensity of the Seventy Years War.[8]

Eighteenth-century British foreign policy was characterised by a persistent tension between European and colonial aims. The virtues of a 'blue-water' maritime policy were relentlessly championed by parliamentary oppositions and the public. Britain should stay out of European conflicts, it was argued, and rest secure behind the wooden walls of a powerful Royal Navy. 'British liberties' were seen as resting on a combination of commercial prosperity and a small and inexpensive standing army that could not be used by a monarch to coerce parliament. A citizen militia could help defend the island in the event of a successful invasion. The dynastic link to Hanover and desire to preserve a balance of power, however, ensured that the Crown's ministers often controversially pursued diplomatic and military intervention on the Continent.

Historians of British foreign policy in the eighteenth century often discuss the relative merits of maritime and continental strategy. Political historians have tended to depict popular blue-water sentiment as reflecting bigoted Francophobia and ignorance of the realities of European diplomacy.[9] Yet, some note that the popularity of blue water policy set significant limits to what ministers could do in relation to Europe.[10] The popular ideal of a commercial maritime empire has also attracted the attention of cultural historians who have highlighted its role in shaping British national identity.[11]

Several political historians have recently argued forcefully that Europe dominated the minds of ministers. While admitting that 'whole swathes of British public opinion continued to be mesmerized by the prospect of colonial wealth', Brendan Simms argues that, prior to the 1760s, when ministers talked of defending 'The Empire' they tended to be referring to the German Holy Roman Empire rather than overseas.[12] In this view, British foreign policy went through three phases in the course of the Seventy Years War. In the 1740s and 50s ministers such as the Duke of Newcastle worked hard to maintain continental alliances, and were rewarded with victories over France. There followed a period of isolationism from the mid 1760s to mid 1780s, in which Britain was humiliatingly defeated by France and its allies in the American War of Independence. Re-engagement with Europe saw Britain eventually triumph at the end of the French Revolutionary and Napoleonic Wars. While there is merit in this view, it oversimplifies a long period of conflict in which opportunities and constraints were constantly changing. As Jeremy Black has observed, in addition to external criticism Newcastle's diplomatic initiatives in Germany were controversial within the government, as other ministers worried about the expense of subsidies. Withdrawal from Europe to focus on colonial empire made sense in the 1760s. The alliance with Frederick the Great could have ended in disaster as he came very close to being crushed by his continental enemies. In light of Britain's miraculous victories in that war, a focus on consolidating gains and reforming imperial administration made sense.[13]

Amidst debate and disagreement, a few key points can be made. First, while there was debate over the means of achieving it, the security of Britain was the primary concern. Second, while deep engagement with the European balance of power was controversial, there was broad agreement on the importance of those parts of Europe linked to Britain's maritime strength and security. The Baltic Sea had to be guarded as a vital source of naval supplies. Gibraltar and other naval bases in the Mediterranean Sea acted as a shield against the southern French fleet. And the greatest strategic priority was ensuring the Low Countries did not fall under French domination. In particular, the Scheldt Estuary and the port of Antwerp could base an invasion fleet only one day's sail from London. While ministers struggled to justify involvement in German affairs, most Britons could see that certain places around Europe were vital to defence of the blue water around Britain. Third, colonies were viewed primarily in light of their contribution to Britain's strategic security. Colonies provided resources and wealth that enabled Britain to defend itself against a much larger France. The most valued colonies were those that boosted Britain's naval power – those with deep and well-placed harbours being highly prized. Thriving maritime commerce was seen as a vital reservoir of skilled sailors who could be pressed into wartime service in the Royal Navy.

Ministers faced no simple choice between pursuing blue-water or continental commitment. Securing Britain in the face of potential invasion was the top priority, and this required both engagement with Europe and the resources derived from empire. The key question was: how much engagement with Europe? Could Britain defend itself against the undivided attention of France, or did it need a continental ally to tie down a significant proportion of French military resources? Would that happen anyway without costly British involvement in continental alliances? If France did manage to secure peace on the continent, how quickly could it convert resources from its army to naval expansion? And how soon would that navy be able to rival the experience and combat effectiveness of the Royal Navy? Such questions provoked much debate in the eighteenth century and among historians since. In an astute essay, Nicholas Rodger has observed:

> The political nation at large may not have realized it, but a plain choice between military and naval strategy was never in fact available, and it is hard to find a British statesman in power who really thought it was. Real policy was based on distribution of commitments afloat and ashore, aimed at preserving the balance of power in Europe and upsetting it overseas.[14]

Historians have traditionally ignored or downplayed the role of religion in eighteenth-century diplomacy. In the Age of Reason, it is argued, enlightened elites were increasingly scornful of the religious passions that had fuelled wars in the previous two centuries. With the rise of new powers such as Prussia and Russia, European diplomacy increasingly focused on state-building and the pursuit of economic and strategic goals. Among the more striking examples of such conduct is the War of the Austrian Succession, in which Catholic France and Protestant Prussia allied against Catholic Austria backed by Protestant Britain and Hanover. Yet if there was arguably a secularisation of international politics in the eighteenth century, religion nevertheless remained a factor. It has recently been shown how the notion of defending a European

'Protestant Interest' remained an important consideration in the early eighteenth century. The Hanoverians sat on the British throne in place of the Stuarts by virtue of their Protestantism, and loyalist propaganda depicted them as traditional 'Protestant soldier kings'.[15] Periods of alliance with Catholic powers could be explained as temporary expedients to aid in countering the main Catholic monarchical threat at any particular time. In the early eighteenth century, according to Andrew Thompson, 'Britain and Hanover played the role of balancer in the European state system partly to preserve their territorial security but also to ensure that Protestantism survived.'[16] In light of the disruptive impact of Frederick the II's Prussia and the increasingly complex nature of diplomacy, from the 1740s British policy makers focused on *realpolitik* and maintaining the balance of power, with limited consideration for religious factors. The idea of a European Protestant interest nevertheless lived on in public perceptions of war and empire. Thus, British decision-makers had to take some account of anti-Catholic sentiment, and found that at times it could bolster the war effort, as in the late 1750s, when Frederick of Prussia, their new ally, was celebrated as a 'Protestant Hero'.

The War of the Austrian Succession, 1740–1748

After many years of peace, in 1739 Britain declared war on Spain in the War of Jenkins' Ear. Robert Walpole, the first and longest-serving British prime minister, had worked long and hard to avoid becoming embroiled in wars. Under relentless criticism by 'Patriots' in parliament, who were keen on colonial expansion, Walpole reluctantly went to war with Spain. That conflict soon merged into the War of the Austrian Succession.

The War of the Austrian Succession (1740–48) was a messy conflict. It started when, upon inheriting the throne of Prussia, the young Frederick II sought to take advantage of a succession crisis in Austria, and invaded the Habsburg province of Silesia. Upon the death of her father, Emperor Charles VI, Maria Theresa had become Queen of Hungary and ruler of the Austrian territories in the Holy Roman Empire. Traditionally the ruler of Austria was elected as Emperor, but the Salic Law forbade this title to a woman. At the Peace of Utrecht in 1713 a 'Pragmatic Sanction' had been internationally agreed by which a future female heir could become Queen of Hungary, and have her husband elected emperor. Allied with Prussia, France saw an opportunity to take advantage of

Habsburg weakness and supported Charles of Bavaria in his bid for election as Emperor. George II of Britain and Hanover raised a 'Pragmatic Army' and led it into southern Germany with an eye to preventing France from making a decisive military intervention in the struggle between Bavaria and Austria.

George II, leading the Pragmatic Army of almost 40,000 Hanoverian, British and Austrian troops, defeated the French at Dettingen in June 1743. Highly visible during the course of the battle, shouting orders to his troops in a thick German accent, George II was the last British monarch to lead his army into battle in person. A narrow victory that only saved the army from possible annihilation rather than securing a significant strategic advantage, news of Dettingen nevertheless sparked wild celebrations in Britain. However, the victory provided George II's government with only a brief respite from fevered parliamentary and public debate over the extent to which Britain should be involved in German affairs. While George's personal courage at Dettingen was widely praised in Britain, there was also criticism of his decision to dress in the colours of Hanover – one ballad was titled 'The Yellow Sash, or Hanover Beshit'.[17] The volume of pamphlets on foreign policy in 1742–44 was not reached again until the start of the Seven Years War in the mid 1750s.[18] Aside from the celebrations following victory at Dettingen, British involvement in the German conflict proved deeply unpopular.

War was officially declared between Britain and France after a French invasion fleet entered the English Channel in early 1744. The threat passed as a large British fleet gathered in the Channel and a storm damaged the French landing craft assembling at Dunkirk. Having long been under intense criticism for their involvement in the German conflict, government ministers were greatly relieved at the public response to the invasion threat. In the words of one pamphlet, *A Warning to the Whigs, and to Well-Affected Tories* (1744), 'however Englishmen may differ and dislike ... one another, they are unanimous against France, against French Falsehood, French invasion, and a King of French creation'.[19] Intense criticism soon resumed, however, as Louis XV's troops advanced into the Austrian Netherlands. George II's favourite minister, the Secretary of State for the Northern Department ('Northern Secretary') Lord Carteret, came under increasing pressure for his pro-Hanoverian approach and eventually resigned in November 1744. Made Lord Granville, he continued to act as an advisor to the King 'behind the curtain', much to the annoyance of the new 'Broad-Bottom' ministry headed by Henry Pelham.

It was a long-standing strategic principle that England should work to prevent the Low Countries from being occupied by a major enemy such as Spain or France, who might launch an invasion from the many ports in the Netherlands. To that end, during the wars against Louis XIV a series of 'Barrier Treaties' had been signed by which Britain promised to help the Dutch defend fortresses located in the Austrian Netherlands. In the course of 1744 Marshal Saxe, a talented general at the head of Louis XV's army, began to lay siege to the fortresses. While the French were diverted south for a time to counter an Austrian advance into Alsace, an opportunistic Allied counterattack into northern France failed. The campaign began to reveal military weakness on the part of the Dutch and a lack of commitment to defending their Low Country territories on the part of the Austrians.

At Fontenoy in May 1745 Marshal Saxe achieved a hard fought victory over the Allied forces in one of the most significant battles of the eighteenth century. The British and Hanoverian infantry proved valiant, marching though withering flanking fire to break the French centre. While the Duke of Cumberland, George II's favourite son, proved a poor commander of the Allied army, his courage in the battle was widely praised, having personally led 'one of the great infantry advances of the eighteenth century'.[20] Seriously ill, Saxe bit on bullets while rallying his troops for a counterattack, and slumped to his knees before Louis XV at the end of the day. After Fontenoy, Barrier fortresses fell to Saxe one after another, until he had conquered most of the Austrian Netherlands by the end of the year.

From the perspective of the British ministry, 1745 was a good time to make peace. Defeat at Fontenoy was followed by news of a surprise success in North America. In June the gateway to French Canada, the fortress of Louisbourg on Cape Breton, was captured by New England militiamen supported by a small Royal Navy squadron from the West Indies. Patriots were ecstatic, seeing conquest of this strategic American bastion as opening the possibility of easy pickings among French islands in the West Indies, 'by which we might much more effectively distress them, and serve ourselves, than by shewing them our B[ac]k S[i]des in Flanders'.[21] Contrary to such popular opinion, however, the Whig ministry viewed Cape Breton as something to be traded for concessions in Europe during peace negotiations.[22]

The French were not inclined toward peace in 1745, however, as a mortal threat to the Hanoverian regime appeared within Britain. At the end of July news spread that Prince Charles Edward Stuart had landed in Scotland and was gathering support among the Highland clans. George II was in Hanover and did not take the threat seriously, only returning to London at the end of August. By late September attitudes had changed, as Charles had raised a small army, occupied Edinburgh and put a government force to flight at Prestonpans. Horace Walpole, son of the former prime minister, wrote to a friend in Italy:

> The confusion that I have found, and the danger we are in, prevent my talking of anything else ... The clans will not rise for the government ... I look upon Scotland as gone! ... There are two manifestos published, signed Charles, Prince Regent for his father, King of Scotland, England, France and Ireland. By one, he promises to preserve everybody in their just rights; and orders all persons who have public moneys in their hands to bring it to him; and by the other dissolves the Union between England and Scotland. — But all this is not the worst! Notice came yesterday, that [the French have] ten thousand men, thirty transports, and ten men of war at Dunkirk. Against this force, we have — I don't know what — scarce fears![23]

The threat of a French invasion was less immediate than Walpole thought, and troops were brought over from the Continent to meet the challenge. Louis XV wanted to see how Britons responded to the prospect of a Stuart restoration before making a substantial military intervention. In October he signed a treaty with Charles' father, 'James VIII of Scotland', and promised French military assistance in reclaiming the throne of England.

The Jacobite army marched south, requisitioning money, food and clothing as they went. English people let them pass, but sympathisers failed to join. It is hard to gauge popular sentiment in times before modern opinion polling, but judging by their actions most of the English seem to have regarded it as a 'rebellion' rather than an 'uprising'. That said, had Charles managed to march into London or win a major battle in England, a substantial number of Britons might have rallied to his cause. Jacobite occupation of London would have had a profoundly destabilising effect on the financial system that underpinned the Hanoverian regime, and would have disrupted supplies to the Royal Navy. The Duke of Newcastle reported that 'we are under the greatest alarms of an immediate invasion from France'.[24] Given widespread anti-Catholic sentiment in Britain, and the fact that many Presbyterian Scots volunteered to fight against the Catholic Charles, this might have led to a widespread and bloody war in Britain.[25]

A miasma of romance, sustained by novels, movies and the tourist industry, surrounds memory of Bonnie Prince Charlie's bid to regain the throne for the Stuarts. The decision made at Derby to retreat to Scotland is often seen as a fateful one that robbed the Jacobite cause of its chance of success. Yet the really decisive moment was in Edinburgh during October when Charles and his close Irish advisors, full of assurances the English would rise and the French invade, persuaded the Jacobite council of war to march into England.[26] By the margin of one vote, the Jacobite army resolved to invade England and leave the major Scottish castles unconquered – including Edinburgh castle, in which the two leading banks of Scotland had stored their funds before closing for business.[27] Had Charles focused on securing the throne of a revived Kingdom of Scotland, the Jacobite uprising would have lasted longer and may have proved successful – with significant implications for the course of British history.

Leaving aside the plausible 'what ifs', the actual course of the '45 had significant strategic implications.[28] Failure to engage and defeat the Jacobite army in England meant the Duke of Cumberland's troops had to spend the winter pursuing Charles' army into the north of Scotland, where it was finally defeated at Culloden in April 1746. The subsequent military 'pacification' of the Highlands was brutal to the point of being called an act of genocide in Scottish scholarship.[29] The coercive 'civilising' tactics applied in the Highlands were repeated in other parts of the empire in subsequent years by those who served in Cumberland's army.[30] More immediately, time spent repressing the Jacobites delayed the return of British troops to the Continent, where Marshal Saxe was gradually conquering the Austrian Netherlands. Possible peace negotiations were delayed during 1745–46 while European diplomats waited to see the outcome of the Jacobite uprising.

The Treaty of Aix-la-Chapelle

By 1747 the British were dominant at sea, and the French were in control of much of the Netherlands. With Europe war-weary and the interruption of Atlantic trade damaging the French economy, the Treaty of Aix-la-Chapelle was concluded in October 1748. To a large extent it returned Britain and France to their pre-war status. In the face of widespread criticism, Cape Breton was returned to France. For their part, the French vacated the Low Countries and returned Madras, which they had captured in late 1746, to the British East India Company. Frederick II of Prussia appeared the biggest winner, retaining Silesia. Popular protest erupted in France, where the phrase 'as stupid as the peace' was coined.[31] In London, George II reluctantly sponsored an elaborate display of fireworks accompanied by Handel's music.

The War of the Austrian Succession saw a revolution in British naval strategy with the creation of a 'Western Squadron', which became the pillar of British naval power throughout the Seventy Years War. In the course of much debate among ministers and naval officers, a strategy was developed whereby a squadron of the Royal Navy would cruise to windward in the western approaches to the English Channel, enabling it to blockade France's Atlantic coast ports while also protecting British merchant shipping. While there were 'horrendous operational and logistical difficulties' in keeping ships at sea in gale force winds, the strategic rewards were immediate and game changing.[32] Two large French convoys were intercepted, and many ships captured, by the Western Squadron in the Battles of Finisterre in 1747.[33]

The French learned the value of naval power as Britain successfully cut-off much of their Atlantic trade. This 'initiated a naval arms race that reached its zenith in the 1790s and constituted a threat that Britain could not afford to ignore'.[34] The swift descent of Europe into a new war was arguably not inevitable, as there were politicians in both Britain and France who were keen on peace. An accommodation of interests might have been achieved, such as developed between Britain and Spain.[35] But there were also hawks on both sides, and clashes continued to occur in India and America. By 1750 'a full-scale guerrilla war' was under way in Arcadia, with the governor of Quebec supporting French settlers against the British military.[36] French commerce recovered rapidly, and there was a growing fear in Britain that this would soon translate into military hegemony.

In the years following the peace of Aix-la-Chapelle the Duke of Newcastle tried to revive the old diplomatic system and build a continental coalition against France. Seemingly obsessed with influencing the politics of the German Empire, within the cabinet he pushed for subsidies to be granted to Austria and various German princes. Newcastle clashed with his brother Henry Pelham, the prime minister, who was committed to fiscal consolidation. As Northern Secretary, Newcastle was a man of considerable experience, having first become a minister in

1724, but he displayed limited flexibility or creativity. The leading voice in mid-century British foreign policy, Newcastle became prime minister following the death of his brother in 1754.

While Newcastle's interest in German affairs pleased George II and Hanoverian ministers such as Baron von Munchhausen, he failed to appreciate the problematic nature of his endeavours in the changing context of the 1750s. Firstly, popular opinion was becoming a more significant factor in British politics, and the Duke, one of the richest landowners in Britain, arguably underestimated the degree to which popular hostility was setting limits to the pursuit of Continental intervention. Secondly, and more importantly, Newcastle failed to appreciate the degree to which European international relations were changing. From the perspective of Britain, France and its empire was becoming a greater threat. This was not the case, however, for continental states, whose eyes were turning toward the rise of Prussia and Russia. The possibility of France dominating Western Europe seemed to be receding as it increasingly focused on global rivalry with Britain. The Netherlands, for generations the crucible of war in Western Europe, had gone quiet. The Dutch, who had led alliances in war against Louis XIV, were financially weakened and keen on peace through neutrality. Austria, burning with a desire for revenge on Prussia, was showing more interest in regaining the wealthy and contiguous province of Silesia than in defending the far-flung and vulnerable Austrian Netherlands.

What Americans call the 'French and Indian War' (1754–1763) merged into another war in Germany that became known as the 'Seven Years War' (1756–1763). During the early 1750s the British and French were increasingly clashing in the Ohio Valley. The French wanted to strengthen their fortifications linking Quebec to Louisiana, while British settlers were pushing westward. British North Americans denounced what they regarded as French efforts to encircle them, and conflict escalated in 1754 when the young George Washington and some Virginia militiamen launched an unsuccessful attack on the French. The last thing George II and his ministers wanted was another full-scale war with France, but in the face of strategic necessity and a bellicose opposition and public opinion (on both sides of the Atlantic), they dispatched troops to North America and ordered the Royal Navy to intercept French reinforcements and supplies.

Conflict between Britain and France in America helped cause a 'Diplomatic Revolution' in Europe. In the 1740s France and Prussia had been allies, and this left Hanover in a vulnerable position. With the

Dutch and Austrians showing little interest in serving British interests, a convention was signed with St Petersburg in 1755 by which, in return for subsidies, Russia promised to attack Prussia if it invaded Hanover. This encouraged Frederick II to reach out to Britain, and in January 1756 a Convention of Westminster was signed by which he promised to support German neutrality. This further promoted the Diplomatic Revolution. The Austrian Habsburg dynasty had secured its leadership of the Holy Roman Empire in the 1740s and had been developing good relations with France, its traditional rival. Both powers nursed resentment toward the opportunistic behaviour of Frederick II and his expansion of Prussia. In May 1756 they announced to a shocked Europe the signing of a defensive treaty. In the same month, French troops landed on the Mediterranean island of Minorca to besiege its British garrison, and war was officially declared between the two states. Thus began the Seven Years War, which was fought on a bigger scale than the War of the Austrian Succession in terms of both resources and geography.[37]

The Seven Years War, 1756–1763

The Seven Years War was justly called 'The First World War' by Winston Churchill.[38] Owing in part to the relatively small size of its standing army, Britain tended to start badly in wars. That was certainly the case in the Seven Years War, with its early years witnessing numerous British defeats. General Braddock was sent to North America in 1755 and advanced against Fort Duquesne, only to be killed along with many of his soldiers by a smaller French and Indian force. During the retreat, George Washington buried Braddock and marched the army across the grave to conceal it so the scalp could not be claimed.[39] After 6000 French Arcadians were deported from Nova Scotia to the Thirteen Colonies, the new British commander, Lord Loudoun, tried and failed to re-capture Louisbourg on Cape Breton in 1757. Plans to seize French forts on Lake Ontario failed; and the French counterattacked into northern New York, establishing Fort Ticonderoga on the Hudson River.

The bad start to the war in Europe forced a change of government. Placed at the head of a poorly equipped force, Admiral Byng failed to relieve Minorca and it fell to the French in mid 1756. His court martial and execution prompted Voltaire's famous quip that the English sometimes execute an admiral 'to encourage the others'. In the face of widespread anger at the Minorca fiasco, Newcastle resigned. George II had to reluctantly accept a new ministry with the Duke of Devonshire as nominal prime minister, and the patriotic William Pitt as leader in the House of Commons. Owing to the king's hostility and its parliamentary weakness the Devonshire–Pitt ministry fell in early 1757. After some weeks in which Britain was effectively without a government, Newcastle returned as prime minister with Pitt leader in the Commons. Despite Pitt's long record of denouncing the influence of Hanover, in office the expectations of George II, combined with strategic necessity, saw him support subsidies for Prussia and the dispatch of British troops to Hanover in 1758. This coalition of Court and Country Whigs led to a few years of domestic political peace while war with France was waged around the globe.

With Britons fearing a potential French invasion, the summer and autumn of 1757 brought very bad news from Germany. In the previous year Frederick II had started war in Germany by launching what he claimed was a necessary pre-emptive strike at Austria through Saxony. This Machiavellian move only encouraged the Austrians and French to sign an offensive alliance in May 1757, and in the following month the Austrians inflicted a heavy defeat on Frederick's Prussians at Kolin in Bohemia. The Russians had joined the war and defeated a Prussian army in August. A large French army invaded Hanover, and after a brief clash at Hastenbeck the Duke of Cumberland signed the Convention of Kloster-Zeven. George II was furious when told his son had agreed to disband the largely Hanoverian 'Army of Observation' and allow the French to occupy his beloved Electorate. A failed British attempt to raid Rochefort in September added to the seemingly endless bad news.

Frederick II saved the situation, however, and closed the year with two stunning victories over the French and Austrians at Rossbach and Leuthen. Horace Walpole declared:

> All England has kept his birth-day; it has taken its place in our calendar next to Admiral Vernon's … and the people, I believe, begin to think Prussia is some part of *Old England*. We had bonfires and processions, illuminations and French horns playing out windows all night.[40]

Frederick was hailed as a Protestant soldier-king, and the Marquis d'Argenson observed that the war was developing the character of 'a general crusade of the Catholic party against the Protestants in Europe … with France as treasurer'.[41] Over the next four years Frederick, supported by British subsidies, battled to survive against the combined might of Austria, France, Russia and Sweden, and was only saved in 1762 when the Prussiaphile Peter III inherited the throne in St Petersburg and transformed Russia from an enemy into an ally. Frederick's survival also owed in part to the assistance of his friend, Ferdinand of Brunswick, who skilfully fought the French in western Germany during these years with an Anglo-Hanoverian army. At the Battle of Minden on 1 August 1759 orders became confused and several British regiments marched forward to attack the massed French cavalry. Seeing a wonderful opportunity, the French cavalry charged. The red line held fire until at ten yards they smashed the charge with a volley, and proceeded to stand firm in the face of counterattacks by French cavalry, infantry and artillery. The French commander, Marquis de Contades, was astonished: 'I never thought to see a single line of infantry break through three lines of cavalry ranked in order of battle, and tumble them to ruin'.[42]

By the end of 1759 the British could look back on an *annus mirabilis* – a year of wondrous victories.[43] Yet it had also been a year in which the new French foreign minister, Choiseul, had worked hard at planning an invasion, whereby large forces would have been landed in both Essex and Scotland. In June a midlands banker, Samuel Kenrick, observed: 'We are daily alarmed with a French invasion: the ministry seem apprehensive of it. 'Tis certain there are orders given for 3 more Battalions of highlanders to be regimented', while in Germany, 'Poor Prince Ferdinand is in a most miserable situation, retreating before the French & must necessarily be forced into an action'.[44] Yet at this time Pitt's global strategy, supported by vast sums of borrowed money, heroism and luck, was seeing Britain's war effort hit its straps. In Canada, Fort Niagara was captured in the summer and, after capturing Cape Breton in the previous year, a sophisticated amphibious operation was mounted against the supposedly impregnable fortress of Quebec on the St Lawrence River. In September, General Wolfe famously scaled the Heights of Abraham and died as his troops defeated the garrison, and in the following year the remaining French forces in New France surrendered at Montreal. France's share in the lucrative slave trade was being damaged, with the capture of West African trading posts in Senegal in 1758. In May 1759 an amphibious operation captured the rich French West Indian island of Guadeloupe, which had an annual sugar production equal to that of all the British Leeward Islands combined.[45]

The British were also ascendant in India. In 1757 Robert Clive had defeated Siraj-ud-Daula and his French allies at the Battle of Plassey, and proceeded to secure British East India company rule over Bengal.

A French force under Comte de Lally landed in Pondicherry with an eye to capturing Madras and expelling the British from Southern India. The timely arrival of a Royal Navy squadron and 600 troops dispatched by Pitt broke the siege of Madras, and British victory at Wandiwash in January 1760 effectively ended French influence in the Carnatic.

In an effort to redress these losses Choiseul pressed on with plans to invade Britain in late 1759. The Royal Navy put an end to this, however, by defeating the French Navy at Lagos off Portugal in August and smashing the invasion fleet at Quiberon Bay on the south coast of Brittany in November. In early 1760, Carrickfergus in Northern Ireland was briefly occupied by 600 French soldiers, but they soon withdrew in the face of a mobilised militia. Quiberon Bay was arguably a more important naval victory than Trafalgar, and has recently been called 'the battle that gave birth to an empire'.[46] In the wake of these victories Horace Walpole wrote to his ambassador friend in Florence: 'You would not know your country again. You left it a private little island, living upon its means. You would find it now the capital of the world.'[47]

The sudden death of the old George II in October 1760 changed the political climate in Britain. 'Born and educated in this country', George III declared in his first speech from the throne, 'I glory in the name Briton'.[48] Amidst the widespread joy that greeted his reign, however, there were early signs of political problems. Full of youthful idealism, George III wanted to rule as a 'Patriot King' and put an end to party factionalism and Whig cronyism. Since the failed '45, Jacobitism had ceased to be a serious threat to the Hanoverian dynasty, and George made a show of welcoming Tories to the Court. This made old Court Whigs 'stand aghast'. The young king and his favourite advisor, the Scottish Lord Bute, were anxious about the ballooning government debt and wanted to end the war. In the text he drew up for the King's first speech to the Privy Council on 25 October 1760, Bute had written that the 'bloody and expensive war' needed to be ended by 'obtaining an honourable and lasting peace'. At Pitt's insistence the wording was changed to 'an expensive but just and necessary war' that should be ended with an 'honourable peace in concert with our allies'.[49] Ironically, Pitt found himself championing continued involvement in the German War against a Patriot King who wanted to abandon Prussia – in parliament he declared 'that America had been conquered in Germany'.[50]

Lord Bute was made Northern Secretary in March 1761 with the hope of negotiating peace with France. Southern Secretary Pitt, however, proved inflexible in peace negotiations during the summer of 1761 – in particular on the issue of French access to the Newfoundland fisheries. Pitt regarded the fisheries as 'a nursery of seamen', and wanted to permanently cripple France's capacity as a naval power. The French envoy, Bussy, wrote of Pitt at this time:

> This minister is the idol of the people, who regard him as the sole author of their success, and they do not have the same confidence in the other members of the council. The court and its partisans are obliged to have the greatest regards for the fantasies of a fiery people, whom it is dangerous to contradict. Pitt joins to a reputation of superior spirit and talent, that of most exact honesty ... With simple manners and dignity, he seeks neither display nor ostentation ... He is courageous to the point of rashness, he supports his ideas in an impassioned fashion and with an invincible determination ... Pitt seems to have no other ambition than to elevate Britain to the highest point of glory and to abase France to the lowest degree of humiliation ... he has few friends in the council, but there is no one there strong or bold enough to try to replace him.[51]

Britons were becoming war-weary, however, with Lord Hardwicke asking, 'is this country to wage eternal war, and run in debt fifty millions more, upon wild imaginary schemes of conquest?'[52] In a widely read tract a thoughtful and informed merchant, Israel Mauduit, argued that money and men were being wasted because France 'cannot be hurt in any material interest' by the 'German War', other than losing some men easily replaced by militia or mercenaries. He estimated that for each year of war Britain was wasting £5 million in Germany and £10 million was being added to the national debt.[53]

One of the successes of British foreign policy in the 1750s had been to maintain friendly relations with Spain, but after the Anglophobe Charles III inherited the throne in 1759 he expressed concern at British colonial expansion and moved to renew the Bourbon 'family compact' in August 1761. Pitt was keen to launch a pre-emptive strike on Spain's empire, but met strong opposition. This brought tensions within the ministry to a head, and in October a shocked public learned that the 'Great Commoner', the architect of victories, had resigned in protest. As it turned out, Spain and Britain went to war in January 1762 anyway. When Russia pulled out of the war following the death of Tsarina Elizabeth in the same month, Bute saw an opportunity to stop paying subsidies to Prussia – something Frederick II branded an act of 'perfidious Albion'.[54]

Newcastle resigned in protest, arguing the move was immoral and left Britain diplomatically isolated. Bute's decision was sensible, however, as the danger had passed for Prussia and Britain had no reason to help Frederick wage a war of conquest against a weakened Austria. [55]

Britain needed to concentrate on fighting the new Bourbon alliance. Spanish timing was poor, however, as they entered the war when the French were weak and the British navy was dominant. 1762 turned into another year of British victories. After the French West Indian island of Martinique was conquered in February, and the islands of St Lucia, St Vincent and Grenada occupied, secret peace negotiations began. Spain's military weakness was revealed when its invasion of Portugal, Britain's ally, met with defeat. A surprise amphibious attack with high casualties saw the British capture Havana, Spain's main West Indian port; and the East India Company cobbled together a force that captured Manila in the Spanish Philippines. Spain soon joined France in the peace negotiations.

The Treaty of Paris

The Treaty of Paris signed in February 1763 proved both controversial and consequential. There was strong criticism of its terms by the likes of Pitt, and popular protests in London, where Lord Bute was 'very much insulted, hissed in every gross manner and a little pelted'.[56] Yet the treaty was endorsed by a very large majority of the House of Commons and many addresses of congratulation were received from a war-weary kingdom. Decisions made with limited geographical knowledge or strategic forethought, however, had significant consequences for the future of Britain and many regions of the globe.

Bute and the Duke of Bedford, the chief negotiator in Paris, were willing to make substantial concessions in order to make a peace they hoped would bring a lasting end to Anglo-French rivalry. Early in negotiations Bedford had advised generosity toward France:

Let us do as we would be done by, the most golden rule ... We have too much already – more than we know what to do with; and I very much fear that if we retain the greatest part of our conquests out of Europe we shall be in danger of over-colonising and undoing ourselves by them as the Spaniards have done.[57]

From a position of weakness, and facing widespread domestic anger at France's abysmal military performance, foreign minister Choiseul proved a skilful negotiator with an ambivalent attitude toward the 'frozen wastelands' of Canada. In North America, Britain gained Louisiana east of the Mississippi River and Canada; and Florida was got for restoring Cuba to Spain. The wealthy West Indian islands of Guadeloupe, Martinique, and St Lucia were returned to France, but Britain retained Grenada, St Vincent, Dominica, and Tobago. In West Africa, Britain gained Senegal, but returned the slave trading island of Goree to France. In India, the French were allowed to regain their trading bases, but without military support. Manila was freely returned to Spain. In Europe, the British regained Minorca in exchange for Belle-Ile. Even after returning much to France and Spain, the British Empire had expanded considerably and Louis XV had been humiliated.

Pitt's calls for a Carthaginian peace that would cripple France ran counter to conventional diplomatic practice, and claims that Prussia had been abandoned lacked substance. Given the heroic nature of Wolfe's capture of Quebec, and its strategic importance, there was no question of returning Quebec to France. When in government, Pitt had accepted that there could be no peace if Britain tried to keep both Quebec and France's main West Indian islands.[58] Bute gave limited consideration to commercial interests, and was guided by strategic aims: to secure North America and conciliate France. In doing so, he was following the common practice of British policy makers in the eighteenth century.[59]

George III and Bute were over-optimistic, however, and probably should have pushed for a better treaty. Pitt complained that 'France and Spain were neither appeased or crushed'. In an age when honour and glory were leading values, it was natural that France would seek to restore its fortunes, irrespective of the terms of the treaty. 'Bute was aiming impossibly high', according to a perceptive study of the treaty, and he 'never seems to have quite grasped that France was not interested in a permanent peace'.[60] While the balance of power had been maintained in Europe, it had been significantly upset in the colonial sphere, where Britain's dominance provoked anxiety and resentment. Pitt was probably right to complain that in restoring access to the Newfoundland fisheries Britain gave France a nursery for deep-sea sailors.

> The ministers seem to have lost sight of the great fundamental principle that France is chiefly, if not solely, to be dreaded by us in the light of a maritime and commercial power...we have given to her the

means of recovering her prodigious losses and of becoming once more formidable to us at sea.[61]

That was certainly the case until 1805, and the Newfoundland fisheries remained a site of Anglo-French tension until the twentieth century. Granted that return of France's main West Indian islands was required to stop the war, Britain might arguably have pushed for some better terms. Florida was a poor swap for Havana; something could have been got for Manila; St Lucia was given away without a clear appreciation of its strategic importance; and the French might have been excluded from the Newfoundland fisheries. Ironically, had some more commercial gains been made in the treaty, the need to tax Colonists in North America might not have been so pressing in the post-war years.

There were soon indications that the ideal of lasting Anglo-French peace and harmony would not become reality. Choiseul was busy strengthening the French alliance with Austria as a means of preserving peace in Europe while he concentrated on preparing for a war of revenge against Britain. The French navy had long been culturally and financially in the shadow of the army, but Choiseul embarked on an ambitious programme of naval expansion in the 1760s.[62] The Bourbon family pact was bolstered by granting Spain western Louisiana, and Choiseul aimed to build their combined fleets to equal that of Britain. Resource and manpower limitations, however, meant that by the late 1760s there had been only marginal reconstruction of the French navy, and the Spanish had proved unable to expand their fleet. As a result, while seeking to improve France's standing, Choiseul had to be careful to avoid provoking war with Britain. An armed struggle for independence by Corsican patriots against French-backed Genoese rule had attracted much sympathy among the British public, however France was able to annex Corsica unopposed in 1768 through clever diplomatic deceit and because the British ministry was distracted by problems in America and Ireland and large-scale rioting in London.[63] When Spain invaded Britain's windswept Falkland Islands in the south Atlantic with an expectation of French support, Louis XV forced Choiseul to resign after Lord North's government threatened war. At the same time, naval explorers such as Louis de Bougainville and James Cook carried Anglo-French rivalry into the south Pacific, as they charted and claimed islands for their respective kings.[64]

British foreign policy in the 1760s and 1770s has been severely criticised by historians for failing to engage with Continental issues and leaving

Britain bereft of allies during the American War of Independence. Hamish Scott has argued that the 'decline of Louis XV's monarchy', along with Britain's imperial gains in the Seven Years War, 'destroyed the strategy of building alliances on the basis of the danger of French hegemony'. British politicians 'were slow to appreciate' the changed nature of geopolitics in Western Europe. Austria and Prussia's priorities were now focused on Eastern Europe and 'if any state threatened to dominate' Western Europe 'it was Britain not France'.[65] This arguably overstates the case, but it is clear that the British failed to appreciate Continental concerns about the degree to which the colonial balance of power had tipped in their favour. But British ministries proved intent on peace and consolidation. Shortly after the 1763 Peace of Paris the new prime minister, George Grenville, expressed concern at the 'exhausted state of the public revenues'. In the following years, governments balked at the potential cost of securing alliances with powers such as Russia or Prussia, which might drag them into wars in Eastern Europe. As Jeremy Black has argued, 'critics of diplomacy in this period fail to explain why foreign policy should have been immune from restraint in terms of commitments and expenditure'.[66]

Having made peace with France in 1763, George III was confronted by growing political conflict over domestic and imperial issues. 'Lord Boot' was subject to a torrent of Scotophobic abuse, especially in John Wilkes's paper *The North Briton*, which argued that Tory men and measures were back in favour at Court. Throughout the 1760s various attempts to prosecute Wilkes and bar him from sitting in the House of Commons saw 'Wilkes and Liberty' become the rallying cry of popular political activists agitating for parliamentary reform. It was a decade of political instability, with several prime ministers serving – Bute (May 1762–April 1763), George Grenville (April 1763–July 1765), Lord Rockingham (July 1765–July 1766), Pitt, made Earl of Chatham (July 1766–October 1768), and the Duke of Grafton (Oct. 1768–Jan. 1770) – before Lord North was able to secure the support of both King and Commons from 1770 to 1782.

The British Civil War in America, 1775–1783

The American War of Independence (1775–83) was a British Civil War. Its origins lay in two key consequences of British victory over France in the Seven Years War. First, France's retreat from North America left the colonists feeling less threatened and less in need of redcoats for defence. Second, the British government needed to tap new sources of revenue.[67]

There was a broad consensus among British politicians that new sources of revenue were required in order to fund administration of the expanded empire and pay down the large public debt. During the War of the Austrian Succession it had cost Britain £148,000 p.a. to defend its American colonies, and that figure had risen to nearly £1 million during the Seven Years War. General Amherst estimated that a standing army of 10,000 would need to be maintained in the Colonies in order to police and defend North America.[68] Grenville started to reform imperial regulations, crack down on smuggling, and sought to raise revenue from the hitherto lightly taxed North Americans. In 1763, Pontiac's War in the Ohio Valley was followed by a Royal Proclamation Line, which aimed to restrict British settlement and thus limit frontier conflict. If Colonials were angered by the Proclamation Line, they were enraged by the 1765 Stamp Act which placed a highly visible stamp duty on printed matter and legal documents. British MPs were genuinely surprised at the storm of protest in the Colonies, with boycotts of British manufactures and declarations of 'No Taxation Without Representation'. Grenville fell from office in the same year, but this owed more to his poor relations with George III than his American policies. In order to pacify the Colonies, Lord Rockingham's ministry repealed the stamp duties but passed a Declaratory Act stating the British parliament's theoretical right to impose taxes on the Colonies. Pitt became prime minister in his own right in 1766, but his position was weakened by accepting the title Earl of Chatham, which removed him from the Commons to the House of Lords. Bouts of severe illness, especially from late 1767, further undermined his leadership. In opposition Pitt had agreed with the Americans that any 'internal' taxes should be raised through their own Colonial assemblies, but that the British parliament had the right to regulate imperial commerce. Taking the Americans at their word, before he died in late 1767 the Chancellor of the Exchequer, Charles Townshend, established an American Board of Customs Commissioners (based in Boston) and imposed duties on imported products such as paint, paper, lead and tea. He hoped this would raise funds that could free colonial governors from dependence on revenue raised by colonial assemblies. In response, Americans denounced the Townshend duties as a tax in all but name and embarked on another round of boycotts and tarring-and-feathering. The British government responded by sending troops to

Boston to counter the riotous 'Sons of Liberty', and by early 1770 moved to repeal all the duties except that on tea. On the day that the new prime minister Lord North was moving to repeal most of the duties, confrontation with a jeering crowd in Boston saw soldiers open fire and kill five men. Violence was a part of everyday life in the eighteenth century, and clashes between troops and rioters were not unusual in Europe. In the politically charged atmosphere of the American Colonies, however, this incident was memorably depicted in an etching by Paul Revere as 'The Boston Massacre'.

While the Thirteen Colonies were proving troublesome, Lord North's government was grappling with a number of imperial and geostrategic challenges: France and Spain were stared down over the Falkland Islands; Britons watched with interest as the rising absolutist eastern powers of Russia and Prussia joined with Austria to partition sections of the Polish 'aristocratic republic' in 1772; the challenge of incorporating 70,000 French-speaking Canadian Catholics into the empire resulted in the Quebec Act (1774), which granted rights to the Catholic Church and established a combination of French civil law and English criminal law. This act of enlightened imperial policy fuelled more anger in the Thirteen Colonies, where it was seen as limiting the progress of Protestantism and British liberties, and as further evidence of the British government becoming authoritarian and Tory.

With the British East India Company in financial trouble, the government allowed it to ship surplus tea direct to Boston. This attempt to help the Company, undercut American smugglers, and raise customs revenue led to the 'Boston Tea Party', in which Sons of Liberty disguised as 'American Indians' dumped the tea in Boston harbour. The British parliament responded to this flagrant attack on property by imposing a series of measures in early 1774, dubbed the 'Intolerable Acts' in America, which shut the port, increased military strength and replaced elected officials with Crown appointments. Rather than isolate and subdue the Boston radicals these measures provoked the election of delegates to a Continental Congress, which met in September to discuss how to coordinate colonial resistance in support of Boston.

George III and his ministers fundamentally misread the American crisis, believing that they were engaged in a large-scale police action. Well into what became the American War of Independence they assumed that the silent majority of Americans were loyalist. This was understandable, as it is clear that Americans were becoming more British in the course of the eighteenth century.[69] War began in April 1775 when General Gage marched out of Boston to seize a stockpile of weapons at Concord and clashed with colonial militia at Lexington. Generations of Americans have learned that Paul Revere rode through the New England country-side calling out 'the British are coming'. But as David Hackett Fischer has noted, that is not what he said:

> Many New England express riders that night would speak of Regulars, Redcoats, the King's men, and even the 'Ministerial Troops'.... But no messenger is known on good authority to have cried, 'The British are coming', until the grandfathers' tales began to be recorded long after American Independence. In 1775, the people of Massachusetts still thought *they* were British.[70]

The lightly taxed Americans knew they were among the most fortunate people on earth, but increasingly felt they were being treated as second-class citizens within the empire. Patriots feared for the future and took up arms to defend their 'British liberties' against what they considered an increasingly authoritarian monarch and corrupt parliament. George III's government failed to see that its half-hearted heavy-handedness was provoking, in the words of John Adams, 'a revolution in the hearts and minds of the people'.[71] The British government failed to realise it was stumbling into the first modern revolutionary war.[72]

The British Civil War in America began slowly – not least because neither side wanted war. Both sides were shocked at the loss of life at Bunker Hill in June 1775, and the Congress sent an Olive Branch Petition to George III. This was rejected and George declared the colonies in a state of open rebellion, but it was not until after the publication of Tom Paine's *Common Sense* in January 1776 that a significant portion of Americans reluctantly embraced the idea of independence. Struggling with a large public debt, Lord North proved reluctant to commit significant resources and forces to quell the rebellion. The government relied to a large extent on German mercenaries, the 29,000 of which constituted approximately 35% of the troops sent to America during the war. Only one new British regiment was raised before 1778, and failure to systematically mobilise American Loyalists left them vulnerable to attack by Patriots and deprived the government of a significant source of manpower. Blockading of the American coast was ineffective because most of the Royal Navy was kept in European waters, and only fully mobilised for war in late 1776 on reports the French were expanding their fleet. General Howe, who replaced Gage in late 1775, proved a cautious commander. Operating at the end of supply lines that stretched back across the Atlantic to Britain, British strategy was poorly coordinated and Howe did not follow up early opportunities to destroy George Washington's Continental Army.[73]

The British Civil War became another British-Bourbon World War when France entered on the side of the rebels in early 1778. Only thirteen of Britain's twenty-six American colonies had rebelled, and the loyal colonies now came under threat. A key aim of the Declaration of Independence had been to create a diplomatic place for the Continental Congress in international relations.[74] British defeat at Saratoga in late 1777 convinced France that the rebellion was worth backing as a means to revenge on Britain. In 1778 General Clinton, the new Commander in Chief in America, was ordered to withdraw 8,000 of his troops and send them to the West Indies and Florida. Lacking any allies, Britain had to implement full-scale military mobilisation and found itself also at war with Spain in April 1779. British resources were stretched further when they declared war on the Dutch in 1780 in an effort to stop them trading with the Americans. War with the Bourbon powers turned the American conflict into just one theatre of a global struggle.

In the renewed world war defence of Britain was the top priority. In 1760 the French had spent £7 million on their army and only £500,000 on their navy. Near the end of the American War, in contrast, they spent £9 million on their navy.[75] Outnumbered by the combined Bourbon fleet, the Royal Navy had to base most of its ships in home waters. Fears of a possible invasion in 1778 were allayed when Admiral Keppel gained a bruising marginal victory at Ushant. In the following year, the French prepared 30,000 troops for an invasion of southern England that aimed to capture the Royal Navy base at Portsmouth and set off a financial panic in London. With the Channel Fleet guarding southern Ireland, where it was feared the majority Catholic population would support an invasion, a numerically superior Franco-Spanish fleet managed to evade the British blockade and appeared off Portsmouth in mid-August 1779. The Dissenting minister Richard Price told his friend Lord Shelburne:

> The present crisis is surely dreadful. It is impossible to think without distress of a kingdom, lately at the head of the world, suffer'd by providence to fall under the direction of infatuated men whose councils are now threatening it with destruction.[76]

Portsmouth's defences were strengthened and volunteer militia raised. Unfavourable winds and caution prevented Admiral Hardy from engaging the numerically superior Bourbon fleet, before sickness, dissention and bad weather saw it retire to the Continent in early September. This failed invasion was, in the words of David Syrett, 'the greatest threat to [Britain's] security to occur between the Armada and the Battle of Britain'.[77]

The invasion threat and anger at the seemingly poor conduct of the war had a profound effect upon domestic politics. In the winter of 1779–80 a network of 'Associations' petitioning for political reform emerged in Britain. The House of Commons, it was argued, had been corrupted by the influence of both Crown and Lords. The remedy was claimed to be a combination of administrative 'economical reform', more frequent elections and extension of the franchise. Pressure on Lord North's government eased after support for parliamentary reform was dampened by the Gordon Riots in June 1780, during which London suffered more damage than Paris experienced during the French Revolution of 1789. A more serious challenge to the status quo emerged in Ireland. With much of the Irish Army overseas, a large-scale paramilitary movement emerged in 1778 to defend Ireland against possible invasion. Inspired by the American example, the overwhelmingly Protestant Volunteers elected their own officers and became increasingly politicised, demanding free trade and an end to the Irish parliament's subordination to Westminster. Worried about a potential Irish Revolution, at the end of 1779 Lord North conceded the right to trade freely with British colonies.

In America, a change in strategic focus to the supposedly more loyal southern Colonies eventually ended in defeat. Building on earlier success in Georgia, key ports in South Carolina were captured in 1780, and in North Carolina in the following year. But a vicious frontier war erupted between Loyalists and Patriots, and once General Cornwallis's forces marched on to Virginia the Patriots recaptured most of Georgia and South Carolina. In August 1781 Cornwallis entrenched at Yorktown on the banks of the Chesapeake where he hoped to be reinforced. Yet he was soon besieged by Washington and isolated by a squadron of the French navy, which repelled an attack by the British navy and allowed more French troops and artillery to land. In October Cornwallis surrendered, and while the war continued for over a year, Yorktown marked the end of offensive operations in America.

Having lost the support of independents in the House of Commons, Lord North resigned as prime minister in March 1782. A period of political instability ensued. The new prime minister, Lord Rockingham, began peace negotiations, but he was ill and died in an influenza epidemic in July. Charles James Fox, a pro-American 'man of the people', served in the new position of Foreign Secretary (which merged the old positions of Southern and Northern Secretary). Rockingham was too weakened to prevent squabbling between Fox and Lord Shelburne, who as Home Secretary was responsible for Colonial affairs. The King detested Fox, who resigned after Rockingham was replaced by the unpopular Shelburne as prime minister. Shelburne proceeded to negotiate the Treaty of Versailles before falling to the Fox–North Coalition in April 1783. After signing the Treaty in September the Coalition were in turn replaced by the younger William Pitt in December 1783, who became prime minister at the age of 24.

While Yorktown effectively ended the conflict in North America, the global war continued. In West Africa the British captured Goree and all of the Dutch bases on the Gold Coast, but called off an attempt on the Dutch Cape Colony when it was reinforced by the French Navy. In India the war see-sawed. While the British East India Company was already at war with the Maratha Confederacy, reinforced by several regular army regiments it managed to capture all of the remaining French factories by 1779. This provoked Haidar Ali of Mysore to attack British interests in the Carnatic, commencing the Second Mysore War (1780–84), and by late 1780 he threatened Madras. The British might have been expelled from southern India if the French had provided decisive assistance. The East India Company successfully counterattacked Haidar Ali and also occupied most of the Dutch bases in India and Ceylon. The French intervened in early 1782 and captured Trincomalee on the east coast of Ceylon before the war ended.

The Caribbean became the main theatre of war after the French entered the conflict.[78] In 1778 less than 10% of British ships of the line were in the West Indies, but by 1780 the figure was over 40%.[79] Troops withdrawn from North America were used to capture St Lucia at the end of 1778, but in the following year the French Navy occupied St Vincent and Grenada. On entering the war, Spain attacked British bases on the Mississippi, while the British made some gains in modern day Honduras and Nicaragua. After declaring war on the Dutch in December 1780, the British took St Eustatius and their other islands. These were in turn captured by the French, who went on the offensive in mid 1781 and also took Tobago, St Kitts and Montserrat. A French invasion of Jamaica was narrowly avoided when Admiral Rodney returned with reinforcements and defeated the French fleet at the Battle of the Saintes in April 1782.

Widespread celebration greeted Rodney's victory, and in part reflected an evolving sense of embattled 'Britishness'. If the American Declaration of Independence destroyed a transatlantic 'Greater Britain', the global struggle against the French, Spanish, American and Dutch forces arguably deepened a sense of British identity within the Atlantic Archipelago.[80] The winter of 1781–82 proved difficult days. In the months following Yorktown Britons received news of a series of defeats in the Caribbean and India, and the surrender of besieged Minorca in February 1782. In the same month, a meeting at Dungannon of the Ulster Volunteers threatened rebellion if the Irish parliament was not made independent. And Admiral Howe's Channel fleet was stretched to the limit in acting as a Western Squadron and also guarding the North Sea against the Dutch.[81] In the days prior to learning of the Battle of the Saintes people were worried about the prospect of a Franco-Dutch invasion of eastern England. Rodney's victory saved Jamaica, boosted national morale and bolstered the British position on the eve of peace negotiations. In the words of the *Cumberland Pacquet*, 'a joy unknown for years past seemed to spread itself amongst all ranks of people'.[82] Throughout the summer of 1782 the British press cheered on General Eliott's defence of Gibraltar in the face of a long Bourbon siege, and the City of London commissioned John Singleton Copley to create one of Britain's largest history paintings to celebrate *The Defeat of the Floating Batteries at Gibraltar, September 1782* (1783).[83]

The Treaty of Versailles

Owing to the military successes of 1782, the peace treaties that brought the war to an end were less disadvantageous for Britain than had been anticipated. As Andrew Stockley has observed, 'the War of American Independence was not so much won by America as abandoned by Britain'.[84] With the global war going badly, the Rockingham Whigs came to power in April 1782. To avert the possibility of a rebellion by the Volunteers in Ireland they granted the Dublin parliament legislative independence, and were committed to granting American independence against the wishes of George III. With George Washington failing to conquer New York, 1782 was militarily an unsuccessful year for the Americans. The bilateral Treaty of Paris concluded in November was nevertheless generous to the Americans: in addition to conceding independence, in the words of Paul Langford, 'the boundary of Canada was defined so as gratuitously to renounce the Old North West and give Congress territories which were to become the heart of the prosperous Mid-West in the nineteenth century'.[85] Newfoundland fishing rights were granted and American loyalists were effectively left at the mercy of the Congress. This owed much to the self-consciously enlightened Lord Shelburne who, as prime minister following Rockingham's untimely death in July, carefully managed the peace negotiations. The Rockingham Whigs, and their leading spokesmen such as Charles James Fox and Edmund Burke, had reconciled themselves to the idea of American independence. Shelburne was one of the small group of 'Chathamites' (the remains of the elder Pitt's faction), who condemned the government for causing the American war but also wished to keep the Thirteen Colonies within the empire.[86] Shelburne inherited leadership of the Chathamites following Pitt's death in 1778, and even in August 1782 he still hoped that the Americans might remain within the empire. If independence must be granted, Shelburne was determined to be generous in an effort to repair cultural and economic ties between Britain and the new republic.

It is notable that, aside from some lamentation, Britons were not traumatised by the loss of America. In addition to the fact that cultural and economic ties soon revived, this owes something to the fact that Britain effectively won the last year of the global war.[87] With the Americans split from their allies, peace was signed with France and Spain in January 1783. While the French Foreign minister, Vergennes, had been keen to overturn the 1763 Peace of Paris, he was also worried by the rising power of Russia and its threat to French allies in the east such as Poland and the Ottoman Empire. Spain's desire to capture Gibraltar had delayed the peace, but Vergennes was keen to conclude the war before Shelburne fell in the face of popular protest at the treaty terms. While Britain's financial system remained strong and its navy was expanding, France was heading toward bankruptcy. As a result, the 1783 Treaty of Versailles was concluded with very limited reversal of the 1763 Peace of Paris. France gained Tobago and regained Senegal. Vergennes persuaded the Spanish to stop eyeing Gibraltar, and settle for Minorca and the Floridas. The Dutch were sidelined during the negotiations. The British proposed an Anglo-Bourbon partition of their colonies, but had to settle for gaining Negapatam in India and the right to sail through the Dutch East Indies.

Setting aside creation of the USA as an independent republic, on the whole the great powers regained territories lost during the war. While the Bourbons could claim to have won, the changes agreed at Versailles hardly matched the scale and cost of the global war. At a gathering in Benjamin Franklin's house after singing the preliminary articles of peace, a Frenchman taunted the British that the new USA would become 'the greatest empire in the world'. One of the Britons replied: 'Yes, and they will *all* speak English, every one of 'em'.[88]

The period 1782–84 was a time of constitutional crisis in Britain. Lord Shelburne was personally unpopular, and he resigned in the face of widespread criticism of the peace treaty. George III was once again forced to appoint a ministry against his will when he made the Duke of Portland nominal prime minister in a Fox–North coalition. This alliance of men who had been determined opponents during the American war struck many Britons as cynical and unnatural. Foxite Whigs openly identified with the American revolutionaries by wearing buff and blue clothes and, as a minister under Rockingham, Fox had openly 'talked of the King under the description of Satan'.[89] When Fox saw a bill through the Commons in November 1783 that gave ministers greater control over the East India Company and its vast revenues, George III let it be known that he would regard as an enemy any peer who supported it in the House of Lords. The bill was duly defeated in the Lords and the King dismissed the Fox–North Coalition.

The independently minded William Pitt (1759–1806) was appointed as the youngest ever prime minister at the end of the year, with the rest of his cabinet in the Lords. Fox boasted of devouring the 'mince pie administration', but his East India Bill had angered both radicals and conservatives. While Pitt lost numerous votes in the Commons in the early months of 1784, the supply of revenue to government was allowed to pass. An election was called, and Pitt was returned with a substantial majority.

Pitt turned his attention to financial reform and rebuilding Britain's international position. He earned widespread respect for his rational administrative reforms: taxes, duties and their collection were streamlined, public debt reorganised, and a 'sinking fund' established to reduce debt over time. An East India Act was passed that created a Board of Control appointed by the crown rather than parliament, and the powers of the Governor-General of Bengal were strengthened. Anxious to undermine Franco-American cooperation, the British ensured post-war negotiations with the USA were held in London. Anglo-American trade boomed in the post-war years, but political relations remained frosty, with disagreement over the Canadian border and treatment of loyalists. A British representative was not resident in Philadelphia until 1791.[90] As usual, post-war demobilisation saw a rise in unemployment and crime. Unable to resume sending convicts to North America, a new destination was sought. Eventually a fleet of 1300 marines and convicts was sent to Botany Bay where, after a voyage of eight months, they began the penal colony of New South Wales in a hot January 1788.

Post-war relations with France were complicated. On the one hand, the Eden Treaty of 1786 improved commercial relations and benefited British manufacturers. Britain and France shared anxiety about the growth of Russian power and the potential for large-scale conflict in Eastern Europe – which was justified in light of the Russo-Turkish War (1787–92) and the abolition by partition of Poland in the 1790s. Developments in the Dutch Republic, however, caused Anglo-French tension. An ongoing struggle between republican champions of the States-General and supporters of the Stadtholder, Prince William V of Orange, flared up in the wake of the American Revolution. French backing of the Patriot Revolt threatened Britain's longstanding strategic principle that the Low Countries and their ports should not fall under the influence of a rival great power. When the Princess of Orange requested help from her uncle, Frederick William III of Prussia, Pitt started mobilising the navy and warned the French against intervening – they must give up their 'predominant influence' in the Republic or prepare 'to fight for it'.[91] In September 1787, with their Austrian allies having just started a war with Turkey, the French stood by as Prussian troops marched into the United Provinces and restored the fortunes of the House of Orange.

Pitt's skilful diplomacy ended Britain's quarter century of isolation, and in 1788 a Triple Alliance was formed with the Dutch and Prussia. Britain began to play a significant role in European diplomacy. When the Austrian Netherlands rebelled in 1789, Prussia wanted to support the creation of an independent Belgium. Fearing that a weak Belgium might become a client state of France, however, Pitt prevented the Triple Alliance from intervening and supported the restoration of Austrian authority. At the start of 1790 news reached London that the Spanish had captured a recently established British trading base on Vancouver Island in Nootka Sound. While San Francisco was the northernmost Spanish settlement, they claimed the entire Pacific coast of North America and wished to prevent Russian and British encroachment. Buoyed by jingo-istic anti-Spanish sentiment, Pitt mobilised the navy and secured Triple

Alliance support for war. In the words of Alan Frost, 'the speed, scale and global range of [British naval] preparations would be impressive even in the twentieth century'.[92] With only inadequate support from France, Spain backed down in October and conceded British rights to fish in the Pacific and Southern Oceans and to settle on the coast north of California.

Pitt's diplomatic triumphs owed much to the weakened state of France, the senior partner in the Bourbon alliance. France's financial crisis did not, however, appear to contemporaries as necessarily weakening their long-term strategic position. On the contrary, the winter of 1788–89 saw British politics convulsed by the Regency Crisis, in which Pitt clung to power hoping that George III would recover from a bout of 'madness', while the Foxites demanded that their friend, the Prince of Wales, be made regent. George III recovered, but at the same time France was buzzing with optimism about the revival of the Estates-General and the possibility of regenerating the nation through a written constitution embodying the principles of the Enlightenment. A revitalised and resurgent France appeared a real prospect, and Britons worried about the French attempt to build a large artificial harbour at Cherbourg in Normandy, a few hours sail from southern England. Revolution in 1789, however, ensured that in the short term France played a negligible role in European diplomacy.

War with Revolutionary France, 1793–1802

In his budget speech in February 1792, Pitt observed that 'while events may arise, which human foresight cannot reach, and which may baffle all our conjectures ... unquestionably there never was a time in the history of this country, when, from the situation of Europe, we might more reasonably expect fifteen years of peace, than we may at the present moment'.[93] This is a fine example of the way in which even informed observers can be mugged by events. A year after Pitt's speech Britain and France went to war in a struggle that would last for more than two decades, and in which nearly a quarter of a million British soldiers and sailors would die from wounds and disease.

Pitt's optimistic assessment of geopolitics in Western Europe was understandable in light of the early years of the French Revolution. The revolution against absolute monarchy in 1789 and the Declaration of the Rights of Man and Citizen had an electrifying effect on enlightened opinion throughout Europe. It seemed a new age of reason and liberty was dawning. Charles James Fox, leader of the parliamentary opposition, reflected a widespread view when he wrote: 'How much the greatest Event it is that ever happened in the World! & how much the best! ... all my prepossessions against French connections for this country will be at an end, & indeed most part of my European system of Politics be altered if this Revolution has the consequences that I expect'.[94] Enlightened progressives on both sides of the Channel claimed that wars were caused by the vanity and ambition of monarchs. Aside from the fact that political divisions hamstrung French foreign policy, the revolutionaries repeatedly denounced the traditional warrior ethos of monarchy and aristocracy, deplored wars of conquest and talked much of the 'brotherhood of mankind'. When Edmund Burke condemned its principles and prospects in his *Reflections on the Revolution in France* (1790), he was dismissed by many as gloomy, wrong-headed and hysterical.

In the early 1790s it was in Eastern Europe that the potential for war seemed greatest. Concerned at the growing power of Russia under Catherine II, Pitt diplomatically overreached himself in the Ochakov crisis of 1791. In alliance with Prussia, Pitt wanted to force Russia to return the strategically important Black Sea port of Ochakov to Turkey. In the face of a divided cabinet and vocal criticism in parliament and press, he abandoned plans for war. This proved a humiliating political defeat for Pitt, and effectively ended the Triple Alliance. Prussia soon allied with Austria, and together with Russia they set about partitioning Poland until it disappeared from the map of Europe in 1795.

At the same time as Pitt was predicting a peaceful future, enthusiasm for war was developing in France. In late 1791 the enlightened Austrian emperor Leopold II, brother of the French queen Marie Antoinette, had asked the major powers to assist Louis XVI. While this appeal to monarchical solidarity met with a lukewarm response, it increased paranoia among French revolutionaries. In the middle of the year Louis XVI had tried to flee Paris in order to avoid signing a constitution that significantly reduced his powers. Under the new written constitution a National Assembly was elected, and by early 1792 there were growing calls for war against Austria, which was harbouring *émigré* royalists. J.P. Brissot argued that war would end the external threats, unite the nation, force the king to make a stand for or against the constitution, and make opposition to the revolution treasonous. For their part, royalists were also enthusiastic for war in the hope it would result in a crushing defeat of the revolution. The National Assembly declared war on the new Austrian emperor, Francis II, on 20 April 1792. With many of its aristocratic officers having gone into exile, the French army was in no condition to wage war. Austria and its ally, Prussia, were distracted by problems in Eastern Europe, but managed easily to repulse a French advance into the Austrian Netherlands and begin a slow march toward Paris.

War radicalised the French Revolution in 1792, but Britain, Holland and Spain remained on the sidelines. Louis XVI was deposed in August and the advancing Prussian army was defeated at Valmy in September. While Burke and his sympathisers were calling for a united monarchical crusade against the revolution, Pitt was keen to stay out of the war. The issue that drew Britain into the conflict was the traditional strategic principle of preventing the Low Countries from falling under the control of France.[95] In November the French defeated an Austrian army at Jemappes, and the new National Convention proceeded to issue several bold decrees, declaring France would 'accord fraternity and help to all peoples who wish to recover their liberty', and that all ships had a natural right to sail through the Scheldt estuary. The River Scheldt began in northern France, flowed into the Austrian Netherlands, through Antwerp and entered the sea via an estuary in the Dutch Netherlands. The Scheldt estuary had been closed to international shipping by the Treaty of Westphalia (1648), something most recently reaffirmed in the Anglo-Dutch treaty of 1788. This prevented Antwerp from becoming a port that would rival Dutch commerce, or help France to launch an invasion of Britain. In a private and amicable meeting with Maret, the French envoy, Pitt warned that the fraternal decree appeared an 'act of hostility to neutral nations' and that opening the Scheldt would lead to war with both Holland and Britain.[96] Pitt's views were relayed to the political hothouse of Paris at a time when the king was on trial and French forces had conquered the Austrian Netherlands and Savoy. On December 15 the National Convention issued a decree that empowered French generals to abolish nobility and feudal dues in occupied territories, implement republican principles, confiscate property and raise revenue to fund the French armies of 'liberation'. The time for subtle diplomacy had passed – indeed, the French Revolutionaries made a virtue of rejecting the traditional 'charlatan' arts of diplomacy in favour of transparency and asserting the primacy of 'natural rights'.[97]

With republican France posing both a strategic and ideological threat, the British government's position hardened. There was growing concern at the spread of radical ideas in Britain and Ireland, but Pitt's government was bolstered by the establishment of a popular loyalist Association for the Preservation of Liberty and Property against Republicans and Levellers, and a deepening split in the parliamentary opposition.[98] In a parliamentary debate on 28 December 1792, Edmund Burke condemned his former Foxite Whig friends for continuing to champion the French revolutionaries as defending liberty against despotism. France 'had always been the natural enemy of this country... the only nation from which we had anything to fear', and he was horrified to see his former friends celebrating its victories over Prussia and Austria. Welcoming Pitt's draconian Alien Bill, Burke hoped it would 'keep out of England those murderous atheists, who would pull down church and state; religion and God; morality and happiness'. Noting that 3,000 daggers were being produced at Birmingham to be sent to the French republic, Burke 'drew out a dagger which he had concealed, and with much vehemence of action threw it on the floor', declaring he wanted 'to keep the French infection from this country; their principles from our minds, and their daggers from our hearts'.[99]

With war looming, Pitt began to use similarly strong language, declaring that the French Revolution was 'founded upon principles that were inconsistent with every regular government – which were hostile to hereditary monarchy, to nobility, to all the privileged orders, and to every sort of popular representation, short of that which would give to every individual a voice in the election of representatives'. The French army in Flanders had 'issued a proclamation, that whoever should not embrace the tree of liberty, should be cut off as a wretch unfit to live'. Working to 'promote rebellion in other countries' the French were waging a new kind of 'war against all legitimate power... a war of extirpation'.[100] Unlike in past wars, the French aimed to change the political systems of territories they 'liberated'.

With Britain mobilising for war, and after guillotining Louis XVI on January 21, the French National Convention unanimously declared war on Britain and the Dutch Republic – urging Britons to rise in republican revolution. After the news reached London, Charles James Fox continued to call for negotiations with an eye to restoring peace, but his support in the Commons shrank to approximately 50 MPs. Opinion in Britain became increasingly polarised, with Francophile radicals forming a vocal minority increasingly subject to repression. While Britain's entry into the war was sparked by strategic considerations, ideology played an important role in intensifying the conflict.[101] Inspired with the idea of a 'crusade for liberty', the French republic added Spain and all of the Holy Roman Empire to its impressive list of enemies.

The War of the First Coalition (1793–97) began with the British government confident it would be short and profitable. The French seemed to have picked fights with more than they could handle. Pitt, Foreign Secretary William Grenville and Home Secretary Henry Dundas planned a traditional strategy of sending a small force to the Continent combined with maritime raids on the French coast and colonies. Dundas confidently predicted that by the end of 1794 'this country having captured the West Indian Islands and having destroyed their existing fleet, may long rest in peace'.[102] By summer the revolutionary state was in serious trouble. After losing to the Austrians at Neerwinden and fearing he would be suspected a traitor, their leading general, Dumouriez, tried to turn the army against the increasing power of the radical Jacobins in Paris. When the soldiers refused to follow he prudently defected to the Austro-Prussian forces that were once again pressing into north-eastern France. In the west a huge royalist counter-revolutionary uprising developed in the Vendée. For their part, the British sent a force under the Duke of York, son of George III, to Flanders where it proceeded to besiege Dunkirk. Admiral Samuel Hood's Mediterranean fleet occupied the southern port of Toulon. Forced to withdraw in December by a besieging Jacobin force that included the young Napoleon, Hood nevertheless burned nine ships of the line and large stockpiles of timber which 'was possibly the single most crippling blow suffered by the French navy since Quiberon Bay'.[103]

If the Allies had acted with speed, focus and cooperation the French monarchy may have been restored and two decades of bloodshed avoided. Instead, they were over-confident and uncoordinated; their interests differed; and their aims were ill-defined. Should they fight on until monarchy was restored? And if so, was constitutional monarchy acceptable, or need it be a return to pre-1789 absolute monarchy? For his part, Pitt was happy to leave such aims ill-defined in order to encourage a variety of royalist and moderate republican anti-Jacobin activists in France. While Pitt favoured Continental commitment, as a wartime leader he failed to develop a clear and consistent grand strategy. In general, he was torn between Foreign Secretary Grenville's demands for a continental focus and the blue-water strategy championed by Henry Dundas, his War Secretary and drinking partner.

The Coalition also underestimated the strength of the revolutionary forces unleashed in France. The Jacobins began ruling through a 'Committee for Public Safety' composed of zealots such as the virtuous

Maximilien Robespierre. In August 1793 'total war' was effectively declared via the *levée en mass* which decreed mobilisation of the nation:

> From this moment until that in which our enemies shall have been driven from the territory of the Republic, all Frenchmen are permanently requisitioned for service in the armies. The young men shall fight; the women will make tents and clothes and will serve in the hospitals; the children will make up old linen into lint; the old men will have themselves carried into the public squares to rouse the courage of fighting men, to preach the unity of the Republic and hatred of Kings.[104]

Any means were justified towards the end of securing universal peace and happiness in a new age of liberty, equality and fraternity.[105] The guillotine was used to execute suspected enemies of the nation, anti-Jacobin uprisings were crushed in cities such as Lyon, and the Vendée was subjected to brutal 'pacification' by Jacobin 'Infernal Columns' that marched in gridlines across it killing tens of thousands in an effort to 'exterminate' counter-revolution. Their general boasted to the Committee of Public Safety: 'I have crushed children beneath my horses' hooves, and massacred the women, who thus will give birth to no more brigands...we take no prisoners'.[106] Mass mobilisation, revolutionary enthusiasm and the rise of competitive young generals saw France successfully counterattack its internal and external enemies.

While the French focused their offensive energy on the north-east, the British dispersed their forces. Navy and troops were sent to the West Indies to capture French islands, and intervene in support of royalist French planters facing a slave revolution in Saint-Domingue. With occupied Toulon and the Vendée uprising calling for British reinforcement, George III warned Pitt: 'the misfortune of our situation is that we have too many objectives to attend to, and our force consequently must be too small at each place'.[107] And so it proved. Toulon was abandoned, help for the Vendeans was too little too late, and lacking the promised naval support the Duke of York failed to secure Dunkirk. With the French 'nation in arms' on the offensive against the allies throughout 1794, Lord Auckland observed that 'all reasonings and all confidence are changed respecting military speculations by the numberless and strange defeats, treacheries, retreats, capitulations, incapacities and disgraces'.[108] The Duke of York was forced to retreat through the Netherlands and into northern Germany where his humiliated army was evacuated from Bremen in April 1795.

In the face of French success, the loose Coalition began to fall apart. Holland was renamed the Batavian Republic under a pro-French government after it was conquered during the eighteenth-century's coldest winter, with French cavalry charging across ice to capture the Dutch fleet in January 1795. With the French occupying Belgium and the left bank of the Rhine, Prussia and Spain made peace in mid 1795. Aided by large British subsidies, Austria fought on until its forces in northern Italy suffered a series of defeats by the young general Napoleon Bonaparte and made peace in early 1797.

There were signs the French regime was moderating. Robespierre and some of his radical associates were executed in July 1794 and a year later another new constitution curbed democracy and created a Directory of five to govern France. With growing opposition to the war and widespread food rioting as a result of two bad harvests, Pitt was keen to start peace negotiations. A despairing Burke condemned the idea in *Letters on a Regicide Peace* (1796), and to an extent George III agreed with him – only very reluctantly approving preliminary peace negotiations in late 1796. Nothing came of these, however, owing to the confidently uncompromising stance of the Directory who spurned the traditional practice of exchanging European gains for the return of colonies conquered by the British. Spain had re-entered the war as an enemy of Britain, Napoleon was winning in northern Italy and plans were afoot to invade Britain and Ireland. In December 1796 a French invasion fleet carrying 15,000 troops eluded the British blockade and arrived in Bantry Bay, south-west Ireland, only to be dispersed by a fierce storm.

George III's ministers faced multiple challenges, but success on the seas enabled them to struggle on. In 1794 the Royal Navy won a victory on the 'Glorious First of June' in which French losses were the heaviest in a single day of battle since 1692.[109] After the Dutch entered the war the British occupied Ceylon and the Cape Colony in southern Africa on behalf of the exiled Prince of Orange. 'What was a feather in the hands of Holland', Dundas said of the Cape, would have 'become a sword in the hands of France'.[110] During the mid 1790s the French republican government allied with insurgent slaves in the West Indies, and Pitt and Dundas sent tens of thousands of troops to the Caribbean in an effort to conquer French colonies. Caught up in a complex conflict, the core of Britain's small army was decimated by tropical disease.[111] Following the near-invasion of Ireland, in February 1797 a small force of 1500 French soldiers landed near Fishguard on the coast of Wales. They soon surrendered, but the incident sparked panic and a run on the banks. Financial meltdown was averted through innovative policies by Pitt, which included allowing banks to issue low-denomination paper notes. Nerves were also steadied when newspapers reported 'VICTORY OVER THE SPANIARDS!!!' by an outnumbered Admiral Jervis at Cape St Vincent.[112] Horatio Nelson became famous as the first flag-officer in nearly 300 years to lead the boarding of an enemy ship, and the scale of defeat inflicted by rapid and accurate British gunnery put an end to the Spanish navy as a major threat.[113]

Concerned at the spread of republican ideas, British loyalists were further panicked by mutinies among the British fleet at both Spithead and the Nore between April and June 1797. While there were some indications of politicisation among the sailors, these mutinies were in essence strikes against poor pay and conditions. They were brought to an end by a combination of royal pardon, concessions and execution of the leading mutineers at the Nore. In October, sailors who had mutinied in turn helped Admiral Duncan win the Battle of Camperdown, which decimated a Dutch fleet that was expected to support the next French attempt to invade Ireland.[114] In the same month Napoleon was put in charge of building an 'Army of England' invasion force along the coast between Normandy and Belgium. Pitt was heartened by the degree to which the British public was galvanised by the threat of invasion, with thousands joining volunteer militia units. Tellingly, when leaders of the radical London Corresponding Society were arrested in April 1798 they were in the midst of debating whether they should join a volunteer unit.[115] They thought the British political system corrupt and in need of reform, but they were not keen for the reforming to be done by the French army.

Ireland, however, was a powder-keg. A republican movement of United Irishmen had formed and wanted French help to make a revolution against British rule. Wolfe Tone, an Irish republican who had accompanied the failed invasion fleet in Bantry Bay, returned to France and lobbied for another invasion attempt. During 1797 General Lake's soldiers, supported by volunteer Protestant 'Orangemen', brutally disarmed and executed suspected republicans in Ulster, their approach heralded by smoke rising from burning houses. Caught between waiting for another French invasion force and increasing repression, the United Irishmen began their revolution at the end of May 1798. In the wake of repression Dublin and Belfast remained quiet, and the uprising was in many ways a short rural civil war limited to the north and south-east. By the time a small French force eventually landed on the remote west coast in August, the rebellion was defeated with up to 30,000 dead. In a large military operation General Cornwallis, a veteran of America and India, sought to quell sectarian conflict, declaring 'the life of a Lord-Lieutenant of Ireland comes up to my idea of perfect misery'.[116] With an eye to the success of the 1707 Act of Union between England and Scotland, Pitt moved to unite Britain and Ireland with an Act of Union that took effect in 1801.

In the face of the Royal Navy's continuing dominance of the English Channel, in mid 1798 Napoleon undertook an expedition to Egypt. He argued it would be a step toward sending military support to Tipu Sultan of Mysore, a determined enemy of the British in India. Successful in conquering Egypt, Napoleon found his army stranded when the French fleet was destroyed in August at the Battle of Aboukir Bay at the mouth of the Nile. 'Victory is not a name strong enough for such a scene', Nelson declared after another brilliant battle that saw all thirteen French ships of the line either burnt or captured. The Nile was one of the most strategically significant battles in history. The Royal Navy became dominant in the Mediterranean, its tonnage began to equal the combined fleets of France, Spain and Holland, and the French navy never regained its confidence.[117] In Vienna Haydn composed a 'Nelson Mass' and Austria eagerly resumed war with France in early 1799.

With France facing a Second Coalition composed of Britain, Austria, Portugal, Russia and Turkey, Napoleon left his army in the Middle East and returned to Paris where he staged a coup and became First Consul in November 1799. In his absence the French had suffered a number of defeats, with a Russian army pushing them out of Italy. Yet tensions soon strained the Coalition. An Anglo-Russian force invaded Holland but had to withdraw after several weeks, and the eccentric Tsar Paul I proceeded to leave the coalition and begin negotiations with France. In early 1800 Napoleon crossed the Alps into Italy where he inflicted another significant defeat on the Austrians at Marengo. By 1801 Britain was once again facing France alone. Angered by British treatment of neutral merchant shipping, Tsar Paul formed a League of Armed Neutrality with Prussia and Scandinavian countries to resist the practice. With the Baltic Sea a vital source of trade, and especially naval provisions, the Royal Navy was sent to attack the Danish fleet. At Copenhagen in April 1801 Nelson led a daring attack that destroyed the Danish fleet and forced them to withdraw from the Russian alliance. Soon after this the League was effectively ended when Tsar Paul was murdered by nobles and replaced by his son, Alexander I.

The war was at a stalemate, with Napoleon master of western Europe and Britain ascendant at sea but lacking Continental allies. Pitt had resigned in February 1801 in the face of George III's opposition to granting full political rights to Catholics following the Act of Union with Ireland. A new ministry under Henry Addington concluded the Peace of Amiens in March 1802, by which all possessions were handed back to France and its allies and the British retained only Spanish Trinidad and Dutch Ceylon, with its valuable harbour at Trincomalee. William Grenville, who had been Foreign Secretary since 1791 and resigned with Pitt, opposed it as a 'disgraceful and ruinous treaty', but was defeated in the Lords by 114 votes to 10.[118] With a ballooning debt, two failed harvests and social unrest, a war-weary nation was resigned to a necessary peace.

Napoleonic Wars, 1803–1815

Addington moved to demobilise Britain's military forces, while a wary eye was kept on French behaviour around the globe. For example, with a French scientific expedition exploring the coast of Australia during the Peace of Amiens, the British governor of New South Wales decided to send settlers to Van Diemen's Land lest Napoleon decide to make it a French colony.[119] With an eye to restoring French power in the Americas, Napoleon charged a small expedition with re-establishing a presence in Louisiana, and sent 35,000 troops to conquer Haiti and restore slavery. With war looming with Britain, however, in April 1803 he sold the USA the vast territory of Louisiana, stretching from the west bank of the Mississippi to the Rocky Mountains. This provided $80 million for Napoleon's war chest.

Addington's ministry was desperate for a sustained period of peace, but Napoleon was clearly eyeing further conquests. 'With my France, England should have naturally finished by being nothing more than an appendix', he reflected near the end of his life. 'Nature had made her one of our islands as much as those of Oleron or of Corsica.'[120] During 1802 Napoleon moved to strengthen his dominant position in Europe contrary to both the spirit and letter of the Treaty of Amiens. Angered by ongoing mockery of him in the British newspapers, Napoleon demanded they be censored by the British government and the exiled

Bourbon princes sent back to the Continent. On more than one occasion he publicly abused the British ambassador. A French officer sent on a reconnaissance mission to North Africa published a report in January 1803 in which it was claimed that Egypt could be easily reconquered. Addington ordered a slow-down of troop withdrawal from Egypt, asked that Britain be allowed to retain Malta, and demanded that Napoleon withdraw from Holland and Switzerland. When these conditions were not met, in May 1803 'the whale went to war with the elephant'.[121]

Aside from Trafalgar, in which Nelson died, the first five years of the Napoleonic Wars saw little in the way of major Franco-British battles. With Napoleon preparing a huge invasion force, an unprecedented mobilisation of navy, army, militia and volunteers began in Britain. Radicals and reformers tended to join loyalists in preparing to resist an invasion by the authoritarian Napoleon. Out of office, William Pitt busied himself as the commander of three battalions of volunteers. By the end of 1803 there were over 200,000 soldiers in the British army and nearly 400,000 in volunteer regiments.[122] In order for his army to cross 'the mere ditch' and invade England, the French navy needed to master the Channel. Contrary to popular belief, the Battle of Trafalgar in October 1805 did not save Britain from immediate invasion – Napoleon had already turned his back to the Channel and proceeded to defeat the Austrians at Ulm. But it did devastate the Spanish and French fleets, and gave the Royal Navy command of the seas – which was crucial to the growing British economy. In the words of Nicholas Rodger, 'Napoleon had no sooner thrown away his fleet than he realised how much he needed it to break out of the strategic limitations of his situation, and spent the rest of his reign in a futile and immensely costly attempt to reconstruct it'.[123] Trafalgar was followed by more years blockading French ports in stormy seas. Many merchant ships were lost to small French warships and by 1813 Napoleon had rebuilt his navy to eighty ships of the line. The Royal Navy had to work hard to maintain the command of the ocean won at Trafalgar.[124]

British politics in the decade following 1801 is a tale of weak ministries, factionalism and scandal. In 1804 Pitt had become increasingly critical of Addington's conduct of the war, denouncing the 'tardiness, languor, and imbecility of ministers in every thing'.[125] In May the King recalled Pitt as prime minister and, at the head of a weak ministry, he worked at developing a Continental alliance. He was aided in this by Napoleon's occupation of Genoa in mid 1805, which ensured that a Third Coalition formed, centred on Britain, Russia and Austria.

Napoleon came to dominate Europe though a series of stunning victories. An Austro-Russian force was spectacularly defeated at Austerlitz at the end of 1805. Austria made a humiliating peace and Napoleon proceeded to reorganise the smaller German states into a Confederation of the Rhine. In return for neutrality, Prussia had been allowed to absorb Hanover. With Napoleon pressing for additional territory in Germany and willing to return Hanover to Britain to secure peace, in September 1806 the Prussian King Frederick William III demanded that the French withdraw from southern Germany. Disaster followed as the heirs of Frederick the Great were swiftly routed at Jena, and French soldiers occupied Berlin at the end of October. Napoleon pressed on into East Prussia fighting hard battles against the Russians in 1807, before meeting with Tsar Alexander I on a barge in the River Niemen to conclude the Treaty of Tilsit in July. Prussia was forced to host French garrisons and cede land to a new Grand Duchy of Poland. Russia agreed to join Napoleon's 'Continental System' which aimed to blockade and break the British economy.

While Napoleon became master of Europe, the British expanded their global empire. Pittite ministries tended to prioritise the war in Europe, only initiating colonial campaigns when expeditions to the continent were not possible. Colonial gains were usually the result of local initiatives. Cape Town had been very reluctantly handed back to the Dutch as part of the Amiens treaty, and in 1805 Pitt sent a force to recapture this strategically important colony at the southern tip of Africa. In the West Indies, after losing tens of thousands of troops in fighting the slave revolt in French Saint-Domingue in the mid 1790s, the British had signed a non-aggression pact in 1798 with the black leader Toussaint l'Ouverture. They switched to a policy of consolidation and local opportunism, creating redcoat regiments of black slaves (collectively emancipated in 1807), 8,000 of whom came to account for a third of the British West Indian garrison.[126] When war renewed with Napoleon, local forces seized Dutch Guiana in 1803, followed by several French, Dutch and Danish colonies. Only in 1809 was a significant force sent from North America to conquer Martinique, and, in the following year, Guadeloupe.

The British East India Company greatly increased its power during the course of the Revolutionary and Napoleonic Wars. Wars against Tipu Sultan of Mysore, who allied himself with France, had ended with his death during the storming of his fortress at Seringapatam in 1799. Expansionist war against the Maratha princes led the imperious Richard Wellesley to boast at the end of 1803 that 'the result of a glorious and uninterrupted course of victories has extinguished the last remnant of French influence in India, and has confirmed the stability of the British Empire in the East'.[127] In Wellesley's short period as Governor-General, 1797–1805, thanks in large part to the military skill of his brother Arthur, British rule was extended across most of India via treaties through which princes were bound to provide subsidies and military aid. Almost bankrupting the Company, Wellesley was replaced in the face of widespread concern about imperial overreach, but he had built up a formidable Indian army. In 1810–11 Lord Minto used it to conquer the French naval base at Mauritius and, after Napoleon annexed the Netherlands, the Dutch East Indies were captured by Stamford Raffles.

Pitt lived to receive the bittersweet news of Trafalgar, but his dying days were clouded by Austrian defeat. He was succeeded by pedestrian prime ministers in the form of William Grenville (1806–07), the aging Duke of Portland (1807–09) and Spencer Perceval (1809–12) at the head of unstable ministries, until Lord Liverpool became a long serving Tory prime minister from 1812 to 1827.

Following Pitt's death George III was forced to accept a 'Ministry of All the Talents' headed by Lord Grenville and including Charles James Fox as Foreign Secretary and leader in the Commons. Long a critic of the wars, Fox failed in his efforts to make peace with Napoleon. When the French invaded Naples a British force withdrew with King Ferdinand to Sicily, which they proceeded to fortify as support for the British naval base on Malta. In mid-1806 Sir John Stuart crossed back into southern Italy with over 4,000 troops and an eye to encouraging a peasant uprising. Before withdrawing he confronted and defeated a slightly larger French army at Maida. While small in scale, news of this victory was greeted rapturously as evidence that British soldiers could beat Napoleon's troops.[128] The Talents pursued a blue-water policy and acted coolly toward Continental allies. Military resources were dissipated in expeditions to the Dardanelles and Egypt, and in trying to secure Buenos Aires with a small force as a step toward conquering Spain's vast South American Empire. Aside from abolishing the British slave trade, the Talents ministry failed to live up to its promise and used George III's unbending opposition to Catholic emancipation as an issue upon which to resign.

'Tory' Pittites returned to government in March 1807 under the aging Duke of Portland and sought to reengage with continental allies.[129] The policy of the Talents combined with Napoleon's victories had left Britain almost isolated, with its only allies being in southern Europe. Appointed Foreign Secretary, George Canning planned to capture the Danish fleet before it fell into the hands of Napoleon. In September the siege of Copenhagen saw 2000 civilians killed by bombardment before the Danes surrendered their fleet.[130] The following year Canning announced:

> We shall proceed upon the principle that any nation of Europe that starts up with a determination to oppose a power which...is the common enemy of all nations...becomes instantly our essential ally.

As Michael Duffy has observed, in saying this Canning in effect 'confessed British diplomatic impotence'.[131] The British faced a number of diplomatic problems, not the least being that the eastern European powers were as worried about each other's expansionist intentions as they were about Napoleon. They did not share Britain's obsession with France, resented its lack of interest in Eastern issues, disliked its maritime hegemony, and regarded the British as unreliable and self-serving.

In 1805 Lord Castlereagh had helped Pitt promote the idea of a 'general concert' of Europe's powers in order to oppose French 'schemes of ambition and aggrandisement'.[132] Together they organised the despatch of thousands of troops to Hanover, only to immediately withdraw them in light of the Austro-Russian defeat at Austerlitz. When the Austrians again went to war in 1809, Castlereagh, as Secretary for War, pushed for an amphibious attack on the island of Walcheren in the Scheldt Estuary. The original cause of war between Britain and Revolutionary France, the Scheldt had become the second largest French naval base – Napoleon described it 'a cocked pistol pointed at the head of England'.[133] Over 40,000 troops in 600 vessels sailed for the Scheldt just as news arrived that Napoleon had defeated the Austrians in a bloody battle at Wagram. Disaster followed. With malaria spreading through their ranks and in the face of French reinforcements, after a few weeks the British had to withdraw from Walcheren, having achieved little and with only 10,000 men left fit for service. Facing a storm of criticism and discovering that the Foreign Secretary had been undermining him within the cabinet for months, Castlereagh resigned and won a pistol duel to which he challenged Canning.[134] In 1812 Castlereagh returned to office under Lord Liverpool, serving as leader in the Commons and arguably Britain's greatest Foreign Secretary until, harassed and overworked, he slit his throat in 1822.

To win the war Britain needed a major uprising they could support in Western Europe, allies who could defeat Napoleon's army in Central Europe, and the diplomatic ability to hold an alliance together until

France was returned to its pre-Revolutionary borders. With the help of Napoleon's overbearing behaviour, to a large extent these three needs were met by Spain, Russia and Castlereagh.

The conflict that began in mid 1808 on the Iberian Peninsula provided the British with their best opportunity to engage in continental warfare. Traditionally a trading partner and ally of Britain, Portugal proved a frustrating leak in Napoleon's Continental System. Having marched an army through Spain to conquer Portugal, Napoleon proceeded to replace Spain's Bourbon monarch with his own brother Joseph. This attempt to rule the Peninsula backfired with serious ramifications. It provoked a popular uprising consisting of both organised armies and partisans waging guerrilla warfare. This brutal conflict became Napoleon's 'Spanish ulcer', tying down and killing hundreds of thousands of French soldiers. It encouraged resistance in other parts of Europe, with Napoleon forced to engage in some very bloody battles to defeat the Austrians again in 1809. The Royal Navy carried the Portuguese royal family to refuge in Brazil, and helped supply those fighting French occupation on the Iberian Peninsula. British merchants gained lucrative opportunities to trade with South America as a result of Napoleon's occupation of Spain and subsequent revolutions for independence in its colonies – something that did much to counterbalance the economic impact of Napoleon's blockade.

The scale of the Spanish uprising encouraged the British to send an army to Portugal in July 1808. Castlereagh was instrumental in ensuring that Arthur Wellesley, the future Duke of Wellington, was placed in command. In addition to his talented military leadership, Wellington exercised great political skill in working with the Portuguese and Spanish in a highly complex conflict. Using his fortified lines of Torres Vedras as a fall-back position, throughout 1809–11 Wellington skilfully defended his position in Portugal. When some French forces transferred to the campaign in Russia in 1812, Wellington went on the offensive. At Salamanca he won a memorable victory, after which he briefly occupied Madrid before retreating to Portugal. In mid 1813 Wellington's celebrated victory at Vitoria in northern Spain saw the French retreat to the Pyrenees.[135]

Involvement in the Peninsular War was subject to sustained criticism in parliament and press as a costly distraction that weakened Britain's diplomatic clout in northern Europe. From the opposition benches Grenville argued that it would be better to marshal forces in Britain in preparation for another opportunity to intervene in the Low Countries or Germany. Contrary to such criticism, however, Wellington's campaign on the Peninsula made a substantial contribution to Britain's war effort. Had Napoleon conquered Spain and Portugal the impact on Britain's maritime strategy would have been significant, and it would have freed up 200,000 French troops for deployment in central Europe. This might have won the war for Napoleon. The Peninsular campaign also forged a battle hardened Anglo-Portuguese army that became the first Allied troops to enter France in 1814. Without Wellington's boots on the ground Castlereagh would not have had a strong diplomatic hand to play.[136]

In 1812 Russia broke the military might of Napoleon. Angered by Tsar Alexander's failure to conform to his Continental System, Napoleon assembled an army of over 600,000 and marched deep into Russia. After the bloody but indecisive Battle of Borodino Napoleon occupied Moscow, but had to withdraw after it caught fire. A horrific retreat ensued as winter descended.[137] With Napoleon having lost hundreds of thousands of veteran soldiers and horses in Russia, Prussia joined a Sixth Coalition.

Napoleon won some victories in early 1813 and the Austrians hesitated as to which side they would join. Behind British backs, Austria's Prince Metternich tried to negotiate a generous peace between Napoleon and the Eastern Powers. This would have left the Rhine as France's border, and thus Antwerp and the Scheldt estuary in Napoleon's hands. After he heard the news of Wellington's decisive victory at Vitoria in June, however, Metternich broke off negotiations with an arrogant and uncompromising Napoleon. Castlereagh ensured the Allies were granted massive and unconditional subsidies – urging that 'we have now the bull pinioned between us, and if either of us lets go our hold till we render him harmless, we shall deserve to suffer for it'.[138]

At Leipzig in October Napoleon lost the 'Battle of the Nations' and began a fighting retreat toward Paris. In the words of Jeremy Black, after the Napoleonic Wars Allied 'cooperation was made to seem inevitable, but it was not, and it was only on 1 March 1814, at Chaumont, that the Allies agreed not to conclude any separate peace with Napoleon and, instead, to continue the war and then join in maintaining the peace'.[139] Castlereagh had crossed on to the Continent to conduct diplomacy personally, in line with the principles he had drawn up with Pitt in 1805. In the words of one diplomat, 'what Castlereagh has achieved is really wonderful. But for him I do believe we should have been off, the Devil take the hindmost'.[140] After Paris fell, Napoleon was forced to abdicate in April and exiled to the island of Elba.

In October 1814 the Allied leadership met at the Congress of Vienna to begin long and complex negotiations over the post-war settlement. While the discussions proceeded amidst concerts and balls, Napoleon escaped from Elba and raised a new army in France, only to be defeated at Waterloo in June 1815. Louis XVIII was restored to the throne, and Napoleon was exiled far away on the island of St Helena in the South Atlantic under British guard. The Congress of Vienna aimed to ensure collective security within Europe by establishing a 'just equilibrium' between the five great powers of Russia, Prussia, Austria, France and Britain. Britain was happy to see the creation of an independent United Netherlands, and Russia was allowed to rule over most of Poland. Metternich and Castlereagh worked with Talleyrand to ensure the treatment of France was not too punitive, in order to help Louis XVIII consolidate his reign. While obliged to return to its 1789 borders, and forced to pay indemnities, France regained some of its colonial empire. In light of the growing power of Russia, a stable France was seen as an important ally in preserving the balance of power. Radicals and reformers criticised the Congress as a reactionary attempt to entrench monarchy and aristocratic privilege. For Castlereagh, however, the primary aim was to preserve peace in a changing world: 'It is impossible not to perceive a great moral change coming on in Europe, and that the principles of freedom are in full operation. The danger is, that the transition may be too sudden to ripen into anything likely to make the world better or happier'.[141]

On the face of it Britain's gains from the Congress of Vienna seemed to fall short of its large contribution to the war. The strategically important harbours of Malta, Cape Town and Mauritius were retained, and in the West Indies the colonies of Trinidad, Tobago and St Lucia. But many colonies were returned to the French and Dutch. Napoleon ridiculed Castlereagh's diplomacy, wondering 'how a sensible nation can allow herself to be governed by such a lunatic ... What great advantage, what just compensations, has he acquired for his country? The peace he has made is the sort of peace he would have made if he had been beaten'.[142] Yet as various historians have pointed out, this was to misunderstand the defensive nature of British aims. While jingoistic imperialist voices were often raised in parliament and press, British ministers worried about imperial overreach. They prioritised pursuit of strategic security via preserving a balance of power in Europe and a friendly Netherlands. As Lord Harrowby declared in early 1814, 'Antwerp and Flushing out of the hands of France are worth twenty Martiniques in our hands'.[143]

Wellington said that Waterloo was 'a damned nice thing – the nearest run thing you ever saw'.[144] The same could be said of the whole Seventy Years War. As Michael Duffy has observed with respect to the final two decades of war, 'Britain owed its *survival* in this long struggle to its national determination to keep fighting, to its financial strength and to its sea power. It owed its ultimate *triumph* to its allies and to Napoleon.'[145] Down to the final months of the war it had always been possible for Napoleon to secure his rule over a large France, had he been willing to compromise with the Eastern powers. Given different diplomacy, Anglo-French rivalry and war might have continued.

Foreign policy played a key role in Britain's fortunes during the Seventy Years War. Cultivation of alliances was crucial, and it is notable that Britain's main defeat occurred when it became diplomatically isolated during the American War. For its part, France squandered opportunities to shift more weight on to its conflict with Britain. Louis XV did not need to agree to neutrality for the Low Countries in 1756, and Napoleon did not need to attack Austria in 1805 or Russia in 1812.[146] Throughout the Seventy Years War Britain swung between defeats and victories, between invasion threats and naval triumphs, between success and fiasco in amphibious expeditions. All the while, taxation and the national debt ballooned, and the economy, politics and culture were profoundly influenced.

Chapter 2: The Fiscal-Naval State

> It is obvious that the present strength and pre-eminence of this country is owing to the extent of its resources arising from its commerce and its naval power which are inseparably connected. – Henry Dundas.[1]

The pressures of the Seventy Years War saw Britain develop a powerful 'fiscal-naval state' based on heavy taxation and a large public debt. In addition to analysing the sources of funding, this chapter shows how the fiscal-naval state contracted resources and reformed its administration in order to increase the efficiency of its military spending. It concludes by assessing the role of the fiscal-naval state in maintaining social order and fostering the first industrial revolution.

Scholarship on early modern European state formation has emphasised the rise of 'absolute monarchies'.[2] Monarchs such as Louis XIV were seen as centralising authority at the expense of the rights and privileges of various corporate groups such as aristocracy, church and regional estates. The concept of a 'military revolution' occurring from the sixteenth to eighteenth centuries was linked to the development of absolutism.[3] Large armies with regimental organisation and weapons fired by gunpowder enabled monarchs to increase their power at the expense of domestic and smaller international rivals. Contemporaries recognised that there had been great change, with a writer in 1788 asking: 'Suppose that the Greeks or the Romans had discovered gunpowder; would that invention in their hands have produced the same revolution in military art that we have seen in our times?'[4] The high cost of modern armies in turn drove monarchs to increase taxation. England/ Britain does not fit the standard definition of the military revolution, as its monarchy remained limited and its army small. While it is clear that profound changes occurred in European warfare over the period 1500–1800, there are problems with the concept of a 'military revolution': can something that occurred over three centuries be called a 'revolution'? And to a large extent military change reinforced traditional social structures. The role of navies has also tended to be neglected, and so 'military revolution' does not explain the success of Britain.

It is often assumed that limits imposed by parliament caused Britain to have a weaker state and lighter taxation than absolute monarchies. Separated from continental land wars by the English Channel, in the words of the historical-sociologist Michael Mann, 'a rich trading country like England could maintain great power status without reaching a high level of tax extraction and therefore without a standing army'.[5] This view has implications for how we understand the origins of the industrial revolution, with free-market liberals holding Britain up as an example of the virtues of small government.

Scholarship in the past two decades has, however, transformed our view of the British state in the eighteenth century. During the long eighteenth century there emerged, in the words of John Brewer, 'a peculiarly British version of the fiscal-military state, complete with large armies and navies, industrious administrators, high taxes and huge debts'.[6] Yet while the term 'fiscal-military state' is appropriate for continental states that devoted their resources to large land armies, Britain is best described as a 'fiscal-naval state', given the Royal Navy's relatively high cost, need for sustained investment, large organisational structure and key role in British military strategy and economic expansion.[7] While its foundations were put in place in the late seventeenth century, during the Seventy Years War Britain's fiscal-naval state was refined and loomed large.

The British state spent similar amounts of money on its army and navy between 1744 and 1815. If subsidies are included, whether to pay for troops serving in an allied army or foreigners under British command, the proportion of expenditure was 55% on soldiers and 45% on the navy.[8] Expenditure on the army and subsidies spiked during times of Continental commitment, skyrocketing during the Peninsular War and final campaigns against Napoleon. While slightly more was spent on soldiers over the course of the Seventy Years War in total, in terms of the relative amount of funds devoted to the navy Britain appears to have been far ahead of Continental 'fiscal-military' states (see the comparative size of navies in Chapter 3).[9] And naval expenditure had important economic feedback loops. In contrast to the army, a greater proportion of naval funds were spent within Britain, thus adding to economic growth; and the navy protected British maritime trade, while damaging that of its rivals. This appears to have given the British fiscal-naval state a significant competitive advantage: its balance of defence spending had a more positive, or at least less negative, economic effect than in army-dominated Continental fiscal-military states.

International relations in the early modern period were highly combative, with states spending most of their revenue on military strength – generally around 70%, but as high as 90% in wartime. Some states thrived, some struggled and others vanished. Historians are hard at work trying to understand the various factors that shaped the path-dependent fates of early modern states. It has long been recognised that some were too small to survive – finding themselves absorbed into larger neighbours. It also seems that many early modern Eurasian empires 'became too large and heterogeneous' to transform into developmental modern states – for example, the Ottoman Empire, Austria, Russia and Qing China.[10] Britain was a middle-size state that had the advantage of ruling over a relatively cohesive and taxable island nation, with a thriving maritime trade. It became exceptional in developing a powerful fiscal-naval state.

Despite having a much smaller population and economy, Britain developed a state that was able to tax and borrow more than France. In 1745 the population of Great Britain was 7 million compared to France's 21 million, and the ratio remained approximately 1:3 throughout the Seventy Years War. In the decade after 1800 the figures were roughly 11 million compared to 30 million people. Traditional depictions of the French economy as moribund have been revised by historians, and French science, technology and manufacturing were well advanced.[11] It was possible for the French finance minister, de Fleury, to write in 1782:

> From any standpoint, England's position is far from being as favour-able as that of France, inasmuch as she has not a third of our money in circulation or our population; nor a soil so extensive or productive; nor as many manufactures of all varieties; nor a geography so favourable, which links us by land and sea to all parts of Europe and the globe.[12]

Economic historians have calculated that France's gross national product was at least twice the size of Britain's.[13] Despite these compara-tive disadvantages, the more effective means of raising revenue devel-oped by the British state enabled it to compete with its larger neighbour. While at the start of the Seventy Years War Britain had one of the smallest armies in Europe, by 1815 it had among the largest number of men under arms in Europe and the world's largest navy.

Britain's public expenditure during periods of open conflict grew significantly over the course of the Seventy Years War. Average annual public spending was £7.3 million in the 1740s. Measured in real terms, during the period 1756–63 the figure rose to £14.8 million, and then to £17.4 million for 1777–83, and £29.2 million for the French Revolutionary and Napoleonic Wars. Most of this was devoted to military spending, or servicing wartime debt. Only 11% of the budget was spent on civil government during the 1740s, dropping to 6% by 1815.[14] At the end of the Seventy Years War, Britons were paying three times more tax per capita than the French; and the per capita burden of public debt was fifteen times larger.[15]

Despite its large-scale revenue and expenditure, it can still be argued that eighteenth-century Britain had a relatively 'small state'. The efficient Excise department and size of the Royal Navy are central to the claim that Britain had a strong state. Yet aside from this, the eighteenth-century British state looks very traditional and unreformed. In the words of Wilfrid Prest, 'Hanoverian government was not merely decentralized, but "polyarchic" – multi-centred – with power widely and almost randomly distributed among an array of agencies and individuals, including Crown, ministry, both houses of parliament, privy council, the Church of England, the law courts, the Bank of England, and the East India Company.'[16] At the local level there were JPs, alderman and various commissioners. Collection of the land tax was in the hands of local elites, the standing army was relatively small and mostly stationed overseas, and home defence depended on militia and volunteers.[17] It can even be argued that the British East India Company had a more impressive bureaucracy than the British state.[18]

Early modern English monarchs, and the Parliamentary Commonwealth, had sought to centralise government, but the Revolution of 1688 marked a reaction against this trend. This is best illustrated by the changing role of the monarch's Privy Council, established under Henry VIII, which aimed to supervise all elements of government. While its powers were limited in practice, under the early Stuarts it increasingly sought to collect information and intervene in local affairs. In light of the seventeenth-century experience of Stuart authoritarianism and Cromwellian military rule, supporters of the Revolution of 1688 sought to make government more accountable to parliament. During the eighteenth century the Privy Council was marginalised, as decision-making and responsibility increasingly rested with specialist departments, most notably the Treasury, Admiralty, and Secretaries of State. Ministers responsible for departments met in 'cabinet', but as war and foreign policy dominated their discussions there was little coordination of domestic government. Different departments were largely left to interact with society in their own spheres of interest. Most domestic affairs were handled by the Secretaries of State; the position of Home Secretary (who was also responsible for colonial affairs) was created in 1782. Government of domestic affairs was 'co-ordinated by more or less informal co-operation between leading statesmen'.[19]

It would be perverse, however, to describe the state that won the Seventy Years War as 'weak'. The problem is that the criteria for measuring 'weak' and 'strong' states were originally drawn up with an eye to continental absolute monarchies, with the number of administrators and size of professional armies as key measures. It is better that we think in terms of the effectiveness of a state in achieving its key aims of defence, domestic peace and order, and where necessary and possible, expansion. The British state was 'strong' because it cooperated with society through parliament, the established churches, the legal system and local government.[20]

Rather than seeing parliament as an institution that limited the state, we can see it as a body that fostered a robust partnership between state and society. The seventeenth-century revolutions enhanced and secured the status of parliament. After 1688 government policy was increasingly implemented by act of parliament, ensuring that decisions were debated and enacted with a degree of support among the social elite. In the ten parliamentary sessions prior to 1688 only 10% of proposed bills were enacted, while the figure was 75% for the period 1688–1800. Along with the increasing success rate there was a dramatic increase in the number of parliamentary acts: there were around 2,700 acts passed in the 200 years before 1688, but over 13,600 between 1688 and the union with Ireland in 1801.[21] In many ways the mid eighteenth century was a golden age of the independent parliamentarian. With the attention of government drawn towards international relations and fiscal challenges, legislation on social policy was often introduced by back-bench members of parliament. Much of this legislation was concerned with local issues, but much was also national in scope – with ministers often consulted informally about proposed legislation.[22]

While ministerial initiation of social legislation increased, government remained dependent on cooperation with local authorities throughout the Seventy Years War. Even after the Home Office was created, its small staff could do little more than monitor, advise and request information from local authorities. The pressures of war and the 'information age' aspect of the Enlightenment, however, combined to foster an overall growth of national administration and policies. Government and parliamentary committees increasingly requested information from local authorities such as the clergy, magistrates and lords lieutenant, and these people often enthusiastically cooperated. There was no shortage of enlightened local individuals and associations keen to collect data, improve record keeping, and promote reform. And national legislation for social reform usually grew out of successful initiatives developed at a local level. The dramatic bureaucratic expansion of the British state in the mid nineteenth century was built upon the modernising processes and data collected by local government in the decades prior to 1815.[23]

Britain was a composite state that governed over the ethnic nations of England, Wales, Scotland, and after 1801, Ireland. While the state was most interventionist in the legal and economic restructuring of the Highlands of Scotland the weight of parliament's legislative activity was focused on England. As the most economically developed and administratively integrated nation, England was the most heavily taxed and regulated part of Great Britain. Parliament acted as a forum in which the applicability of policies to the United Kingdom's constituent nations could be debated, and in the clash of accents and interests the distinctiveness of ethnic national identities was in some ways enhanced.[24] The state nevertheless became more 'British' as Scots, Welsh and Irish migrated to London and filled civil service and military positions.

Parliament facilitated the growth of the fiscal-naval state and rooted it in a degree of public deference and support. This enabled the state to maintain domestic order while raising significant funds to fight France. If government as a whole was polyarchic, its parts nevertheless became stronger under the pressures of the Seventy Years War. Where the state did not undertake activities itself, it directed funds as a contractor or encouraged patriotic efforts.

Taxation

A crushing and inequitable tax burden is usually cited as a main cause of the French Revolution. Thus, it was surprising when detailed research revealed that the British were more heavily taxed. For most of the Seventy Years War French taxation remained around 11–12% of national economic output, not even rising under Napoleon's modernising regime – which relied on extracting resources from occupied countries. The British population paid nearly twice that rate of tax, rising even higher during the war against Napoleon.[25] Viewed over a longer term, in 1640 – at the start of the decade in which England experienced a civil war and executed Charles I – its per capita taxation equalled 14 grams of silver, compared to 30 grams in France. At the start of the French Revolution 150 years later the roles had reversed: In 1789 French taxation per capita was 75 grams of silver, compared to 188 in England.[26] If high taxation was a significant cause of revolution the historical roles should have been reversed, with a republican regime created in mid-seventeenth-century France (rather than the absolute monarchy of Louis XIV), and George III facing revolution and execution in Britain at the end of the eighteenth century.

Following the Glorious Revolution of 1688, two decades of war against Louis XIV placed enormous financial strain on the British state. The new regime's wars for survival were initially funded by an increase in taxation. It appears that England had been relatively under-taxed throughout the sixteenth and seventeenth centuries, despite the continual protests of parliament and eventual civil war. The revolution of 1688 secured parliamentary control over legislation and taxation, and politicians proceeded to vote increased revenue in order to defeat Louis XIV's expansionism and prevent a Catholic Stuart restoration.

There were three phases of growth in the level of taxation raised from the British economy in the long eighteenth century: initial escalation during the wars against Louis XIV, a gradual rise from the 1740s to 1790s, and then a sharp rise in the wars against the French republic and empire. In 1680, total tax receipts were £1.5 million, but rose to over £5 million in the first decade of the eighteenth century. In real terms receipts from taxation hovered around £5 million until the 1740s, rose during the Seventy Years War to £10.8 million in 1795, and then almost trebled to £28 million in 1815. Some of this reflects growth in the British economy, but most came from improved administration and the extension of taxation – especially Pitt's introduction of income tax in 1799. Over the course of the Seventy Years War the British economy grew, but tax revenue grew faster: taxation remained around 10% of national income from the 1740s to 1780s, and then rose to 18.2% in 1810.[27]

The pillars of Britain's eighteenth-century tax regime were put in place before the revolution of 1688. Tudor and Stuart monarchs confronted significant administrative difficulties and repeatedly clashed with parliament in their efforts to raise taxes. They were never able to raise revenue above an average of 2–3% of national income. Resort to indirect taxes by royal prerogative provoked resistance and resulted in revolution in the 1640s. Chastened by regicide and republican rule, parliaments accepted some growth in indirect tax under the restored monarchy of Charles II, while resisting any significant expansion in direct tax on property. Importantly, the Restoration period saw the establishment of a relatively efficient excise tax bureaucracy.[28]

During the eighteenth century, direct tax was collected by local elites according to the traditional practice of quotas based on the wealth of regions. The quotas for this 'land tax' were based on valuations made in the 1690s, and thus in the course of the eighteenth century the tax failed to tap the new wealth generated by urbanisation and industrialisation, particularly in the booming north of England. With the land-tax as low as 5% in peacetime, parliament nevertheless allowed it to rise to 20% during the frequent war years. Yet any hint of reforming the land tax, or having it collected by a department of state, provoked heated political resistance from the landed gentlemen in parliament. As a result, while direct tax had accounted for 47% of total tax revenue in the 1690s, it averaged only half that proportion for most of the Seventy Years War. Only when British finances were near breaking point at the end of the eighteenth century was William Pitt able to introduce an income tax, which saw direct tax rise to more than 30% of total tax revenue.[29]

During most of the Seventy Years War 70–80% of tax revenue was raised indirectly, mainly through customs duties on imports and excise duties on domestic goods. Customs duties, which were collected in an inefficient manner, accounted for approximately 25% of total tax revenue. The approximately 2,000 customs officials were often appointed as an act of patronage by the Treasury, and in addition to a small wage they drew income from fees, which encouraged corruption. Customs duties were highest on imported manufactured, foreign and luxury goods, which encouraged smuggling of these products. Revenue from customs duties stagnated because eighteenth-century trade grew fastest in imports of food and raw materials from the empire.[30]

The Excise department proved the fiscal-state's most effective arm, collecting around 50% of total tax revenue during the Seventy Years War.[31] By the 1780s the fiscal bureaucracy had nearly 8,000 employees, and around 5,000 of these collected excise duties.[32] Created in 1683, the Department of Excise was distinctive in developing some of the attributes of a modern professional civil service. Excise officials were paid a salary, sat exams, were promoted on merit and received a retirement pension. Tom Paine worked as an excise assessor and his first publication was *The Case of the Officers of the Excise* (1772) in support of an unsuccessful campaign for a salary increase. He noted that 'no set of men under His Majesty earn their salary with any comparison of labour and fatigue ... the station may rather be called a seat of constant work than either a place or an employment'.[33] The efficiency and reliability of excise officers saw government broaden their reach over the course of the century. Walpole tried to make the Excise department responsible for some customs duties in 1733, but a storm of protest forced him to back down. After the younger Pitt managed to make excise officers responsible for collecting duties on imported tea, spirits, wine and tobacco in the 1780s, total customs revenue began to rise.

It was the nature of tax collection, rather than the scale of the burden, that made the difference between Britain and France. Taxes in France were highly visible, irritating and inequitable. There were internal customs barriers. There was a heavy reliance on direct taxation, but with privileged exemptions. Tax was collected by 'tax farmers' who acted as agents of the state and creamed off profitable fees. For all this, the French state failed to increase its tax revenue in real terms in the decades prior to the Revolution. In the words of Richard Bonney, 'the weakness of the *ancien régime* was not too much, but too little taxation'.[34]

British taxation was more universal and accountable. In contrast to France's numerous jurisdictions and corporate privileges, Britain's parliament provided 'a single powerful institution capable of making decisions that were binding on the whole realm'.[35] There was an internal free market in Britain, with customs duties only provoking opposition in coastal communities. Most exports were duty-free, so a producer could avoid the excise by selling overseas. The rate of direct land tax was universal, without privileged exemptions, and was self-administered by local elites. Excise duties were collected at point of production, which largely hid them from consumers, enabling the state to raise rates and broaden the excise net. And in an effort to mitigate their inherently regressive nature, British politicians calibrated their application of indirect taxes. Commodities regarded as 'necessities' of the poor were generally exempt, and 'luxuries' targeted – for example, cheap tallow candles were exempt from the excise, while wax candles were taxed. As a result, a growing burden of taxation fell upon the rising incomes of the industrious middling sort – the same people who benefited disproportionately from the commercial and colonial gains of war. The younger Pitt declared it 'justice to tax the wealthier in preference to the more indigent part of the community', and so over 60% of the additional taxation in the period 1793–1815 fell on the incomes of the wealthy and on luxury goods.[36]

All early modern states in Eurasia faced political and administrative difficulties in taxing their populations, but Britain was among the most successful in meeting the fiscal challenges. Effective taxation requires a monetised market, and in this the British state had an advantage given the relatively advanced state of capitalism and free trade within its borders.[37] Nevertheless, it is estimated that around 40% of the British population remained outside of the effective tax base owing to evasion, poverty, customary practices and administrative difficulties – thus the Celtic regions were relatively lightly taxed, and governments concerned about political stability prudently allowed this to continue. If total revenue is compared to the roughly 60% of the economy that was taxable, then by the end of the Seventy Years War the British state was extracting approximately 30% in tax from its economic base (a figure similar to that of a modern state).[38] While Britons often grumbled and at times rioted about tax, there was no revolution. It was only the lightly taxed Britons in North America that made a revolution in response to heavy-handed efforts to impose highly visible indirect taxes.[39]

National Debt

A reliable and expandable tax base was primarily used to secure and service loans. Most of Britain's Seventy Years War was funded by borrowing, and at its end the national debt had reached eye-watering levels, above two and a half times the size of the British economy. By 1815 over 50% of tax revenue was committed to paying interest on the national debt.[40] This staggering debt was gradually paid down during the relatively peaceful international environment of the nineteenth century, through financial reforms and the economic benefits of the industrial revolution and a global empire. The story might have been very different had the defeat of Napoleon not been so resounding.

The public debts of Britain and France dwarfed those of other European states. Many Enlightenment thinkers worried about where the growing scale of debt and military force would lead – particularly in a nation as large as France. Some thought that unless political reform was enacted it would lead to the 'emergence of a highly militarized dictatorial regime', which would default on all debt and 'destroy much of the civility, culture and liberty that had been built up in Europe since the Age of the Renaissance'.[41]

The rise and rise of Britain's public debt caused much worry and criticism. On the face of it, in the wake of the American War of Independence the finances of Britain appeared in worse shape than France. The French economy was more than twice the size of Britain, and its debt was smaller. In 1788 the public debt of France was 65% of its national income, while Britain's was over 180%.[42] At that time it was the French state, however, that was in the grip of a financial crisis that led to revolution. While Britain's debt was larger, it paid less in annual loan payments – for the first five decades of the Seventy Years War the British state was able to borrow at an interest rate 2% lower than France.[43] As a result, in 1788 Louis XVI had to spend the equivalent of £12.2 million on debt payments, while the figure for Britain was only £8.1 million. Despite having a smaller economy, lower total tax revenue and larger debt, in that year Britain had almost £2 million more than France to spend on its military.[44]

The French monarchy relied on traditional means of raising loans and managing debt. A bewildering array of loans and life annuities was part of a French financial structure that was largely veiled from the public until the shocking state of the deficit was revealed in the 1780s. The root cause of French fiscal problems were that the state controlled spending but not income – its tax revenue was limited by corporate privileges and resistance, particularly from the aristocracy. As a result, *ancien régime* France was usually forced to raise loans to fund war, and then borrow again to service its debts, which tended to lead to financial crisis. Default was a traditional means of defusing a crisis, and Louis XV resorted to this in 1759 and 1770, and the republic did so in 1797. The interest rate for private loans was similar in Britain and France, but creditors demanded higher interest rates from the French state because it had proved willing and able to default. Default was never total or indiscriminate – loans and interest were usually revised down. The fiscal crisis of the late 1780s led to revolution because Louis XVI suspended payments but ruled default out as an option. Assuming that default was probable, creditors had already priced the risk into their high-interest loans.[45]

The 'financial revolution' that created Britain's successful system of public debt began in the late seventeenth-century, but became fully developed during the Seventy Years War. Along with a Dutch monarch the revolution of 1688 brought Dutch finance to London. The fragility of the new regime and strains of war in the 1690s fostered financial innovation. In return for approving creation of the Bank of England, parliament gained control over the Crown's borrowing. This parliamentary check on state debt lowered the possibility of default, and thus improved the confidence of investors – many of whom had direct or indirect influence in parliament. The new financial system as a whole proved volatile, however, until the accession of George I, and was not really secure until the Jacobite threat was finally defeated in the 1740s. Tories complained long and loud that the country's taxes were being used to make financiers in the City of London rich. The Whig Daniel Defoe in turn warned that Jacobites saw a Stuart restoration as a means to default – 'a political sponge to wipe out the debts of the nation'.[46]

If taxes appeared less intrusive in the daily lives of Britons, parliamentary scrutiny of the Treasury's accounts proved a key strength of the British financial system. In the words of Martin Daunton, 'Britain was the first European state to complete a full statement of its financial position, which meant that its operations were visible'.[47] This increased the confidence of creditors, for whom the security of their investment was as important as the rate of return. While public debt was 'immature, experimental and innovative in 1700', by the middle of the eighteenth century it had become an established part of the British economy, and credit crises became associated with the private sector.[48] The Treasury usually had little trouble securing loans from British and Continental investors through personal negotiations with leading financiers in the City of London – who were often also members of parliament who supported the government.[49] The British state was able to borrow at relatively low interest rates because it was seen to be transparent, reliable and operating according to the rule of law. Default was abandoned as a fiscal tool after 1688, and during periods of peace ministers tried to run budget surpluses and reduce debt.

In the late 1740s Henry Pelham completed Britain's financial revolution by reorganising the national debt. During the wars against Louis XIV both short and long-term loans were mostly self-liquidating. Walpole favoured a policy of converting such loans into interest-bearing government stock that was redeemable but need not be paid off. This approach was followed by successors such as Pelham, and most of Britain's borrowing during the War of the Austrian Succession was in the form of low-interest government stock. By 1748 the national debt had risen to £76 million – most of it held at 4% interest. After the Treaty of Aix-la-Chapelle, money became cheaper and in 1749, in the face of hostile vested interests, Pelham carried through parliament a scheme that would reduce the 4% interest debt to 3% within eight years. Many in Europe were impressed by the ability of the British state to achieve a 25% reduction in the cost of servicing its debt. In 1751 Pelham proceeded to reform the administration of the national debt, consolidating four-teen different stocks into five. 'Consols' at 3% interest traded until the late nineteenth century.[50] In France the state tended to raise fixed term loans that were paid off over time like a modern house mortgage. In contrast, the British national debt increased financial liquidity within the economy as stocks were traded at a market price, and could be used as a substitute for cash.

While the national debt became more stable during the Seventy Years War, critics focused on its growing size. In 1752 David Hume was sure that national bankruptcy loomed at some time in the not so distant future:

> Let the time come (and surely it will come) when the new funds, created for the exigencies of the year, are not subscribed to, and raise not the money projected. Suppose, either that the cash of the nation is exhausted; or that our faith, which has hitherto been so ample, begins to fail us. Suppose, that, in this distress, the nation is threat-ened with invasion; a rebellion is suspected or broken out at home; a squadron cannot be equipped for want of pay, victuals, or repairs; or even a foreign subsidy cannot be advanced. What must a prince or minister do in such an emergence?[51]

Twenty years later the Dissenting philosopher, Richard Price, told Lord Chatham: 'All that I converse with are persuaded that the national debt is one of our greatest evils, and that, if not soon put upon a *fixed* course of redemption, it must terminate in all the calamities of a public bankruptcy.'[52]

Despite such concerns, ministers borrowed around 80% of the addi-tional revenue needed during wartime operations.[53] At the start of the Seventy Years War the national debt stood at £50 million; it proceeded to balloon. By 1763 it had risen to £133 million, which led George III's ministers to seek new indirect tax revenues in the American colonies. Unexpectedly heated colonial protests led to open revolt and war that nearly doubled the national debt to £245 million. The younger Pitt undertook a series of reforms aimed at debt reduction, including improvements in revenue collection. From 1786 £1 million per year was earmarked for a Sinking Fund that would purchase government stocks, and the compound interest earned would enable the Fund to buy back national debt over time. In 1792 Pitt was confident that Britain faced more than a decade of peace in which the public debt would be substantially reduced. Instead, war with Revolutionary France saw the national debt climb almost vertically toward £750 million by 1815. Estimated to be 270% of national income, Britain's national debt was higher in 1819 than the end of the Second World War.[54]

Throughout the Seventy Years War French strategists hoped to defeat Britain by provoking a financial panic in London. 'This credit on which everything hangs in England, hangs itself on very little, despite the false glamour from which it benefits', wrote Francois Chaumont in 1760.[55] The threat of financial panic loomed on numerous occasions. The retreat of the Jacobites in 1745 probably saved the City of London from financial catastrophe.[56] In October 1757, while worrying about a potential invasion, Lord Holderness observed that 'public credit is our very being, and there is no answering for the effects which a panick taken here might have upon those objects which are the basis of our strength and grandeur'.[57] In the 1790s Kersaint told the revolutionary National Convention that 'the credit of England rests on fictitious wealth', and several invasion attempts hoped to give a shock to British finance. The French republic defaulted on its own national debt and Napoleon proceeded to fund his wars through taxes and wealth extracted from conquered territories. Napoleon was thus able to be a bullionist, who regarded his enemy's national debt as a 'gnawing worm' that would ultimately see Britain collapse.[58] In addition to his Continental blockade of trade, Napoleon tried to hasten the day of downfall by extending state sponsorship to smugglers in the English Channel as an aid to draining Britain of gold.[59]

Britain funded its Seventy Years War by shifting the largest share of the burden onto future taxpayers via the national debt. Owing in part to luck, Britain's financial system avoided collapse, as there were various points at which a successful invasion could have caused chaos. And what might have happened if Austria had made a separate peace that allowed Napoleon to stay ruler of an expanded France in 1814? Napoleon's aversion to borrowing led to a striking contrast in relative debt burdens by 1818: with the public debt in Britain equivalent to 1,210 francs per capita, the figure for France was a mere 80 francs.[60] Two economic historians have concluded that, as late as 1811, 'French finances appeared victorious'. But they were destroyed by the cost of the Russian campaign and the burden of reparations after Waterloo.[61]

In addition to luck, however, much was owed to the credibility of the British financial system, built up by men of numbers like Pelham, Lord North and the younger Pitt. The latter, in particular, managed to steady and reform government finances in the wake of the American Revolution, and helped Britain avoid financial meltdown during its most dangerous crisis. In the mid 1790s, tax revenues were rising, but interest payments were rising faster. At the same time, the possibility of a successful invasion loomed. Only a storm prevented a large French invasion force from landing in Ireland in December 1796. When a small force landed at Fishguard in Wales the following February it set off a run on the Bank of England. To avoid collapse, it stopped converting paper notes into coin – and Britain did not return to the gold standard until 1821. Pitt proceeded to dramatically increase indirect taxes on luxuries, such as wigs, servants and carriages, and then took the radical step of introducing an income tax. This struck at the heart of English notions of privacy and the sanctity of private property. Yet it was accepted as an emergency measure and, despite widespread evasion, yielded significant revenue that enabled Britain to continue fighting, borrowing and subsidising allies until Napoleon was defeated. In the words of Joel Mokyr, 'management of the government debt can be seen as one of the triumphs of eighteenth-century British institutions'.[62]

Large public debt made it *possible* to defend the Atlantic Archipelago and build a global empire. It made it *possible* for Britain to triumph in its long struggle with France, and to help at Vienna in 1815 to create the international conditions in which potentially crippling public debt could be paid down in a more peaceful nineteenth century. Yet much depended on how money was spent.

The Caring Contractor State

At the end of the eighteenth century Henry Dundas observed that 'all modern wars are a contention of the purse',[63] and it is easy for historians to regard finance as the fundamental explanation for British military success. Thus Lawrence Stone has written: 'At bottom, victory in war was a question of money, not men, since money could always be used to hire men and Europe was full of mercenaries willing to serve a reliable paymaster'.[64] In two ways this is a limited explanation of British success: firstly, it diminishes the role of individuals and contingent events. Secondly, it underestimates the importance of how that money was deployed. While there are now many studies of how states raised money, historians have only recently begun to focus on the difficult task of assessing how efficiently money was spent.[65] Political leadership, effective administration, and cooperation between state and society were needed in order to maximise the translation of money into military power. To continue fighting its long struggle with France the British state had to care for its military forces; and it did so largely through contracting work to the private sector.

Erica Charters has argued that Britain's state was of necessity a 'caring' state.[66] There is abundant evidence of patrician distain for the "unwashed masses" in the eighteenth century. The 'mob' were seen as impulsive and ignorant – described as 'two-legged brutes' by one gentleman.[67] Attitudes nevertheless softened as the public sphere expanded over the course of the Seventy Years War. Rankers and tars, seen as among the lowest and most desperate of the low at mid century, became, to some extent, sentimentalised as sturdy patriots. This owed much to the increasingly fashionable humanitarian ideals of the Enlightenment and evangelical Protestantism. Yet it also owed something to the pragmatic needs of the fiscal-naval state. Manpower was hard to recruit, and maintaining health and military effectiveness required a lot of care and effort.

As the struggle with France seemed to stretch Britain's resources to breaking point, leaders could not afford to neglect or waste military manpower. More soldiers and seamen were killed by disease than by weapons in the eighteenth century, and leaders showed a high degree of concern about limiting the spread of disease. Naval commanders were fanatical about the cleanliness of ships. Political and military leaders tried to plan campaigns outside of 'sickly seasons' and to use locally acclimatised troops. Yet, given limited medical knowledge, high casualty rates from disease were often unavoidable. Thousands fell ill in Quebec in the winter of 1759–60 and again in Havana in 1762, despite efforts to minimise the impact of disease. Commanders nevertheless tried to keep men fit and healthy. General George Townshend claimed that disease among British troops in Portugal in 1762 was 'occasioned merely by climate & not to be imputed to any inattention in officers nor irregularity of the men'.[68] During the American rebellion an officer observed that General Burgoyne's army at the start of the Saratoga campaign 'were in a high state of discipline, and had been kept in their winter quarters with the greatest of care'.[69] Another officer reported from New York in early 1777 that the troops 'have been remarkably healthy from the great Attention pay'd them. They swim in the Sea most mornings & in the Evenings have foot Races & other manly Exercises'.[70] Wellington's correspondence from the Peninsular War is full of pleas for more supplies for his troops. He paid close attention to logistics, declaring it was 'very necessary... to trace a biscuit from Lisbon into the man's mouth on the frontier, and to provide for its removal from place to place by land or water'.[71] Soldiers and seamen were sometimes treated poorly and their lives wasted in flawed campaigns like the West Indies in the 1790s and Walcheren in 1809. Of course, even the best plans can end in disaster, and incompetent leadership is not necessarily uncaring leadership.

British leaders also had to be *seen* to be caring for their men at arms. Aside from the immediate damage done to military strength, reports of epidemics had a negative impact on recruitment and relations with colonies that were asked to supply troops. When they could not stop the spread of disease, admirals and generals sometimes tried to censor news of epidemics by halting the dispatch of mail. The storm of criticism that wasteful operations attracted reflected the high public expectations that Britain's military should be deployed with wisdom and care. Perceived incompetence and uncaring leadership could seriously damage an individual's reputation and career. As Charters has concluded, 'the effectiveness of the British fiscal-military state, and hence its long term strength, relied on it caring, and showing that it cared, about the welfare of its armed forces'.[72]

Britain acted as a 'contractor state' in order to maintain its expanding military effort. Early modern European states were to a large extent dependent upon hiring mercenaries and contracting private-sector merchants to supply armies and navies.[73] In the late eighteenth century France and Spain moved away from commercial competition, preferring to grant a private monopoly or have government officials directly purchase supplies.[74] The British state, however, worked at making better use of market forces to secure the best value contracts.

Contractors and administrators had a terrible image in the eighteenth century. There was endless complaint about corrupt government officials and commercial contractors getting fat on ballooning state taxation and debt. Government officials received a fee on contracts they granted – a system clearly open to abuse. With the army often having pressing needs, there were many opportunities for contractors to increase the profit margin on supplies. During the mid eighteenth-century wars a number of agents and merchants became rich through contracting to supply the army and navy. Richard Oswald, for example, provided the army in southern England and Germany with bread, straw, firewood, wagons and forage for horses – making over £116,000 profit on the bread contracts in Germany alone.[75] Lawrence Dundas, a Scottish merchant, was appointed commissary to the army on a salary of £780 during the Culloden campaign and went on to amass a fortune that was estimated to be a staggering £900,000 at his death in 1781.[76] Thus it is not surprising that suppliers of the armed forces were often scorned in parliament and print. Reflecting popular suspicion of profiteering merchants, in 1793 the French republic guillotined two contractors and tried to nationalise its system of military supply.[77]

High-profile corruption scandals have obscured the reality of the workings of the contracting system. Some delays and inefficiencies can be attributed to the inherent limitations of administration in an age of quill pens and rudimentary communication systems. Yet, Britain's war machine could not have worked without the support of contractors. While Oswald made immense profits, he worked hard and delivered the goods, earning praise from Prince Ferdinand of Brunswick, who declared that 'the British have sent me Commissaries fit to be Generals, and Generals not fit to be Commissaries'.[78] Lawrence Dundas, ridiculed as the 'Nabob of the North', nevertheless earned praise from the Duke of Cumberland for his fulfilment of huge contracts for the German War totalling nearly £2 million.[79] While wealthy London merchants had an advantage in securing large contracts, many smaller and provincial merchants were able to act as sub-contractors, or win contracts in their own right as competition and scrutiny increased.[80]

Over the course of the Seventy Years War the state improved its military administration in order to increase efficiency and cope with the growing scale of conflict. Navy and army administration in the eighteenth century was often the subject of criticism from officers who were frustrated by delays and supply failures. These criticisms have been echoed by historians who have depicted the polyarchic nature of military administration as corrupt and inefficient. In 1896 a naval historian, Admiral Vesey Hamilton, wrote of the 'gross corruption, profligate expenditure and supine negligence' of eighteenth-century naval administration, which was 'a mass of iniquity and corruption almost incredible'.[81] While accepting there were things to criticise, recent scholarship is highlighting the successes and improvements in administration that enabled Britain to successfully wage world-wide war.[82] It is important that a focus on inefficiencies and failures not distract attention from the thousands of soldiers and seamen who were successfully fed, clothed and shipped around the world.

By the mid eighteenth century the Admiralty had a well-developed system of contracting for ships and supplies. The building of ships was increasingly contracted out to private shipyards. Essential raw materials such as hemp, timber and masts were sourced from countries around the Baltic Sea. Naval weaponry and equipment was contracted from Britain's manufacturers. The Victualling Board developed efficient contracting practices that enabled it to successfully feed thousands of seamen and soldiers serving around the globe. Thus, around 80,000 men were fed higher-quality victuals during the 1750s, at less cost, than 45,000 men in the early eighteenth century.[83]

Administration of army supply was confusingly divided between several government departments. The Board of Ordnance organised barracks and equipment; the Secretary at War provided medical supplies and uniforms; the Paymaster-General provided money. Food was traditionally supplied by the Treasury, working through commissaries who contracted merchants to supply some basics such as bread and biscuit, with soldiers left to purchase or plunder additional food. In the late 1750s the Treasury expanded its role in order to manage supply of over 60,000 British and German troops fighting on the Continent. In doing so it brought 'to a notoriously fragmented system some measure of rationalization'.[84] One contractor was dismissed for poor supply of German troops, and replaced by a state-owned and operated bakery. By expanding the number of commissaries and improving supervision, a civilian 'Commissariat' slowly came into existence, employing many commissaries, inspectors, clerks, craftsmen and labourers. By the end of the war, the accounts and supervision branch was considered in 'Variety & Extent of Business & Numbers of Persons' to be 'equal to the office of Excise'.[85]

The work of building up a Commissariat was marred by corruption and, to a large extent, the Commissariat was dismantled in the cost-cutting drive that followed the peace treaty of 1763. In May 1761 the Duke of Newcastle had ordered an enquiry into corruption and it appears that there was widespread profiteering by commissaries in Germany.[86] The corruption was recognised and mocked in the character of Zachary Fungus in the comic play *The Commissary* (1765), who went to the German war 'very little better than a driver of carts' but returned with 'a whole cart load of money'.[87] During the American Revolution the Commissariat was rebuilt and many of the old lessons relearned.[88] Scope for petty corruption remained, but the Commissariat became increasingly efficient as the pressures of global war grew. During the Peninsular War the Commissariat's credit account was fully stretched in sourcing food locally and from the Mediterranean, United States and Britain. After the Battle of Salamanca Wellington wrote:

> Notwithstanding the increased distance of our operations from our magazines, and that the country is completely exhausted, we have hitherto wanted nothing, owing to the diligence and attention of the Commissary-General, Mr. Blissett, and the officers of the department under his direction.[89]

In America, the Commissariat relied largely on contracting colonial merchants to supply the army. This became problematic during the War of Independence, and in 1779 the Navy Board took over the role of supplying food to the soldiers. With the Navy Board overworked in the 1780s, the task devolved to the Victualling Board. These were important developments in streamlining the combined-arms operations that were necessary to wage global war successfully.

Reliable transportation was increasingly important to Britain's war effort. Competition for contracting transport ships between the boards of Treasury, Navy, Victualling and Ordnance caused inefficiency and inflated costs.[90] To solve this problem a central Transport Board was established in 1794 to improve the organisation and allocation of shipping. By 1813 the Transport Board was contracting up to 10% of Britain's merchant fleet. This enabled Britain to have 45% of its armed forces stationed or operating in parts of the world beyond Europe.[91]

Enhanced military strength depended on improvements in administration that enabled the state to better tap the resources of Britain's robust financial, maritime, agricultural and industrial markets. Roger Morriss has argued that the growing number of commissioners, secretaries and clerks were 'the unsung heroes', as it was 'the competence of this bureaucracy, at the head of a cascade of agents, officials and merchant contractors who worked to their figures, that was central to the military and naval achievements of Britain'.[92]

The 1780s were a point at which the pressures of war, combined with Enlightenment and Evangelical values, sparked substantial cultural change in British government and military administration. While there had been condemnation of corruption during the Seven Years War, this was counterbalanced by stunning victories and imperial expansion. Britain's poor performance in the American war, and loss of a large part of its empire, led to widespread calls for fundamental reform. In the midst of agitation for parliamentary reform, Edmund Burke made a famous speech calling for 'economical reform'. Under both political and financial pressure caused by war, Lord North established a Commission on the Public Accounts in 1780. This began a wave of commissions and reports that, over the following decades, fostered reform of government administration.[93]

Economical reform started a process whereby military finance was made more transparent and accountable, and civilian bureaucratic authority strengthened. Some reforms aimed at ensuring money brought good-quality weapons, equipment and infrastructure. For example, the Board of Ordnance appointed inspectors of artillery and gunpowder production in the 1780s. In the mid 1790s the Admiralty appointed an Inspector General of Naval Works to supervise systems and infrastructure, and a Hydrographer of the Navy to supply accurate charts.[94]

Making the earnings of government positions transparent and cost effective was a key aim of economical reform. Salaries for administrators were often very low, and so fees and perquisites had become their main form of income. These offered wide scope for corruption and often failed to match the practical importance of a position. As prime minister, the younger Pitt did much to advance the cause of administrative reform, speaking eloquently of the importance of efficiency, accountability and public service. In those departments that were under his control Pitt gradually moved to replace sinecures and fees with adequate salaries for clearly defined roles. Yet while the Public Accounts commission had recommended fundamental legislative reform, Pitt did not want parliament to interfere with management of the Crown's departments. Major legislative reforms were only implemented during the struggle with Napoleon – often by Pittite politicians who had been inspired by their mentor's ideals of efficiency and public service.[95]

Changes to the army office of Paymaster General illustrate the nature of military administrative reform. Traditionally this was a lucrative post for profit, fees and patronage beyond its £3,000 salary. When Pitt the elder became Paymaster in 1746 he approached the job with a strong sense of civic virtue. Working hard, and not lining his own pockets, he inspired his subordinates and helped Chelsea Pensioners by ending payment in arrears and legislating payment six months in advance.[96] In contrast, one of his successors, Henry Fox, built on traditional practice and creamed off hundreds of thousands of pounds.[97] In 1782, Edmund Burke moved to legislate the elder Pitt's practice, ensuring funds for the Paymaster General were paid into an account at the Bank of England, from which they were to be withdrawn for specific purposes, with Treasury receiving monthly accounts of the expenditure. Salaries were fixed and fee-taking was abolished.[98] The huge amounts of expenditure in the last decades of the Seventy Years War led to delays in accounting and created opportunities for money to leak into private pockets. Various efforts culminated in the 1808 Pay Office Act, which simplified administration, tightened supervision of accounts and strengthened subordination to the Secretary at War.[99]

Taken together, the various reforms to administration that began in the 1780s amounted to a significant transformation in the bureaucratic culture of the British state. Administrative positions had traditionally been seen as opportunities for profit – as forms of personal property. The last decades of the Seventy Years War forced a dramatic growth in the size of government, with the number of public officials rising from 16,267 in 1797 to 24,598 by 1815. Sinecures, waste and corruption continued, and were magnified in the unrelenting scorn of radical journalists like William Cobbett.[100] Yet as fee-taking was gradually replaced by salaries fitted to the responsibilities of a position, a culture developed of individual accountability and 'civil service'. As a navy administrator, Samuel Bentham was one of the key promoters of this profound shift in bureaucratic culture and had a close relationship with his philosopher brother. During these years Jeremy Bentham was developing the ideas for fundamental rational reform that would come to be known as 'utilitarianism' and exert a profound influence on the culture of nineteenth-century Britain. Thus, the principles of utilitarianism were arguably first introduced into the British state via navy reform during the war with Revolutionary France.[101]

The origins of Britain's modern professional civil service lay in war and politics, rather than in a middle class rising out of economic change. War forced change on conservative Pittite politicians. For two main reasons they worked to implement practical reforms that can be called enlightened and rational. Firstly, in the struggle with France they needed to maximise the military power they got for money spent. Secondly, as Chapter 5 will show, they needed to respond to intensified party politics and the rise of popular political activism by heavily burdened taxpayers. In order to conserve the fundamental structure of British politics in an age of revolution, Pittite conservatives engaged in economical reform with an eye to making government more efficient and respectable. After 1815, they moved to rapidly reduce the size of the state, hoping to dampen the fire of critics and maintain aristocratic hegemony. Believing the state only needed to be large during wartime, the architects of Britain's fiscal-naval state worked to shrink it to an efficient and limited laissez-faire state in the relatively peaceful nineteenth century.[102]

State and Society

The state worked in partnership with local elites to maintain social order in an age of revolutionary change. Social stability was a necessary condition for economic growth and the raising of resources for war. Very little of the state's money was spent on domestic policies and administration. For example, judges were appointed to the superior royal courts and parliament enacted a 'Bloody Code' of harsh laws to deter violence and theft, but most of the cost of the legal system fell on individuals and communities. Policing and poor relief were likewise organised and funded at a local level. Society was largely left to provide for itself in areas such as health, education and town planning. The state helped maintain social stability by passing laws and deploying the army in a police role when necessary.

Population growth and bad weather were the main causes of social stress and strain during the Seventy Years War. Population had stagnated in the late seventeenth century through a combination of plague, harsh winters, and delayed marriage; while in the first half of the eighteenth century 'the hare of population growth was slumbering and the tortoise of food supply had a sizable lead'.[103] In 1751 the population of England reached 5.8 million, a height it had previously reached in 1300 and 1650 before being reduced by famine and plague. In the late eighteenth century, however, the growth of wage labour and 'putting-out' work in cottages enabled people to marry younger and have more children. In the absence of widespread famine, the population of England started to grow rapidly, reaching 8.7 million by 1801. In the first half of the eighteenth century there had been few harvest failures, wages and prices remained stable, and England was an exporter of grain. Wheat prices reached a century low in the 1740s, but then began to climb in line with population increase, and Britain became a net importer of grain in the 1760s. In the second half of the eighteenth century, failed harvests became more common as a result of several freezing winters and stormy summers. On a number of occasions when the price of grain spiked, the government was forced to ban exports and suspend import duties – most notably for the duration of the French Revolutionary and Napoleonic Wars. In the years around 1800 average wheat prices recorded at Winchester College were fluctuating between four to seven times the 1744 price.[104]

This put increasing pressure on the living standards of the poor and increased social tensions. Since the late seventeenth century the land-owner-dominated parliament had fostered a free-market within Britain, but had passed 'corn laws' to regulate the price of grain via a mix of bounties for exports and duties on imports. These were designed to ensure farmers received a consistently good price for their grain and would thus continue to produce bread for the nation. Import duties prevented cheap foreign grain from flooding the market, and when prices dropped too low farmers were paid a bounty to export grain. As a result, taxpayers gave money to the state either through funding the bounty or paying the inflated price of grain caused by import duties.

Riot was a key means by which plebeians protested, and the military played an important role in their suppression. Various things provoked protest, such as the activities of press gangs, but food riots were the most common and they increased dramatically from the 1750s onward. E.P. Thompson influentially argued that eighteenth-century riots were fundamentally protests against the expansion of capitalist market economics, and aimed to enforce a 'moral economy' of customary rights and just prices.[105] Yet while it is true that plebeians had a strong sense of customary rights, it is wrong to see them as rejecting capitalism. British people were increasingly engaging in a market-based consumer economy. An 'industrious revolution' of the early eighteenth century saw people seek to enhance their cash incomes in order to purchase 'luxury' goods such as coffee, tea, sugar and tobacco. The Scottish economist, James Steuart observed in 1767 that 'men are forced to labour now because they are slaves to their own wants'.[106] Rather than a protest against capitalism, riots are better viewed as attempts to make market economics work properly – to stop price inflation caused by market-distorting corn laws, monopolies and grain hoarding.[107] Without an established police force, the state relied on magistrates reading the Riot Act with the support of soldiers.[108] Militiamen remained connected to their communities and they sometimes joined rioters – most notably in the crisis year of 1795. Regular army units, however, proved reliable as a police force. Even in the politically febrile 1790s, Roger Wells has concluded, 'no evidence exists of refusals by the regulars to oppose the crowd in the manner determined by their officers'.[109] As a result, merely the presence of army units was often enough to discourage rioters.

War exacerbated the problems of population growth and harvest failure. Prices rose further because trade was often interrupted and the military mobilisation increased demand for food and other goods. In turn, when thousands of servicemen demobilised after a peace treaty competition for work increased dramatically. For example, the 200,000 demobilised in 1763 were only 3% of the total population of England, but accounted for approximately 30% of the adult male labouring class. In light of this, it is not surprising that Douglas Hay's study of indictments for theft in Staffordshire revealed a 35% higher rate of crime in times of peace compared to war.[110] These crime waves led to 'moral panics'. In the years following 1748, for example, propertied people worried that London was descending into mayhem. The *Whitehall Evening Post* declared that 'the frequency of audacious Street Robberies repeated every Night in this great Metropolis call aloud on our Magistrates to think of some Redress; for, as the Case is now, there is no Possibility of stirring from our Habitations after dark without the Hazard of a fractured skull'.[111] The leading historian of crime and the courts, J.M. Beattie, has observed that, in stimulating some sectors of the economy and soaking up unemployment, 'wars undoubtedly had a broadly beneficial effect for the working population in London'.[112]

Post-war crime waves prompted development of police and penal policies. The cabinet was directly involved in the criminal justice system because it was responsible for granting or refusing pardons to those sentenced to death in London. To help combat the 1750s crime wave in the metropolis, financial support was granted to Henry and John Fielding after they established the Bow Street Runners, the forerunners of the modern police.[113] Yet, such limited policing made little overall impact. The War of Independence ended convict transportation to America and was followed by another crime wave in the 1780s. Felons were crowded into decommissioned navy hulks anchored in the Thames, and the number of hangings rose dramatically. Some were put to work digging canals, building coastal fortifications and loading navy ships.[114] With prisons crowded and crime rising after the war, the rate of executions peaked in the mid-1780s. Alternatives were sought as those of enlightened sensibility became critical of the 'Bloody Code' as both inhumane and ineffective. Magistrates throughout the realm moved to implement John Howard's ideas for prison reform.[115] As High Sheriff of Bedfordshire, Howard had become intensely interested in the poor condition of English prisons, and having been thanked for his evidence before a committee of inquiry, he dedicated his influential *State of the*

Prisons in England and Wales (1777) to the House of Commons. Faced with the immediate problems of a post-war crime wave, however, a new destination for transportation was sought. After deciding on Botany Bay the state spent £1 million in the first ten years transporting convicts to Australia.[116]

Poor laws also helped maintain social stability. England's long-established poor laws provided public funding to support destitute people, and became central to alleviating social problems aggravated by war. The poor laws are a good example of the working partnership between government and society. Poor relief was mandated by statute law, but the tax rate was determined, and relief administered, at the individual parish level. In the eighteenth century able-bodied paupers were often required to live in workhouses, but with growing pressure on the system by 1803 around 90% of poor relief was given to people in their own homes, much of it via the Speenhamland system.[117] With dearth causing the price of bread to skyrocket in 1795, the Speenhamland magistrates in Berkshire decided to augment the wages of labourers according to a sliding scale based on the price of a loaf of bread. This enabled agricultural labourers to keep working on estates, and the system was soon adopted widely in rural English parishes, helping to avoid a scale of discontent that could have turned revolutionary.[118]

While charity rates were similar throughout Europe, Protestant states provided significantly more government aid to the poor than Catholic states. Peter Solar has observed that England had a 'long lived, national system of tax-financed relief' which, in comparison to other early modern states, was 'relatively certain and relatively generous'.[119] With the Speenhamland system added to the poor laws, and Dutch institutions disrupted by French conquest, Britain became by far the largest supplier of poor relief in Europe until reform of the poor laws in 1834.[120] At any one time between 5 and 15% of the English population were receiving poor relief. It probably also acted as a form of insurance for the much larger proportion of the population that lived on the margin of poverty, allowing people to take economic risks in employment, migration, early marriage and procreation.[121] The French Revolution occurred in the context of population growth and harvest failures. In contrast, poor relief, higher agricultural output, and possibly better immunity to disease as a result of greater population mobility and urbanisation, contributed to Britain's mortality rate being substantially lower than France's.[122]

War aggravated the social problems of population growth, harvest failure and industrialisation, but it also generated large numbers of

soldiers, militia and volunteers who could be deployed in a police func-
tion. Over 12,000 soldiers were deployed to counter the Luddite riots
in northern England – a larger force than had been sent to Portugal in
1808.[123] Social stability was necessary for the state to raise resources for
war, and the military were in turn used to help police a society under-
going profound structural change.

The Fiscal-Naval State and Industrial Revolution

The industrial revolution was one of the most significant transitions in
human history, and Britain was the first to industrialise. On the basis
that cotton manufacturing rose rapidly in the 1780s, it was once argued
that there was an industrial 'take-off' in that decade. Detailed research
has shown, however, that national economic growth was gradual, with
the annual rate of manufacturing output growing steadily from 1740
through to 1820.[124] Yet, despite some attempts to reject the concept, it is
clear that by the mid nineteenth century there had been an industrial
revolution in Britain, with profound structural change and rapid growth
in key industries such as textiles and iron manufacturing.[125]

The relationship of British industrialisation to global economic development is the subject of many volumes of detailed research and contentious debate. Historians have argued about the relative importance of
long-term structural changes to the economy compared to short-term
change such as the invention of high-impact technology like the steam
engine. With most historians now stressing the importance of long-term
changes, there is also debate as to the relative importance of domestic
(endogenous) developments, such as improved agricultural productivity and cultural change, compared to external (exogenous) factors
such as the economic stimulus provided by colonial resources and
markets. There is also the question of the broader relevance of British
industrialisation: was it the product of a unique economic path, or does
it provide a model of the essential elements of industrial revolution?
Historians of the industrial revolution tend to see war as something that
detracted from the 'normal' process of economic development. Yet war
was so frequent that it should be considered a key component in early
modern economic development. This chapter will conclude by considering the ways war both damaged and stimulated economic activity, and
assess the role of the fiscal-naval state in helping to cause the industrial
revolution.

Business was risky in the eighteenth century, particularly in times of war. The American rebellion put a stop to trade with the thirteen colonies, and the British lost over 3,300 merchant ships. In the period 1793–1815 over 11,000 ships were lost, carrying cargo valued at over £60 million. Given such large-scale loss of ships and property it is not surprising that ocean-going merchants had the highest rate of bankruptcy.[126] This explains in part the intense newspaper interest in foreign policy developments. When war disrupted the supply of raw materials and access to overseas markets it could have a devastating impact on some sectors of the British economy. The American Revolution proved especially disruptive to trade, as important markets were shut off and the Royal Navy found itself outnumbered at sea. Napoleon's continental blockade also caused economic dislocation in some manufacturing sectors. Further, war led to rises in taxation and the burden of public debt. While acknowledging that war grew the empire and added new markets, T.S. Ashton concluded that if there had been no wars then the British people 'would have been better fed, better clad, certainly better housed', they could have focused more energy on building 'an efficient network of main roads and inland waterways', and 'the Industrial Revolution might have come earlier'.[127]

There is ongoing debate as to whether heavy wartime borrowing 'crowded out' private investment in peaceful production. At the very least, there might have been some more cotton production, with associated export income, if there had been less gun production.[128] Yet, aside from notable industrialists, Britain's propertied elite tended to either save or spend their profits on consumption. So, wartime taxing and borrowing may have tapped idle capital and invested it in the navy and expansion of empire.[129] Larry Neal has even argued that there was some 'crowding in' during the French Revolutionary wars as Continental investors sought a safe haven in shares of British public debt. It was between 1793 and 1815 that London 'replaced Amsterdam as the financial center of Europe'.[130]

The ideals of liberal capitalist economic theory had little chance of realisation in the combative mercantilist world of the long eighteenth century. All states pursued mercantilist policies of economic regulation, seeking to harness and tax colonial trade, while using customs duties to protect important sectors of their domestic economy. The rise of Britain's cotton and pottery industries owed much to tariffs put on imports from India and China. And avoiding war was probably not possible in Europe's competitive balance-of-power international relations. Isolation was certainly 'never a serious political option' in the face of French republican and Napoleonic expansionism.[131] Adam Smith himself recognised that Britain could not disconnect from Europe and that security had to come before prosperity.[132] If the British nation had not armed itself and competed for empire, it could have suffered the conquest and economic dislocation that was the fate of many other regions of Europe.

In a number of ways Britain's fiscal-naval state appears to have helped foster the world's first industrial revolution. In the words of Patrick O'Brien, it is possible 'to sum up Britain's famous transition as a "conjuncture" in the global history of material progress that occurred when and where it did largely as a result of the Island state's favourable national endowments and massive investments in naval power'.[133] Britain's path to industrialisation was dependent upon fortunate geology and geography. Without abundant and easily accessible reserves of cheap coal, easily transportable by rivers, canals and coastal shipping, there would have been no industrial revolution in Britain.[134] This was a central feature of the industrial revolution: the gradual transition from organic to mineral sources of power. Burning of coal enabled improvements in iron production and the harnessing of efficient steam power. By the early 1800s Britain was burning 15 million tons of coal, compared to 3 million for the rest of Europe.[135] Coal had, however, been sitting in British ground for centuries without being used to make an industrial revolution. Development of a dynamic economy in the eighteenth century created demand and the ability to use coal, and this was linked in various ways to the rise of Britain's fiscal-naval state.

Some scholars stress the importance of the revolution of 1688 in creating a limited constitutional monarchy and secure property rights.[136] As the first half of this chapter has demonstrated, however, eighteenth-century government was larger and more active than traditionally thought. And although propertied men in parliament ensured that the state was sensitive to the interests of agriculture and commerce, the English legal system remained complex and costly. Many improvements in commercial law had to wait until the 'law making' cases that Lord Chief Justice Mansfield presided over in the later eighteenth century.[137] And property rights were probably as secure in France as they were in Britain. Indeed, in *ancien régime* France privileges and property rights sometimes blocked the development of large-scale infrastructure. In contrast, as William Blackstone noted in his influential *Commentaries on the Laws of England*, the British parliament had authority to wield 'absolute despotic power'.[138] And it often did, passing laws that impinged on the property rights of particular individuals in order to enclose land or enable the construction of turnpikes and canals – not to mention new and higher taxes.[139] Property rights were nevertheless vaunted in Britain, and individuals were often compensated – most famously in the millions paid to owners in compensation for the abolition of West Indian slavery in the 1830s. Rather than its limitations, it was the activities of the state in defending the island and private property, and promoting improvement, that most contributed to economic growth.

The fiscal-naval state's public debt did much to foster the development of financial systems in Britain. Through massive borrowing, the state increased financial liquidity and spent money in ways that stimulated the economy. In addition to this, the public debt had a number of beneficial effects. As late as 1873, shares in British government debt accounted for 38% of the activity of the London stock market. This added great depth to Britain's financial market, enabling brokers and stock-jobbers to invest and trade in public stocks. While often denigrated, these men fostered financial liquidity by giving people confidence that they could always find a buyer of stock – they encouraged economic activity in a way similar to how warehousemen act as a point of trade between primary producers and retailers. This aided the rise of an insurance industry, as insurers liked to hold liquid public debt that could be cashed in order to pay claims. Thus, shares in public debt accounted for 22% of the Royal Exchange Assurance's assets in 1734, and rose to 54% in 1784. Savings banks, which developed in the years after 1810, relied to a large extent on investing in public debt.[140] British economic growth owed much to the development of financial markets that promoted risk-sharing, as opposed to reliance upon individual credit institutions and financiers, as was the case in France after the failure of John Law's financial experiment in the early eighteenth century.[141] A recent study has concluded that, to the extent that wartime borrowing did 'crowd out' private sector investment, the effect was short term and easily outweighed by the key role public debt played in fostering the development of Britain's private banks and financial markets.[142]

The British economy was stimulated by the particular ways in which the fiscal-naval state spent its money. Economic historians of the industrial revolution generally ignore military spending or depict it as a wasteful cost. In doing so, they play down the degree to which the fiscal-naval state engaged in a mercantilist form of Keynesian economic stimulus.[143] The navy received approximately half of Britain's expenditure on its armed forces, and the largest share of that was spent in Britain.[144]

During the Napoleonic wars the construction and repair of warships alone accounted for 15% of total military expenditure.[145] Spending a relatively large amount on its navy ensured that a substantial portion of military spending returned to stimulate capital-intensive industries to a far higher degree than in states oriented towards land warfare.

An 'agricultural revolution' peaking in the late eighteenth century has traditionally been accorded an important role in causing the industrial revolution. This owed much to Marxist historians who argued that industrialisation was rooted in a change to England's social structure, with traditional feudal relations giving way to modern capitalist market-mediated relations. It was argued that the Enclosure Acts, which turned common farmland into private pastures, encouraged use of agricultural technology and increased output and profits. As landless labourers were pushed from rural areas into growing cities, they became wage-dependent factory workers who in turn increased the demand for food produced by land-hungry capitalist farmers. There is some truth in this, but studies have revealed that enclosure was not inherently more efficient compared to traditional forms of farming, and there was limited redeployment of rural labourers into factories. During the period 1700–1850 the agricultural workforce declined as a proportion of the population, but the total number remained steady at around 1.5 million, with an increasing proportion of them being adult men. During that period agriculture was 'the slowest growing economic sector'.[146] Timing is important. In 1600, 74% of England's population was engaged in agriculture; by 1750 that proportion had dropped to 45%. At the same time, agricultural output increased by 54%.[147] An agricultural revolution did occur, but it happened gradually, and mostly in the century before the industrial revolution.

In combination with imported grain, however, late-eighteenth-century improvements in agriculture kept Malthusian famine at bay and allowed Britain to urbanise and industrialise. In 1600 around 10% of the populations of France and England lived in towns of more than 5,000 people. By 1800 the figure for France was 11% while the English figure was 28%, and rose steeply in the nineteenth century.[148] In essence, Britain's farmers responded to the growing urban demand for food by enhancing productivity through various means: manuring fields, breeding better animals, improving grains, adopting new technology, and bringing marginal land under cultivation.

In addition to urbanisation, war appears to have contributed to the price rises that encouraged agricultural improvement. Prices rose when the army and navy increased their demand for food and import of grain was disrupted by war. The navy's Victualling Board, in particular, did much to stimulate the growth of grain and livestock markets in London. Many black cattle were walked from the Scottish Highlands, and sheep driven from Wales to London, to be bought and processed as food for seamen and soldiers. Economic historians have paid very little attention to the impact of military demand and food-processing innovations on agriculture – which is surprising, given that the navy purchased approximately 20% of produce sold on the national agricultural market during the American war. The Victualling Board appears to have encouraged the development of large produce merchants, while also seeking to maintain competition by encouraging the development of provincial suppliers.[149] Population growth, urbanisation and industrialisation during a time of war put enormous strains on British society. While living standards slipped in the last decades of the Seventy Years War, improvements in agriculture helped ensure there was no widespread famine and contributed to the growth of (taxable) capitalist market relations.

The urbanisation of England and lowland Scotland was fuelled by three main factors: agricultural surplus, manufacturing, and international trade. Agriculture was taxed and the money spent in ways that stimulated urbanisation – such as courtly display in London or naval infrastructure in Portsmouth. The propertied elite spent money on urban lifestyle, for example driving the growth of Bath as a place of leisure and pleasure. Textile-producing towns grew in regions such as East Anglia, where fine woollen 'new draperies' that undercut Italian textiles were produced, and cotton manufacturing drove urbanisation in Lancashire in the late eighteenth century. Overseas trade also fostered urbanisation, as important southern port cities oriented toward Europe were joined in the eighteenth century by rapidly growing Atlantic-oriented cities such as Bristol, Liverpool and Glasgow. These ports acted as dynamic hubs of trade and communication.

Economic dynamism saw cities act as magnets for internal migration. From the middle of the seventeenth century, real wages in London appear to have been around twice as high as other areas of England. In the late eighteenth century, wages in provincial towns rose substantially, but a large gap opened up between urban and agricultural wages. With an eye to emulating rising urban living standards, farmers who stayed on the land worked harder and smarter in order to increase productivity and profit.[150]

The agricultural revolution and urbanisation fostered consumer demand and an early-eighteenth-century 'industrious revolution' that was a key cause of the later Industrial Revolution. Increasing opportunities to consume luxury goods encouraged people to work harder to increase household cash incomes. This imposed longer working hours, and encouraged whole-family engagement in cottage industry production to earn additional income. The macro result was steady economic growth and rising demand for affordable manufactured goods. A consumer revolution, including the origins of modern shopping and advertising, increased the market demand that, in turn, stimulated industrialisation in the late eighteenth century.[151]

Historians of industriousness and consumerism tend to see war as having an overwhelmingly negative economic impact, but there were important ways in which the fiscal-naval state stimulated key sectors of the economy. If growth in some areas of private consumption, such as building and brewing, was dampened during war, there were other sectors of the economy that continued to grow. Iron and armaments producers won contracts to supply both the British and foreign governments. Textile manufacturing, the fastest-growing sector in the industrial revolution, supplied clothing for soldiers, seamen and volunteers, and military service probably led to some of the working class being better clothed. If overall economic growth tended to slow during some periods of conflict, the scale and efficiencies of some important sectors appear to have benefited.

A 'transport revolution' was essential to the increasing integration of markets, facilitating cheaper movement of larger volumes of goods. Britain had the advantage of many navigable rivers, substantially augmented by canal-building in the late eighteenth century. There was also a boom in building turnpike roads between the 1750s and 1770s. While much of this was initiated by individuals, parliament played an important role in promoting construction of canals and roads via numerous Improvement Acts. Jo Guildi has gone so far as to argue that the construction of military roads through the Scottish Highlands saw Britain begin to develop an 'infrastructure state'.[152] Roads were needed to counter rebellion or invasion, but they also improved trade, travel and communication by mail. So the state encouraged improvement and extension of 'the King's highway' throughout Britain in the century after 1750. A thriving coastal trade was also important, and it depended upon Royal Navy protection of the coast and ports – despite which, French privateers remained a serious threat. Coastal trade grew substantially, with the tonnage of ships rising from 154,000, in 1760 to 833,000 by 1824.[153]

An expanding empire made a substantial contribution to British economic growth. Claims have been made that the profits of empire, particularly from slavery, caused the industrial revolution.[154] There are problems with this. Overseas trade accounted for only 10 to 15 per cent of national income in the late eighteenth century, and the profits of West Indian slavery tended to be spent on conspicuous consumption or reinvested in trade.[155] That said, imperial trade played an important role in fostering a dynamic economy. It aided development of systems of finance and insurance, and many of the goods at the heart of the consumer revolution were the products of colonial trade. People worked hard to afford the produce of slave plantations, such as tobacco and sugar. Slaves gained a little revenge when sweet tooths decayed painfully in European heads.[156] In addition to providing 'ghost acres' that supplied agricultural produce and raw materials for Britain, the empire provided expanding markets for British manufactures. Aside from the growth of consumerism in North America, slaves were often clothed in textiles and chained in irons made in Britain. It is significant that it was some of the key sectors of the industrial revolution, such as textiles and iron, that bulked large in Atlantic trade.[157]

Growth of the empire, and overseas trade generally, was symbiotically linked with the Royal Navy and success in war. While the start of renewed Anglo-French fighting disrupted trade, each period of conflict ended with British overseas trade larger and stronger. The one exception was the American War of Independence, when British trade in 1778 was 26% smaller than it had been in 1774.[158] After the end of hostilities, however, trade with the new United States roared back to life. Overall, naval victories and amphibious operations enabled the rise of an economically dynamic global empire.

The creation of the Western Squadron in 1747 had a crucial impact on the relative development of British and French trade. It enabled the Royal Navy to contain France's navy and intercept its trade, while protecting Britain and its merchant ships. As a result, French ocean-going trade was repeatedly disrupted. French imports from outside Europe were cut by two-thirds in the late 1740s, 1756–63, and the late 1770s. By 1770 British exports to the non-European world had grown to more than five times that of France. The gap narrowed to near parity in the early 1780s, before Britain streaked ahead as trade was renewed with the USA and French overseas trade was devastated during the Revolutionary and Napoleonic wars.[159] Blockading the French coast in stormy seas was very difficult and dangerous, and French navy ships and privateers were still able to destroy many British merchant ships. Aside from during the American war, however, British trade continued to flow and grow.

There were other positive spin-offs from the Royal Navy for Britain's merchant marine. The navy invested in improving the infrastructure of ports. Merchant shipping also benefited from naval improvements in navigation techniques, charts, efforts to combat scurvy, copper bottoming of ships and so on. During wartime, the navy also turned many landsmen into skilled seamen. With the total pool of seamen larger at the end of each period of conflict than at the start, it is clear that war and the navy itself served as Britain's 'nursery of seamen'.[160]

War and the fiscal-naval state clearly played a central role in fostering the political, financial and economic conditions that were necessary to make industrialisation possible. In short, Britain's dynamic organic economy owed much to the Royal Navy. The remainder of this chapter will consider the extent to which the fiscal-naval state helped to light the fires of industrial revolution in the late eighteenth century.

Invention of new technologies by 'men of genius' has traditionally been seen as the primary cause of the industrial revolution. A 'wave of gadgets' such as Richard Arkwright's cotton-spinning water frame and James Watt's separate condenser steam engine were given pride of place in the story. Birmingham's 'Lunar Society', in which scientists like Watt and Joseph Priestley dined and talked with enterprising industrialists such as Josiah Wedgwood and Matthew Boulton, has been depicted in a recent popular history as 'the friends who made the future'.[161] While the idea of inventions as a causal factor is now widely discounted, technological change remains one of the defining elements of the industrial revolution. Military technology changed little over the course of the Seventy Years War, and so there was limited scope for technological spin-offs that could benefit the broader economy. Surveying the impact of war on innovation and technology, H.V. Bowen concluded that 'little tangible benefit was derived by way of a return on the nation's considerable wartime expenditure'.[162]

Military spending did, however, provide significant stimulus to one of the leading sectors of the industrial revolution: iron production. Iron production stagnated in the peaceful decades prior to 1740, but Britain's wartime needs saw the granting of large contracts for muskets, cannon, shot, and various equipment. This helped the iron industry to build capacity and refine technology and operations.[163] It is even possible that the iron industry would not have developed without large-scale war contacts. A cotton factory could be built for around £10,000, but an ironworks cost £50,000 in 1812.[164] It is surely not a coincidence that expansion of the iron industry accelerated during the Revolutionary and Napoleonic wars. And it is also worth noting that the first place to industrialise on the Continent in the early nineteenth century was modern-day Belgium – a long-established centre of armaments manufacture. In Britain, over three million small guns were manufactured between 1793 and 1815. Pig iron output rose from 70,000 to 395,000 tons in the period 1788–1815, and in the first decade of the nineteenth century Britain ended its dependence on importing refined bar iron. Military demand consumed nearly 20% of iron output during the French Revolutionary and Napoleonic wars and the industry went into recession for several years following 1815.[165] Challenging the traditional neglect of war by economic historians, Priya Satia argues strongly in *Empire of Guns* that Birmingham developed as the heart of a 'military-industrial society'. Dramatic expansion of the iron industry seems to have been sparked by the fiscal-naval state's carrots, and then after 1815 the stick of post-war recession forced peacetime product innovation that carried the industrial revolution forward.[166]

Military contracts fostered innovations in wrought iron production and the steam engine that were at the heart of Britain's industrial revolution. After a decade of work on military ordinance, John Wilkinson developed a cannon lathe that, in addition to making better artillery, was able to bore cylinders accurately enough to make Watt's steam engine work.[167] More broadly, according to A.H. John, 'wartime pressure on mineral- and coal-mining gave a powerful impetus to the development of the steam engine', and 'of the sixty-six steam pumps erected by Boulton and Watt between 1775 and 1785, twenty-two were placed in copper mines and seventeen in iron works'.[168] Also crucial was the development of 'puddling and rolling', which greatly improved the process of turning pig-iron into finer quality bars of wrought iron. Its inventor, Henry Cort, was a naval pay agent who invested in an iron forge. A contract to provide the navy's Victualling Board with iron hoops for their barrels encouraged Cort to develop and patent his puddling process in 1784. During the mid-1780s the quality of chains, anchors, hooks and bolts made from his iron were rigorously tested in the royal dockyards.[169] Phyllis Dean has described the steam engine and iron puddling as the two 'crucial inventions which made the industrial revolution possible'.[170] They allowed Britain to build the machines, railways and iron ships that enabled a transition to sustained 'modern economic growth' in the nineteenth century.[171]

The traditional emphasis on technology, in a revised form, has been given a new lease of life in some important recent studies that focus on a broad Enlightenment scientific culture. In this view, the important thing about the science of Isaac Newton, Robert Boyle and other men of the Royal Society is that their knowledge was popularised and applied in the eighteenth century. Across the course of the Seventy Years War technical literacy and mechanical knowledge was increasingly diffused throughout Britain via print and sociability.[172] Joel Mokyr has depicted Britain's inventive and enterprising businessmen, scientists and artisans as leaders of a 'European Industrial Enlightenment'.[173]

The fiscal-naval state played a role in cultivating and popularising scientific culture. Despite neglect by scholars, as the next chapter will show, soldiers and seamen were often agents of Enlightenment values. Many soldiers, particularly artillery officers, were skilled in mathematics and surveying. In charting oceans, naval officers were at the cutting edge of the Enlightenment pursuit of geographical knowledge. The naval dockyards were the largest industrial sites in the world, with a fully fitted 74-gun warship costing around £80,000 – the equivalent of building at least eight cotton factories.[174] These wooden ships were built with costly iron nails, bolts, chains, hooks, anchors and cannon. Large-scale dockyards contributed significantly to demand for industrial products and helped develop a skilled workforce in Britain. One difficult technical and logistical innovation alone, the copper-bottoming of warships, had various positive linkages to the broader process of industrialisation.

A combination of cheap coal and high wages appears to have sparked the use of industrial technology. Urbanisation, fuelled by thriving European and Atlantic trade and supported by agricultural revolution, created demand for labour and energy. A shortage of wood for heating in London saw the expansion of coal mining in the seventeenth century. By the eighteenth century Britain had a well-developed coal mining and trade sector, with a young James Cook starting his famous seafaring career carrying coal from Newcastle to heat the homes of London. In addition to colonial 'ghost acres', coal provided the British economy with a dramatic increase in its energy resource base, enabling it to push beyond the limits of an organic economy.[175]

In addition to the low cost of energy from coal, Robert Allen has recently shown that Britain had the highest wages for labourers in the eighteenth-century world. Calculation of real wages for selected cities in Europe suggests that, after the mid-fourteenth-century Black Death, living standards were three to four times the level of subsistence. From then on, with the exception of Britain and Holland, population growth appears to have caused a steady and substantial decline in wages. Real wages remained between three to four times the level of subsistence in London through to the eighteenth century, with the agricultural revolution and overseas trade lifting rates in rural and regional Britain. High wages fuelled consumerism and created an incentive for manufacturers to invest capital in labour-saving technology, whether driven by water wheel or steam engine. While early industrialisation was often driven by traditional organic sources of power, it was use of coal, iron and steam that constituted the big structural change at the heart of the industrial revolution. France had many inventive scientists and skilled artisans, but lacked the combination of cheap coal and high wages that encouraged the British to develop steam powered industries.[176]

The fiscal-naval state made both a broad and a specific contribution to high wages. It protected and expanded the overseas trade that did much to fuel urbanisation and economic growth. In addition, the manpower needs of the fiscal-naval state helped maintain high wages in a time of population growth. Owing primarily to a combination of population pressure on resources and more frequent bad harvests, price rises saw real wages stagnate in the late eighteenth century, and even dip in the years around 1800. Yet for real wages to remain relatively stable during a period of rapid population growth, price rises and structural change required a substantial rise in nominal wage rates. Measured in grams of silver, the wages of labourers in London rose steeply after 1775, while wages in Amsterdam, Vienna, Florence, Delhi and Beijing stagnated or declined. [177] During the Seventy Years War the fiscal-naval state repeatedly recruited large numbers of men, including some of the unemployed – something borne out by the social problems that accompanied post-war demobilisations.[178] At the very least, war helped to maintain high wages during a time of population growth.

In multiple ways the fiscal-naval state played a key role in Britain's path to industrial revolution. It defended the island from invasion, extended empire and protected trade. Fiscal policy fostered a robust financial system, tapped some idle capital and stimulated key sectors of the economy. For a state in Britain's position, war was unavoidable in the eighteenth century – the failure of Robert Walpole to keep Britain free of war in the 1730s is testimony to that. Given that war had to be fought,

Britain's fiscal-military state fought in a way that fostered economic growth and helped spark industrial revolution.

The traditional and still influential idea that Britain had a small and limited state has been turned on its head by recent scholarship. In the words of Harling and Mandler, 'we now see that by the end of the French wars the British state was one of the largest and most efficient in Europe'.[179] The degree to which research is revealing Britain's state to be strong and active is reflected in the various terms being coined as alternatives, or complimentary, to Brewer's 'fiscal-military state'. We now have scholars suggesting Britain had a 'fiscal-naval state', a 'caring state', a 'contractor state', a 'bureaucratic-military state', a 'entrepreneurial state' and even an 'infrastructure state'.[180] Roger Morriss has gone so far as to argue that the impact of a reforming military bureaucracy on society and economy amounted to a 'military revolution'.[181] While 'fiscal-military state' is appropriate for most Continental states, Britain is best described as having a 'fiscal-naval state', while using the other concepts to highlight aspects of its operation. Taken together these concepts highlight the ways a fiscal-naval state, under the pressures of war, grew substantially in size, professionalism and in its impact upon British society and economy.

Chapter 3: Britain's Armed Forces

While every man was as busy as he could be the greater order prevailed. A serious cast was perceived on every face but not a shade of doubt or fear. We rejoiced in a general action; not that we loved fighting, but we all wished to be free to return to our homes and follow our own pursuits. We knew there was no other way of obtaining this than by defeating the enemy. 'The hotter the war the sooner the peace,' was a saying with us. When everything was cleared, the ports open, the matches lighted and guns run out, then we gave them three such cheers as are only to be heard in a British man-of-war. This intimidates the enemy more than a broadside, as they have often declared to me. It shows them all is right, and the men in the true spirit baying to be at them.

Start of the battle of St Vincent,
as remembered by John Nicol,
seaman on the *Goliath*.[1]

With increased funding and parliamentary scrutiny, Britain's armed forces grew in size and professionalism. The army was augmented by militia and volunteer units to the point Britain had nearly one million men armed at the height of the struggle against Napoleon. Nevertheless, the core of the army was largely deployed to help keep France committed to Continental land warfare, and thus tie down resources that might have been diverted into enhanced naval power. And the army was heavily dependent on the navy in conducting operations to defend and expand maritime empire – even the Peninsular War was to some extent a combined forces operation. In fact, the degree to which the army and navy learned to work together became an essential strength of the British war effort. The navy was popularly seen as the defining national military institution. A 'blue-water' foreign policy was conceivable (if impractical), while an army-based policy was inconceivable for an island nation. This chapter shows how the British fiscal-naval state's armed forces developed a war-winning capacity over the course of the Seventy Years War.

The Royal Navy

Navies were expensive both to build and maintain, requiring enormous amounts of investment and logistical support. In the late eighteenth century a large cotton factory cost £10,000, while the 104-gun HMS *Victory* cost over £63,000 to build in 1765. To keep a 'ship of the line' (two or three gun-decks) operational for six months cost £13,000.[2] The number of ships of the line in the Royal Navy remained stable at around 120 to 140 during the Seventy Years War. Their size, however, doubled over the course of the eighteenth century – which increased their firepower, but also their cost. There was substantial growth in Britain's fleet of cruisers (single gun-deck ships), which more than quadrupled in number between 1740 and 1810, from around 40 to 180. Cruisers were useful for patrolling and blockading ports – the main work of the Royal Navy.

The British navy had greater political and financial support than the French navy.[3] Although there was increasing popular support for the navy in France, which included patriotic societies raising funds for individual ships, generals tended to find more favour than admirals at Versailles. Along with the prestige and popular support the British navy attracted came high expectations and scrutiny. Detailed accounts appeared in the newspapers soon after naval battles and could result in the disgrace or even execution of an admiral.[4]

Domestic criticism of the Royal Navy was particularly harsh from the 1740s through to the 1780s, some of it by notable admirals who became members of the parliamentary opposition. A common complaint was that a large amount of the money voted for the navy was squandered through corruption. This was encouraged by a lack of clear reporting of the navy's real costs. The dire state of the fleet in 1749, which had been reduced to only thirty-three seaworthy ships of the line, was largely concealed from the public (and Britain's enemies). With the growth of popular politics and newspapers, however, scrutiny and accountability increased to the point that Lord Sandwich, First Lord of the Admiralty from 1771 to 1782, was subject to relentless denigration during the unpopular American war. Although Britain lost the American colonies, recent scholarship has praised Sandwich as an administrator who faced a 'naval crisis' owing to a rapidly aging fleet, and whose reforms enabled an outnumbered Navy to fight several opponents to a standstill – his 'achievement was overshadowed by misinformed criticism, a lack of communication, and an unsuccessful war'.[5] The victories of Nelson's navy owed more than a little to the reforms of Sandwich in the 1770s.[6]

As the size of the navy grew during the eighteenth century, the administrative challenge of keeping it afloat also grew. Parliament tried to keep a tight hold of the purse strings in order to exercise and preserve its hard-won role in the British constitution. As a result, while large amounts of money were devoted to the Navy, a recent study has concluded: 'It is clear from the naval estimates that parliament almost never granted sufficient money to cover the Navy's annual expenditure.'[7] Always short of funds, and under the critical eye of an emerging public sphere, the Navy's leadership worked hard at improving the systems and management of the world's largest industrial complex.

In addition to broad public support, the Royal Navy had a centralised administration that gave it an advantage over the French navy. The Admiralty became a permanent department of state in the 1690s, and the First Lord of the Admiralty became a member of cabinet, thus giving the Navy a direct say in national decision making. Sometimes the First Lord was an Admiral, such as the important lordship of George Anson (1751–62); but when it was a civilian, admirals were brought into cabinet discussions when naval expertise was required. While the Board of Admiralty conventionally had one or two naval officers, those in active service were at sea for much of the time during war. When at war, the Admiralty was a hive of activity, issuing hundreds of orders every day. The Admiralty was directly responsible for manning ships and appointing officers, with subordinate boards reporting on other key administrative tasks. The Navy Board, headed by a naval officer and a master shipwright, administered shipbuilding, dockyards and all naval finances. The Victualling Board was in charge of feeding the navy; and in the 1740s a Sick and Hurt Board was made permanent, and construction of the first naval medical hospital began in 1745. At the cost of three battleships, Haslar Hospital near Portsmouth was one of the largest brick buildings in Europe, and became 'the prototype of a new regime in treating sick seamen, under professional care, in buildings designed for the purpose, carefully isolated from the temptations of drink and desertion'.[8]

Sea officer complaints about the design of Royal Navy ships became more vocal in the 1740s. British ships were too cramped and slow, and the lower-deck of three-deckers could not open their gun portals in rough weather. Disquiet increased in light of sleek scientifically designed French ships that were captured, but attempts by the Admiralty to reform ship design were frustrated by entrenched conservatism at the Navy Board. In 1755 George Anson was finally able to appoint a new Surveyor of the Navy, Thomas Slade, and the Royal Navy proceeded to emulate French-style two-deck 74-gun ships. The British did not, however, adopt the lighter, longer and faster style French hull, which performed poorly in rough weather and needed more frequent repair. Royal Navy ships were built for durability: shorter, heavier and with more storage, enabling longer time at sea. In the hands of a skilled crew, a well-rigged and main-tained British ship was able to catch a technically faster French ship.[9]

There are various ways of assessing the relative strength of navies in the eighteenth century. In an impressive feat of archival research, Jan Glete calculated and compared the size of navies in terms of ship displacement tons. This revealed, for example, that in 1780 the Royal Navy of 372,000 tons was outnumbered by the combined 467,000 tons of the Bourbon allies, France and Spain.[10] This measure has its limitations, however, as it was not used by strategists in the eighteenth century, and, arguably, it favours fleets that tended to have larger ships, such as France and Spain. To compare Britain against France (and its sometime ally, Bourbon Spain), it is probably best to compare the number of ships (Figure 3.1).[11] As a general trend, most growth was in the lighter cruiser class.

When comparing total number of ships a few key points stand out. First, while France's navy collapsed and Spain was only beginning to build off a small base in the 1720s, Britain invested considerable money in maintaining its peacetime fleet. While there was widespread hostility to a 'standing army', a 'standing navy' was seen as necessary. Second, Britain's maritime success in the late 1740s was followed by a naval arms race. Between 1730 and 1790 the French tripled their number of ships, while the British doubled theirs between 1740 and 1805. Third, British belt-tightening following the peace of 1763 coincided with Bourbon naval investment to see parity achieved in the 1770s. Going to war with the Dutch in 1780 saw Britain outnumbered at sea in the last years of the American war. Fourth, the naval arms race continued after the peace of 1783, contributing to the collapse of French finances. That Louis XVI's regime continued to pour money into its navy on the eve of revolution underlines the degree to which the French state had turned its strategic

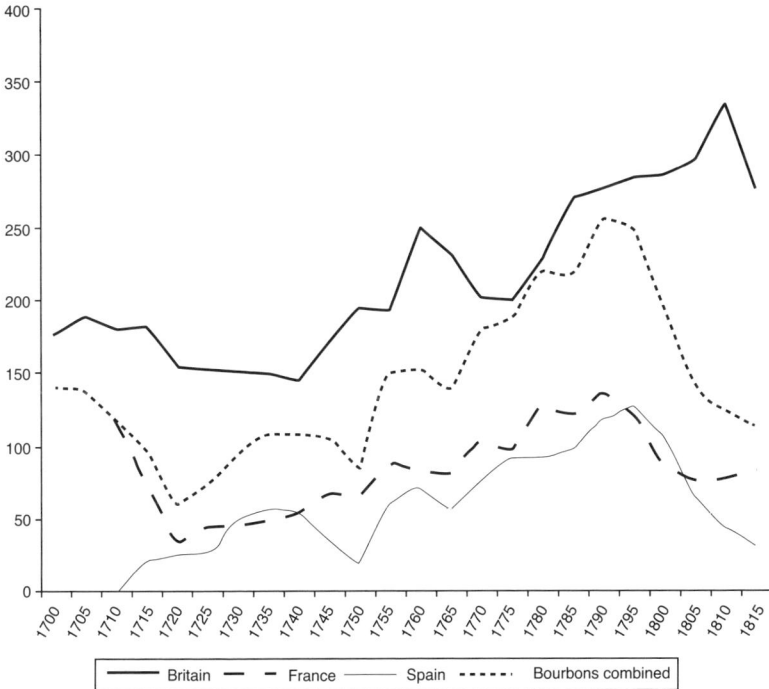

Figure 3.1 Total number of listed ships of the line and cruisers

Source: N.A.M. Rodger, The Command of the Ocean: a Naval History of Britain, 1649–1815 (2005), pp. 606–9.

attention toward maritime rivalry with Britain. Fifth, British victories in the 1790s, combined with the disruptive impact of the revolution, started a decline in the French navy.[12] Napoleon arrested the decline, but his shipbuilding programs failed to return the French navy to growth.

Statistics can be revealing, but are never the full story. A simple comparison of ship totals does not reflect the relative number of ships built, as over the course of the Seventy Years War the British increasingly captured and re-deployed more ships than their opponents. More importantly, in the words of Nicholas Rodger: 'No navy ever had all its ships available for service, and the proportion which might be made fit for service was variable and unpredictable'.[13] Mobilising three-quarters of its listed ships was the best the Royal Navy could achieve. Buoyed by political and financial support, it developed a number of organisational advantages that acted as a 'force multiplier', enabling it to keep more ships at sea, for longer, and more operationally effective than its rivals.[14]

To turn ships on paper into ships at sea required dockyard support, and here the British had a distinct superiority. While large ships of the line (90 guns or more) were built in the royal dockyards, construction of frigates and other cruisers was usually contracted out to private yards, as was building of smaller ships of the line after 1755. In the words of Daniel Baugh, 'building warships, even very good warships was rather easy. Consistently repairing and replacing them over the years was harder'.[15] Wooden ships had a limited life span and needed regular maintenance. During the 1740s the royal dockyards struggled to keep up with a growing demand for repairs. Unsystematic use of timber from unsheltered piles combined with a period of warm winters in the 1730s to increase the rate at which ships rotted during the War of the Austrian Succession. An attempt by the Admiralty to reform inefficient work practices at the royal dockyards ran into stiff opposition, and instead the workforce was reduced during the Treasury's economy drive in the early 1750s. In light of this, Admiral Anson planned to contract-out an increasing amount of shipbuilding to private yards after he succeeded Sandwich as First Lord of the Admiralty in 1751. Being able to draw on an extensive network of private dockyards enabled the Royal Navy to build new ships rapidly in the early years of future conflicts.[16] It also allowed the royal dockyards to focus on repairing and refitting ships – with ships in reserve during peacetime given a triennial repair in dry-dock. While Britain's large number of ships at sea during peacetime was an advantage, it always took time to fully mobilise the navy during conflict, as many ships in reserve had to be checked and repaired before putting to sea. Once operational, ships needed regular refitting and scraping of barnacles from hulls. Copper coating of hulls was an important technical advance in 1779, increasing the speed of ships and reducing time spent in port.[17]

Large amounts of money were spent on developing an impressive system of dockyards. The royal dockyards were the largest industrial sites in eighteenth-century Britain. Those in the Thames estuary (Deptford, Woolwich, Sheerness and the largest at Chatham) tended to be used for shipbuilding and major repairs. Following the peace of 1763, £680,000 was spent on improving the south coast dockyards at Portsmouth and Plymouth.[18] By the 1770s there were over 8,000 men working in the Royal Navy's dockyards. To these British home bases, the Royal Navy added strategically valuable dockyards overseas. In the Mediterranean there was Gibraltar and Port Mahon on Minorca, to which was added Malta in 1800. In the West Indies, Port Royal in Jamaica and English Harbour in Antigua were developed as naval bases. Halifax in Nova Scotia was established as a base in 1749 and expanded after American independence. Royal Navy ships seldom ventured into the Indian Ocean before the 1740s, but as imperial rivalry intensified the East India Company built Britain's only overseas dry-dock at Bombay in 1750. This helped the Royal Navy to play an increasingly influential role in the Eastern hemisphere in the late eighteenth century. In 1788 the British established a settlement in the South Pacific at Sydney Cove, one of the world's finest natural harbours. In comparison, the French were slow to invest in dockyards, with the important port of Toulon not having a dry-dock until the 1770s. The French dockyards also suffered supply problems during wartime, as the Royal Navy interrupted the flow of timber and other naval resources from the Baltic Sea.

According to Jan Glete, 'naval history may be rewritten as campaigns against epidemics and problems with food preservation'.[19] Epidemics tended to be more frequent in the early years of war as fresh recruits were brought together and exposed to shipboard diseases. Sickness accounted for approximately three-quarters of wartime deaths in the Royal Navy. Overseas bases helped to mitigate this problem, by allowing acclimatised squadrons to operate for long periods of time.

Recent scholarship has highlighted the vital role of the Victualling Commissioners in sustaining the activity of a large and widely disbursed navy. The quality of the food supplied to seamen was bland, consisting largely of salt meat, bread, hard cheese and a ration of beer, wine or rum. Scurvy remained a problem until the late eighteenth century. Yet the poor quality of the naval diet needs to be considered in light of the generally bland and low-quality diet of the eighteenth-century lower orders. British seamen probably ate more meat than many of Europe's poor, and the phrase 'square meal' probably derives from the navy's square platters.

Starting in the 1740s, the Victualling Board made heroic efforts to supply fresh meat and vegetables to ships operating off the southern coast of England. In rolling seas, live cattle were hoisted in slings from transports on to warships blockading the French coast in the late 1750s. Without such efforts ships would have spent less time at sea, and British blockades during the Seventy Years War would have been far less effective.

With the Admiralty declaring it was 'their intention that the seamen should be supplied with the best of everything in its kind', the Victualling Board developed sophisticated systems of quality control and delivery.

At the Victualling Office bases at Tower Hill, Portsmouth and Plymouth, biscuits were baked and packed in bags, along with casks of salt beef, pork, peas and other consumables. By the 1750s spoilage rates were less than 1%, which is astonishing given the technical difficulties of preserving food at sea.[20] A Mrs Dubois in London perfected the production of meat stock cubes, and the navy started contracting for large quantities in 1757. As seamen developed a habit of adding vegetables to this portable soup it inadvertently had a large impact in lowering rates of scurvy.[21] A French historian, Christian Buchet, has shown how the Victualling Board's improving, flexible and well-financed logistics provided Britain with a decisive superiority over France and Spain during the mid-century conflict. In addition to its central operations, the Victualling Board used contractors when possible in various regions of the globe, while maintaining strict quality-control inspections. Britain's booming agricultural market and reliable financial system provided a solid base for the construction of this war-winning system of naval supply. The capabilities of the Victualling Board grew along with the empire, and by the time of the Napoleonic Wars it was aiming 'to promote a fair and open competition for contracts', with foreign merchants able to bid for business.[22]

Improvements in logistics underpinned the expansion of the British Empire. The Victualling Board employed contractors in major theatres of conflict such as the Mediterranean and Caribbean, and ensured that the spoilage rates of food dropped until they were negligible. In contrast, when Bourbon fleets managed to leave port, their operations on the high seas were often hampered by food shortages and outbreaks of disease. Supplying the British navy and army across the Atlantic during the American War proved a major logistical feat.[23] Lessons learned and systems developed enabled the British to undertake major operations such as the Peninsular campaign against Napoleon. As Alan Frost has argued, in 1788 no other European power had the capability to found and supply a settlement in Australia.[24]

Naval Manpower

Naval performance was heavily influenced by the quantity and quality of crews. The growing size of ships of the line and the increasing number of cruisers caused the manpower of the Royal Navy to nearly triple over the course of the Seventy Years War. At peak wartime mobilisation, naval manpower was 48,000 in 1748; 82,000 in 1762; 95,000 in 1782; 118,000 in

1800; and 138,000 in 1812.[25] Large ships carried several hundred men, with Nelson's *Victory* having over 800. Not all of these were experienced seamen, as all nations faced recruitment difficulties. Given that ships often had inexperienced crews, Europe's navies were generally conservative in their approach to battle tactics – standard practice was to form a line and deliver broadsides. Relatively more experienced sailing crews and rapid gunnery enabled British commanders to be more innovative and risky in their tactics. Thus, in a gale and unchartered waters, Hawke could successfully chase and smash a French fleet in Quiberon Bay; and Rodney at the Saintes and Nelson at Trafalgar could dangerously cut into the enemy line of battle to win celebrated victories.

The press gang seizing drunken men and forcing them into a hellish life on His Majesty's ships is a common image from the eighteenth century. Unlike the French, the Royal Navy lacked a central register of available seamen, but it had the advantage of a much larger pool of commercial shipping from which to draw manpower. Recruitment was, however, always a serious problem. Efforts to establish a national registry were widely opposed, mainly owing to fears that trade would be damaged, with dire consequences for the British economy and tax revenue. Merchant ships paid higher wages during wartime, which encouraged the Royal Navy to press gang when it needed to rapidly mobilise its ships. Press ganging became increasingly regulated, with the Impress Service established in the 1750s and placed under the leadership of an admiral in 1793. From the 1750s press gangs cast their net beyond the major ports in an effort to capture seamen who had moved inland. 'Landsmen' were also drafted, as they could be put to work as gunners or labourers on ships. Rather than press a disgruntled seaman, one captain declared, he would prefer 'a willing and contented landman, who with a little time, and his own endeavours, I could make a seaman'.[26] As a result, the Royal Navy always ended wars with near or more men than the total pool of British seamen at the start of the conflict.[27]

Impressment provoked many forms of opposition, including more than a few riots, and was at best seen as a necessary evil.[28] *Memoirs of a Seafaring Life* (1796) by William Spavens provides a particularly revealing insight into the attitudes of one seaman. Impressed into the Royal Navy himself, Spavens also took part in press gang operations, and in turn evaded press gangs by wearing the 'long clothes' of a landsman when he deserted a ship to avoid serving under a 'haughty' officer. While outward-bound ships were conventionally left alone, merchant ships returning from an Atlantic voyage were sometimes intercepted before reaching port and a portion of their crew impressed into the Royal Navy – to the dismay of sea-weary sailors. This was the main source of pressed seamen. Spavens described boarding a merchant ship bound for Dublin:

> but finding the men had taken close quarters, we scuttled their decks with axes, and fired down amongst them, while they kept firing up at us where they saw the light appear. After having shot one of our men through the head and another through both his thighs, they submitted, and we got 16 brave fellows.... Such are the methods frequently made use of to obtain seamen for the service in this land of liberty... it is a hardship which nothing but absolute necessity can reconcile to our boasted freedom.[29]

The destination of this ship points toward the ethnic mix of the Royal Navy, which drew seamen from around Britain, Ireland, Europe and Atlantic ports. In his study of a large sample of seamen and petty officers in the 1790s, Jeremiah Dancy found the following breakdown of nationalities: 51% English, 19% Irish, 10% Scottish, 3% Welsh, 8% Foreign and 9% unknown.[30] Though race was not identified in muster records, it is clear that there were more than a few Africans. The Royal Navy provided better working conditions than plantation slavery and could protect a runaway slave from being reclaimed by his owner.[31] Olaudah Equiano, in his remarkable autobiography of a man who worked his way from slavery to freedom in the eighteenth century, speaks warmly of the multi-racial comradeship and adventure he experienced during years as a seaman in the Royal Navy.[32]

Rum, sodomy and the lash is the traditional popular image of life on eighteenth-century ships. This owes much to nineteenth-century writings that, for polemical or entertainment reasons, tended to spotlight violence and depravity in naval life. A comparison can be drawn with the way unjustifiably negative images of the convict system in Australia are rooted in sensationalist novels and writings by anti-transportation campaigners in the nineteenth century.[33] Some historians confidently assert that Royal Navy ships 'were, of course, floating prisons in which press ganged labour was exploited with notorious cruelty'.[34] And some are also keen to depict the lower decks of eighteenth-century ships as the birth site of a self-conscious international working class – with the immense demand for manpower in the 1790s causing 'hundreds of thousands' to experience the 'shock of proletarianization at sea'.[35]

While there was undoubtedly rigorous and brutal discipline on ships, the traditional view seriously distorts the nature of life in the navy. Ships were complex hierarchical microcosms in which teamwork was essential for survival in dangerous seas. The 'old man', as captains were often called, was expected to be skilled, disciplined and respectable. Seaman had various ways of expressing disapproval at their treatment, including petitions to the Admiralty to complain about an incompetent or overly brutal captain. After the 1797 mutinies over poor pay and treatment, which occurred against the background of revolutionary ideas of equality, relations on Navy ships became stricter and more class conscious. The authority of officers was strengthened by the growing presence of armed marines. The 1806 *Regulations and Instructions* removed the 12 lashes limit, but in practice the tendency was toward sparing the lash. Admiral Collingwood, a stern paternalist, thought excessive flogging 'big with the most dangerous consequences, and subversive of all real discipline'. Lord Eldon once found Collingwood with tears in his eyes in the Strand: 'He said that a few days before his Ships Company were paid off – that he had lost his children – all his family – that they were dear to him, and he could not refrain.'[36] During the mutinies of 1797 Collingwood declined the command of a larger ship: 'for I know I am known here, which, in these ticklish times, I hold to be of much consequence'.[37] Officers who treated their crews with respect were in turn respected. One captain declared: 'that ship which gives the most leave will ever have the least desertion'.[38]

By the end of the eighteenth century it was not uncommon for the wives of some seamen to accompany them on Royal Navy ships. These women seem to have worked at washing clothes, participated in amateur theatricals and acted as powder monkeys during battle. Famously, at the Battle of the Nile, Captain Thomas Foley, in the *Goliath*, cut across the French line in shallow water and led five ships down their unprepared landward side. Less well known, it has been estimated that as many as 100 women were on board *Goliath*: several were wounded, one killed and another gave birth during the battle.[39]

In the absence of detailed research, it was traditionally estimated that more than half of naval seamen were press ganged into service. However, it now appears that most seamen in the Royal Navy were volunteers. In a recent study of over 27,000 seamen, Jeremiah Dancy has revealed that between 1793 and 1802 only 16% were pressed, and over 80% were volunteers.[40] The tough life in the Royal Navy must be considered in the context of the generally hard life of labouring people in pre-industrial

societies – particularly in a time of population growth and price inflation. Although Royal Navy wages were lower than on merchant ships
(and a key reason for the 1797 mutinies was that wages had been frozen
since 1686), there were a number of benefits in being on a navy ship,
aside from pride in serving king and country. Unlike merchant seamen,
those in the navy did not lose their wages as a result of shipwreck or
capture. Food supply and medical treatment were more reliable than in
many other places of work. Royal Navy captains' fanatical attention to
cleanliness ensured that disease was less prevalent than in other navies
and merchant ships. Navy ships needed enough men to man guns in
battle, so the daily work of sailing was probably easier than on merchant
ships which had much smaller crews. All seaman paid 6d of their wage to
support 'the Royal Hospital at Greenwich, which magnificent building
is not to be equalled in the world', according to Spavens. This provided
a retirement home for those 'most disabled by loss of limbs or other
extreme hurts sustained in the service, and also those who have worn out
their best days and spent their strength Britannia's weal to save'.[41] Less-
injured seamen could draw a pension from the Chatham chest.

A key motivation was the prospect of prize money from the sale of a
captured ship and its contents. In 1740 parliament began to grant Royal
Navy ships £5 'head money' for each man on board an enemy ship that
was captured or destroyed.[42] One surgeon received £100 for participating
in the capture of three ships in two days.[43] While in reality seamen only
received a small share, the prospect of earnings from taking 'a prize'
was a greater hope than could be had in most eighteenth-century walks
of life.

In an age when many were born and died in the same village, the navy
also provided an opportunity for travel. One able seaman recalled that
as a boy he 'read *Robinson Crusoe* many times over and longed to be at
sea'.[44] Captain Matthew Flinders, the first to circumnavigate Australia,
and the man who proposed its name, joined the navy 'against the wishes
of my friends from reading *Robinson Crusoe*'.[45] William Cobbett was
born to farming, but when he first saw 'riding at anchor at Spithead'
the 'wooden walls of Old England', he 'stood lost between astonish-
ment and admiration'. With a head full of tales of naval victories 'over
our natural enemies, the French and Spaniards' that 'true Englishmen
never fail to relate to their children about a hundred times a year', he
tried to enlist on HMS *Pegasus*. He was turned away by a captain who
'had more compassion than is generally met with in men of his profession' (the captain's response would probably have been different had

post-war demobilisation not been looming). Reluctantly returning to the plough, Cobbett was 'spoiled for a farmer' and, desperate 'for a sight of the world', ran away to London and joined the army.[46]

The brutality and harshness of life in the Royal Navy is evident, but it probably appears more shocking to modern middle-class sensibilities than it did to seamen drawn from the eighteenth-century poor. In a conversation about war and sailors, Dr Johnson expressed the horrified reaction of an urban intellectual:

> *Johnson*: '... as to the sailor, when you look down from the quarter-deck to the space below, you see the utmost extremity of human misery: such crowding, such stench!'
>
> *Boswell*: 'Yet sailors are happy.'
>
> *Johnson*: 'They are happy as brutes are happy, with a piece of fresh meat, – with the grossest sensuality. But, sir, the profession of soldiers and sailors has the dignity of danger. Mankind reverence those who have got over fear, which is so general a weakness.' ...
>
> *Scott*: 'We find people fond of being sailors.'
>
> *Johnson*: 'I cannot account for that, any more than I can account for other strange perversions of imagination'.[47]

A soldier who had the 'irksome and uncomfortable' experience of being crammed aboard a transport ship nevertheless thought that life on ships was 'not quite so forlorn as Doctor Johnson has portrayed it'.[48]

The Royal Navy grew in professionalism during the Seventy Years War. Uniforms were introduced in 1747 for officers, but not for ordinary seamen, who nevertheless wore distinctive clothes consisting of trousers and short coat. A man could rise from humble origins through acquiring experience and skill – James Cook being one of the most famous examples. While classed as gentlemen, British sea officers were often noted for their rough manners and heavy drinking. Nelson advised a young man: 'Recollect that you must be a Seaman to be an Officer, and also that you cannot be a good Officer without being a Gentleman.'[49] Gentlemanly manners were desirable, but skill in seamanship was essential. Commenting on an 'odd Man' who was taking command of his old ship, Nelson observed that it was possible to be a *'respectable gentleman ... and a bad captain of a man of War'*.[50] Technical skills and mathematical knowledge were acquired from a young age through long years at sea, under instruction from experienced seamen. A naval officer started his career as a boy, doing low-ranked tasks in order to 'learn the ropes'. To become a commissioned officer required six years' experience at sea and an oral examination in seamanship. As in all areas of eighteenth-century life, patronage played an important role, but the navy was notable for the importance accorded to professional merit – expensive ships and many lives depended on the seamanship of a captain.[51]

Ruling the Waves

The naval dominance Britain attained was far from preordained. Louis XIV had the biggest navy at the end of the seventeenth century, but allowed it to decline as he focused on fighting the Grand Alliance in the Low Countries. In the words of Jan Glete, Britain thus became 'the largest naval power in the world...partly by default'.[52] In addition to its larger population and economy, as a naval power France had some advantages: ports on both the Mediterranean and Atlantic coasts gave it the ability to intercept British merchant shipping. British politicians and public always had an anxious eye on French shipbuilding. In terms of rivalry with Britain, France's major problems were a lack of deep-water ports on the English Channel – which Louis XVI tried to solve by starting construction of a large artificial harbour at Cherbourg – and the fact that vital naval supplies from the Baltic Sea were vulnerable to disruption by the British.[53] Added to these geographic disadvantages, France's financial and policy inconsistency was not conducive to developing a powerful navy, with French monarchs only showing 'spasmodic interest in sea power'.[54] Bursts of shipbuilding were not supported by similar investment in dockyards and cultivation of a large pool of seamen. Thus, the quality of the French navy declined as it grew in size during the American war. This owed in part to a shortage of officers, with aristocrats resisting the appointment of non-noble auxiliary officers. As a result, for example, in the days of manoeuvring prior to the Battle of the Saintes in 1782 there were several embarrassing collisions between French ships.[55]

The French navy's strategy and tactics were designed to fit its priorities and limitations. French admirals focused on escaping blockaded ports in order to guard a convoy, whether it be merchant ships or an invasion force, and success was measured in their ability to avoid engagement with the British navy. With growing rivalry between the rising powers of Eastern Europe, after 1763 France encouraged peace in its Continental diplomacy, enabling it to focus on naval development and the contest for colonies. Had Louis XV adopted this stance earlier, from the late 1740s, and more consistently pursued a 'blue-water' policy, then the history of Anglo-French rivalry might have been very different.

The Royal Navy was primarily deployed to defend the coasts of Britain and Ireland, and important sea routes for trade around Europe. Only small detachments of ships could be spared for colonial operations. The creation of a Western Squadron in the late 1740s was a very significant development in the deployment of the British navy. Its consequences were so profound that Daniel Baugh has called it a naval 'military revolution'.[56] The primary task of the Royal Navy was to prevent invasion of Britain and Ireland, which required the stationing of ships in ports along the south coast and in the mouth of the Thames. Only in the eighteenth century did ships become big and strong enough to stay at sea in all seasons, making the strategy of continuous blockade of enemy ports possible.[57] At the urging of Admiral Anson, the Royal Navy started to have a squadron cruise in the western approaches to the English Channel. By doing so, it could guard the Channel against invasion, protect inbound British merchant convoys, and attack ships sailing in and out of the French Atlantic ports. This was a dangerous strategy, as it exposed ships to wear and tear, and possible destruction in Atlantic gales. But it reaped immediate rewards as it strangled French shipping and encouraged Versailles to talk peace. The great naval battles of the age of sail were all the more famous for being rare. The Royal Navy won command of the ocean through the tireless, dangerous and unheralded work of blockading French ports.

In addition to striving to deny its opponents use of the sea, the Royal Navy supported offensive amphibious operations with the army. In Europe these tended to be well resourced and designed to aid Continental allies who were hard-pressed fighting large French armies. They were notoriously expensive, difficult to execute and often failed. Henry Fox described coastal raids on France in the 1750s as 'breaking windows with guineas'. Although there were failures – the most spectacular being at Walcheren in 1809 – the British made some technical and operational improvements in their conduct of amphibious landings over the course of the Seventy Years War. The Peninsular campaign began as a large-scale amphibious operation. In colonial theatres, amphibious operations tended to be opportunistic. The capture of Louisbourg in 1745, an attack planned by colonial New Englanders and facilitated by a small Royal Navy squadron, provided advocates of a 'blue-water' strategy with an inspiring model for future campaigns. Colonial operations were best conducted by regionally based forces that were acclimatised to local conditions and diseases. When large-scale forces were shipped into a colonial theatre, losses to disease could be horrendous – as in the capture of Havana in 1762 and the British intervention in the Haitian Revolution in the mid 1790s.

The technical difficulties of conducting amphibious operations during the age of wooden sailing ships were never solved. During a landing, with seamen ferrying troops ashore, ships were vulnerable to attack by an enemy with wind in their sails. Thus, amphibious operations were most successful in periods when the Royal Navy had command of the ocean, most notably 1759–63 and 1805–15.[58]

Britain's Armies

The Seventy Years War made the British army. In 1745 the army was small and had an image problem not helped by defeat at Fontenoy and the Jacobite invasion of England. By 1815 a growing list of battle honours for a truly British army was crowned with Waterloo.

The experience of military rule under Cromwell in the 1650s entrenched a phobia of a professional standing army in English culture. As a result, aside from invasion scares, the presence of regular soldiers in England was kept to a minimum. During peacetime Britain's professional army was small compared to Continental states, and most troops were stationed in Ireland or colonial posts. Between the wars of Louis XIV and the 1740s the decline of the British army mirrored that of the French navy. Parliament voted funds for 144,000 soldiers in 1712, but in 1718 the figure had dropped to 16,000.[59] There were only nine regiments stationed outside the Atlantic Archipelago – seven of these were in Gibraltar and Minorca, with only one each in North America and the West Indies.[60] This was a small imperial military footprint, especially considering regiments were usually not at full strength owing to disease, desertion and limited recruitment. This changed profoundly during the Seventy Years War, by the end of which there were tens of thousands of troops stationed throughout a global empire.

Britain's regular army remained small in comparison to France throughout the Seventy Years War. At times army officers expressed a desire to copy Continental-style conscription, but this was never a serious possibility under the British constitution. In France there were army barracks in more than 300 towns by the 1740s, and the peacetime army stood at 200,000 soldiers in the late eighteenth century. In both 1745 and

1760 France fielded approximately 350,000 soldiers; in comparison the figures for Britain were 50,000 and 100,000.[61] Even at its peak of 250,000 in 1812, with units fighting in Europe and scattered around the globe, the British army was considerably smaller than Napoleon's legions – over 600,000 men followed him into Russia. Napoleon had the advantage of conscripting many soldiers from conquered European states, and the population of France itself was more than twice the size of Britain and Ireland. Napoleon's armies, however, were involved in larger battles and suffered more casualties than the British, which put a great strain on French society through a highly organised system of conscription. For example, in the period 1800–1805, before the impact of large casualties, Napoleon conscripted 78,000 men per annum.[62] By the end of 1813 conscription had virtually stripped French society of its unmarried able-bodied men.[63] In comparison, over the period 1803–1815 the British army directly recruited an average of only 12,000 per year.[64]

While the British army as a whole was relatively small, the proportion of troops available for offensive operations was even smaller. George Canning told General Moore that the 32,000 troops allocated to the Peninsular campaign in 1808 were 'not merely a considerable part of the disposable force of this country. It is, in fact, the British army'.[65] Most of the army was tied down by the need to defend Britain, Ireland and a growing empire. In addition to garrisons in the Mediterranean and Canada, in 1811 there were 76,000 troops stationed throughout the West Indies, Africa, Asia and Australia. Added to this were 56,000 troops stationed in Britain and Ireland. Thus, even in 1813, when the army was at its height of 250,000 men, only a quarter were serving under Wellington in Spain.[66]

Owing to parliamentary suspicion of professional soldiers as a potential threat to liberty, the army had a deliberately divided organisational structure, which has been criticised for causing inefficiency and petty rivalry. A Commander-in-Chief was only appointed during wartime, and his authority was limited. He had to work with the Adjutant-General, a permanent position that was responsible for managing personnel and promotions. The government's Secretary *at* War, a junior minister only sometimes included in cabinet discussions, was in charge of army finance. In addition, a cabinet level Secretary *for* War was created in 1794, which became the Secretary for War and the Colonies in 1801. The Secretary for War had a strong influence on British policy, particularly when the position was occupied by men such as Henry Dundas and Lord Castlereagh. Artillery and engineer units were under the authority of the Master-General of the Ordnance, which was usually a cabinet level position during the Seventy Years War. The complex and inefficient organisation of the army helped ensure it remained subordinate to parliament and also allowed for a multitude of economic links to British civil society.[67]

While there was no root-and-branch structural reform of army administration during the Seventy Years War, there were incremental improvements to institutions and practices, an expansion in size, and growing professionalism that amounted to substantial change. The story of the army was one of boom and bust. During periods of conflict a rapid expansion would occur, with attendant teething problems. On the signing of a peace treaty a rapid and large-scale demobilisation would leave the army gutted. With the resumption of hostilities another desperate scramble for NCOs and rankers would ensue. There was growth over time, however, as the army was bigger in each new period of mobilisation or demobilisation; and Scotland and Ireland played important roles in recruitment.

Scotland made a disproportionate contribution to the British army. With only 10% of the population of the Atlantic Archipelago, Scotland provided over 15% of the soldiers in the British army, and approximately 30% of its officers. Loyal Scottish regiments had helped defeat the Jacobite '45. In 1751 the young James Wolfe, who fought at Culloden and served as part of the military occupation, observed that some Highland units would be a good addition to the British army:

> they are hardy, intrepid, accustomed to a rough country, and no great mischief if they fall. How can you better employ a secret enemy than by making his end conducive to the common good? If this sentiment should take wind, what an execrable and bloody being should I be considered here in the midst of Popery and Jacobitism?[68]

The sentiment did take wind, with the elder Pitt pushing for the recruitment of Highland regiments for service in North America. They soon distinguished themselves fighting under Wolfe at Quebec – though their dress was unsuited to the harsh Canadian weather: the wearing of the kilt led to their death by disease in greater numbers than other troops.[69] In addition to their bravery on the battlefield, Highlanders were thought better-behaved than most British regiments, with one general declaring during the American rebellion: 'the Highlanders are thrifty, consequently sober & therefore less likely to get into squabbles'.[70] With their kilts, broadswords and Gaelic language, the Highland regiments were the most distinctive units in the British army in the 1750s. Over the following years, however, they tended to adopt the weapons and dress of normal regiments on campaign, reserving the kilt for ceremonial occasions. Scotland also provided several Lowland regiments and recruits for other British army units. Of 35 infantry battalions raised between 1775 and 1781, 12 were 'distinctively Scottish'.[71] As a result, Scots made up approximately 30% of the British soldiers who fought in North America between 1757 and 1783.[72]

In the decades of peace before the Seventy Years War half of Britain's small army was stationed in Ireland, and was paid for by the Irish parliament.[73] The peacetime establishment was fixed at 12,000 troops until it was raised to over 15,000 in 1769.[74] The British state used these units as a strategic reserve 4,000 were shipped to America to combat the rebellion. The garrisoning of this nominally Protestant force among a largely Catholic population has led historians to debate whether Ireland was an 'occupied country' in the eighteenth century.[75] The Duke of Wellington, a Protestant Irishman, certainly thought so, declaring in 1807 that 'Ireland, in a view to military operations, must be considered an enemy's country'.[76] In the late eighteenth century some British politicians took a less hostile view. There were signs that the Catholic population, or at least elements of its elite, was becoming grudgingly reconciled to British rule. It is possible that Ireland could, in the words of the nineteenth-century Catholic politician Daniel O'Connell, have developed into 'a kind of West Britons'.[77] The manpower needs of the army encouraged British politicians to consider relaxing the penal laws against Catholics. It appears that in the 1740s Irish Catholics were being illegally recruited into regiments.[78] On the initiative of George Townshend, a reforming lord-lieutenant, open recruiting of Catholics began in 1771, with an oath of allegiance replacing the traditional religious test. While this was criticised by conservative Irish Protestants, the British government became keen on the idea of relaxing the penal laws against Catholics, with an eye to making recruitment into the army easier and more attractive.[79] The Catholic Relief Act of 1793, which removed many Catholic civil disabilities, owed more than a little to military considerations at the start of war with Revolutionary France. At the end of the Seventy Years War, and in line with its proportion of the population of the United Kingdom, Ireland was the birthplace of nearly a third of the British army.

The army thus became increasingly British during the Seventy Years War – before the nineteenth-century elite obsession with 'The Queen's English', it talked in multiple national and regional dialects. In the 1740s English people unthinkingly referred to their army as composed of 'Englishmen', despite the significant number of Scotsmen and others in its ranks.[80] By the 1750s its British character was increasingly recognised, and during the American War it was unmistakable. In the 1770s over half the officers in the British army were Irish or Scottish.[81] The birthplace of recruits was not systematically recorded until 1765, but studies of scattered evidence reveal that the manpower demands of the 1750s saw an increase in the ethnic diversity of the army. Lauded for its professionalism, the recently created 58th Foot regiment served with distinction at Quebec in 1759. Of its 553 men with identifiable birthplaces, the ethnic breakdown was: English 55%, Scots 17%, Irish 16%, Welsh 10%, with the remaining 2% foreign and American.[82] While Irishmen were only 4% of regiments stationed in Britain, they were 27.5% of the 14,772 soldiers in North America in 1757 for whom enlistment data has survived.[83] This reflects the fact that a number of the regiments had spent time stationed in Ireland. Over the following decades, Celts, including Irish Catholics, played an important role in the expansion of the British army. A study of 7,250 soldiers who enlisted between 1790 and 1815, sampled from twenty regiments, provides the following statistics: English and Welsh 53%, Irish 30% and Scottish 16%.[84] A verse of the soldier song *The British Bayoneteers* ran:

> The English arm is strong, boys,
> The Irish arm is tough.
> The Scotsman's blow the French well know
> Is struck by sterling stuff.
> And when before the enemy
> Their shining steel appears,
> Goodbye, goodbye, how they run, how they run,
> From the British bayoneteers.[85]

One soldier reported that Colonel Mainwaring, 'full of chat', inspired the 51st Foot prior to the Walcheren campaign: ' "Here" he exclaimed, "is John Bull from England; Swaney from Scotland, and Paddy from my own country. By J—s, we will not only beat the French but we will eat them afterwards." '[86] With its multinational ranks and officers, the army was central to the forging of a British identity.[87]

Growing manpower needs saw the ethnic diversity of the British army develop beyond the peoples of the Atlantic Archipelago. Europeans and European Americans were an established minority in the ranks of British regiments. Non-Europeans were recruited into regiments that helped expand Britain's military power. By 1770 the East India Company had

20,000 Indian sepoys in battalions under British officers – a figure that doubled in the following decade and continued to rise so that there were 227,000 men under arms in 1815, of whom only 31,000 were European.[88] By mid century it was common for British regiments to have African drummer boys and musicians, and there is evidence that some indigenous Americans were recruited into the ranks; and both Africans and indigenous Americans bore arms in ranger companies and provincial regiments.[89] During the American war, Lord Dunmore, on his own initiative, offered freedom to slaves who escaped rebel owners and served in the British army. Most of these were employed as labourers, but some fought in defence of Savannah in 1779 and a black 'Carolina Corps' was formed.[90] Some free and enslaved Africans were armed as auxiliaries in the West Indies during the American war. Pointing to the success of sepoy regiments in India, General John Vaughan argued persistently for the formation of black regiments in the mid 1790s in the face of strong opposition from West India planters. The British government eventually agreed to arm slaves after British troops sent to fight the revolution in Saint-Domingue were decimated by disease. Two West India regiments were raised in 1795 and within three years there were twelve. In 1799 the government ruled that black troops should form one-third of each island garrison in the West Indies.[91] With Africans filling the ranks up to sergeant, they received the same pay and equipment as other British army regiments.

Given the political limits placed on the size of the army, Britain resorted to allies and auxiliaries to augment its military power. Indigenous people in North America proved valuable allies during conflicts in the colonies.[92] Outside the period 1763–83, British statesmen were careful to cultivate European allies. Until 1756 these were primarily Austria and the Dutch Republic, followed by Prussia, and then, after 1792, anyone who would fight France. Alliances usually involved a substantial subsidy to pay for troops to fight a common enemy. Despite their best efforts to attach conditions to subsidies, and pay them in instalments dependent upon progress, it was hard to ensure that enough troops were employed in a manner that served Britain's interests. Continental alliances were controversial, with critics complaining that they cost Britain more in blood and treasure than they were worth. Yet British statesmen generally thought them necessary to draw a sizable portion of French military resources away from focusing on a Channel invasion or colonial conquest.

The British army was augmented by foreign regiments, most commonly German, and foreign troops were at times used to top-up British regiments. During the '45 Hessian soldiers in British pay participated in the Battle of Culloden. In 1756 Hanoverian troops were stationed in southern England to counter a potential French invasion – which triggered English xenophobia and paranoia about standing armies, and led to calls for a new English militia.[93] British soldiers, however, developed respect for regiments from their King's Electorate of Hanover. Contemplating defeat on the 'field of blood & slaughter' at Fontenoy in 1745, Captain Philip Browne noted that 'true English courage hath been exercised & displayed in as high a degree as is possible for mankind to act and by the behaviour of the Hanoverians they may henceforward justly be stiled of the same nation'.[94] Of the 70,000 strong British-funded army in northern Germany under the Duke of Brunswick in the late 1750s, only 20,000 were British soldiers.[95] German troops hired from Hesse-Cassel, Brunswick, Hesse-Hanau, Waldeck, Anspach-Bayreuth and Anhalt-Zerbst provided around 35% of the force George III sent to fight the American rebellion.[96] Colonel George Hanger thought there were 'no braver or better disciplined' troops than the Hessians, who in America 'behaved with the greatest gallantry and fidelity, and the most sincere *attachment* to the cause'.[97] In Europe, in addition to Germans, Portuguese regiments under British officers formed a significant portion of Wellington's army during the Peninsular War. Foreign and colonial troops accounted for 20% of Britain's 250,000-strong army in 1813.[98]

Militia and Volunteers

Harking back to Anglo-Saxon times, county militia units were popularly seen as the appropriate form of military defence for the 'English constitution'. On English soil, the argument ran, guns should be in the hands of citizens rather than the monarch's soldiers. Whig governments were reluctant to mobilise militia in the first half of the eighteenth century because they feared they might side with the Jacobite cause.[99] Having been caught under-armed by the rebellion in 1745, and with invasion threatening again in 1757, the British government began to create a 'new militia' of 32,000 men. The militia was designed to provide an additional force for home defence that could also free regular regiments to serve overseas. Militia service required 28 days of annual training in summer, and service was full-time at army rates of pay when fully mobilised. Each county was assigned a quota in proportion to its population, and men were selected by ballot. There were numerous exemptions, such as for clergy and teachers, and militia service could be avoided by hiring a substitute or paying a fine of £10.

The legislation was met with widespread rioting as the burden fell on the lower orders and there were fears that militia units might be sent overseas. Rioters at Chesterfield declared they would 'rather be hanged in England than scalped in America'.[100] In response to popular protest, the militia legislation was modified in various ways, including an exemption for those with three or more children under 10 years old. When embodied, the new militia performed a number of tasks, such as guarding prisoners of war, combating smuggling and suppressing riots, with nine militia battalions involved in quelling the Gordon riots of 1780.[101] A proposal to double the size of the militia was strongly opposed by parliament during the American war. As tensions escalated with Revolutionary France, and popular radicalism seemed to be spreading in Britain, the militia was mobilised in December 1792. With Britain's military stretched, the militia became the backbone of home defence in the 1790s. As militia were drawn from the community, and their service only temporary, they sometimes proved reluctant to follow orders. During 1795 militiamen participated in at least 16 food riots, but in subsequent years they generally proved reliable in enforcing order.[102] As invasion threatened in the late 1790s, the militia was expanded to around 100,000 men.

In order to get around the strict limitations placed on direct recruitment for the army, Lord Castlereagh instituted incentives, such as bounties, to encourage large-scale transfers from the militia to regular army regiments. As Kevin Linch has demonstrated, this marked a significant advance in the scale and quality of recruitment. As a result, total army recruitment rose from an average of 12,000 to an average of 30,000 for the years 1807–1813 – which is close to the estimated maximum of 35–40,000 recruits Britain could have raised through a Continental style system of conscription.[103] Men who transferred from the militia entered army regiments with a degree of basic training and familiarity with the military that made them ready for combat.

Raising militia in Scotland and Ireland proved controversial. A popular campaign to raise militia in lowland Scotland in the 1750s was resisted by government out of concern that Jacobites might be armed in the process. For loyalist Scots, the militia issue became an important measure of their civic virtue and status as Britons.[104] Despite the Highland regiments proving among the best in the British army, however, a militia was not raised in Scotland until the invasion crisis of 1797.[105]

Owing to the presence of a large standing army, the government showed little interest in the question of militia units in Ireland. Until the rural Whiteboy violence of the 1760s, Ireland, with its large but unarmed Catholic population, appeared relatively secure under Protestant rule. The clan system that underpinned the Jacobite uprising in Scotland had long ceased to exist in Ireland. During the '45 the government felt confident enough to send Irish regiments to help suppress the Jacobites in Scotland. Lord Chesterfield, the lord lieutenant of Ireland, accepted declarations of loyalty by leading Catholics, and mocked the concerns of Irish Protestants who were 'still at the year 1689, and have not shook off any religious prejudice that prevailed at that time'.[106] Dublin Castle allowed the old Irish militia to lapse in the 1760s, and the creation of a new militia became a point of hot contention between government and its Patriot opponents in parliament. Eventually, along with enfranchising Catholics, in 1793 the government created a new militia raised by ballot, three-quarters of whom were Catholic under mainly Protestant officers. With revolutionary republican ideas circulating there were serious concerns about the reliability of the militia, but following some courts martial and executions, and at the urging of the hierarchy of the Catholic Church, they generally followed orders to suppress the 1798 uprising.[107] At the Battle of New Ross, 'Black Bob' Craufurd, a tough Scottish officer, was astonished to see the militia 'shew the most inconceivable inveteracy against their rebellious countrymen'. He blamed their 'licentious, irregular, uncontroulable' behaviour on poor leadership by ignorant, drunken, bigoted Protestant militia officers. Impressed by the ruthlessness of the militia and the bravery of the rebel pikemen, Craufurd was convinced Irish peasants would make excellent soldiers if recruited into British line regiments under officers who 'are obliged to behave like gentlemen and men of honour'.[108]

With the new militia in England effectively an arm of the state, independent gentlemen increasingly formed volunteer corps during invasion crises. This occurred most spectacularly in Ireland when, with some Irish regiments posted to America, Protestants rushed to form volunteer corps in 1778 to counter a potential invasion. Some of these units included some Catholics, but they were overwhelmingly composed of Protestants – both Dissenters and Church of Ireland. With the Irish Volunteers talking of greater political rights, Lord North's government was reluctant to encourage similar units in Britain. Volunteering spread, however, as men banded together to create uniforms, bear arms and parade their readiness to defend Britain. Owing to the sketchy nature of the evidence it is hard to gauge the scale of this activity, but it is estimated that there were around 60,000 Irish Volunteers and as many as 30,000 volunteers in Britain toward the end of the American war.[109] This has led Stephen Conway to argue that the scale of British military mobilisation that began in 1778 was 'revolutionary'.[110]

The French Revolution had a significant impact on volunteering. In Ireland, the Volunteer movement finally came to an end with the creation of militia regiments. In order to counter the growth and seeming convergence of the Catholic Defenders and revolutionary United Irishmen, and at the risk of fanning sectarianism, in 1796 the government reluctantly endorsed the creation of volunteer yeoman cavalry that had strong links to the Protestant Orange Order. Fearing a revolution backed by a French invasion the Crown turned a blind eye while its small force of regular soldiers, augmented by predominantly Catholic militia and Orange yeomanry, set about waging a brutal counterinsurgency.

In Britain, the government worried about the risks inherent in a proliferation of armed vigilantes outside of its authority. Pitt reluctantly approved the formation of self-funded volunteer corps in 1794, in the hope that they would be composed of 'respectable' men. As a result, for example, 40% of a volunteers in Edinburgh were lawyers; and in the words of Linda Colley, 'of the seventy-five heroes who volunteered to defend Ely in Cambridgeshire, sixty-nine were farmers, or attorneys, or snug tradesmen, butchers, blacksmiths, victuallers, and the like; only six were labourers'.[111] The ongoing threat of invasion saw Pitt's government pass a 'Defence of the Realm Act' in April 1798 that ordered each county to report on how many men it had who were willing and able to enlist as volunteers. While some of the responses were disappointing, this began a dramatic increase in volunteering – predominantly by the middling sort.

This resort to national mobilisation, according to John Cookson, makes 1798 'a turning point in the history of the oligarchy'.[112] When Napoleon again threatened invasion in 1803–5 over 400,000 men joined volunteer units. The sheer scale of volunteering saw it draw in many who were outside the formal political nation as defined by the franchise. While the real and present danger of invasion by Napoleon acted as a powerful stimulant to patriotic unity, there were more than a few among the elite who worried about the long-term political implications of this mass mobilisation. Pitt and Dundas did their best to extend state control over the volunteers – instituting government pay, military uniforms, inspection by army officers and mandatory oaths of allegiance. With officers lacking the authority of military law, however, the volunteers retained their civilian character, and many corps appeared disorderly and without 'gentlemen of rank and property'. George Tierney, a Foxite Whig politician and champion of liberty, quit command of his corps because they demanded the right to elect their officers. In the years following Trafalgar enthusiasm for volunteering waned, and Castlereagh encouraged its replacement by expansion of new county regiments of local militia.[113]

Redcoats

The growing use of auxiliaries enabled Britain's regular army to focus on garrisoning the empire and conducting offensive operations. With a quarter of the army stationed overseas, in 1749 the Duke of Cumberland instituted a process of rotating units to prevent regiments from decaying and melting into communities in corners of the empire. There were significant limitations on the ability of the British army to engage in training, with regiments posted around the empire as garrisons or acting as police within Britain. Stationing regiments in southern England during the various invasion scares provided rare opportunities to engage in large-scale manoeuvres.[114] When mobilised for active service, British regiments became among the best in the world.

'Scum of the earth' was how the Duke of Wellington described the men who enlisted as redcoats. He made such statements on a number of occasions, particularly in the post-war years when he became a Tory prime minister.[115] This view has been widely recycled by historians as evidence of the nature of British soldiers in the age of the musket. In a widely read history of the eighteenth century, Europe's armies were depicted as composed of 'criminals, vagabonds and...misfits' commanded by aristocratic officers.[116] In the words of the American military historian, John Shy, the British soldier was treated 'little better than an animal, and...behaved like one whenever he dared'.[117] This traditional view has been challenged by recent research. The negative caricature of British officers and rankers in popular films like Mel Gibson's *The Patriot* is a gross distortion of the true nature of the Georgian army.

Some men were pressed into the army, especially during the early years of conflict when regiments were trying to rapidly build to full strength. The Vagrancy Act of 1744, and various Recruiting Acts, authorised the impressment of beggars and unemployed men. At times those convicted of crime were pressed into the army, particularly into regiments bound for dangerous duty in tropical climes. It needs to be noted, however, that traditional ideas of a 'criminal class' have been challenged by research that shows convicts, in a society in which many struggled to survive, were representative of the labouring classes as a whole – and those guilty of the most serious crimes tended to be hanged.[118] Aside from the elitist prejudices of officers who wrote about them, negative images of British soldiers owed more to circumstances than to the character of those recruited into the ranks. For example, the inherent difficulties of waging war against an insurgency account for clashes between soldiers and civilians during the American war. Plundering by Wellington's troops on the Peninsula owed much to persistent shortages in supplies and delayed payment of wages.[119]

The traditional negative image of soldiers also owes much to contemporary criticism by civilians. Aside from popular prejudice against standing armies, resentment at their drunken behaviour and role as police, soldiers were in some ways seen as lesser Britons. In an age when English/British liberties were boasted, soldiers were denied some of these rights by being subject to military law. Most visible and shocking, whipping was prominent among the forms of punishment inflicted on soldiers. Countless witnesses attest to the horrifying sight of a flogging. One retired soldier, who had seen public hangings as a young man, recalled witnessing a flogging soon after he joined the army at the age of seventeen: 'the spectacle made a lasting impression ... I cried like a child'.[120] The sense in which this set soldiers apart from 'free born' Britons is illustrated by the commander of a regiment stationed in South Carolina who noted that civilians saw 'no great difference between a soldier & a Negro'.[121]

If British officers often spoke harshly about their troops, they also made many positive comments. Wellington himself, after the Battle of Waterloo, described the British infantry as 'the best of All Instruments'.[122] The writings of British officers during the American Revolution contain much praise of their troops. An Irish officer was proud of the way none of his seven men wounded at Harlem Heights wanted 'to be taken precipitately off and some continued to fire after being severely wounded'; and during a long and tiring march to Brandywine his troops 'never murmured'.[123] When it came time to farewell his company of Royal Highland Grenadiers after six years of fighting the American rebellion, Captain Peebles told the 'very clean' ranks of his great 'satisfaction & pleasure' in serving with them. He offered to help them in future in any way he could, concluding: 'And Gentlemen ... I sincerely wish you all, that honour, Success, & happiness which your merit & good behaviour so well deserves'. Noting in his diary:

> I could hardly make an end to this little speech, my voice faulter'd, and my knees shook under me. I was glad to get into my room where my heart swelled at the thoughts of it. I saw the poor fellows were affected too – I ordered them five gallons of Rum.[124]

That Peebles addressed the ranks as 'gentlemen' should not surprise, as Josiah Woodward wrote in a frequently republished tract, *The Soldiers Monitor,* that 'the meanest Person that truly answers the Character of a *Good Soldier,* deserves the name of a *Gentlemen*'.[125] Hannah Smith has observed that soldiers 'may have internalised their position as servants of the Crown, and seen their profession of arms as conferring upon them a quasi-gentlemanly status and political authority' that other plebeians lacked.[126] That soldiers often engaged in drunkenness and womanising is no bar to such a self-perception in light of the riotous behaviour of young men at the universities and licentious reputations of many aristocrats.

Recent studies reveal that the ranks of the British army reflected a broad cross-section of the British lower classes.[127] Study of a sample of 7,055 soldiers from Wellington's army shows that 42% were labourers, 29% were textile workers and 29% were in other skilled trades.[128] In other words, nearly six in ten were skilled workers. Volunteering for the army was influenced by a range of push and pull factors. While army pay was very low, it came with benefits such as food and accommodation, and volunteers often received a substantial bounty for enlisting. As a result, joining the army could be seen as preferable to living in poverty. Skilled workers who joined the army, such as weavers, tended to come from occupations in which wartime disruption or structural change owing to industrialisation was causing unemployment.[129] During times of severe food shortage, joining the army could become a last resort. 'People can scarcely live here', it was reported in Northamptonshire in 1801, 'the young ones go for soldiers and the old ones starve at home'.[130] In addition to those who enlisted out of desperation, or were press ganged into the armed services, bounties were increasingly used to encourage poor men to enlist. A good example is the Scottish Highlands, which became a key source of soldiers for the British army. It has traditionally been assumed that clan chiefs worked with the British state to force Highland men into the army. Yet, study of Highland recruitment reveals that the elite were divided on the issue, while many among the poor bargained for bounties.[131] Some Highlanders became soldiers as a means of migrating to America to gain land and liberty.[132]

Various personal inclinations could also encourage a man to join the army, such as a sense of patriotism, a desire to look good in a brightly coloured uniform and a sense of adventure. As Kevin Linch has observed, 'wanderlust appears particularly conspicuous in the accounts of some soldier's biographies, coupled with a desire to escape parental control'.[133] Edward Costello, for example, after growing 'tired of my occupation' as an apprentice cabinet maker in Dublin, fled his master and found work as a shoemaker alongside

> an old soldier, who had lost a leg, fighting under Sir Ralph Abercrombie, in Egypt. From this old blade, I think it was, I first acquired that martial ardour that so frequently infects young men in time of war. There was, indeed, no resisting the old pensioner's description of glory. I became red hot for a soldier's life.

Too young to join the army, Costello listed in the Dublin militia and later volunteered for the 95th rifles, feeling 'highly delighted with the smart appearance of the men, as well as with their green uniform'. In this he reflects the fact that recruits tended to be young and single, and the militia became an important conduit for recruits into the regular army. He received a bounty of eighteen guineas for volunteering, and found that in turn he could earn two pounds for each man he recruited to his regiment. Developing a 'serious attachment' to a 'remarkably pretty girl' saw him consider quitting the army, but war had 'claimed me with her iron grasp as her proselyte'.[134]

Many of the officers of the British army came from the landed elite, particularly among the upper echelons. This played an important role in ensuring that the army remained subordinate to civil society. In 1744 Henry Pelham boasted: 'Has it not always been with good reason urged that our liberties are in no danger from our standing army because it is commanded by men of the best families and fortunes?'[135] This is borne out by statistics which show that 27% of British generals in 1769 were members of the peerage; and just over 40% of colonels were from aristocratic families. In France aristocratic domination of the army was stronger; for example, the 181 senior officers that served in Germany in 1758 reads like a list of France's leading noble families, with two-thirds of these men having aristocratic titles. Prior to the revolution, for a Frenchman to rise above lieutenant he had to prove all four grandparents were from noble families. In contrast, only 30% of British officers had titles in 1780, with members of the landed gentry mixing with men from the middling sort, and even a few promoted from the ranks.[136] Ironically, while an emphasis on gentlemanly manners became stronger, the social composition of the British army became less aristocratic. In the last years of the struggle against Napoleon, of 10,000 officers on full-pay only 283 had attended one of the elite public schools. One officer in Wellington's army observed that 'we had but a slender sprinkling of the aristocracy among us'.[137] While there was a higher proportion of officers from the landed elite in Guards and Cavalry regiments, most officers in Wellington's army were non-English and from middle-class families.

An officer's commission in a British regiment was a form of property, to be bought and sold. The Crown tried to regulate this by preventing officers from rising more than one rank at a time, limiting the price and requiring purchase of a commission to be authorised by the Commander in Chief or Secretary at War. Commissions started at £400 for ensign rising to £3,600 for lieutenant-colonel.[138] When an officer retired it set off a chain reaction as an officer purchasing a higher rank in turn created a vacancy. The system of purchasing army commissions offends modern sensibilities as discriminating against the meritorious poor. Yet there were some strong arguments in its favour. It enabled the old or unfit to cash in their commission and retire without the need for a taxpayer-funded pension. It also ensured that the unenthusiastic or incompetent were not trapped in a job for life to which they found themselves unsuited – they could sell out. It was possible for the commander of a regiment to encourage unfit officers to leave by demanding exacting standards and rigorous drill. The system of purchase also restrained the crown's ability to make the army an instrument to coerce parliament, as when James II replaced Protestant officers with Catholics in the 1680s. To remove officers who had purchased commissions would involve the unthinkable act of robbing men of their property.[139]

Many officers took advantage of military, administrative and economic opportunities in the empire. There were few crown positions to fill in the Americas, given that most government was local, but the East India Company's civil service steadily expanded thanks to Bengal tax revenues – the average annual income of a Bengal civil servant was £2,250 in 1783. The military experienced the greatest expansion in opportunities. Garrison requirements for the expanded empire saw 24 regiments stationed in the Americas, which kept a high number of officers on full pay – many of whom married colonial wives. The East India Company's army continued to grow; by 1772 it had 1,560 officers, compared to 2,800 in the regular British army.[140] The mid-century expansion of empire significantly increased opportunities for migration and military careers, and led to widespread 'imperial careering'.[141] One example of many was Loftus Cliffe, an army officer and poor relation of a leading Anglo-Irish family, who died soon after being sent to India – he had hoped to make a fortune and return home 'independent'.[142]

Promotion opportunities opened up during wartime, and could be had without purchase, as the army expanded and officers died on campaign. At the start of the American Rebellion, Lord Barrington received so many requests to serve in active regiments that he was like 'a Baker in a famine his Shop crowded with Customers, & very little bread to give 'em'.[143] After the Battle of Bunker Hill, in which a number of officers were casualties, a young lieutenant in the 52nd Foot rose 'five steps, which brings me within three of being the Eldest Lieut: I am in great spirits, and expectations, of getting a Company before matters can possibly be concluded'.[144] Only 20% of new entrants to the officer class during the Peninsular War were through purchase.[145] Commissions were not heritable property, so they could not be sold by a widow or filled by an inexperienced son; and a commission that was gained without purchase could not be sold. The frequency and growing scale of conflict during the Seventy Years War ensured that the officer class of the British army did not ossify or simply become a patronage plaything. It was possible for dynamic young men like James Wolfe to rise quickly up the hierarchy through a combination of experience, skill and determination.[146] In the words of one expert, during the eighteenth century British 'regiments were trained and led by an officer corps which was careerist, long-serving, notably experienced, and capable'.[147]

Improving the Army

The British army became increasingly professional, and regiments developed strong identities over the course of the Seventy Years War. Until 1745 the army was seen as a tool of the Hanoverian dynasty and politically aligned with the Whigs. Following the military defeat of Jacobitism the army developed a reputation as politically neutral. In 1750 some officers were punished for cheering an election candidate while they were on duty.[148] While soldiers remained officially 'the King's men', they increasingly identified as servants of the nation.[149] Sergeant Major Cobbett reflected this changing attitude, in extreme form:

> Soldiers are taught to believe every thing they receive, *a gift from the Crown; –* cast this notion from you immediately...you are not the servant of *one man* only; a British soldier never can be that. You are a servant of the whole nation, of your countrymen, who pay you, and from whom you can have no separate interests.[150]

It has been argued that, as most of the ranks were demobilised following peace treaties, there was only limited development of regimental identities prior to the 1790s, and these were primarily the work of small groups of officers who established traditions such as 'Minden Day'. Evidence suggests, however, that the frequency of conflict throughout the Seventy Years War saw more than a few regiments develop strong identities around a core of old soldiers. Sylvia Frey has argued that British regiments that fought in the American war developed strong identities.[151] Study of the 58th Foot reveals that over half of its identified rankers in 1759 spent their whole career in that regiment, and twenty years later 48 of them were still serving during the regiment's defence of Gibraltar.[152] By the end of the eighteenth century, regimental identities were well established. The day after landing on Walcheren in 1809, Private Wheeler, a recent recruit to the 51st regiment, wrote home:

> 1st of August, a remarkable day, it being the fiftieth anniversary of the *Battle of Minden*. Colonel M–– could not let this opportunity slip without addressing us. I wish I could give you his speech, that is impossible. He told us that all the pleasure and happiness he had ever felt fell short of the pleasure he now felt at the head of our Corps, who on that day fifty years had by their native valour repulsed and defeated the whole body of the enemy's Cavalry before *Minden*. He shewed us the word *Minden* on our Colours, and reminded us it was inscribed on our breast plates. He said it was probable we would fall in with the enemy that day, and if we did not give them a good drubbing, how could we ever return home to our Fathers, Mothers etc. Our country expected much from us, the Regiment in its infancy had performed prodigies of valour on that day, and now we had grown grey (some of us) in the service, would it not be expected we should eclips them in glory etc. etc. etc.[153]

In addition to inspiring fighting qualities, strong regimental identities were increasingly fostered as the key to attracting and retaining recruits. Creating county depots met with mixed success, as recruits often travelled to join a particular regiment based on factors such as reputation or personal connections – but this in its own way helped build regimental cohesiveness. Army administration came to see that getting a recruit settled into a regiment as a new 'family' as soon as possible was key to ensuring they did not desert.[154] The centrality of regiments to effective recruitment encouraged the development of distinctive identities through uniforms, social conventions and commemoration of past deeds.

To the extent that there was reform of the army as a whole, it was driven by particular individuals on behalf of the Crown. Parliament traditionally showed little interest in the army beyond the hot-button issues of finance and the militia. As the last British king to lead troops into battle, George II took a keen interest in improving the army. In 1741 he established a Royal Military Academy for training artillery officers. A royal command in 1751 required all regiments to have numbers; and he kept a book by which he could monitor and scrutinise officer commissions. New *Regulations* (1748) and *Standing Orders* (1753) were promoted by the Duke of Cumberland. During the campaigns in America there was impressive innovation on the part of some regiments in developing 'light infantry' style skirmishing tactics. This led, however, to a lack of uniformity across the army, with some officers training according to the 'American way of war' while others demanded conformity to 'German' drill and tactics. While both approaches had their merits, it was clear that employing American tactics on European battlefields would lead to disaster. Of the incoherent practices of the disbursed and reduced regiments following the American war, one expert has observed it may 'be questioned whether taxpayers ever supported a more useless body of men than the British army in the early days of the younger Pitt'.[155] Colonel David Dundas sought to remedy this with his influential *Principles of Military Movements* (1788), which was based upon extensive military experience, wide reading and visits to Europe to observe Prussian training methods. This book was used as the basis for a comprehensive *Rules and Regulations* that was issued to all British regiments in 1792 and remained in use until the Crimean War. This ended the latitude officers had exercised in deciding how their soldiers should operate and began a period of substantial military reform.

The Duke of York became a driving force behind reform of the army. With the French Revolution spreading ideas of equality, and inflation greatly eroding the meagre and long-unaltered salary of British soldiers, it was thought prudent to grant three pay rises during the mid 1790s. York and the Adjutant-General Harry Calvert, along with enlightened commanders in the field such as Lieutenant-General John Moore, built on this through a series of reforms aimed at improving the status of British rankers. They promoted better organisation and the introduction of Light Infantry regiments. With Britain lagging behind continental practice in educating officers, a Royal Military College was established in 1801. Officers were encouraged to promote reformation of manners by establishing regimental libraries and schools. Improvements were made to army medicine and hospitals, and an Asylum School attached to the Chelsea hospital was established to educate over one thousand orphans and children of soldiers.

The reform impulse spread to army administration, with sinecures gradually replaced by salaried careers. The vast expansion in wartime expenditure came under increasing civilian authority and scrutiny. The Secretary at War became the 'the linchpin of the Army', responsible for Army estimates, financing of regiments, and approval of troop movements.[156]

Much of the army's structure and practice nevertheless remained traditional, and there were undoubtedly inefficiencies. Yet, modern meritocracy and rational bureaucracy can have their own forms of waste and inefficiency. As an institution that operated according to paternalism and patronage, the army nevertheless became a highly effective instrument of war. To an extent what Britain's military lacked in formal organisational structure was compensated by cultural codes and values: personal ties, regimental identities, concern for reputation, ideals of honour and courage, and patriotism.[157] While there were more than a few time-servers, such cultural values drove a general movement to make Britain's army an effective fighting force.

Leadership played an important role in the success or failure of British arms. Edward Costello noted that his fellow soldiers during the Peninsular War distinguished between 'come on' and 'go on' officers, and idolised a captain who displayed 'affability and personal courage' until the day he was killed in action.[158] One of the best textbook guides to governing a battalion observed that during times of danger soldiers always looked at their commander

> to see how he feels himself, whether he is unperplexed and seems to be easy; and from his looks they will often augur good or bad

success...actions or appearances of officers should never tend therefore to give soldiers room to doubt, or form unfavourable conjec-
ture...Animation, like electricity, is communicative, is catching; and
the officer who is animated himself will inspire others.[159]

Reading such guides, and books like Caesar's *Commentaries*, saw British
officers become imbued with ideals of honour and heroism. An expectation that they should lead from the front saw officers suffer a disproportionately high rate of casualties during the American Revolution. At
Guilford Court House two of General Cornwallis' horses were shot and
he was one of only two general officers not wounded in the battle.[160] On
the Channel island of Jersey in January 1781 a young officer refused an
order to surrender and proceeded to die leading troops in recapturing
the capital – subsequently immortalised in Copley's painting *The Death of
Major Peirson* (1784).[161] Major-General 'Black Bob' Craufurd was buried
in the breach where he died leading a attack on Ciudad Rodrigo in 1812.
In addition to such inspirational courage, officers were expected to
demonstrate tactical skill and cool judgement. Soldiers admired talented
commanders, even if they were aloof and authoritarian like the Duke
of Wellington, as bad leadership could cause hardship, defeat and high
casualties. Wellington's ability, when possible, to gain victory at minimal
cost in casualties inspired confidence. According to Captain John
Kincaid, 'the sight of his long nose among us was worth ten thousand
men any day of the week...there was not a heart in the army which did
not beat more lightly when we heard the joyful news of his arrival'.[162]
'If I had had an English army, I would have conquered the universe',
Napoleon declared during his exile.[163] The British army tended to start
conflicts poorly, but develop into an impressive fighting force once fully
mobilised and battle-hardened. In the words of Tony Hayter, 'in terms of
martial qualities, particularly dogged persistence in attack and defence,
and the ability to improvise and to develop new tactics, the British army
was second to none'.[164] To an extent this reflects the fact that most of
the British army were on garrison duty and only the best regiments
with the fittest troops were committed to offensive campaigns. Different
armies developed reputations for particular characteristics and qualities. The French were renowned for their courage and élan – which was
only enhanced by the meritocracy created by the revolution. The British
infantry were known for their steadfastness and firepower – their first
volley at Fontenoy was said to have caused 700 French casualties.[165] It
was a reputation that became self-reinforcing and reached its height
when the British squares at Waterloo withstood repeated charges by

Napoleon's cavalry. A soldier who served with the 71st Highland regiment on the Peninsula reflected:

> How different the duty of the French officers from ours. They, stimulating the men by example, the men vociferating, each chaffing each until they appear in a fury, shouting to the points of our bayonets. After the first huzza, the British officers restraining their men, still as death. 'Steady, lads, steady' is all you hear, and that in an undertone.[166]

British soldiers were generally working-class men, accompanied by female camp followers, who formed tightly bonded primary groups that fought, foraged, ate, played football and laughed together.[167] A British officer who commanded in the King's German Legion admired the endurance and professionalism of his troops, and, while praising them, shed light on the nature of British soldiers: 'before the enemy a German moves on silently but mechanically, whilst an Englishman is all sarcasm, laughter and indifference'.[168] They lived within a broader regimental 'family' in which they expected their commander to be a good 'father'. The frequently impressive combat performance of the British army owed much to the self-respect and the 'moral economy' that existed among regiments. 'It will be remarked by those who live among soldiers', Moyle Sherer observed,

> that they are charitable and generous, kind to children, and fond of dumb animals; add to this, a frequent exposure to hardship, privation, and danger, make them friendly and ready to assist each other...the worthless characters who are met with in every regiment (and society) are generally shunned.[169]

'I like soldiers as a class in life, better than any other description of men', William Cobbett declared,

> Their conversation is more pleasing to me; they have generally seen more than other men; they have less vulgar prejudice about them; to which may be added, that, having felt hardships themselves, they know how to feel for others.[170]

Sampson Staniforth, an early Methodist soldier-preacher who served in Flanders in the 1740s, 'frequently remarked' that 'there is a kind of affection in the army toward one another, which is hardly to be found elsewhere'.[171]

While the citizen soldiers of Revolutionary France were often lauded, awarded and promoted, British rankers, as subjects of a monarch, and commanded by gentlemen with an aristocratic ethos, had limited opportunities for promotion or official recognition. Only at the end of the Seventy Years War was a medal struck for all ranks who served in the Waterloo campaign, which provoked anger among those who had served long years in the Peninsula. In his influential *History of the Peninsular War* (1828–1840), William Napier complained that

> Napoleon's troops fought in the brightest fields, where every helmet caught some gleam of glory; but the British soldier conquered under the cold shade of the aristocracy; no honours awaited his daring; no dispatch gave his name the applauses of his countrymen; his life of danger and hardship was uncheered by hope, his death unnoticed.[172]

Posterity has perpetuated condescension toward the redcoat rank and file. As Linch and McCormack have observed, during the revolutionary era 'the soldier experience, broadly defined, is more representative of the working-class experience than that of the millhand, but is disregarded by labour history'.[173] Eighteenth-century social historians have only recently turned their attention toward the military, and are finding much work to be done.

Home from the War

In contrast to the modern welfare state, the eighteenth-century warfare state made limited efforts to assist demobilised seamen, soldiers and their families. They often returned to hard and uncertain plebeian lives. Family breakups increased 40% during times of war, and a 1796 study of beggars in London found that most of them were women who claimed their husbands were serving in the armed forces.[174] Limbless men became a common sight as the scale of warfare grew. In mid 1762 one journal noted the 'swarms of miserable maimed Highlanders' living on the edge of London 'with scarce any vestige of the human form'.[175] There were clearly also some female walking wounded, given that many accompanied the army as camp followers, and a smaller number were below deck on navy ships. One veteran of the Peninsular War recalled that a comrade, Tom Plunket, after Waterloo

> had wedded a lady remarkable for being deficient in one essential to beauty – she actually had no face, or, at all events, was so defaced, it amounted to the same thing. This slight flaw in the beauty of Tom's wife, who had gallantly follow'd the camp through the war, arose from the bursting of an ammunition-wagon at Quatre Bras... by which her countenance was rendered a blue, shapeless, noseless mass.

In compensation the government granted her a shilling per-day pension; and Tom would say: 'It was an ill blowing up of powder that blew nobody good'.[176] Black humour was one of the ways plebeian Britons coped with their harsh lives.

Hospitals and pensions became an important source of assistance for wounded servicemen. Wounded or disabled seamen could draw a pension from the 'Chatham Chest', and the naval hospital at Greenwich housed 2,000 men by the 1780s, along with over 3,000 'out-pensioners'. The army hospitals at Chelsea and Kilmainham in Ireland had room for fewer patients. In the 1780s Chelsea hospital had less than 500 in-pensioners, but over 20,000 out-pensioners drawing 5d per day to live in the community at large – more men than the peace-time army in Britain.[177] To qualify for this basic subsistence pension a soldier had to be recommended by his commander as worthy and be examined by the hospital board. The bar was set high, with Lord Barrington declaring in 1771 that no soldier would be considered 'under Twenty years Service, except as are Wounded, Disabled, or Worn out in the Service'.[178] Travelling to appear before the Chelsea Board to present their case was arguably most difficult for Gaelic-speaking Highlanders.

During peacetime, officers had to live on half-pay, but most demobilised tars and rankers were left to fend for themselves. With Britain's maritime trade expanding, seamen had a better chance of gaining employment. The poor laws provided those who struggled to find employment with basic subsistence relief in their home parish. Some soldiers received a little charity upon discharge, such as volunteers in the 51st Foot, who were given £5 each by Lord Rockingham and Sir George Savile for their heroism at Minden. John Manners, Marquess of Granby, an immensely popular cavalry commander in the German war, became renowned for his charity toward old soldiers, many of whom he was said to have given money to open a pub.[179] Yet this did little to ease the plight of most demobilised men and their families. After the Peninsular War ended, Edwin Quin, of the Irish Charitable Society, estimated that seven in every twelve applicants for charity were discharged soldiers. Government did little to help other than grant soldiers and sailors the right to work in restricted trades and license them to beg under the Vagrancy Act of 1744.[180] Magistrates complained that public generosity encouraged begging, with one London observer noting that 'black people, as well as those destitute of sight, seldom fail to excite compassion'. Beggars sometimes faked physical disability to attract sympathy, and 'one old soldier plastered his leg with a mixture of sheep's blood and flour to simulate "mortification"'.[181] Some returned servicemen played music for money in street and tavern. The most famous was Billy Waters, an African who had served in the navy during the American war, lost a leg, and proceeded to play the fiddle and perform 'peculiar antics' dressed in a navy uniform with feathered hat. Declared 'King of the Beggars', Waters was immortalised in caricature, literature and porcelain.[182] When possible, ex-servicemen tried to tap public sympathy through print. At mid century, William Catton, an old ex-soldier, wrote and performed ballads celebrating war heroes in order to make a living – being unwounded he had received no pension.[183] The few memoirs written by soldiers and sailors need to be handled with care as they were often motivated in part by a desire to make money from sales, or attract charity.

In one way or another, war touched the lives of millions of Britons between the invasion scare of early 1744 and the Battle of Waterloo. Defeats in the Low Countries in the 1740s were counterbalanced by naval dominance. During the 1750s manpower was mobilised to fight in Asia, America and Europe, with large numbers of Irish and Scots recruited into the British army. At the end of the American war there were nearly 220,000 men serving in the army and navy, and over 100,000 in various militia and volunteer units around the Atlantic Archipelago. Allowing for deaths and deserters, it has been estimated that during the course of the American war as many as half a million men served in Britain's armed forces.[184] As a proportion of the adult male population, that was probably around one in seven. At the height of the Napoleonic wars, Britain probably had a million men under arms – as many as one in four of the adult male population during the invasion crisis of 1803–5.[185] Mobilisation for war on this scale influenced many aspects of British culture and politics.

Chapter 4: Enlightenment, Evangelicalism and War

War has received little consideration as both subject and setting of the British Enlightenment and the rise of evangelical religion. Roy Porter's otherwise excellent survey of Enlightenment in Britain only mentions war in passing; and Michael Snape has observed that there has been little study of 'the religious impact of the massive and prolonged intercontinental wars of the eighteenth and nineteenth centuries'.[1] Even Jeremy Black, who has written widely on military history, has little to say about war in his study *Culture in Eighteenth-Century England* (2005).

Enlightenment in Britain

The Enlightenment has long been seen as a movement championing reason, science, natural rights and freedom as means of emancipation from traditional ideas and institutions. In providing the intellectual origins for the American and French Revolutions, the Enlightenment is popularly seen as the intellectual origin of modern secular liberal democracy. There are problems with this conventional view. Recent scholarship has expanded, enriched and complicated our view of the Enlightenment in three important ways: a diverse range of sometimes contradictory intellectual positions can be seen as 'enlightened'; Enlightenment varied according to national and other particular contexts; and Enlightenment was a social and cultural phenomenon as much as an intellectual one.

The traditional view of the Enlightenment was Franco-centric and focused on a small number of bewigged men who waged intellectual war against the *ancien régime* in the name of reason, science, scepticism, individual rights, religious liberty and freedom of expression. In Peter

Gay's influential histories of the Enlightenment, Voltaire loomed large, with his humorous ridicule of established institutions and practices, especially aristocracy and the Catholic Church. The *philosophes* were depicted as a *Party of Humanity* whose ideas helped cause the French Revolution.[2] This traditional view originated in conservative criticism of the French Revolution by the likes of Edmund Burke, and is best illustrated by the nineteenth-century *Oxford English Dictionary* definition of 'Enlightenment' as 'shallow and pretentious intellectualism, unreasonable contempt for authority and tradition, etc., applied *esp.* to the spirit and aims of the French philosophers of the 18th c'. It is a view that seems to be held by more than a few British military historians.

The means of spreading Enlightenment values have attracted a great deal of research into topics such as salons, coffeehouses, freemasonry, theatre, newspapers and the book trade – such that it can be seen as an early 'information age'.[3] The way various individuals and social groups experienced and were positioned within Enlightenment culture is also being studied. Women, for example, found themselves classed as 'naturally' weaker and less rational than men, but also benefited in some ways from the development of sensibility, sociability and participation in print culture.[4] We are only in the early stages, however, of research into the relationship between war and Enlightenment.

While at a general level we can identify some core pan-European Enlightenment values, we have become sensitive to the distinctive nature of national, regional and confessional 'Enlightenments'.[5] The 'French Enlightenment', with its fierce anti-clericalism, now sits alongside other enlightenments that had different issues and priorities. In addition to the diverse ways it manifested in different contexts, there were inherent tensions within Enlightenment values. Ideals of reason and order could be in conflict with liberty and equality. In various ways, thinkers tried to balance differing enlightened values. In an influential recent interpretation, Jonathan Israel has sought to organise thinkers into two broad camps of 'Radical Enlightenment' and 'Moderate Enlightenment'.[6] While Israel's approach is overly schematic, leads to some odd grouping of thinkers and holds radicals up as the more enlightened, it nevertheless reflects the way Enlightenment could be advocated in either radical or conserving forms.[7]

The overarching Enlightenment impulse was optimistic confidence in the capacity of human reason to improve the world. Henry May has provided a good definition of Enlightenment based on two core propositions: 'first, that the present age is more enlightened than the past;

and second, that we understand nature and man best through the use of our natural faculties'.[8] Before the eighteenth century people venerated traditions and ancient knowledge (the word of God in scripture and the works of classical philosophers), and tended to equate change with decay. The seventeenth-century Scientific Revolution made stunning advances in natural philosophy, particularly in the field of astronomy. Enlightened thinkers wanted to build on this and extend scientific methods of reason, experiment and calculation to all fields of knowledge. While enlightened minds differed as to whether particular ideas and institutions should be replaced or just modified, they believed that the use of reason made progress possible, that modern knowledge was superior to ancient knowledge and that the world was becoming a better place.[9] Enlightened Christians even claimed that knowledge of God's word was being improved by critical study of the Bible and history.[10] In the late eighteenth century, however, calls for fundamental change became more widespread and insistent, and in an era of revolutions radical and moderate enlighteners became polarised.

Enlightenment was promoted in Britain by the Whig elite as the path to orderly progress. In the wake of the Reformation and religious conflict of the preceding centuries, a dominant Moderate Enlightenment championed the established partnership between crown, parliament and established church as the basis of peace and prosperity.[11] The Revolution of 1688 had secured the rights of parliament and the established church, while granting toleration to Protestant nonconformists. The Church of England, combining Protestant doctrine with ecclesiastical hierarchy headed by the monarch, was championed as a sensible middle ground between sectarian 'enthusiasm' and Papal authority. The lapse of the Licensing Act in 1695 led to a vibrant print culture and ensured a disgruntled intelligentsia did not develop in opposition to the established order. Many of Britain's Enlightenment thinkers were latitudinarian Anglican, Dissenting or Church of Scotland clergy, and debate focused on issues such as the true nature of religion, the sources of morality, and the proper extent of toleration. Many members of the Royal Society for the Advancement of Science were clergymen, and the scientific achievements of 'natural philosophers' such as Isaac Newton were used to bolster Christianity as revealing the wondrous design of God's works. While *philosophes* attacked the privileges of key French institutions, in Britain the Whig elite acted as patrons of enlightened thought with an eye to promoting agricultural, commercial and civic improvement.[12]

Enlightened Britons were generally empiricist and inductive, distrusting 'systems' that claimed to explain everything – whether it be the systematic theology of the Roman Catholic Church or Cartesian rationalist philosophy. Following Francis Bacon, British philosophers such as John Locke and David Hume tended to stress the mind's limitations, and focus on developing methods for observing, collecting and categorising knowledge as a means to discerning 'Nature's laws'. Enlightened Britons, whether clergymen or sceptical philosophers, were united in their opposition to religious 'enthusiasm', arguing that the civil wars of the previous century were in part caused by rebellious Puritans claiming to know truth through individual spiritual inspiration. By 1789 an evangelical, Isaac Milner, was complaining that 'reasoning to excess' was 'the spirit of the age'.[13]

Polite manners and sociability were central to Enlightenment values. Traditional Christianity saw this world as a vale of tears rooted in original sin – a testing ground before life after death. With the mind increasingly seen as a Lockean *tabula rasa*, attention shifted from belief in original sin to optimism about the human capacity for moral improvement through science, education and sociability. Enlightened Protestants could focus on Jesus as a moral teacher and exemplar. Polite manners were championed as the means of preventing conflict, and facilitating progress, in a society in which ideas were circulating and people and goods were increasingly mobile. Polite manners aided commerce, and in turn commerce fostered more progress in the arts and sciences. In a 1769 election speech, Edmund Burke declared: 'An English gentleman... has no rank above his fellow citizens – but what his manners, his affability, his knowledge, his justice, the popular use of his fortune give him'.[14] And when denouncing the French Revolution, he observed: 'The law touches us but here and there, and now and then. Manners are what vex or sooth, corrupt or purify, exalt or debase, barbarize or refine us, by a constant, steady, uniform, insensible operation, like that of the air we breathe in. They give the whole form and colour to our lives.'[15] The participation of women was seen as essential to polite society, and their status came to be used as a measure of society's level of civility. Enlightenment thinkers depicted nature as tending toward balance, and the moderate British Enlightenment depicted harmony between church, state and commerce as underpinning the progress of manners.

The Enlightenment invented the term 'civilisation' and popularised the idea of progress.[16] Scottish thinkers took the lead. Access to empire after the 1707 Act of Union saw commerce boom in the Lowlands, and a vibrant Scottish Enlightenment flowered after the Jacobite '45 was defeated. In a 1762 lecture, Adam Smith outlined a 'Four Stage Theory of Development' that 'mankind pass thro: - 1st the Age of Hunters; 2ndly, Age of Shepherds; 3rdly, the Age of Agriculture; and 4thly, the Age of Commerce'.[17] For Smith, history revealed 'the natural, or rather the necessary course of advancement from rudeness to polish'.[18] Enlightened Scots saw the military destruction and legal abolition of Highland 'feudalism' after the '45 as a transition to modernity. Summarising enlightened attitudes to property and the past, J.G.A. Pocock has written: 'when the polite man of commercial and cultivated society looked back into his past, what he necessarily saw there was the passions not yet socialised, to which he gave such names as "barbarism" and "savagery" '.[19] A number of the leading Scottish Enlightenment thinkers had witnessed the march south of the Jacobite clans in 1745. Thinking the Highlanders represented the past, enlightened minds were induced by the '45 to concentrate on the nature of social change. The idea that all societies can be classified according to stages of development, and that eighteenth-century Europe was at the most advanced stage, proved enormously influential, forming a key part of the outlook of British soldiers, seamen and colonisers.

Moderate Enlightenment in Britain was increasingly challenged in the late eighteenth century. Evangelicals rose and declared the Church of England spiritually deficient – a line of attack joined by secular Romantics at the end of the century. Branded dangerous enthusiasts by worried bishops, most evangelical Methodists nevertheless proved politically conservative. From the opposite direction, 'Rational Dissenters' began to campaign for toleration to be replaced by full religious liberty, and praised the constitutional separation of church and state in the new United States of America. When leading Rational Dissenters cheered the French Revolution as inaugurating an era of worldwide radical reform, Edmund Burke drew on the ideological toolkit of the Anglican Enlightenment to denounce the 'enthusiasm' of radical intellectuals as a threat to the pillars of modern European civilisation. In the words of J.G.A. Pocock, Burke 'was an Enlightened figure, who saw himself defending Enlightened Europe'.[20] While British radicals called for Anglo-French peace and cooperation, Burke urged continuing war against the 'armed doctrine' of the French Revolution.[21] While radicals saw the French Revolution as beginning an age of greater light and liberty, Burke saw darkness descending in the wake of attacks on the monarchical, aristocratic and clerical patrons of eighteenth-century Enlightenment. If to some extent he became idiosyncratic and extreme, Burke nevertheless helped create modern conservatism out of a Moderate Enlightenment response to the radicalism of the French Revolution.

Military Enlightenment

There were many points of contact and mutual influence between war and Enlightenment in Britain. As the multi-ethnic armed forces were instruments of state-building and imperial expansion, it is surprising that the connections between Britain's military and the modernising culture of Enlightenment have attracted little attention. Some recent studies have begun to address this gap in historiography, but they have tended to reflect traditional views of the Enlightenment.[22] As a result, there is a tendency to distinguish between the influences of 'Enlightenment' and 'traditional' attitudes, with the latter accorded more importance. Yet such a binary opposition is an oversimplification and misunderstands the British context, where Enlightenment usually involved modifying and improving traditional ideas and practices. Viewed in light of cultural history and the importance of national context, the army and navy can be seen as leading agents of Enlightenment in Britain.

Enlightenment thinkers were generally critical of war. Voltaire's most famous novella, *Candide* (1759), ridiculed its brutality and wastefulness. Some leading Enlightenment thinkers dreamed of a world without war, arguing that it could be achieved if people were able to trade freely in goods and ideas, and with national disputes resolved in an international assembly. Yet aside from such high hopes, enlightened thinkers generally accepted that war was at times unavoidable.

Historians have recently begun to talk of a 'Military Enlightenment' that developed notions of 'just war' and scientific approaches to the conduct of war. In *The Law of Nations*, the influential Swiss jurist Emer de Vattel declared, when criticising the use of poisonous weapons, that 'the law of Nature ... does not allow us to multiply the evils of war beyond all bounds'. War was only justified by necessity, and in waging it 'let us never forget that our enemies are men' and 'not destroy that charity which connects us to all mankind', so that 'victory will not be tarnished by inhuman and brutal actions'.[23]

If enlightened war should be limited according to natural law, it should also be waged according to mechanistic scientific principles. The 'linear warfare' of the eighteenth century was partly determined by technology, with muskets best used by soldiers massed in ranks. Yet it

was also influenced by the Enlightenment's emphasis on reason, calculation, mechanical movement and regulated manners.[24] Henry Lloyd
was 'the only British military thinker... to influence the development
of European military thought' prior to the twentieth century.[25] He was
a Welsh soldier of fortune who started in France, accompanied Prince
Charles in the '45, and served most of the major European powers in
the course of the mid-century wars. Lloyd returned to Britain the 1760s
and published an influential *History of the Late War in Germany* (1766).
Heavily influenced by the French Enlightenment, and a great admirer
of Marshal Saxe, Lloyd aimed to combine the writing of history with
instruction in military theory. His major contribution was to help shift
attention from the organisational system and tactics of an army to its
operation in particular landscapes. Controversially criticising Frederick
the Great's strategic decisions, Lloyd shifted attention to the importance
of geography and the need for large modern armies to operate along
lines of supply and communication. Widely read in his time, the cosmopolitan Lloyd has been neglected by historians until recently.[26]

Given that Britain lacked major philosophical theorists and lagged
in establishing military colleges, the focus of work on the military
Enlightenment has been on continental developments. Yet what Britain
lacked in heavyweight theorists and new institutions, it made up in
informal diffusion of Enlightenment, with British officers espousing
moderate Enlightenment values that emphasised reason, order and
politeness.

Books became a key means of military improvement and professionalisation. A detailed study of officers during the mid eighteenth century
concluded that: 'British officers bought, read and recommended
hundreds of books on war... they were particularly attracted to histories, biographies, and memoirs; texts on artillery and engineering; clas-
sics of Greece and Rome; and Continental treatises on the art of war.'[27]
Reading was one way army officers filled long hours in barracks and
bivouac. Many officers had impressive libraries. And while it was difficult to obtain books on campaign, some favourites could be carried in
the large baggage trains. Thomas Moyle, an officer in the 28th Foot,
had 84 volumes with him when in America in 1777, including novels,
poetry and literary periodicals.[28] Reflecting professionalisation of the
army, from the 1740s military books made up a growing proportion of
the libraries of soldiers.[29] While naval officers tended to be blunt and
practical men, absorbed in the task of keeping ships afloat, there were
many hours to fill on long voyages. One navy second lieutenant, with

a library of over 300 books in multiple languages, was described by an army surgeon as possessing 'a highly cultivated mind, and has so great a taste for reading, that during the whole passage when not on duty I scarcely once observed him without a book in his hand'.[30] The late eighteenth century saw a growing number of British army officers translate Continental texts or write their own books on the art of war.[31] Officers in both forces also increasingly produced books and pamphlets when they felt the need to defend their conduct in the public sphere. For example, generals Clinton and Cornwallis publicly disputed who was to blame for the loss at Yorktown.

The importance Enlightenment accorded to independence, politeness and women posed some problems for military officers. Naval officers were particularly limited by the nature of life at sea; a former chaplain remembering his experiences in the 1750s said: 'Nothing could be more shocking, and mortifying to me, or to any mind which possessed a particle of moral delicacy, or of intellectual improvement, than the manners, and conversation of the sea-officers…I hope they are better now.'[32] When popularly lauded, admirals tended to be seen as representing middle-class values of plain speaking, virtuous, hard-working masculinity. Army officers had more scope to play the gentleman, and skill as a dancer became an essential accomplishment. As readers of Jane Austen know, army officers were prominent at balls in England, and when on campaign in America or Europe they hosted balls in which they danced with local ladies.[33] In addition, dance was promoted by authors of military manuals as a way of complementing and reinforcing military drill. As Matthew McCormack has observed, both dance and drill epitomised 'distinctively eighteenth-century rationalities concerning the body and the self'.[34] Military service could even be a means of making men genteel. In 1760, Isabella Carr wrote that some militia NCOs 'are now downright polite gentlemen, and seem as well accustomed to a sword and bag [wig] as if they had always been used to them. Tis astonishing what a change and improvement a military life makes.'[35]

The Enlightenment had a mixed impact upon the status of women. On the one hand, it developed the idea that gender inequality was rooted in essential 'natural' qualities: masculinity was associated with reason, strength and the public sphere, while femininity was associated with emotion, weakness and the domestic sphere. This was reinforced by the growing professionalisation and prominence of the military, and by the near-hysteria about British men becoming 'effeminate' that flared at times of poor military performance in the mid eighteenth century. An ideology of separate spheres developed in part, however, because women were increasingly visible participants in Enlightenment sociability and print culture. The expanding field of English literature, in particular, was to a considerable extent driven by women as both readers and writers. The ideology of separate spheres was in large part a response to 'gender panic' caused by the growing public visibility of women and discussion of their status. If women were increasingly subject to a discourse of separate spheres, they nevertheless continued to participate in various sites of sociability, print culture and philanthropy.[36]

Louise Carter's study of 'scarlet fever', as female admiration of men in uniform was called, illuminates aspects of the status of women at the end of the eighteenth century. With uniforms to some extent sacrificing practicality for display, 'military men were amongst the best dressed and most smartly turned out in Georgian society'. Scarlet fever caused moral anxieties about 'licentiousness', but it was also promoted as a means of encouraging recruitment, and men were frequently told they had a duty to defend their women folk against invasion. Female agency in pursuing military men is yet more evidence that qualifies the extent to which women were passive and confined to a domestic sphere. At the same time, scarlet fever reflected the degree to which gender limited the ways women could express patriotism: 'next to the supposed patriotic glory of putting on a red coat yourself, admiring a man wearing one might just have been the next best thing'.[37]

While military officers were inherently authoritarian, some advocated more humane treatment as a means of producing better and more motivated soldiers and seamen.[38] During the American war some commanders developed light infantry tactics suited to bush warfare, which involved troops exercising a degree of individual initiative. Those who championed 'German drill', however, dismissed such tactics as inapplicable to Europe. Yet the north-west European landscape was changing, with land increasingly enclosed by fences and hedgerows. As a result, against the mass citizen armies of Revolutionary France, which included numerous free-ranging skirmishers, the British army performed poorly in the 1790s. The Duke of York ordered the training of several regiments in light infantry tactics, and this was done at Shorncliffe under Sir John Moore when the army gathered in southern England to face the threat of invasion in 1803.[39] In the words of Hew Strachan, light infantrymen 'became the beau ideal of the British soldier, the heroes of the Peninsular War, and its officers adopted an influential system of training which suffused the ethos and disciplinary code of the army with paternalism and enlightenment'.[40] Moore was inspirational, and ensured that officers trained along with their men, noting in his diary: 'it is evident that not only the officers, but that each individual soldier, knows perfectly what he has to do; the discipline is carried on without severity, the officers are attached to the men and the men to the officers'.[41]

The navy had its flogging captains and the army its harsh authoritarians, but such behaviour was not encouraged. General Thomas Picton, the highest-ranking officer killed at Waterloo, had been criticised for excessive brutality during his stint as governor of Trinidad.[42] Regarding Picton as one of his bravest and most reliable generals, Wellington nevertheless described him as 'a rough, foul-mouthed devil'.[43] Yet a study of regimental courts has shown that flogging was often mitigated or used as a last resort, with many milder forms of discipline used first in order to correct conduct.[44] Naval commanders who made excessive use of the lash were not respected by their peers or crews – it was a sign of weakness, of a commander unable to generate genuine respect and cooperation. A detailed case study of discipline in Royal Navy ships stationed in the Leeward Islands concluded that less than 10% of seamen were flogged, with 'the principles of gentility, paternalism and detached justice' leading commanders to deploy the 'awesome disciplinary powers at their disposal with moderation and restraint'.[45] On the whole, officers in both the army and the navy regarded punishment as a necessary evil and tried to restrain their use of its most severe forms.

Cleanliness was increasingly championed during the Enlightenment, and the military, in particular the navy, became key agents of its promotion. Bathing was traditionally very limited in European culture, with people able to live for decades without being 'wett all over at once'. But the Enlightenment 'produced a public health education movement and a gospel of cleanliness and hygiene' that came to be used as one measure of civilisation.[46] It was not until the nineteenth century that this campaign, and the means of being clean, was extended to the unwashed masses. The writings of army officers are peppered with observations on the cleanliness of barracks, houses and towns. In eighteenth-century medical knowledge disease was associated with bad air, and Royal Navy commanders became renowned for their scrubbed and ventilated ships. Keeping seamen clean was more difficult, and in trying to wash clothes twice each week, urine was used as a detergent when soap was lacking.[47] If personal hygiene remained a challenge, seamen in the navy nevertheless worked in some of the cleanest worksites in the eighteenth century. And the need to keep military manpower healthy spurred developments in medical knowledge.[48]

Reflecting the evolutionary nature of Enlightenment in Britain, there were gradual and practical advances in military technology rather than revolutionary change. The spread of science and technology amongst the middling sort, and the associated improvements in manufacturing, were key features of Enlightenment in Britain.[49] This bore military fruit. For example, Benjamin Robins, a teacher of Newtonian mathematics, published an influential *New Principles of Gunnery* (1742). At the end of the century, Henry Shrapnel invented the artillery shell that explodes with pellets. The British army first used 'Shrapnel shells' in the first decade of the nineteenth century, and their manufacture was a jealously guarded secret until well after Waterloo.[50] Encouraged by government sponsorship in the form of prizes, the key naval problem of measuring longitude was gradually solved through the invention of the marine chronometer, which was in wide use by the early nineteenth century. Improvements in manufacturing saw navigational instruments such as sextants, compasses and chronometers become more affordable and numerous.

Advances in the natural sciences were entwined with the growth of state power. Geographical mapping grew at a pace during the Enlightenment, and within the British Empire much of it was done by soldiers and seamen trained in the art of surveying. Most mapping of Britain's expanding rule in India was done by military men, including Colonel Colin Mackenzie, the first British Surveyor General of India. Another characteristic example: in 1791 William Dawes, a marine officer, surveyor and the first British astronomer based in Australia, marched into the bush around Parramatta in an effort to map the land, counting 2,200 paces to measure a mile.[51] Knowledge is power, and maps are particularly powerful ideological tools, facilitating the physical colonisation of lands and depicting them as possessed by Britain.

The voyages of captain James Cook best illustrate the close links between science and state power. In three voyages starting in 1768 Cook charted large areas of the Pacific and fed the growing European fascination with Tahiti – where people were imagined to be living in a happy state of nature. Cook's first voyage in HMS *Endeavour* was initiated by a request from the Royal Society that the transit of Venus be observed from the antipodes. What Daniel Baugh has called 'protective maritime imperialism' saw the Admiralty embrace the Royal Society's request as an excuse to send another expedition to the South Pacific. France was engaged in a programme of naval expansion in the 1760s, and naval manpower depended on the ability to draw seamen in times of war from a thriving merchant marine. If there were large unexplored lands in the Southern Ocean, continued naval strength required their future trade be secured for the British Empire and denied the French.[52] The young gentleman botanist, Joseph Banks, accompanied Cook's first voyage and later became president of the Royal Society, where he devoted his life to promoting science in the service of empire.[53]

The navy and army provided crucial points of contact between Britain and the world. When soldiers and seamen wrote or returned home they spread stories of people and places beyond Britain, complementing the growing demand for works of travel writing. Military men and their partners were to some extent tourists, espousing Enlightenment ideas of civilisation and its different stages as displayed in the 'Great map of Mankind'.[54]

The prominence of the military reinforced the hierarchical nature of the multi-ethnic empire, in which people were judged primarily by social status, manners and religion. For example, after serving with the army in India, Lachlan Macquarie returned to Britain overland via Persia and Russia. His journal records observations on the cleanliness of towns, the 'savage' Kurds compared to civilised Persians, with his harshest comments reserved for provincial Russian police and Napoleon's envoys to Persia. He was most impressed with the Armenian wife of Samuel Manesty, the British Resident at Basra, describing her as 'by Birth of a respectable family', and after having 13 children, 'still a beautiful woman and very pleasing in her manners'.[55] A few years later, as Governor of New South Wales, Macquarie was friendly toward 'Billy Blue', an African ferryman on Sydney harbour with whom he might have shared military experience in the American war.[56]

Enlightenment categorisation and imperial expansion worked together to foster a growing sense of 'difference', which contributed to the origins of modern 'scientific racism'. Established racial and caste hierarchies were reinforced by imperial practices, institutions and laws, and justified by Enlightenment ideas of natural differences between races and nations.[57] Africans were widely identified as savages and slaves. While the insatiable manpower needs of the Royal Navy saw it become a haven for escaped slaves, Africans remained vulnerable to re-enslavement. When recruited for the army, they found themselves in 'black regiments' under white officers. Indigenous Americans were defined as 'noble savages' when serving as allies, or 'barbaric savages' when opponents.

India proved a key site in construction of an imperial racial hierarchy. Soldiers and civil servants of the East India Company often had children with Indian women in the eighteenth century – though they usually tried to hide the fact from family back in Britain. Many lighter-skinned children were sent to Britain for education, and so the British elite came to include people of Anglo-Indian descent, including the prime minister Lord Liverpool. A Bengal Military Orphan Society school established in 1782 removed many children from Indian mothers in order to raise them according to European norms. With concerns about Company men 'going native', and former Governor-General Warren Hastings being prosecuted for corruption in the 1780s, his successor, General Cornwallis, instituted bureaucratic reforms that sought to secure white rule in British India and make the empire 'respectable'. People of mixed race, who had hitherto been central to relations between the Company and Indian society, began to be excluded from the bureaucracy. Syncretic practices by officials and soldiers increasingly gave way to displays of chauvinistic British patriotism and ideas of racial superiority.[58]

Britain's armed forces were central to the spread of both Enlightenment and empire. To varying degrees agents of moderate Enlightenment values, officers in both the army and navy played a prominent role in the conquest and defence of empire, and as colonial governors.

Enlightenment and War

The French Revolution changed how war was waged. The question is: how much? At the very least, the mass citizen armies of Revolutionary France dramatically escalated the scale of conflict. It has long been argued that there was also a notable change in the culture and conduct of war. Enlightenment commanders engaged in limited war, it is argued, based on cautious, calculated, chessboard style strategy and tactics. Leading Enlightenment theorists argued that battle should be avoided as much as possible, and an enemy defeated through a process of manoeuvre and carefully staged sieges that pushed him into a position of checkmate. The ideal was Frederick the Great's stunning victory with minimal casualties at Rossbach, won by out-manoeuvring a larger enemy, of which he famously said: 'I won the battle of Rossbach with most of my infantry having their muskets shouldered'. Such a mode of war suited the importance accorded to gentlemanly conduct by eighteenth-century elite culture. The French Revolution, however, started what David Bell has called 'The First Total War'. After 1792, bloody and decisive battles were sought by the ambitious officers and ideologically enthused soldiers of the French Republic. While there is some truth in this contrast, it also needs significant qualification, especially when applied to the case of Britain.

War in the eighteenth century hardly seemed limited to those caught up in the fighting. One of the most famous examples of the supposedly genteel nature of eighteenth-century warfare is the story of a British Guards officer, Lord Charles Hay, toasting the French Guards and asking them to fire first, with the French politely declining the offer. Yet this is misleading, as he was undoubtedly goading the French because firing first was disadvantageous – something stressed by leading authorities such as Saxe and Frederick the Great. Those who fired first were enveloped in smoke, fumbling to reload, and thus more likely to break as they were struck by their opponent's reply volley, which might be followed by a bayonet charge.[59] Eighteenth-century battles could be hard fought, with soldiers suffering horrific wounds and limited medical treatment; armies often lived off the land and the plundering of civilians was common.

While Enlightenment theorists developed notions of just war, they allowed for brutal behaviour in cases of 'necessity'. Thus, George Hennell, a soldier and Rational Dissenter, wrote after his first experience of battle at the siege of Badajoz that 'by the laws of war we are allowed to kill all found in a town that stands a storm, but an Englishman cannot kill in cold blood'.[60] Brutality was especially licensed against 'uncivilised' or rebellious people. Enlightenment thinkers were obsessed with categorising, and those people categorised as 'savage', such as Indigenous North Americans, could be treated savagely. In addition, those seen as rebelling against legitimate authority could also be repressed with measures that did not spare women and children. Seeing the Jacobite clans as both rebellious and uncivilised, British repression of Highland clans following the '45 was particularly unsparing.[61]

In a number of contexts there were pragmatic reasons for British commanders to order their forces to show humanity and restraint. As commanders in chief during the American war, Lord Howe and Henry Clinton tried to wage limited war with an eye to facilitating reconciliation. Yet as the war dragged on, and particularly after the Declaration of Independence, middle-ranking British officers increasingly called for brutal measures in order to end the war quickly – and at times practised them. In mid 1777 John Bowater, an officer in the marines stationed in New York, thought all Americans untrustworthy and advocated genocide: 'They swallow the Oaths of Allegience to the King, & Congress, Alternately... I think nothing but a total Exterpation of the Inhabitants of this Country, will ever make it a desirable object of any Prince or State.' Expecting that the British would soon win the war, he hoped the army could first 'cut them up a little in the Northern Colonies... as they have been Foremost in this Rebellion, & as yet have felt none of the Horrors of War'.[62] A captain of the King's Own Regiment, who regarded Americans as 'upstart vagabonds, the dregs and scorn of the human species', argued that a war of devastation, 'almost extirpating the present rebellious race', was needed in order to restore British rule.[63] There were officers who behaved in such a ruthless manner, such as Banastre Tarleton's notorious use of fire and sword in the southern campaign. Yet they did so in the face of an official policy that, however much it failed, commanded moderation with an eye to not hurting loyalist civilians and further alienating the population.

A similar situation occurred during the Irish Rebellion of 1798 when, in the midst of sectarian conflict, General Gerard Lake allowed his troops to engage in brutal repression and reprisal. A few months after being appointed Commander in Chief, the respected Scottish general Sir Ralph Abercromby issued an order criticising the army in Ireland for being 'in a state of licentiousness, which must render it formidable to every one but the enemy'; and demanding that officers enforce discipline and 'restore the high and distinguished reputation the British troops have been accustomed to enjoy in every part of the world'.[64] After Abercromby resigned, the Lord Lieutenant replaced him with Lake, who unleashed a reign of terror in the counties around Dublin. With open warfare raging by mid-year, Pitt in turn replaced Lake with Cornwallis, who criticised Protestant loyalist forces (for whom 'murder appears to be their favourite pastime'), tightened discipline in the army, and after suppressing the rebellion argued for policies that would 'soften the hatred of the Catholics to our Government'.[65] Cornwallis advocated union of Britain and Ireland combined with Catholic emancipation – an approach both pragmatic and enlightened, if only partially implemented.

In addition to practical considerations, Enlightenment values influenced the way British officers waged war. British soldiers aspired to fight opponents they saw as their equal in manners, preferring war in Europe to service in the colonies. In December 1758, bound for glory at Quebec, Wolfe wrote to a friend: 'It is my fortune to be cursed with American services, yours to serve in an army commanded by a great and able prince [Ferdinand of Brunswick].'[66] The peoples of Europe were in turn viewed as occupying different levels of civilisation. As Gavin Daly has shown, British soldiers in the Peninsular War tended to see their Portuguese allies as a degenerate race and the Spanish as proud but in decline, while positively admiring their French opponents.[67] The few scholars who have written on Enlightenment and war tend to distinguish between the influence of traditional chivalry and Enlightenment, but this ignores the degree to which polite manners were woven into Enlightenment values such that it makes little sense to distinguish between the two.[68]

The American Rebellion reveals much about Enlightenment attitudes to war. There were arguments in favour of adopting a guerrilla war strategy against George III's forces, but George Washington adopted the British 'Articles of War' and worked hard, with French and German help, to build a European style army.[69] The rebellious Britons in North America worked at building a more virtuous version of the British army. Like other initiatives, such as the Declaration of Independence and Thomas Jefferson's *Notes on the State of Virginia*, Washington's way of war aimed to win recognition of the new American states as equal to Europeans in the international order. When British troops or their Indigenous allies committed massacres, the Americans highlighted such behaviour as a 'barbarous' contrast with their own 'virtue'.[70]

It also appears that British officers were influenced by Enlightenment writings in the conduct of strategy and tactics. It is one thing to show that many soldiers had books, but another thing to demonstrate that books influenced their behaviour. Nevertheless, Ira Gruber has made a good case for the development of a distinctive British attitude toward war based on analysis of the popularity of particular books, and scattered evidence of their influence on some officers. In short, he has shown that in addition to modern Continental writers, who stressed caution, manoeuvre and siege, British officers were also keen on classical texts. Julius Caesar advocated aggression and destruction of the enemy, and his *Commentaries* was the most popular book among British officers. This has led Gruber to suggest that a tension in the minds of British generals, between Enlightenment caution and Classical aggression, was one reason for their indecisiveness during the American War. The best example of this was Henry Clinton, commander-in-chief from late 1777 to 1782, whose detailed notebooks reveal that he was a wide and thoughtful reader. Having served in Germany under Brunswick, he was a great admirer of Frederick the Great's ability to win by skilful manoeuvre. Clinton was consistently critical of aggressive generals, observing that even during an offensive campaign, 'a general action should be avoided...except in certain situations for be it remembered, one victory obtained by the assailing army does not decide the contest; one battle lost by him does too often'.[71] During the American war, Clinton continually found reasons for avoiding a decisive battle. When criticised by a historian of the war for 'desultory movements' in the northern theatre, Clinton characteristically responded: 'Surely that Gentleman might have known, that all those desultory movements were necessary preludes to others more solid, which could not be carried into execution for want of promised and adequate reinforcement.'[72] When the more aggressive Cornwallis marched into Virginia, Clinton commanded him to entrench at Yorktown, where his army was surrounded, cut off and forced to surrender. If Clinton was one of the most widely read and cautious of generals, there were others who appear to have shared his enlightened 'prudential art of war'. Cumberland in the 1740s and 50s, and York in the 1790s campaigned with caution and prudent retreats. Cornwallis, in the febrile environment of rebellious Ireland, moved very cautiously when confronting a small French invasion on the west coast.

While British generals often had to be cautious, the navy developed a culture of risk-taking. Navies tend to be set aside by scholars who argue for a transformation of warfare following the French Revolution – with David Bell acknowledging that 'naval warfare changed much less than land warfare during this period'.[73] If there was a revolutionary moment in naval warfare, it was Britain's creation of a Western Squadron in 1747. At mid-century, Admirals Anson and Hawke helped build a highly skilled navy that enabled commanders to risk radical manoeuvres. According to an important recent study: 'the greatest difference between the naval policy of Britain and its rivals was in the extent to which British admirals sought battle when opportunity offered'. While France and her allies sometimes gained numerical superiority, they failed to match 'British levels of seamanship and gunnery, and especially aggressive leadership'.[74] Revitalised by Nelson, it was a style of warfare that strove to capture or destroy as many enemy ships as possible. At the crucial Battle of Quiberon Bay in 1759, for example, Admiral Hawke chased the enemy into a dangerous, unfamiliar part of the French coast on a darkening, windy, winter afternoon. Trusting the French to know their way through the shoals and reefs, Hawke risked his squadron in order to catch and destroy their fleet. According to Nicholas Rodger, 'probably no British admiral has ever risked battle in such dangerous circumstances'.[75] If the French had escaped and Hawke's ships been wrecked on rocks, then Britain would have laid open to invasion.

Enlightenment ideas of linear and limited war arguably overlapped and gave way to 'Military Romanticism' at the start of the nineteenth century. John Lynn has argued that Napoleon's crushing victory at Austerliz in 1805 created a 'cult of the decisive battle', won through genius and hero-ism.[76] While this might be true, it requires qualification in the case of Britain. While the Royal Navy's command of the waves owed much to the unglamorous job of continuous blockade of French ports, since the mid eighteenth century commanders often sought decisive battles – some-thing encouraged by the execution of Admiral Byng for failure to engage the enemy. If the Royal Navy was practising a cult of the decisive battle in the half-century before Napoleon, the relatively small British army continued with an Enlightenment emphasis on prudence, manoeuvre and alliance through to Waterloo.

British officers during the Seventy Years War can be compared to the 'Enlightened Despotism' of Frederick the Great (a figure greatly admired in Britain).[77] For example, 'Black Bob' Craufurd was renowned as among the harshest of disciplinarians, but also had enlightened characteristics. In the 1780s he attended manoeuvres held by Frederick the Great, and later translated Tielke's *Art of War*. During a short stint in parliament Craufurd displayed 'enlightened political and social principles', calling for rational reform of the army and full emancipa-tion for Catholics in Ireland.[78] Similarly, in a traditional view of the Enlightenment, Wellington appears a leading anti-Enlightenment Briton: born to an Anglo-Irish landed family, scathing in his assess-ments of the poor, an authoritarian general, a champion of aristoc-racy, and Tory prime minister in the 1820s. Yet like Burke and Pitt, Wellington was one of those conservative eighteenth-century Whigs who came to be labelled 'Tories' in the changing political context of the revolutionary era. Wellington can be properly located within the moderate British Enlightenment: a cool, clear, calculating, rationalist in his defence of the established order in Church and State. Wellington began serious study of the art of war while serving in Ireland in the late 1780s; and after a marriage proposal was refused owing to his limited finances, he burned his violins and dedicated himself to life as a professional soldier. Wellington became renowned for his careful assessment of terrain and positions, attention to detail and careful timing of movement – he was arguably an Enlightenment general fighting the Revolutionary officers of France. Preparing to face the formidable French army in the Peninsula, Wellington reflected that they have, 'it seems, a new system of strategy, which has outmanoeuvred and overwhelmed all the armies of Europe'. Yet he was confident he could fight them:

> They may overwhelm me, but I don't think they will outmanoeuvre me. First, because I am not afraid of them, as everyone else seems to be; and secondly, because if what I hear of their system of manoeuvres be true, I think it a false one against steady troops. I suspect all the continental armies were more than half beaten before the battle was begun. I, at least, will not be frightened beforehand.[79]

'Damn the fellow', an officer remembered Wellington saying of Napoleon at Waterloo, 'he's a mere pounder after all'. Wellington made his usual enlightened use of the terrain to position his army while Napoleon tried to overwhelm the redcoats with repeated heroic but costly charges. Enlightenment calculation narrowly defeated revolutionary zeal at the end of the Seventy Years War.

Tars and Rankers

Britain's military forces played a role in the spread of print culture among the lower classes. Along with the broader population, only half of eighteenth-century British soldiers and seamen could sign their name – though this compares favourably with the figure of 37% for the French population in 1800.[80] If literacy is measured by the ability to write extended texts, then the rarity of published work by ordinary soldiers and seamen in the eighteenth century could be seen as evidence to support traditional depictions of them as illiterate 'scum of the earth'. Yet writing was a difficult skill to acquire and practice in an age of quill pens, coarse paper and communal living. Only in the glow of victory after Waterloo, and with peace, prosperity and technological improvements, did a significant number of memoirs by common soldiers and sailors issue from printing presses. Yet if we take the ability to read as the measure of literacy, and add the fact that many illiterate people had newspapers and books read aloud to them, then the lower decks and ranks need to be considered an important element in the diffusion of Enlightenment print culture.

Navy ships to some extent acted as schools. Naval officers started life learning the ropes as boys on ships, rubbing shoulders with the various ranks of seamen, and gaining knowledge through both books and experience. Mathematics and basic literacy were essential to becoming an officer, and could aid an ordinary seaman ambitious to rise in rank. There are scattered references to seamen reading in hammocks, many became multilingual during their travels, and their degree of literacy is indicated by the fact naval officers communicated with crews via notices posted in newspapers.[81] Robert Wilson, who had been press-ganged, described seamen off duty: 'Those who are not employed sewing and mending, you see them either learning to read or write, or cyphering, or instructing others.'[82] A guide to letter-writing published in 1754 provided examples of how a sailor and his sweet-heart should write to each other.[83] In the eyes of one navy chaplain, many a press-ganged sailor had 'been taken out of a merchant ship, filthy, and so ignorant of God and the Bible, as not to be able to distinguish his letters', and 'not a few of these have found all the advantages of schools, and cleanliness, and order, and discipline, in the ships of war'.[84] The autobiography of Olaudah Equiano, one of the most significant publications by an African in the eighteenth century, provides an example of how a slave became literate while serving on Royal Navy ships. Purchased by a lieutenant as a servant boy, Equiano befriended a bookish white boy servant who 'instructed me with pleasure' in the art of reading. Although still a slave, Equiano delighted in feeling part of a community on the multiracial decks of the Royal Navy and 'embraced every occasion of improvement'. During a stay in London he received his first formal education when some of his master's female cousins sent him to school and 'took great pains to instruct me in the principles of religion'. At sea again on the 90-gun *Namur*, which like many large navy ships had a schoolmaster, Equiano was able to continue his formal education. Becoming captain's steward after his master gained command of a smaller ship, Equiano was 'very happy, for I was extremely well treated by all on board, and I had leisure to improve myself in reading and writing'.[85]

While Equiano is an outstanding example in the distance he travelled from slavery to published author and gentleman, it is clear that reading became more common on navy ships during the Seventy Years War. When being carried to Portugal in 1811 on HMS *Revenge*, commanded by a pious captain, a soldier described Sunday on deck:

In one place might be seen a sailor sitting on a gun reading to his shipmates, others reading to themselves, in another place a party could be listening to the hair breadths escapes and wondrous deeds of some well fought battle, while others...offering up prayers and singing Hymns of praise.[86]

The combination of literacy and sailing the world's seas could prove particularly mind-expanding. In *Moby Dick*, Herman Melville describes hours spent on lookout in the tropics as 'delightful' for a 'meditative man...there you stand, lost in the infinite series of the sea, with nothing ruffled but the waves'.[87] William Spavens provides a good example of how an eighteenth-century seaman developed a fascination with scientific knowledge. Undoubtedly augmenting his knowledge with wide reading in the years after he retired injured from the navy, including learning of William Herschel's 1783 discovery of Uranus, Spavins included extensive discussion of astronomy, navigation and geography in his *Memoirs of a Seafaring Life*. Thus, when describing the solar system, he observed 'it is natural to imagine' that Jupiter's moons each 'have an atmosphere, and are habitable systems or worlds, as they are found subject to the same laws of nature as this in which we live'. If that was the case, however, 'the inhabitants must have constitutions very different from ours'.[88]

The social divide between gentlemanly officers and common rankers was undoubtedly sharp in the army, but to some extent they shared an interest in print and plays, and some soldiers possessed basic writing skills. For example, when Captain John Peebles said goodbye to his company of Highland Grenadiers at the end of the American war he offered to carry any letters they might write back to Scotland.[89] During a winter in Boston, one officer reported, 'some Ladies and Officers for diversion, and for the benefit of the sick and maimed Soldiers in this Army, have Acted Plays' in a hall 'fitted up very Elegantly for a Theatre'.[90] John Stevenson, a Methodist soldier, observed that soldiers had more time to read and reflect than civilian workers: 'the soldier cannot always have the whole of the Sabbath, but then he may make every day partly like a Sabbath, when others cannot'.[91] When Wellington's army entered Madrid, Private William Wheeler strolled in the royal gardens and was delighted to find a summerhouse with a large collection of books. Unable to carry away all of the books in English, he 'distributed them amongst my comrades who I know are fond of reading'.[92]

It is hard to know what tars and rankers read. When available, newspapers seem to have been valued. A soldier, drunk on guard duty, tried to see the newspapers being read by officers, tripped over a tent rope, fell at the feet of Earl Dalhousie, and asked 'What news from England?' – he was severely flogged.[93] Johann Seume, a Saxon student pressed into a

Hessian regiment, kept a copy of Caesar's *Commentaries* in his coat when sent to serve George III in combating the American rebellion.[94] During the Peninsular War, Captain Adam Ferguson found soldiers enjoyed listening to him read Scott's *Lady of the Lake* out loud. Judging by his letters, Private Wheeler appears to have been familiar with the works of Shakespeare. Another soldier noted that, as a young man in Glasgow, 'novels, romances and fairy tales, were my favourite books'.[95] Yet such insights are rare in the surviving evidence and tend to come from the second half of the Seventy Years War. Research has shown that the Bible, cheap chapbooks and ballads dominated the reading habits of the poor until a judicial decision in 1774 replaced perpetual copyright with a limit of 14 years. There followed an 'explosion of reading' as cheaper and abridged editions of canonical books poured from printing presses, with Shakespeare for the first time 'available to readers of all classes and ages'.[96] In addition to novels and travel writings, the Bible and religious literature such as John Bunyan's *Pilgrim's Progress* remained among the most popularly available texts in the Age of Reason.

Religion

The role of religion in the eighteenth-century armed forces has received very little attention until recently, and historians have tended to follow contemporary critics in depicting soldiers and sailors as drunken blasphemers.[97] There is plenty of evidence that Britain's armed forces often displayed ungodly behaviour. A doctor tending the army in Flanders in the 1740s observed that officers spent 'each possible moment' in 'Convivial meetings' engaged 'in Mirth and Jollity with Women and Wine'.[98] One of the few poorly-paid navy chaplains lamented that on ship 'I was fed, coaxed, and stared at – if in my den, forgotten; if at large in every body's way; of no manner of use – and at best, endured.'[99] Andrew Burn, an evangelical marine, published his *Christian Officer's Panoply* (1789) to help those 'with just sentiments of religion...defend themselves against the daily attacks of military deists and infidels, who are but too numerous'.[100]

Chaplains were a weak point in both the army and navy. While historians have done much to revise the traditional negative image of the eighteenth-century Church of England, it remains true that many clergy held multiple benefices and employed poor curates to perform duties in their absence.[101] The system of regimental chaplains deteriorated over the course of the Seventy Years War, with chaplains increasingly absentee and holding plural commissions. There were only seven chaplains with the 21 regiments in America in 1757, and only one chaplain accompanied the Duke of York's campaign in Flanders in the early 1790s. Owing to such systemic failure, regimental chaplains were abolished in 1796 in favour of granting officers money to hire clergy as needed. Under the new system, chaplains were appointed at brigade level and under supervision of a chaplain-general.[102] Similarly, efforts were made to improve the diligence and discipline of chaplains in the navy, but by the early nineteenth century it remained a low paid position of last resort for a gentleman.[103] Reform of the chaplain systems had only limited effect, and the degree to which religion was fostered depended largely on the efforts of the officers and men.

In a number of ways, however, religion played an important role in the military. Britain was a confessional state and the armed forces served a monarch who was also head of the Church of England.[104] Authority was couched in religious language and rituals, and in George II the armed forces served a 'Protestant soldier-king'. If religious tempers cooled somewhat in the 'age of reason', Protestantism nevertheless remained a defining element in British identity and enlistment in the armed forces drew thousands into at least a basic engagement with Christianity.

Army and navy officers, with varying degrees of commitment, fostered a sense of religion. In 1743 a naval officer noted that he had only once heard prayers read on ship.[105] This gradually changed during the Seventy Years War. During the voyage of the 43rd Foot to North America in 1757, John Knox observed that

> The duty of chaplain was performed by an officer, who read the service of the church every Sunday upon deck, when weather permitted; and was very decently attended by the greatest part of the men and women on board... the master of our ship, who was a very sober moral man, always attended divine service with great decorum, and answered the responses with much devotion; but, if unfortunately (which was sometimes the case) the attention of the man at the helm was diverted from his duty, and consequently the ship yawed in the wind, or perhaps was taken a-back, our son of Neptune interrupted our prayers with some of the ordinary profane language of the common sailors, which immediately following the Litany, provoked some of our people to laugh, seemingly against their inclination; while others remained steady and attentive to their devotions.[106]

While many officers lacked personal piety, they often saw the value of setting an example of religious observance. James Wolfe considered Presbyterian ministers 'blockheads', but nevertheless regularly attended the Kirk on Sundays when stationed with the army in Scotland.[107] Roger Lamb, a sergeant in the Royal Welch Fusiliers during the American rebellion, went so far as to claim the 'salutary restraints and strict submission' imposed by army life gradually 'render a considerable part of the soldiery not only moral, but truly pious'.[108] Colonel George Hanger expressed the characteristic Enlightenment attitude of most officers:

> Priests may be of this or that opinion, but mankind are now arrived at that enlightened period to have an opinion of their own, and no longer to be affrighted at the fulminating anathemas of the Church, or the dread of excommunication. Priests are very necessary, and very good members of society, when *they pray for us*, and *pray with us... There is no possibility of keeping society together without religion, but it may be done without priestcraft.*[109]

Most British officers displayed an Enlightenment distain for religious fanaticism. During the American war British army officers blamed religious sectarianism and 'enthusiasm' for the social 'levelling' ideas and behaviour they encountered. After being taken prisoner, Thomas Hughes observed that 'people here have not the least idea of a gentleman. Our servants are treated just like ourselves, and they are surprised to find our men won't eat at the same table with us'.[110] John Bowater declared the Americans 'such a Levelling, underbred, Artfull, Race of people that we Cannot Associate with them'. When an American 'of very good property' asked to speak with 'Mr. Percy', Bowater corrected him that it was 'Lord Percy', to which he replied that 'he knew no Lord but the Lord Jehovah'.[111] When France entered the war, Bowater thought it ridiculous to see 'the Presbyterian fanatic Clergy of New England praying publickly for their great Ally the French King, as the great protector of Civil and Religious Liberty'.[112]

After the loss of America there were widespread calls for national moral reform in the 1780s, and religious observance began to increase in the armed forces. The identity of Britain's army and navy as arms of a Christian state was further strengthened in the course of war against anti-Christian French Revolutionaries. Leading admirals made a show of observing religious formalities, particularly in the wake of the 1797 mutinies. A study of ship logbooks has revealed a notable increase in the frequency of shipboard religious services from the 1780s.[113] Nelson, who was, like many navy officers, the son of a clergyman, displayed an Enlightenment Anglicanism that appears to have placed equal weight on service to God, king and country. In a latitudinarian tone, he thanked a society that sent Bibles for the crew of *Victory*: 'a ship where divine service is regularly performed is by far more regular and decent in their conduct than where it is not, and in this ship only 2 men have been punished for upwards of two months'.[114] While Nelson's private life was unconventional, his public image as a Christian warrior helped inspire young naval officers with a sense of the importance of religion.

While officers to varying degrees encouraged orthodox Anglican religious observance, the start of the Seventy Years War coincided with the emergence of evangelical Methodism, which appealed to some soldiers and seamen. Uninspired by established Anglican practice and worried about the state of his soul, the young clergyman John Wesley had a conversion experience in 1738 in which his heart was 'strangely warmed'. He became a leading itinerant Methodist preacher, travelling throughout Britain and Ireland, ministering to people in churches, halls and homes, and also in town squares and fields. Finding the doors of many churches shut in his face, Wesley declared that 'the world is my parish', and in the open air preached repentance, salvation by faith and an emotional engagement with Jesus. To both conservatives and progressive 'rational Christians' it sounded like the Puritan religious 'enthusiasm' that had caused civil war and revolution in the previous century. Starting in the 1740s, Methodism spread until, after Wesley's death, it formally broke away from the Church of England and became a distinct denomination. Wesley applied 'close reasoning' to daily decisions, with his father observing that John 'would not attend to the most pressing necessities of nature unless he had a reason for it'.[115] Yet in contrast to the dominant rationalism of the Enlightenment, Wesley was a firm believer in the supernatural and divine intervention. In the words of Grayson Ditchfield, this helped Methodism to spread in a popular culture that 'was still steeped in the supernatural, in magic, in the physical reality of the devil, in the fear of hell'.[116]

A Methodist subculture emerged in the army in Flanders in 1744, and some of the most notable early Methodist preachers were soldiers. Spiritually tortured, John Haime abandoned his family and joined the army, finding inspiration in John Bunyan's *Grace Abounding to the Chief of Sinners* (1666). While passing through London he was encouraged by Charles Wesley to start preaching to his fellow soldiers. Haime took up the task with enthusiasm, with 'three armies against me: the French army, the wicked English army, and an army of Devils'.[117] By the end of 1744 there were 300 members of a Methodist society within the army camped in Flanders, and around 1,000 were listening to Haime's open-air preaching; some undoubtedly only attended for the spectacle. Dismayed by the 'ignorant profaneness' of soldiers in the streets of Newcastle, John Wesley was granted permission to preach to them but found that, while they listened, 'I could not reach their hearts'.[118] Having been raised with little sense of religion, Sampson Staniforth recalled that when he first heard Whitefield preach 'several times' while stationed at Glasgow, 'I had no conception of what he said, nor any desire to profit by it' – in Flanders, however, he had a conversion experience after which he could not 'drink, swear, game, nor plunder any more'.[119] Some officers complained that the Methodists were mad and a disruptive influence. Yet the Duke of Cumberland allowed the revival to continue after hearing Haime preach that soldiers should obey orders and 'if needful, fight up to the knees in blood' for their good king and cause. At Fontenoy the Methodists 'stood the hottest fire of the enemy', some died 'praising God with joyful lips', and they showed 'such courage and boldness in the fight as made the Officers, as well as soldiers amazed'.[120] Amidst hard fighting, Staniforth declared that 'all day I was in great spirits, and as composed in my mind, as if I had been hearing a sermon'. While a number of Methodists were killed at Fontenoy, including four preachers, Staniforth fondly remembered gathering afterwards with his brethren and thinking: 'This state of life is the only one to love and serve God in: I would not change it for any other under the sun, upon any consideration'.[121]

While Methodism never became more than a subculture, the army played a role in the spread of evangelical religion. Methodism was strong in mining and fishing communities where daily work was dangerous, and thus it had a similar appeal to some in the military. Presbyterian soldiers in Scottish regiments such as the Black Watch proved particularly receptive. Significantly, several of the biographies in Thomas Jackson's *Lives of Early Methodist Preachers* (1837) were ex-soldiers.[122] Soldiers bonded in primary groups that were suited to the formation of Methodist cells, and they had time to read some of the literature published and distributed for their benefit.[123] Josiah Woodward's *Soldier's Monitor: Being Serious Advice to Soldiers, to Behave Themselves with a Just Regard to Religion and True Manhood* (1715) appeared in several editions throughout the century, and the Society for Promoting Christian Knowledge sent 3,000 copies to soldiers fighting the American rebellion. Philip Doddridge, a leading moderate Calvinist nonconformist, fostered a 'cult of Colonel Gardiner' with his multi-edition biography of a pious officer killed fighting the Jacobites at Prestonpans in 1745.[124] John Wesley published his sermon *A Word in Season, or, Advice to a Soldier* (1744), the philanthropic reformer Jonas Hanway published *The Soldier's Faithful Friend* (1761) and a Methodist 'Naval and Military Bible Society' was established in 1779. With such encouragement via print, it is not surprising that in the Peninsular War a godly sergeant reported there were over ten Methodist societies in the army, with soldiers happily 'assembled in quarries, fields, groves, on the banks of rivers, or in old buildings, for the purpose of worshiping Jehovah'.[125] Reflecting enlightened concern about popular religion, Wellington worried that Methodism was 'spreading very fast in the army' in February 1811, and hoped 'a respectable clergyman ... would moderate the zeal and enthusiasm of these gentlemen, and prevent their meeting from becoming mischievous'.[126] Yet while there were moments when enthusiastic preachers gained a following, and pockets of strength like the garrison on Gibraltar, Methodists remained a minority in the army.

In the 1780s, Evangelical Anglicanism began to spread among the officers of the Royal Navy. This owed much to the efforts of Charles Middleton, appointed Comptroller of the Navy in 1778, who formed a circle of evangelical anti-slavery activists in the village of Teston, southeast of London. Middleton worked to promote evangelical 'Blue Lights' to positions of command in the navy, and when he became First Lord of the Admiralty (1805–06) he substantially revised and reinforced the 1731 *Regulations and Instructions for His Majesty's Service at Sea* with an eye to enforcing regular prayers.[127]

On the lower decks Methodism spread among seamen during the last decades of the eighteenth century. Seamen were highly superstitious owing to the dangerous nature of life at sea, but there is limited evidence of formal religiosity in the mid-eighteenth-century navy.[128] The hard-living world of seamen was cramped, communal and conformist, and displays of 'vital religion' could attract merciless ridicule. That said, John Wesley exclaimed in 1768: 'What a desire to hear runs through all the seaport towns whenever we come!'[129] By at least the 1790s small groups of navy seamen began to gather, 'screened round with a few old hammocks or a piece of worn-out canvas', to read the Bible and discuss heaven and hell, the judgement of sins, and 'the sufferings, the love and death of Christ'.[130] 'Bo'sun' Smith recalled that Methodists were often abused, and when meeting to pray among the cannon 'their enemies sent in prostitutes to interrupt them, threw various things at them, and rolled shot in among them'.[131] The ability of seamen to sing hymns, which was central to Methodism and other nonconformist varieties of Protestantism, depended on the indulgence of their commander. That 'psalm singing' was allowed on many ships during the Napoleonic Wars is one instance of how Methodism below decks was aided by a growing number of 'Blue Light' officers.

Along with the spread of evangelical Protestantism, growing official toleration of Catholics added to the religious diversity of Britain's armed forces. Even the most impious of British soldiers tended to manifest a crude Protestantism in the form of deeply entrenched bigotry toward 'papists' – with many admiring the French Revolution's attack on the Catholic Church. Many British soldiers had their Protestant identity strengthened when ridiculing the pervasive Catholicism they encountered in Portugal and Spain. Yet at the same time, some displayed admiration for aspects of Iberian Catholic culture and envied the hospitality shown toward Irish Catholic troops.[132] The influx of Irish Catholics into the British army encouraged a degree of religious toleration in the face of entrenched traditional bigotry. St Patrick's day, for example, could become an occasion for ecumenical revelry; in 1811 all of the 95th Rifles, 'English and Irish duly celebrated the event, by a proper attention to greens, and not having shamrocks, leaves, grass, and boughs of trees were substituted; thus ornamented we commenced our march.'[133] Indeed, it appears that the British army played an important role in the origins of modern St Patrick's Day celebrations. Irish officers of the 47th Foot appear to have staged the first St Patrick's parade in Boston in 1775, and the British army did much to spread the practice in the revolutionary era.[134] One historian has gone so far as to declare the army 'a model of national confessional tolerance'.[135]

War as subject and metaphor echoed through religion in Britain during seventy years of struggle with France. While this owed something to prevalence of war in the Bible, both Anglican and Dissenting clergy delivered, and at times published, countless patriotic sermons chastising national weakness, urging virtue or giving thanks for victory. Methodists talked of themselves as being at war with sin, with John Fletcher urging them to behave like 'a soldier of Jesus'.[136] In addition to echoing the pervasive language of war during its formative years, John Stevenson claimed that soldiers established Methodism in many towns during the Napoleonic era.[137] Charles Wesley penned hymns like 'Soldiers of Christ,

Arise' and 'The Taking of Jericho', and one of his short hymns published in 1761:

> Not like the warring sons of men,
> With shouts and garments roll'd in blood,
> Our Captain doth the fight maintain;
> But lo! the burning Spirit of GOD,
> Kindles within a secret fire,
> And all our sins, as smoke, expire.[138]

Even the most enlightened rational Christians were influenced by living in a time of war; the Rational Dissenting clergyman and scientist, Joseph Priestley, described a human Jesus as 'the captain of our salvation'.[139]

War and Culture

Rumours of war and accounts of war were common in the print culture of Enlightenment Britain. Newspapers breathlessly reported international politics, speculated about future developments and reprinted letters that provided details of military clashes. Delivery of news quickened in the late eighteenth century with better roads and 'flying coaches' often decorated with ribbons when carrying news of a victory. Reports were often inaccurate and it usually took some time for people to develop a reliable picture of events. When news of Trafalgar first reached Newcastle, for example, Admiral Collingwood's wife was out shopping and fainted when told that all of the admirals had been killed. She had to wait for official reports to arrive before she could be sure her husband was still alive.[140] In towns and villages news of military developments sparked sadness or public celebration, and much discussion.

There was no major battle on British soil after the 1740s, but the persistence of conflict combined with the growth of print to ensure that war increasingly influenced culture. Mary Favret has argued that most 'Britons encountered warfare primarily at a distance' – attending plays, viewing paintings, hearing stories, and through reading letters and publications. While the fighting happened overseas, people increasingly read about war and wrote in military metaphors. With war becoming 'unbounded' during the French Revolution, she argues, 'British writers began to contemplate the routines and habits of everyday life as engaged at almost every turn with the conduct of global war', to the extent that 'war infiltrated, even determined, the representation of everyday life'.[141]

Sitting at the fireside reading about war encouraged individuals to imagine themselves as part of a British national community – whether they were happy about it or not. Favret's argument is convincing, but needs two qualifications: first, we should not underestimate the degree to which war impacted on British culture in the decades prior to the French Revolution. Second, more than a few British writers had limited personal exposure to war that could leave a lasting impression.

History became an innovative and popular genre in the eighteenth century, with war a central topic. Most of the important writers of history in Britain were Scots, some of whom had personally witnessed the Jacobite uprising of '45. William Robertson, arguably the most influential eighteenth-century historian, joined the Edinburgh militia in 1745. Adam Ferguson, who published an important *Essay on the History of Civil Society* (1767), had served as a chaplain to the Black Watch regiment during the '45. While he sympathised with the American colonists, he denounced their resort to violence in a pamphlet. Appointed secretary to the Carlisle peace commission in 1778, he tried to pass through the American lines with a letter for Congress but was rebuffed. David Hume, who was best known as an essayist and historian, travelled through Germany 'in the uniform of an officer' as secretary to General St Clair on a diplomatic mission in 1747; and served again as a diplomatic secretary in Paris in the early 1760s.[142] The monumental *Decline and Fall of the Roman Empire* by Edward Gibbon, England's most famous historian, was influenced by his active service in the Hampshire militia in the years 1759–62. While encamped at Winchester he resolved that in pursuing a literary career, 'my own inclinations as well as the taste of the present age have made me decide in favour of history'. Considering war and politics 'the principle subjects of history', Gibbon was sure that in reading the *Decline and Fall* 'the most voracious appetite for war will be abundantly satisfied.' Of his ability to write about ancient armies, he reflected that 'the captain of the Hampshire Grenadiers has not been useless to the historian of the Roman Empire'.[143]

Visual representations of war and empire were common, with paintings depicting historical events the main form of public art. From the 1740s, at places like Southwark Fair, people could view models representing or re-enacting famous battles. Public and private monuments were erected to commemorate heroic deeds. With William Hogarth promoting painting, mid-century Britain became a 'net exporter' of art, with paintings increasingly visible to the public via shop windows, cheap reproductions or in exhibitions.[144] The creation of an 'English school' of art was in large part a response to the mid-century struggle with France, and art became a key medium through which Britons were encouraged to imagine and identify with an expanding empire.[145] By the early nineteenth century one visitor complained that art exhibitions were becoming too popular 'with the lower orders of people ... even sailors in their jackets with their doxies on their arms, now elbow the first people of rank at these spectacles with the utmost familiarity'.[146]

In the 1760s, a distinctive British school of history painting emerged. Edward Penny's *The Marquis of Granby Relieving a Sick Soldier* (1766) was innovative and proved immensely popular. Lord Granby, after whom many pubs were named, had distinguished himself as a cavalry officer in the German war and was renowned for his charity toward soldiers. Granby was depicted as a model of aristocratic civic virtue in an age when many of his peers were being criticised as self-serving and wallowing in luxury. Granby was painted in his contemporary uniform, unlike the traditional practice of depicting military heroes in classical scenes.[147] This painting was soon followed by Benjamin West's Christ-like depiction of *The Death of Wolfe* (1770), in which characters in this epic event were also depicted in contemporary rather than classical clothing. John Singleton Copley's *Death of the Earl of Chatham* (1781) provided a group portrait of Britain's peers as Pitt the Elder collapsed when speaking in support of continuing the American war. Helping to avert eyes from the loss of the North American colonies, the Boston born John Singleton Copley celebrated British victories against the old Bourbon enemies with *Death of Major Peirson* (1783) and *The Siege of Gibraltar* (1783). Both paintings depicted British soldiers as heroic, humane and self-sacrificing.[148] At nearly 40 meters wide, and displayed in a semi-circle to record breaking crowds, Robert Ker Porter's *The Storming of Seringapatam* (1800) was only one spectacular example of many paintings that brought war and empire home in romanticised form. This genre of epic historical war painting became increasingly popular and central to the construction of an imperial British identity.

Theatre was very important in eighteenth-century culture and military themes were popular. *The Recruiting Officer* (1706) was one of the most frequently staged plays and in 1789 was probably the first European play performed in Australia.[149] The young marine officer Watkin Tench described the scene:

> The anniversary of his majesty's birth-day was celebrated, as heretofore, at the government-house, with loyal festivity. In the evening, the

play of 'The Recruiting Officer' was performed by a party of convicts, and honoured by the presence of his excellency, and the officers of the garrison. ... The exhilarating effect of a splendid theatre is well known: and I am not ashamed to confess, that the proper distribution of three or four yards of stained paper, and a dozen farthing candles stuck around the mud walls of a convict-hut, failed not to diffuse general complacency on the countenances of sixty persons, of various descriptions, who were assembled to applaud the representation. Some of the actors acquitted themselves with great spirit, and received the praises of the audience.[150]

Theatre was valued by officers and men serving overseas as a means of entertainment and reinforcement of British identity. For audiences in Britain, plays provided a key means by which they could engage with military re-enactments and celebrate victories. Theatres could be sites of dispute, particularly during the polarised political environment of the French Revolutionary war when army and navy officers often demanded that the audience sing 'God Save the King'.[151]

Music pervaded eighteenth-century British society. Ballad singers roamed streets and villages singing of war and politics, with 'the Birmingham poet', John Freeth, publishing over 400 songs that he often sang for patrons of his pub. As Jeremy Black has noted, 'provincial towns which nowadays enjoy no live music (other than karaoke in the local pub) had regular instrumental concerts, and could boast their own amateur musical societies'.[152] Along with the Church and theatre, the military 'provided the bedrock of the nation's music'.[153] Military bands entertained both soldiers and civilians, and military themes were common in popular songs. Toasts and communal singing were important means of celebration and demonstrating political views, and 'Rule Britannia' and 'God Save the King' became popular in the 1740s. While Britain was notable for its lack of high-quality indigenous composers in the eighteenth century, Continental musicians produced and performed music that served patriotic purposes, most famously when Handel produced his 'Music for the Royal Fireworks' to help celebrate the peace of 1748. Composed for a London audience in the early 1790s, Haydn's Symphony 100 became known as 'Military' for its stirring drums and trumpets.[154]

The eighteenth century gave birth to the English novel, and war was often present in the form of context or military characters. In addition to being in some eyes the father of the novel, Henry Fielding was one of the Whig government's most satirical polemicists in the 1740s struggle with France and Jacobitism. His father was a career soldier who fought at Blenheim and rose to command a regiment, but then lived through three decades of peace on half-pay. This system of state-subsidised idleness on low pay attracted criticism in his son's novels, with one character in *The Humours of the Army* exclaiming 'Oh, for a Battle! to send a Pound of Lead into my body, or a Pound of Gold into my Pocket'.[155] Fielding's greatest novel, *Tom Jones*, is set in the context of the Jacobite rebellion of 1745. Tobias Smollett's ability to describe the horrors of war in literature was rooted in his experience as a Royal Navy surgeon in the early 1740s. Some of the greatest novels of the eighteenth century reflect the influence of war. In Laurence Sterne's innovative comic novel *Tristram Shandy* (1759–67) a central character is uncle Toby, a retired officer with a groin wound, who spends hours of 'infinite delight' building scale models and re-enacting sieges on his bowling green. Soldiers and seamen appear frequently in Jane Austen's novels and letters, and in the words of Gillian Russell, 'the hum of wartime, if not the blast or cry of battle, pervades her fiction', which illustrates 'how print culture spread news about war, shaping and influencing public opinion'.[156]

The Romantic writers could not escape being influenced by the French Revolutionary and Napoleonic wars, including some personal experiences of the military. For example, the translator and reviewer, Henry Crabb Robinson, was sent to Spain in 1808 as *The Times* correspondent, and described witnessing the arrival of a fleet of British troops in Corunna as a 'stirring spectacle' and 'the first of a series of events...which mark one of the most memorable periods in my life'.[157] Three of Samuel Taylor Coleridge's older brothers became army officers, with two serving in India, fostering both feelings of inferiority and a fascination for travel literature on the part of the young romantic poet. His dreamy 'Kubla Khan' probably owes something to the vivid letters his brother John sent back from the foothills of the Himalayas. While a student at Cambridge in 1793, in a moment of dejection Coleridge enlisted as a private in the 15th Light Dragoons under the name Silas Tomkyn Comberbache. A misfit in military life, he was put in charge of nursing a dragoon with smallpox, survived, and was extracted by family and sent back to college. Nevertheless, in the words of a biographer, life as Trooper Comberbache gave Coleridge 'a chance to be himself' and is the first time we 'can really hear the voice of the frantic young poet and intellectual, dramatising and over-dramatising himself'.[158] Another leading Romantic, Robert Southey, was on a small ship bound for Lisbon in 1800, when what appeared to be a larger French ship bore down on them. 'You may imagine Ediths terror', he wrote to Coleridge,

> awakened on a sick bed – disturbed, I should have said, with these tidings! the Captain advised me to surround her with matrasses in the cabin, but she would not believe herself in safety there; I lodged her in the cockpit & took my station on the quarter deck with a musket. – how I felt I can hardly tell – the hurry of the scene – the sight of grape shot – bar shot & the other ingenious implements of this sort – the novelty of my fighting – made an undistinguishable mixture of feelings. I was going to fight without any one motive but that of taking my share in the business.

Thankfully the ship turned out to be British with a crew from Guernsey:

> You will easily imagine that my sensations at thus ending the business were very definable – one honest simple joy – that I was in a whole skin! I laid the musket in the chest with considerably more pleasure than when I took it out. I am glad this took place – it has shown me what it is to prepare for action.[159]

Turning conservative during the Napoleonic Wars, Southey was made Poet Laureate in 1813 and published a number of influential romantic nationalist works, among which his *Life of Nelson* was most popular.

Poetry was a key form of literary expression and war was a common subject in the eighteenth century.[160] Poems and verse were often used in parliamentary speeches and popular politics. A surge of aggressive patriotism in the 1750s was reinforced by bellicose poetry that championed British claims in Europe and America (with little mention of India), while war weariness in 1762 was reflected in the publication of many poems lamenting the destructiveness of global conflict.[161] The mixed emotions generated by the British Civil War in North America were expressed in poems that reflected the culture of sensibility. The liberal-minded Anna Seward, for example, admired the American cause and opposed the war:

> Long did my soul the wretched strife survey,
> And wept the horrors of the deathful day;

Through rolling years saw undecisive War
Drag bleeding Wisdom at his iron car;
Exhaust my country's treasure, pour her gore
In fruitless conflict on the distant shore

Yet she was shocked and angered when the American Congress formed
an alliance with France and rejected Britain's offer of peace after

She gently waves the long disputed claim;
Extends the charter with your right's restor'd,
And hides in olive wreaths the blood-stain'd sword;
Then to reject her peaceful wreaths, and throw
Your Country's freedom to our mutual foe!

In doing so, the Americans had hitched their cause to

Rapacious avarice, superstition vile,
And all the Frenchman dictates in his guile
Disgrace your Congress! – Justice drops her scale!
And radiant Liberty averts her sail![162]

Transformation of the American war into a global struggle with France
and Spain enabled poets like Seward to display 'a renewed if chastened
patriotism', as in her 'Ode to General Eliott' following his successful
defence of Gibraltar.[163]

The war against the French Revolution started with public opinion
polarised between loyalists and 'Friends of Peace'. This period saw
the flowering of introspective Romantic poetry, in which Wordsworth
'wandered lonely as a cloud' and contemplated dancing daffodils. War,
however, was probably the leading poetic topic during these years.[164]
Newspapers and journals published jingoistic verse, such as John Mayne's
popular 'English, Scots and Irishmen' (1803):

ENGLISH, SCOTS, and IRISHMEN,
All that are in VALOUR'S ken!
Shield your KING: and flock agen
Where his sacred Banners fly!
Now's the day, and now's the hour,
Frenchmen would the Land devour—

Will ye wait till they come o'er
To give ye Chains and Slavery?

Who would be a Frenchman's slave?
Who would truckle to the Knave?
Who would shun a glorious grave
For worse than death, for—infamy?
To see your Liberties expire—
Your Temples smoke, your Fleets on fire!
That's a Frenchman's sole desire—
That's your fate, or Liberty!

There were critics of any involvement in war, like William Blake who lamented how 'the hapless soldier's sigh/runs in blood down palace walls'. Yet the weight of poetry was patriotic in one form or another. Robert Burns was one of many radicals inspired by the early years of the French Revolution. He produced, nevertheless, patriotic poetry when Britain came under threat of invasion, while remaining a radical individualist critic of both British aristocratic corruption and French militarism. Some other leading radical poets, such as Wordsworth and Coleridge, became conservative in the course of Britain's struggle for national survival against Napoleon. Radicals focused their criticism on mismanagement of the war effort, such as the disease-ridden Walcheren campaign where 'foul delays...More dang'rous than the foe' saw thousands 'Lay still on the swampy shore'.[165] When the respected Rational Dissenter Anna Laetitia Barbauld criticised involvement in the wars against Napoleon and predicted Britain's demise and America's rise in her poem 'Eighteen Hundred and Eleven', patriotism and misogyny combined in a wave of heated criticism.[166]

If romantic poetry was to a large extent turned to patriotic ends, it often took the form of a critical loyalism. Realism and sentimentalism combined to depict and lament the harsh effects of war and economic dislocation on the poor. War against Napoleon, who became the great bogeyman of British imaginations, required national mobilisation, and this encouraged loyalist poets to depict the British masses in a positive manner.[167] Traditionally only officers had been singled out for individual praise, but both radical and conservative poetry increasingly dwelt on the plight or virtues of tars and rankers. Though most of these men lacked property or the right to vote, and were often coerced, they were increasingly portrayed as valued members and representatives of the British community. In the words of Betty Bennett, it was 'the popular war poetry that, for the first time in British literary history, put the common man centre-stage'.[168]

The modernising cultural developments of the late eighteenth century occurred in the context of war and rivalry with France. Enlightenment values evolved in the context of Anglo-French struggle and in turn influenced the way war was waged. The growing scale of war, combined with expanding print culture, engaged an increasing portion of the population in the process of imagining themselves as part of a British nation. That Britain should be an enlightened nation was widely agreed, but what constituted Enlightenment was contested between conservatives, reformers and radicals. Evangelical Christianity rose, often contesting, but at times complimenting Enlightenment ideas of social organisation and reform. If the enlightened and evangelical differed at the macro level of metaphysics, they tended to agree on the need for more reason and regulation at the micro level of daily life and reformation of manners.

Years of warfare saw Britons increasingly think and write in military metaphors. Thus, by 1808, in a nature poem 'To the Clouds' Wordsworth described an 'Army of clouds! Ye winged Host in troops/Ascending from behind the motionless brow/Of that tall rock.'[169] Linda Colley has rightly argued that war with France fostered a 'cult of heroic endeavour and aggressive maleness' in Britain.[170] Triumphant or self-sacrificing military men were increasingly held up as models of British virtue, culminating in the cult of Admiral Nelson.

In this cultural context Captain James Cook became an icon of Enlightenment and Empire. Cook rose through the ranks of the Royal Navy in the 1750s and participated in Wolfe's conquest of Quebec, where he displayed impressive skill as a surveyor and cartographer. His three voyages exploring the Pacific saw him lauded as a scientific naval officer who outshone his French rivals, advanced the universal cause of Enlightenment and enhanced the power of the British Empire. From humble origins in Yorkshire, through hard work, discipline and courage, the self-taught Cook became a national hero celebrated on stage, in paintings and in print. 'His renown reverberated at many social and political levels', says Kathleen Wilson, as a 'hero who embodied and extended his country's genius for navigation and discovery, aptitude for science, respect for merit, love of liberty, and paternalistic regard for humanity'.[171] Cook was killed in Hawaii in 1779 and Britons keenly immortalised him as a self-sacrificing enlightened naval officer who spearheaded the extension of science and empire in the Pacific. Rev. Andrew Kippis, a Rational Dissenter, concluded his biography of Captain Cook by listing his qualities as genius, application, knowledge, fortitude, perseverance, reason, self-possession and humanity, and claimed that there was an 'essential difference' between the 'horrid cruelties' of the Spanish conquest of the Americas and the British desire to extend science and commerce. Glossing over the disease and destruction that inevitably accompanied British imperialism, and reflecting Enlightenment ideas of the stages of social evolution, Kippis enthused that Cook's 'voyages may be the means appointed by Providence of spreading, in due time, the blessings of civilisation among the numerous tribes of the South Pacific Ocean, and preparing them for holding an honourable rank among the nations of the earth', which would free 'millions of our fellow-creatures from that state of humiliation in which they now exist'.[172] While religious pilgrims and economic opportunists had pioneered Britain's American colonies, a mix of enlightened and evangelical navy and army officers led colonisation in the South Pacific. After the loss of 13 American colonies, the 1780s saw widespread calls for reform and revitalisation of the British empire, and Cook became a model of how Britons wished to represent themselves as enlightened imperialists.

Chapter 5: War and Politics

There was no fundamental change in the institutional structure of British politics during the 'long eighteenth century' from 1688 to 1832. Even the acts of union with Scotland and Ireland, while significantly impacting those countries, were accommodated within the established constitution of Westminster politics. The culture of British politics was, however, very different in 1815 to what it had been in 1744. Institutions such as parliament and the cabinet strengthened under the pressures of war. But most importantly, popular politics became increasingly significant and a modern British nationalism developed. Change in British political culture was caused as much, if not more, by the pressures of war as it was by social change.

Crown and Parliament

Law and historical convention define the British constitution – unlike many modern nations there is no single written document. The relative powers of the Crown, House of Lords and House of Commons have been the subject of debate and modification over centuries. In the centuries prior to 1688, parliament sat when called by a monarch in need of money. In effect, there was 'no representation without taxation'.[1] Disputes over tax and religious policy, such as whether the established church should have bishops or not, led to civil war, execution of Charles I and abolition of the monarchy and House of Lords in 1649. After a decade of republican rule the monarchy was restored, but the revolution of 1688–89 imposed clear limitations on the Crown, without spelling out its rights.

176

The monarch retained important prerogatives in the eighteenth century. Monarchs appointed ministers, conducted foreign policy, commanded the armed forces, and could dissolve parliament. In practice, these powers were largely administered by ministers who had to defend their conduct in parliament. But there were occasions when a difference of opinion between monarch and ministers led to a change in government.

The Hanoverians identified strongly with their military forces. In 1743, as a Protestant soldier-king, George II was the last British monarch to lead an army into battle. 'Militarism', Hannah Smith has argued, was an 'integral part' of George II's 'self-fashioning'.[2] Princes like the Duke of Cumberland and Duke of York served as field commanders during the Seventy Years War. George III never led his army into battle, but enjoyed visiting dockyards and army camps. Military uniform became his habitual form of dress, and was common among the British elite by the end of the eighteenth century.[3] His second son, Frederick, Duke of York, became a reforming general; and the third son went to sea as a midshipman during the American war, and was nicknamed the 'Sailor King' when he became William IV (r. 1830–37).

In the course of the Seventy Years War the public image of the monarchy improved. George II was a grumpy old German who often fought with his ministers and liked to spend time in his homeland of Hanover. There was widespread rejoicing when the young George III came to the throne in 1760, declaring: 'born and educated in this country, I glory in the name of Briton'. Inspired by the ideal of being a 'Patriot King' who would rise above political factions and unite the nation, George III provoked hostility from those Whigs who had hitherto monopolised power. The 1760s saw political instability and a succession of prime ministers. The end of the American war provoked a political crisis in which the king considered abdicating when forced to accept a ministry that included Charles James Fox, a populist opposition Whig whom he detested. From this low point, however, George III's public image rose as people sympathised with his bout of mental illness in 1788 and identified more strongly with monarchy in the face of the French Revolution.[4] And serving in the armed forces forged a personal link to the monarch for hundreds of thousands of men who broke the king's bread, swore oaths and sang patriotic songs.

While at least grudging approval of the monarch was necessary, ministries generally stood or fell on their ability to manage parliament. To bolster their monopoly of government after the accession of George I, the Court Whigs had passed a Riot Act in 1715, which facilitated use of soldiers in repressing popular protest, and the Septennial Act of 1716 changed parliamentary terms from a maximum of three years to seven. With elections less frequent, Whig ministries used Crown patronage, in the form of pensions and government positions, to help secure the votes of a majority of MPs. Under Walpole there were over 180 placemen and pensioners in the House of Commons who provided a relatively reliable block of votes for his ministry.[5] While this fostered relative political stability in the second quarter of the eighteenth century, it became a focus of opposition criticism and prompted calls for parliamentary reform to secure the independence of the House of Commons. There were approximately 50 government office-holders in parliament throughout the Seventy Years War, but after Burke's economic reforms in 1782, the total number of placemen and pensioners dropped to around one hundred. While this remained a sizable block of the 558 member House of Commons, government patronage could not save a failing ministry. As one placeman, William Jolliffe, reflected in early 1778:

> In questions of small importance, if every man was to follow his own caprice no government could last a day, the business of this empire would be anarchy and confusion; but when the fate of thousands is at stake, when millions may be wasted, and an empire lost, he ill deserves to sit here who can from any motive sacrifice his opinion. It is not in the power of the Crown to bribe a man of property on such occasions.[6]

It was this attitude that saw many changes of ministry in the eighteenth century, including the fall of Lord North's administration near the end of the American war.

Patronage and bribery were also used to influence the outcome of elections. Around 300,000 voted during an election, but these were very unevenly distributed, and voting qualifications varied according to constituency. English electorates had been established in the middle ages, and by the eighteenth century there was a serious imbalance in the distribution of population compared to representation. As a result, areas of economic growth in the midlands and north tended to be under-represented compared to the south. Most notoriously, the medieval town of Old Sarum in Wiltshire had long been abandoned, but with only seven voters it still elected an MP. It was only one of a number of 'rotten boroughs' that effectively represented the interests of particular landowners. In contrast, the boomtowns of Manchester, Birmingham, Sheffield and Leeds lacked their own representatives. Thus, the proportion of the population who could vote decreased between 1754 and 1831 – the total population more than doubled, while the number who voted rose by only 20%.[7] Some electorates had a relatively high number of voters, such as the 12,000 in Westminster, and these contests could be expensive, with beer and beef lavished to sway votes. While politicians of all persuasions sought to influence elections, the Crown's ministers had more patronage at their disposal. No government lost an election during the Seventy Years War.

Yet the eighteenth-century constitution lasted into the nineteenth century because it was vigorously defended and in many ways it worked. It is easy to criticise the 'corrupt' nature of the eighteenth-century electorate, and reformers campaigned for more frequent elections, equal electorates and the secret ballot (to prevent bribery or bullying of voters). Yet the eighteenth-century electorate was in many ways vibrant and participatory. Political vitality does not necessarily equate with the extent of the franchise, as attested by the many disengaged twenty-first-century citizens who fail to vote. In the eighteenth century, many who lacked the right to vote nevertheless discussed politics, petitioned, protested and pressed their views on family and friends who possessed the vote.[8] Most voters were of the middling sort, with around 60% being retailers or skilled craftsmen. They were proud of their rights and independence, and did not sell their vote cheaply. 'Outside the few score seats which were totally under nomination, nobody behaved as though elections were foregone conclusions', Frank O'Gorman has noted, and 'electoral support had to be earned by extensive work, organization and favour'.[9] Elections were festivals of liberty that could stretch over several weeks, with parades, ribbons, banners, music, speeches, feasts and liberal quantities of alcohol. Around two-thirds of electorates were uncontested during a general election, but this was not a measure of political passivity. The largest electorates, accounting for the majority of voters, tended to witness fierce contests. And the lack of a contest was usually because extensive canvassing of voters had led to a prior agreement on the outcome. For example, Yorkshire was one of the largest and most politically active electorates but did not have a contest in the bitterly fought general election of 1784. According to one agent 'the inferiors in many parts' had turned against the Foxite Whigs, believing that through the Coalition with Lord North, 'Mr. Fox was attempting to dethrone the

King and make himself an Oliver Cromwell' – to contest would have been a waste of Foxite time and money.[10]

When Americans called for no 'taxation without representation' in the 1760s, champions of the British parliament argued that, like the majority of non-voting Britons, they had 'virtual representation' by the proper-tied elite of the empire. As one writer observed: 'the people of every province, even the most remote, have by our constitution the happiness to have some gentleman in the neighbourhood' who was an MP and by whom 'their complaints must be regarded'.[11] While many on the other side of the Atlantic understandably rejected this argument, politicians in Britain had a genuinely expansive view of their role as representatives.

Governments could usually count on the support of a number of military MPs. From 1715 to 1790, 15% of MPs were officers in the armed forces, which was a larger percentage than in any other professional group – a third were in the navy and the rest in the army.[12] For the period 1790–1820, while naval officers remained around 5%, nearly 20% of MPs served in the army – and half of army MPs were Scots or Irish. In addition, around half of all MPs served in the militia or volunteer corps in the last two decades of the Seventy Years War.[13] Military men tended to be more conservative in their views – especially army officers, who were generally aristocrats or landed gentry, some of whom were prominent defenders of the slave trade. Navy officers appeared less reliable, as they were often at sea and seldom spoke when they did attend parliament, and, while most supported government, as many as 20% sided with the opposition Whigs.[14]

The increasing financial and administrative pressures of war encour-aged the development of cabinet government. Decisions were made by regular meetings of a small cabinet of around 10 senior ministers and the role of prime minister was strengthened. The term 'prime minister' was largely pejorative in the early eighteenth century. The younger Pitt, however, argued that there needed to be a 'first minister', and tried to ensure he was the only point of contact between the cabinet and the crown. The financial and administrative pressures of war transformed the looser peacetime ministerial structure of the Walpole era into the emerging modern prime minister and cabinet of the younger Pitt.

The polarised nature of debate over the American conflict did much to foster the origin of modern political parties. The triennial parlia-ments of 1695–1715 had witnessed a 'rage of party' between Whigs and Tories. While partisan conflict continued in many constituencies during the mid eighteenth century, at the level of high politics party conflict gave way to factional jockeying among the Whig oligarchy. In the 1760s, however, Lord Rockingham took over leadership of the old Duke of Newcastle's group of Whigs and developed a commitment to gaining government as a united party with some clear policies – a key one being conciliation toward the American colonies. Rockinghamites were paranoid that Britain was being governed by a 'double cabinet', with coercion of America promoted by a shadowy group of Tory friends of the king, including the former prime minister, Lord Bute.[15] During the war, Charles James Fox and other young Rockinghamites started wearing blue coats and buff waistcoats in allegiance with the uniform of Washington's army. Importantly, the party continued to exist after Rockingham's death in 1782, with Fox becoming leader and continuing to advocate peace and moderate parliamentary reform during the era of the French Revolution. Party divisions between Pittites and Foxites became deep. While Pitt and many of his followers were a variety of Whig, their opponents branded them 'Tories' and the name was eventually embraced by their nineteenth-century heirs.

War enhanced the power of parliament. As noted in Chapter 2, a strength of the British state was the unusual degree to which its finances were open to public scrutiny. The annual debate on the army estimates occasioned some of the most memorable parliamentary debates, such as when Burke first denounced the French Revolution. Debate over war finance spilled over into the public sphere. For example, Israel Mauduit's *Considerations on the Present German War* (1760) became a best-seller, and in estimating the cost of the ongoing war in Europe it fuelled public demands that Britain withdraw from its alliance with Prussia. Parliamentary control of the purse strings ensured that Britain's military forces remained under strengthening civilian authority.

Monarchs and ministers had to take account of parliamentary and public sentiment. With most spending devoted to the military and subsidising allies, foreign policy was the main subject of debate in parliament. Parliament could be managed, yet funding for unpopular measures had to be argued and could be defeated. The strong link between rising taxation and foreign policy fuelled growing public interest in national politics. As the Seventy Years War proceeded, demands for greater accountability in the spending of vast sums of taxation and debt inspired efforts to make the 'voice of the people' heard through protest, petition and parliamentary reform.

Riot was a key means of plebeian political expression. As noted in Chapter 2, riots were frequent and usually about food prices. But people also rioted in response to local and national political issues. If for no other reason, Britain's leaders had to consider public sentiment with an eye to their personal safety. The eighteenth-century elite often rubbed shoulders with the masses without the sophisticated security that surrounds modern politicians. George III survived being stabbed in 1786 and shot at in 1800. Popular politicians were cheered and carried on high by crowds, but politicians who inspired anger could find themselves subject to verbal and physical abuse. Lord Bute was hissed and pelted by crowds in the early 1760s. During the Gordon riots, peers and MPs were jostled on their way into parliament, and the houses of unpopular politicians attacked. A bag of muck was thrown at Charles James Fox when speaking in Westminster Hall in early 1784.[16] Spencer Perceval, the prime minister, was shot and killed by an angry merchant when entering the House of Commons in 1812. After publically casting his vote on the hustings in Covent Garden in 1818, Lord Castlereagh walked through a surging crowd, with drunken 'men squaring their fists in our faces', and had to seek refuge in a drapers shop that was pelted with rotten fruit and mud.[17] While riot continued to be an important element in British political culture, it was the increasingly organised and nationally oriented nature of popular politics that was a major development during the Seventy Years War.

The Growth of Popular Politics

War fuelled the growth of popular politics. Criticism of government in the age of Walpole came from Tories and Jacobites, on the one hand, or opposition Whigs on the other. While differing in their views on the constitution, by the 1740s Tories and self-styled 'Real Whigs' were part of a broad 'Country' or 'Patriot' critique of the 'Court Whigs' who monopolised government and supported George II's pro-Hanover foreign policy. There was heated debate in pubs and pamphlets over issues such as Jacobitism, relations with Hanover, the militia and the growth of public debt caused by war. Opposition politicians claimed to be voicing the concerns of 'the people', and as Jacobitism waned radical popular politics waxed and exploded in the 1760s.

After the lapse of the Licensing Act in 1695, Britain's free press fuelled popular politics. The mid-century witnessed growth in the number of newspapers and the emergence of what would become long-lived periodicals such as the *Monthly Review, Critical Review* and *Annual Register.* While authors had to avoid prosecution for seditious libel or blasphemy, discussion of politics and religion was wide-ranging. The contrast was frequently drawn with censorship in France. For example, Joseph Priestley noted that the translator of his scientific treatise on the discovery of oxygen was forced to omit a paragraph on 'the consequence of the spread of knowledge with respect to religion', while the translation of his *Essay on the First Principles of Government* had to be printed in Holland and sold clandestinely in France.[18]

The growth of popular politics and the 'public sphere' has long been linked to the rise of the 'middle class' in the eighteenth century. Some historians are sceptical about the significance of an emerging middle class, characterising Britain prior to the late eighteenth century as a society of plebs and patricians.[19] While most people were plebs, and the aristocracy dominated politics, urbanisation nevertheless saw the 'middling sort' expand, and by the end of the eighteenth century the term 'middle class' was coming into use. It was a concept that owed as much to political rhetoric as to social change. While eighteenth-century radicals championed the cause of 'the people', in light of the French Revolution moderate reformers argued that the British constitution should be strengthened by enfranchising a virtuous middle class. So, to some extent, the very concept of a middle class was a product of the changing language of British politics.[20] And that change occurred under the pressures of war.

The intellectual origins of political radicalism have been hotly debated. The concept of popular sovereignty advanced in John Locke's *Two Treatises of Government* (1690) was influential among radicals. This text, however, was only part of a broader Whig political discourse in which the principles of the revolution of 1688 were both revered and contested.[21] Aristocratic Court Whigs argued that the revolution had secured Protestantism and government by Britain's natural rulers among the landed elite. Real Whigs, however, argued that the revolution was incomplete. Inspired by Roman republican notions of propertied independent men embodying 'civic virtue', and the radical ideals of the mid-seventeenth-century Commonwealth, they argued for expansion of voting rights to make the House of Commons more representative. Real Whigs imagined a golden age in which the Anglo-Saxon 'ancient constitution' had given the people greater representation. The Norman invasion of 1066, it was argued, had placed a monarchical and aristocratic yoke on the people. The centuries since had witnessed struggles to regain the rights of the people, especially during the civil wars and revolutions of the seventeenth century. Real Whigs worried that the gains made at the Glorious Revolution were being eroded as the House of Commons was being corrupted by crown patronage.[22] Yet while some were critical of government, Whigs tended to unite in the early eighteenth century in face of the Jacobite threat. As a result, in the 1740s 'Church and King' Tories opportunistically, and somewhat paradoxically, tended to lead urban popular protest against Court Whig 'corruption' of the political system.[23] As Jacobitism subsided, however, radical Whigs and Dissenters became increasingly vocal.

Religion also played an important role in the rise of popular politics. In England, Presbyterians and other Dissenters provided a solid congregational core of radical popular politics – in a way similar to that which their Puritan forebears had done for the parliamentary side in the civil wars. Granted toleration in 1689, Dissenters supported the Whig ascendancy. As the threat of a Jacobite restoration passed, non-conformists became more critical of limited toleration and increasingly called for full religious liberty in the late eighteenth century. Many Dissenters championed political reform as a step toward gaining religious liberty.[24] J.C.D. Clark has gone so far as to argue that political radicalism was fundamentally rooted in religious dissent.[25] At the very least, it is notable that those who developed heterodox theological views, such as Joseph Priestley, Richard Price and John Jebb, were among the leading advocates for political reform.

Scholars have shown how national identity and popular politics were heavily influenced by war with France. Yet the role of war can be even more strongly emphasised. Linda Colley's thesis that the struggle with France forged a British national identity has been criticised by those who emphasise the strength of regional and country identities.[26] Thus, Katrina Navickas has argued that there was a distinctive 'Lancashire Britishness' that was hotly contested by loyalists and radicals.[27] It is true that domestic politics was overwhelmingly local in the eighteenth century. But the high stakes of foreign policy and war drew attention toward national politics. In addition to the threat of invasion, war increased taxes and impacted on business. The rising tax and debt burden fuelled campaigns for parliamentary reform.

Along with skilful deployment of patronage, Walpole had played upon fear of Jacobitism to stay in power, and his Whig heirs did the same in the 1740s. Opposition Country Whigs and Tories played to patriotic prejudices and voiced popular grievances. Yet public opinion had limited influence on political leadership prior to the 1750s. Government was forced to back down on some deeply unpopular legislation such as the 1733 Excise Bill and the Jewish Naturalisation Act of 1753. But the king's confidence and parliamentary support remained the pillars of any ministry. Thus, despite the public being ecstatic at the capture of Louisbourg in 1745, it was handed back to France in the subsequent peace treaty, and the Duke of Newcastle proceeded to play expensive politics within the German Empire.

In 1756, however, popular politics forced George II to accept the elder Pitt, an eloquent Patriot Whig, as a minister and leader in the House of Commons.[28] Pitt had once described Hanover as 'a despicable Electorate', and rode to power on a wave of public anger at military disasters, most notably the loss of Minorca. The expanding urban middling sort, entwined with imperial commerce, were frustrated by aristocratic Court Whig conduct of war. Ministers and the military were denounced in newspapers, pamphlets, petitions, and burnt in effigy. Patriotic associations formed and electors sent instructions to MPs. There were calls for more frequent elections and reform of the militia and parliament. Hailed as 'The Great Commoner', Pitt helped devise a war-winning strategy that balanced German and American aims and resulted in spectacular colonial gains. In the eyes of many, patriotism and the aggressive commercial imperialism of the middling sort had been empowered by Pitt.

The accession of George III in 1760 unsettled politics. The opportunity to serve in government posts was opened to old Tories. Eager to promote Lord Bute, his Scottish tutor and friend, and to make concessions to obtain peace, George III's policies soon saw Pitt and old Whig oligarchs like the Duke of Newcastle resign. As prime minister, Lord Bute concluded a peace agreement in 1763 that returned some colonial gains to France.

The cause of 'Wilkes and Liberty' started with anger at the peace treaty of 1763 and became the first modern campaign for parliamentary reform.[29] John Wilkes had been set on the conventional path to power through patronage links to the old Whig oligarchy, but this path was closed by the resignations of Pitt and those associated with the Duke of Newcastle. Wilkes started a newspaper called *The North Briton*, anonymously attacked Lord Bute and denounced the number of Scotsmen in government positions. *North Briton* no. 45 ridiculed George III's speech on the peace treaty. Wilkes was arrested for seditious libel under a general warrant while the government searched for evidence of authorship. This was widely condemned as an attack on 'English Liberties' and general warrants were ruled illegal by the Court of Common Pleas. Over the following decade Wilkes was charged with blasphemy for his *Essay on Woman*, spent time in exile and was excluded from parliament despite being repeatedly elected. In 1768 a Wilkes and Liberty crowd was fired on by soldiers in St George's Fields, and around seven were killed. Wilkes was consistently supported by radicals in the City of London and the electorates of Westminster and Middlesex, and his treatment inspired anger about threats to 'English liberty' and the corruption of parliament – especially by ambitious Scots and 'Tories'. Wilkites heaped criticism on naval impressment and sought to obstruct the operation of press gangs within the City of London.[30]

Wilkites established a 'Society of the Supporters of the Bill of Rights' in 1769, and petitioned for 'a more fair and equal representation'. No fan of popular politics, Edmund Burke observed that Lord North's ministry 'respect and fear that wretched Knot beyond anything you can readily imagine'.[31] Wilkites made skilful use of the courts to champion free speech. The official ban on publishing parliamentary speeches was increasingly ignored in a competitive newspaper market, and Wilkites used the jurisdiction of the City of London to shelter printers from prosecution until the ban was allowed to lapse after 1771 – though accurate reporting had to wait until note-taking was allowed in the Commons gallery in 1783.[32] Popular politics before 1760 was dominated by the urban middling sort, but Wilkes and Liberty drew in some from the lower classes. In the words of Peter Thomas, 'after Wilkes British politics would never be the same again: his career permanently widened the political dimension beyond the closed world of Westminster, Whitehall and Windsor'.[33] 'Every coal-porter is a politician', observed an Irish visitor to London in 1774, and 'claims the privilege … of damning the ministry and abusing the king'.[34] In 1786 a French visitor was amazed to see a pub brawl start among seamen arguing over speeches by Pitt and Fox.[35]

The cause of Wilkes had been sparked by argument about the end of the Seven Years War, and had formed a transatlantic alliance with the American Patriot campaign for 'no taxation without representation'. John Adams famously observed that the American Revolution had happened in the minds of the people during the 15 years before shots were fired in 1775. While this might have been true for some, it was the experience of war that led a large portion of the American population to embrace independence.[36] The British Civil War in America also had a big impact on popular politics in Britain and Ireland.

When the North American colonies rebelled, the course of the conflict and parliamentary debates were reported in detail. By the 1770s the British market was crowded with newspapers. The words and decisions of politicians, and conduct of soldiers and sailors, became subject to increasing public scrutiny and criticism.[37] Following the defeat at Saratoga, one officer wrote home: 'We are Anxious to hear how it is Reciev'd in England as well by Parliament as the Mobility, who are in general very Violently agitated with a Reverse of fortune.'[38] Recalling life as a farm-boy in Surrey, William Cobbett wrote: 'As to politics, we were like the rest of the country people in England; that is to say, we neither knew nor thought any thing about the matter. The shouts of victory, or the murmurs at a defeat, would now-and-then break in upon our tranquillity for a moment.' Things changed, however, during the American war. People were 'nearly equally divided in their opinions', and his father 'was a partisan of the Americans: he used to frequently dispute on the subject with the gardener of a nobleman who lived near us. This was generally done with good humour, over a pot of our best ale.' In 1776 Cobbett's father took him to a hop-harvest fair where, while sitting down to dine with 'a great company' of farmers and merchants, a newspaper arrived announcing the British capture of Long Island. Placing a chair on a table, a merchant sat in it to read the news aloud. Argument began and the Cobbetts retired with some fellow American sympathisers to another room, where 'Washington's health, and success to the Americans, were repeatedly toasted'.[39]

The controversial, expensive and unsuccessful nature of the war against the American Patriots and their Continental allies led to the creation of an organised nation-wide movement of 'Associations' for political reform. Writers such as the Dissenting minister James Burgh and Major Cartwright argued at length for parliamentary reform and extension of the franchise.[40] Drawing on their arguments, the radical activist John Jebb told the electors of Middlesex in December 1779 that when the House of Commons 'ceases to express the people's will...it becomes us not to reason, but to act. The voice of the people is, and ought to be, a voice of terror to a bad government', and the parliament should be reformed according to 'the general sense of an enlightened people'. Jebb proposed the election of delegates to a national 'convention' that could 'new-model the constitution'.[41]

Following an invasion scare, in the winter of 1779–80 political associations formed throughout Britain to petition for parliamentary reform. According to Christopher Wyvill, the Associations were formed by 'FREEMEN alarmed by the misfortunes of an ill-fated and expensive War, and justly offended by the servility and corruption of their Representatives'.[42] Forty constituencies petitioned in support of 'economical reform', containing the signatures of a quarter of the English electorate.[43] Herbert Butterfield once described this as a potentially revolutionary moment.[44] Lord North's government certainly felt under pressure in 1780 when the Commons passed John Dunning's motion that 'the influence of the Crown has increased, is increasing, and ought to be diminished'. But the invasion threat passed, the large scale anti-Catholic Gordon Riots dampened interest in parliamentary reform, and good news arrived of victories in the Carolinas. As a result, Lord North called an early election and his ministry was returned to power.

The surrender of Cornwallis's army to a Franco-American force at Yorktown prompted widespread calls for peace and sparked a period of constitutional crisis. George III demanded that Lord North continue the war, but with his majority in parliament whittled away North presented an angry king with his resignation in March 1782. George III was forced to accept Rockingham as prime minister. He soon died and was succeeded by Lord Shelburne, which in turn prompted the resignation of Fox and friends. Taking advantage of anger at concessions in Shelbourne's peace treaty, Fox forced his way back into government in early 1783 via an opportunistic alliance with Lord North. Unable to choose his preferred ministers, George III drafted a letter of abdication declaring he would retire to Hanover, but then decided to stay on the throne. Fox had been lauded as 'the man of the people' for his support for America and parliamentary reform. His coalition with North, the man who had led the king's war against the American patriots, shocked, dismayed and disorientated many radicals and reformers. When the Coalition passed an East India Company bill that would dramatically increase the revenue and patronage at the disposal of ministers, George III let it be known he wanted it blocked in the House of Lords. He then dismissed the Coalition and appointed the 24-year-old William Pitt prime minister. Lacking a majority in the House of Commons, Pitt struggled through the winter, refusing to resign in the face of a no-confidence motion and other parliamentary defeats.[45]

The 1784 election marked the triumph of popular politics in determining government. As Ian Christie has observed, 'to hold a general election only three and a half years after the previous one was unprecedented in the Hanoverian period'.[46] Having learned the power of patriotism from his father, Pitt swung it behind government. While he stood firm in the face of parliamentary defeats, petitions arrived encouraging MPs to support the ministry. The Foxites were branded a self-interested faction and their parliamentary majority dwindled before an election was called in March. Because he had spoken in favour of parliamentary reform, Pitt received support from radicals as well as conservatives. The result was a resounding victory for his ministry. A bitter contest in the large electorate of Westminster saw Admiral Hood returned for the government and Fox narrowly win the second seat, only to have the result challenged by Cecil Wray, a reform candidate who supported Pitt. The 1784 election consolidated the development of party and popular politics during the American revolutionary era. Henceforth, candidates in contested electorates needed to identify with one of the major parties, and popular mobilisation became essential to electoral success.[47]

Constitutional crisis and the 1784 election set the stage for British politics in the final decades of the Seventy Years War: Pittites versus Foxites, morphing into Tories versus Whigs, with popular politics playing a central role. During the Regency Crisis of 1788–89, occasioned by George III's first bout of 'madness', party divisions were reinforced. Disagreement over the French Revolution saw the Portland Whigs break with Fox and reinforce Pitt's government in 1794.

While undoubtedly significant, the initial impact of the French Revolution on British politics has been over-emphasised. The stakes were higher in the American war, as the empire faced potential collapse during a global struggle. In contrast, although the French Revolution was hotly debated after Burke published his *Reflections* in 1790, the early years of Britain's war effort from 1793 to 1796 only resembled a large-scale 'police action against a revolutionary regime'.[48] The volume of political publications increased, most spectacularly in the more than 100,000 copies sold of Tom Paine's *Rights of Man* (1791). Setting that book aside, however, the contrast with the American war period is not so great. While Burke's seminal *Reflections* sold 30,000 copies within a few years, Richard Price's earlier *Observations on Liberty* (1776) had sold over 60,000 copies.[49]

The most important development in the 1790s was the rise of working-class political clubs and the government's repressive response. It is this, along with the flowering of romantic poetry, which explains the vast scholarly industry that has developed around this decade. With historians, especially Marxists, seeing the French Revolution as the origin of modern politics, E.P. Thompson argued that the *Making of the English*

Working Class (1963) began in the 1790s. His book was the most influential twentieth-century work of English social history, and inspired scholars to pore over the publications, language and events of that decade.[50] The plain and forceful prose of Paine's *Rights of Man* encouraged working-class men to establish a London Corresponding Society in early 1792, and a network of clubs arose devoted to promoting political education and petitioning for extension of the franchise. Yet this formal organisation of working class political agitation was only a step in the evolution of popular politics. During the American war many artisans and shop-keepers had engaged in radical petitioning and protest.[51] The Society for Constitutional Information (SCI), founded in 1780, had distributed many pamphlets – including William Jones's *Dialogue between a Scholar and a Peasant* (1782), remembered by one loyalist as 'that prototype of the Rights of Man'.[52] Reading SCI pamphlets inspired Thomas Hardy, a shoemaker, to found the London Corresponding Society (LCS).[53] And a leading member of the gentlemanly SCI, John Horne Tooke, acted as a mentor to the LCS. But working-class radicalism ran beyond the consti-tutional comfort zone of many middle-class reformers. In Yorkshire, Christopher Wyvill was dismayed that Paine's writings had 'formed a party for a Republic among the lower classes of people by holding out to them the prospect of plundering the rich'.[54]

Pitt's government moved to repress popular radicalism as war loomed with France. Royal proclamations were issued against seditious writings. After he had escaped to France, Tom Paine was prosecuted *in absentia* and in many places was burned in effigy by enthusiastic crowds that probably amounted to more than half a million people.[55] Pitt's ministry employed informers, suspended *habeas corpus* and prosecuted leading radicals for seditious libel and treason. After up to 100,000 people attended LCS speeches in a London field in 1795, and George III had a window of his coach broken, two 'Gagging Acts' were passed to make speech and writings treasonous and ban large public meetings. Often referred to as Pitt's 'reign of terror', these were temporary measures in the tradition of exemplary punishment, and justified by the wartime context. The approximately 200 prosecutions for sedition in the 1790s were far fewer than during the Jacobite '45.[56] The repressive atmosphere nevertheless damaged the careers of many writers and reformers.[57]

With political reform branded seditious, and some middle class reformers spooked by plebeian radicalism, critics of government united around opposition to the war. Within the bounds defined by repression, a heated 'war of ideas' raged about the nature of republican France and whether Britain should make peace with regicides.[58] Burke urged an ideological crusade against republicanism, arguing that the old regime must be restored. Pitt and mainstream loyalists were open to negotiation with any regime provided it proved stable and willing to make concessions. With taxes rising, harvests failing and economic hardship spreading, Foxite Whigs and other 'Friends of Peace' called for an immediate end to hostilities.[59]

As war with France loomed in late 1792 a large 'Loyalist Association' emerged throughout Britain to counter popular radicalism.[60] As leaders of an oligarchical political system, Pitt's ministry were ambivalent about popular loyalism. It gave many at the margins an opportunity to affirm their status as part of the political nation. Their proposals for fostering 'vulgar conservatism' were not always welcome, such as the frequent proposal that pay rates be raised for soldiers and seamen.[61] Yet, as John Cookson has argued, because war increasingly impacted on society 'Pitt and his government needed to be backed by a public that accepted its necessity, felt involved, and whose actual participation was maximised'.[62] In addition to Loyalist Associations, as noted in Chapter 3, widespread raising of Volunteer corps played an important role in defending the established constitution in church and state, particularly during the years of hardship and invasion threat from 1797 to 1805. At the same time, its practical effect was to extend public participation in politics. Members of militia and volunteer regiments who were prepared to defend Britain against Napoleon might in time of peace demand a greater say in government. Robert Burns, for example, ended *The Dumfries Volunteers* (1795) with the lines: 'And while we sing *God save the King/*We'll ne'er forget the people.' As Cookson has argued, patriotism was a 'variegated thing' and so we should not simply equate volunteers with loyalism. Some volunteered for money in hard times, and many were motivated by a 'national defence patriotism' rather than loyal support for the status quo.[63]

Military mobilisation on a large scale nevertheless appears to have played an important role in limiting the spread of radical politics in Britain. A former sergeant, Roger Lamb, declared that army discipline formed 'not merely good soldiers, but good citizens and subjects to benefit the commonwealth'.[64] Samuel Bamford, a young Lancashire weaver and radical, went to Knightsbridge barracks to visit a childhood friend who was a colour sergeant in the Foot Guards and had served in the Peninsular War. Invited into the canteen, Bamford and a fellow radical were 'soon in a free conversation on the subject of parliamentary reform' with a group of sergeants. The soldiers stated objections to reform and

> listened candidly to our replies, and a good humoured discussion, half serious, half joking was prompted on both sides. I and Mitchell had with us...a few of Cobbett's Registers and Hone's political Pamphlets, to which we sometimes appealed, and read extracts from. The soldiers were delighted; they burst into fits of laughter; and on the copies we had, being given to them, one of them read the Political Litany through, to the further amusement of himself and the company. Thus we passed a most agreeable evening, and parted only at the last hour.[65]

Another example, from Scotland, illustrates how military men could act to counter radicalism among plebeians. Having served in the Royal Navy during the French Revolutionary wars, John Nicol married and settled as a cooper in Edinburgh. When war started again with Napoleon, and having promised his wife he would never go to sea again, to avoid the press gang he left town to work in lime quarries. In the evenings, he read newspapers to the other workmen, who 'were not friendly to the government', except for an old soldier who had served in India. Nicol argued with them: 'I had broke His Majesty's bread for fourteen years and would not...hear his government spoken against...when they spoke of heavy taxes, I spoke of China. When they complained of hard times, I told them of West Indian slaves'. When a press gang was near they taunted him, asking 'what I thought of British freedom', to which he replied that pressing was justified by necessity, as it was hard to make 'perfect seamen'. A veteran of the battles of Cape St Vincent and the Nile, Nicol recalled that when 'news of the victory of Trafalgar arrived I had my triumph over them in return. None but an old tar can feel the joy I felt. I wrought none the next day but walked about enjoying the feeling of triumph.'[66]

More broadly, military men played an important role in the rise of popular politics over the course of the Seventy Years War. The centrality of the Royal Navy to British identity saw admirals become focal points around which popular politics developed. The navy became a focus of popular attention in the 1740s, with admirals becoming heroes and people beginning to sing of Britannia ruling the waves.[67] This culminated in the iconic popularity of Nelson, and thousands lined the streets to view the passing of his coffin after Trafalgar.[68] If sea officers were generally regarded as uncouth by the aristocratic elite, they became heroes to the middling sort. The Royal Navy extended and protected commerce, and captains lived on wages that were barely enough to maintain gentle status – they could only prosper through prize money. To a large extent the navy was a meritocracy, and those who were seen to fail in their duty were punished. Lieutenant Philips was executed in 1745 for surrendering his ship to the French and Admiral Byng was famously executed in 1757.[69] Successful admirals could get themselves elected to parliament, and at times played to the public, joining opposition criticism of management of the navy. In the 1740s the Court Whigs came to regret hailing Admiral Vernon as a national hero after he sided with the opposition Patriots to condemn government corruption.[70] Admiral Augustus Keppel openly sided with the Rockingham Whigs, and when he faced a court-martial trial at Plymouth in 1779 he attracted widespread popular support from those opposed to the American war.[71] During the Napoleonic War, Thomas Cochrane became famous as a daring captain at sea and vocal radical MP.

Two of the most influential leaders in radical popular politics had served in the armed forces. Major John Cartwright, among the first to champion universal manhood suffrage in the 1770s, was started on the path of political activism by his refusal to fight the American rebellion. He lived to be an old man and united generations of radicals. Born into the Nottinghamshire gentry, Cartwright's family served the fiscal-naval state: he and two brothers joined the armed forces, one of whom served as aide-de-camp to the Marquis of Granby in Germany;[72] while the eldest brother gained a position at the Treasury and another became a clergyman and inventor of the power loom. John Cartwright joined the navy, participated in Hawke's victory at Quiberon Bay and rose to command a ship before ill-health saw him return home to rest in the early 1770s. While tensions grew between the king's ministers and the American colonies, Cartwright was planting oak trees on his estate, reading widely and beginning to write on politics. In *American Independence, the Glory and Interest of Great Britain* (1774) he rejected the concept of virtual representation, and argued that the Americans should elect their own parliament based on universal manhood suffrage while being united with Britain in a commonwealth under the Crown. Cartwright became a major in the Nottinghamshire militia and proceeded to write a short guide for officers and NCOs which urged them to act as a model of civic virtue for their men. He designed a regimental button showing a cap of liberty resting on a book under a sword, and with the motto 'Pro legibus et libertate' (for laws and liberty). With the navy mobilising for war Admiral Howe asked Cartwright to serve as a lieutenant on his flag-ship, but he reluctantly declined entering the 'fairest field for promotion that can be imagined', and also declined a request to serve in the fledgling navy of the American states.[73] Instead, while commanding in the militia, Cartwright continued to advocate parliamentary reform and helped establish the Society for Constitutional Information in 1780, which established the basic platform that British radicals championed until the mid nineteenth century: calling for universal manhood suffrage, frequent elections, equal electorates and the secret ballot.

Cartwright was an English gentleman radical, one of the eighteenth-century 'Commonwealthmen' who looked forwards by looking backwards: to an imagined ancient Anglo-Saxon constitution and the heroes of the parliamentary cause in the seventeenth-century revolutions. With the spread of plebeian radicalism inspired by the French Revolution, Cartwright was dismissed from the militia in 1792, when it was claimed that militiamen were reading some of his radical pamphlets. Nevertheless, in addition to his more than 80 political publications, and in stark contrast to the course of the French Revolution, Major Cartwright encouraged organisation, discipline and restraint on the part of British reformers. In the early nineteenth century he encouraged the founding of 'Hampden Clubs' as a means of promoting education and activism within an Anglocentric tradition of reform. Samuel Bamford, an early-nineteenth-century radical, recalled that 'Hold fast by the laws' was the maxim of 'Major Cartwright, our venerable political father' and was 'adhered to with a religious observance'.[74]

Son of a farmer and raised to walk behind a plough, William Cobbett, the greatest of popular political writers, and possibly the most prolific English wordsmith of all time, spent nearly a decade in the 54th Foot, much of it stationed in Canada. In the barracks Cobbett completed his self-education by reading throughout the long winters, and, after returning as a Sergeant Major with his regiment to Britain, he started a publishing career with *The Soldier's Friend* (1792). This anonymous tract demanded better pay and conditions, in the blunt and cutting language that would make him famous. But requesting the court martial of officers he claimed were corrupt put him in danger of a backlash, and prompted emigration to France and then the United States. Returning to Britain in 1800, Cobbett became a powerful voice for loyalism during the threat of invasion, but gradually came to side with Cartwright as a critic of corruption and champion of parliamentary reform. Cobbett served during a 1780s low point in the standards of the army. Later in life he recalled that when charged with exercising the troops he always had them

> on the ground in such time as that the bayonets glistened in the *rising sun*, a sight which gave me delight, of which I often think, but which I should in vain endeavour to describe. If the *officers* were to go out, eight or ten o'clock was the hour, sweating the men in the heat of the day.[75]

Among many things, Cobbett condemned the flogging of soldiers at Ely in 1809, for which he was sentenced to two years in prison for seditious libel.[76] No political writer came close to the influence exerted by Cobbett, and his colourful criticisms of the British elite were in part rooted in his experience of serving in the army under the '*Epaulet* gentry' and their 'profound and surprising ignorance'.[77]

As men who had broken the king's bread, Cartwright and Cobbett promoted a radicalism that was patriotic. They criticised corruption of the British constitution, and wanted to reform it as a means of avoiding revolution.

Gender and the Nation

A traditional *English patriotism* had long been a core element of opposition politics. From the 1740s a modern *British nationalism* emerged, and was eventually harnessed to support the crown. War with France influenced some of the key issues that were debated in Britain's increasingly public politics. War both united and divided the British Empire, and raised questions as to the status of various Britons. Gender became an issue of anxiety. The treatment of Indians and African slaves became central to debate about the nature of the British Empire, and was linked to military performance. Relations with Ireland were dramatically impacted by war, and the struggle with Napoleon reinforced a British nationalism based on Enlightenment, Christianity and constitutional monarchy.

Affluence caused anxieties in the mid eighteenth century. As the middling sort grew in prosperity they increasingly consumed luxury goods such as tea and tobacco. Concern about the 'gin craze' among plebeians, and the crime wave of 1749–53, saw the founding of many patriotic associations to strengthen the nation and promote British arts and sciences. In 1745, London tradesmen established the Laudable Association of Anti-Gallicans to discourage consumption of French imports and promote British manufactures. The Society for the Encouragement of Arts, Commerce and Manufactures in Great Britain was established in 1754. The Marine Society, founded by Jonas Hanway in 1756, raised money to take orphaned children off the streets and prepare them for a life in the navy. The society was spectacularly successful, and by 1763 it had over 1,500 subscribers and had sent 10,000 boys and men into the navy. As Linda Colley has observed, such charity aimed to 'regenerate the donors as well as their beneficiaries' by spreading a spirit of patriotic virtue.[78]

Following the American War, another crime wave and crisis of empire sparked widespread initiatives aimed at 'reformation of manners'. William Wilberforce, MP for Yorkshire and friend of young prime minister Pitt, became an evangelical and dedicated himself to 'suppression of the slave trade and the reformation of manners'.[79] Having suggested that George III issue a 'Proclamation for the Encouragement of Piety and Virtue, and for the Preventing and Punishing of Vice, Profaneness and Immorality' in mid 1787, Wilberforce established a 'Proclamation Society'. It sought to coordinate efforts among the political and administrative elite to counter social atomisation and 'moral decay' in a commercialising society via such initiatives as Sunday schools and prison reform.[80] Such efforts developed even more momentum as war with the French Revolutionaries placed British society under increasing strain.

In addition to being the greatest military power, France was Europe's cultural trendsetter.[81] Aristocrats in Britain were deeply and fashionably influenced by French culture. Deeply in the sense that many traced their ancestry to the Norman invasion of 1066, as a result of which many words in the English language are of French origin, particularly those related to aristocratic interests such as hunting, war, food, card games and dancing. The Enlightenment added French supremacy in polite manners and print culture. A sense of cultural inferiority led many among the British elite to invest in French-language tutors and dancing instructors. This Francophilia drew widespread criticism from Francophobe middle-class English patriots in the mid eighteenth century. An article in the *Gentleman's Magazine* (1766) summed up the situation: 'Those who have conversed with persons of different ranks, that have been in France, will find the account favourable, in proportion as their rank is high. The man of fashion is always captivated with his journey to France; the man who moves in a lower sphere always disgusted.'[82]

'In Contradiction to all known Example', John Brown declared, a strong tradition of military honour, and the ability to unite 'all Extremes' under a strong monarchy, had enabled France to become powerful 'while she seemed to lead the Way in Effeminacy'.[83] But with the defence of Britain dependent upon the civic virtue of its population, it was argued, the importation of French manners would prove fatal. Military defeats appeared to confirm concerns about the moral fibre of the nation and its masculinity. This was particularly so at the start of the Seven Years War, when General James Wolfe complained that 'gaming, eating, & the pox, are the Vices of the effeminate...& have loosen'd the morals, & ruined the constitutions of half our Country-men'.[84] Brown's multi-edition *Estimate of the Manners of the Times* (1757) denounced 'the luxurious and effeminate Manners in the higher Ranks, together with a general Defect of *Principle*' that was corrupting society, so that the 'ruling Character of the Times' was 'a vain, *luxurious*, and *selfish* EFFEMINACY'. Calling for the reformation of manners, Brown declared that Britain's rulers would only wake 'from their fatal Dream' when 'either the Voice of an abused People rouse them into Fear; or the State itself totter thro' the general Incapacity, Cowardice, and Disunion of those who should support it'.[85]

Critics of the Court Whigs and modern manners 'turned to the militia as a cure-all for England's moral, political and military ills'.[86] A citizen militia, it was argued, would provide cheaper and more enthusiastic defence than redcoats or hired German mercenaries. It would also foster manliness and independence among the citizenry. Englishmen, it was argued, were naturally plain speaking, candid, and practical. Forming militia units would prevent the spread of effeminate manners. As discussed in Chapter 3, when the new militia was created in 1757 it proved a disappointment to Patriot Whigs, as it was under tight government regulation and lower-class men filled its ranks. The strong link posed by radicals between citizenship and bearing arms, however, saw Scots and Irish campaign hard for the establishment of their own militias, and saw the formation of volunteer corps become widespread in the Atlantic Archipelago.

The militia debates were central to expanding the concept of an 'independent man'.[87] Independence was a key value in eighteenth-century politics, and until the 1760s it referred to a man of substantial property who could act free of patronage obligations. John Wilkes and his followers began to redefine 'independent man' to include all those of modest means who displayed the patriotic virtues of 'Englishmen'. The American rebellion encouraged radicals to take an even broader view of political rights; one that was tied to militia duty but less inflected with English chauvinism. Richard Price reflected radical visions when he wrote that, 'if I am rightly informed', in the New England states all men were 'nearly on a level, trained to arms, instructed in their rights, cloathed in homespun, of simple manners, strangers to luxury, drawing plenty from the ground...the rich and the poor, the haughty grandee and the creeping sycophant, equally unknown'.[88] The inspiring example of the American militia and Irish Volunteers encouraged some British radicals to argue that the right to vote, in the words of John Jebb, should be 'as extensive as the obligation of bearing arms for the common defence'.[89]

In line with Enlightenment notions of natural rights, during the French Revolution a new generation of radicals increasingly emphasised the personal qualities of independent manhood, such as reason, sincerity, plain speaking, simplicity and virtue – values that were within the reach of all adult men, regardless of rank or nationality.[90] But old Commonwealthman radicals continued to champion the traditional emphasis on militia duty as a pillar of citizenship. In *England's Aegis* (1804) Cartwright argued that Napoleon's invasion should be met by an armed nation, as 'making every citizen a soldier' was 'inseparably interwoven with civil freedom in the very texture of our CONSTITUTION'. The tract offered advice as to how Britain could survive the 'present conflict for empire and existence'. All male taxpaying householders should be armed, many with a 'Britannic spear' invented by Cartwright, and they should elect their officers according to ancient Saxon custom.[91] Cartwright personally demonstrated use of the Britannic spear for visitors to his estate.[92] Along with Enlightenment ideas on gender, the importance accorded to an armed citizenry ensured the radical vision of political rights was highly gendered as 'universal *manhood* suffrage'.

Emphasis on a link between military service and political rights helped frame the context in which women lived. Politically engaged women, such as the republican historian, Catherine Macaulay, and the Rational Dissenting poet and pamphleteer, Anna Laetitia Barbauld, among others, presented themselves as voices of the nation calling on men to behave with civic virtue, and were in turn compared to matrons of republican Rome.[93] They joined reform-minded men to condemn meddling in European power politics and aggressive wars for empire. In *A Vindication of the Rights of Woman*, Mary Wollstonecraft declared that 'the present system of war has little connection with virtue ... being rather the school of *finesse* and effeminacy'. In contrast to a citizen warrior like Washington, who 'returned to his farm ... our British heroes are oftener sent from the gaming table than the plow'. Only defensive war was justifiable, and if this 'were alone adopted as just and glorious, the true heroism of antiquity might again animate female bosoms'.[94] Only three paragraphs after writing this, Wollstonecraft dropped her hint that some women should have the right to vote. As Arianne Chernock has shown, many Rational Dissenting and radical men supported female education, and a few even advocated female political rights.[95] It was from among these circles that Wollstonecraft emerged as a writer. This helps explain her withering, and to an extent misogynist, attacks on frivolous 'effeminate' aristocratic manners, and her hope that women would become more 'masculine' – by which she meant independent and rational.[96] Yet the republican feminism of Wollstonecraft won few followers in the context of a war for national survival and an increasing emphasis on the 'separate spheres' of men and women.

The Seventy Years War nevertheless helped foster female activity in the public sphere. During the eighteenth century aristocratic wives had played important roles in high politics, helping with electioneering and maintaining and managing political alliances.[97] While such salon engagement in high politics was increasingly criticised in the early nineteenth century, women became more prominent in popular politics and humanitarian causes. In the late eighteenth century, women of both radical and conservative inclination wrote and agitated in support of a range of causes. For example, Hannah More, an evangelical, wrote *Cheap Repository Tracts* (1795–97) that were disseminated in the millions, presenting plain language arguments for loyalism. John Cartwright was a friend of Ann Jebb, a strong-minded Unitarian 'politicianess' who wrote in support of religious and political reform, and corresponded with him about political developments in London during the American War.[98] Thus, when he dismissed the idea of women voting, Cartwright pointed to their inability to act as magistrates or 'military defenders of their country', rather than any notion of intellectual inferiority.[99]

Within defined areas, women became increasingly active and profoundly influenced the culture of British politics. The mid-eighteenth-century wars and the associated panic about the supposedly increasing effeminacy of British men deepened a sense of gender difference. As the reformation of manners made headway, however, in the late eighteenth century women were increasingly able to act patriotically.

During the American war, women subscribed money in support of individual regiments, engaged in festivities around the many military camps established to defend the isles, attended debating societies and some took to wearing military style outfits.[100] In the 1790s, as Linda Colley has noted, women made many 'socially acceptable' contributions to the war effort. They knitted warm flannels for soldiers sent to Flanders, made flags and banners and delivered patriotic speeches while presenting these colours to military units at open-air parades.[101]

Women of all religious and political persuasions criticised libertine masculinity, promoted reformation of manners and claimed a central role in creating a moral and patriotic populace. The decades around 1800 saw the 'discursive public sphere' increasingly influenced by the domestic sphere's 'moral virtue and an ethic of care'.[102] In many ways a prime minister for the times, the younger Pitt was heavily influenced by his politically savvy mother Hester Grenville – described by a banker as 'the cleverest *man* of her time in politics and business'.[103] Boyd Hilton has gone so far as to say that, in his championing of 'household virtues' as a model for economic, administrative and moral reform of government, Pitt established 'the ruling regime of the first half of the nineteenth century as a type of gentlewomanly capitalism'.[104]

Empire and Identity

The dramatic mid-century expansion of empire prompted anxieties and posed questions. The status of settler colonists lay at the heart of this. Was the crown and parliament of Great Britain to simply rule over its colonies? Or were American colonists part of an emerging 'Greater Britain', with a status equal to those living in the 'mother country'? Many on both sides of the Atlantic favoured the latter view, and supported the American campaign for 'no taxation without representation'. This presented practical problems: should Americans simply be represented in their own assemblies? Or should they elect representatives to the British parliament? The latter was proposed by some, but dismissed as impractical. While some rejected the claim that colonists were 'virtually represented', the weight of opinion in Britain swung behind the sovereignty of parliament. Though the Rockingham Whigs repealed the offending Stamp Act taxes to promote imperial harmony, they also passed a Declaratory Act that asserted the right of the parliament to tax Americans. This political fix failed to stop an evolving dispute over the status of Britons in the American colonies. While 13 of those colonies declared their independence in 1776, 13 other colonies in the Americas remained within the British Empire and under the supremacy of parliament.[105]

As the empire grew and became more cosmopolitan, so did a sense of things being different beyond the shores of Britain. The conquest of French Canada was important because it highlighted a key problem of the expanding empire. Should French-speaking Catholics be forced to live like protestant Britons? To do so could provoke rebellion. So instead, under the Quebec Act of 1774, they were allowed to maintain their French civil laws and to live as Catholics, with more rights than Catholics in Ireland. In modern eyes this appears an enlightened act, but to paranoid Patriots in the rebellious east coast colonies it appeared as further evidence that the British government was on the path to continental style despotism.

The loss of 13 American colonies prompted widespread public debate and soul searching about the nature of the British Empire in the 1780s. The nature of British rule in India had long been controversial, and this came to a head in Burke's prosecution of Warren Hastings for corrupt and despotic behaviour as Governor-General of Bengal (1774–85). At the same time, Britain's leading role in the Atlantic slave trade became widely condemned by a large abolition movement that became a pioneer model of pressure group politics.

Mercantilist conflict with France expanded British rule in India. It has become historical orthodoxy to stress the many ways Indian society shaped the nature of British East India Company rule. As Sudipta Sen has argued, however, a tension between mercantilism and liberalism lay at the heart of British East India company rule, and it was rooted in the nature of Britain's 'fiscal-military state'.[106] In 1765 the Company secured the Bengal *diwani* in 1765 – the right to collect tax. At around 20 million people, Bengal's population was twice Britain's, but its tax revenue was only a quarter of that raised in Britain.[107] Many Britons had made fortunes by engaging in private trade while working for the Company. When the spectacularly wealthy Robert Clive and other 'nabobs' returned to Britain, and spent lavishly on estates and buying seats in parliament, it fuelled anxiety about corruption.[108] Engaged in complex Indian diplomacy and expensive wars to defend and extend British rule, the Company sought to increase its tax revenue. In the 1770s Governor-General Hastings contracted 'tax farmers' in an effort to increase revenue, with little success. Hastings could speak Urdu, and developed a deep interest in Indian culture, helping to establish an Asiatic Society of Bengal in 1784, and to a large extent he tried to govern according to Indian customs. In the words of P.J. Marshall, he displayed 'an appreciation of Indian culture and a regard for individual Indian people' that was 'unusual in any British official in high office at any time'.[109] However, complex personal rivalries saw Hastings accused of corruption and exploitation of the Indian population. In Britain, he was widely criticised for engaging the Company in expensive wars, and after he resigned as Governor-General in 1785 Hastings was prosecuted for 'high crimes and misdemeanours' by Edmund Burke.

The impeachment of Warren Hastings became one of the greatest public scandals of the eighteenth century.[110] Hastings claimed that he was too busy 'preserving India to Great Britain, from the hour in which I was informed that France meant to strain every nerve to dispute that empire with us, to bestow a thought upon myself or my own private fortune'.[111] This was either deluded or disingenuous, as he sent a large fortune home to Britain and developed a five hundred acre estate in Worcestershire. Yet he was a reserved and scholarly man, and saw much of his lavish expenditure in India as a necessary part of conducting traditional princely politics – in which he also acted ruthlessly toward opponents. This left him open to Burke's condemnation when the trial opened before the Lords in 1788 for behaving like an 'oriental despot' who practiced a 'geographical morality'. By the time a diminished Hastings was acquitted in 1795 the trial had sat for 148 days. In its early years people lined up for tickets to the gallery and the trial was widely discussed in print.

It was war with France that occasioned British expansion in India, military expense that prompted attempts to squeeze more revenue from Bengal and anger at the conduct of war in India that occasioned the impeachment of Hastings. In turn, the Hastings trial became a stage on which the nature of British imperialism was debated and its ideology modified. After Hastings the trend was to increase rules and regulations that strengthened boundaries and differences between Britons and Others. General Cornwallis was appointed Governor-General in 1786 and set about cracking down on corruption, enforcing British legal principles and excluding Indians from senior positions. Ironically, both Hastings and Burke had shown respect for aspects of Indian culture. A patron of Indian arts, Hastings liked to sing 'Hindostannie airs'. Burke praised the ancient and sophisticated nature of Indian society, and declared privately that he would prosecute Hastings 'whether the white people like it or not'.[112] In the wake of the trial, however, there was an increasing emphasis on Britain's civilising mission as a ruler of 'coloured people'. The trend was toward governing new colonies via 'proconsular despotisms' in the form of military governors like Cornwallis.[113]

While public debate raged about the Hastings trial, a campaign to abolish Britain's slave trade loomed large. This too, ironically, fostered a sense of racial and cultural difference between Britons and others in their empire. Josiah Wedgwood's 'Am I not a Man and a Brother?' medallion, depicting a manacled slave on his knees, became one of the most popular images of this campaign. It reflects the fact that abolition was primarily about how Britons wished to see themselves: as humane and civilised people granting mercy to grateful black people.[114] Africans might be men and brothers, but they were seen as different and not necessarily equal to white Britons.[115]

The fiscal-naval state defended British slavery and captured additional plantation colonies from the French and Dutch. Britons prided themselves on living in a land of liberty, but at the same time they became the world's largest trader in slaves. During the eighteenth century the British shipped around three million Africans into slavery across the Atlantic.[116] The growing wealth of the sugar islands made the West Indies a key theatre of conflict that became a 'violent world of marchlands...in which relatively little space opened up for amicable relations between people of different cultures'.[117] Jamaica was more valued by British politicians and public than any of the North American colonies. While Britons grew uneasy about the brutal nature of the slave trade, the idea that this valuable sector of the imperial economy could be abolished was almost unthinkable until the 1780s.

Although the navy extended and defended the slave trade, some of its officers also played an important role in its abolition. The Somerset Case of 1772 is famous for Lord Mansfield's ruling that slave ownership was not recognised by the law in England, and that slaves could not be compelled to accompany masters back to the Americas. Anticipating this, in 1758 the Admiralty received a letter from a black seaman who had been seized in Portsmouth by the master from whom he had fled. The Admiralty responded: 'the laws of this country admit of no badges of slavery' and declared that naval officers should resist any attempts to re-enslave black seamen.[118] The insatiable wartime manpower needs of the Royal Navy created a refuge from plantation slavery for many African seamen, and some of these ended up as free men in Britain.

Gustavus Vassa, better known to history as Olaudah Equiano, was one who came to play an important role in the abolition movement. As noted in the previous chapter, serving in the Royal Navy started Equiano on the path to literacy and liberty, and he settled as part of the free black population in London. It was Equiano who alerted Granville Sharp to the shocking *Zong* case which, combined with debate about the nature of the empire at the end of the American Revolution, started the emergence of an organised movement to abolish the slave trade.[119] Equiano contributed in a number of ways to the abolition campaign, most notably by publishing an account of his life that illustrated the horrors of slavery, testified his conversion to Christianity and countered racist depictions of Africans as inferior.

Two evangelical navy officers were central to the rise of the abolition campaign: Charles Middleton, who eventually became First Lord of the Admiralty, and Rev. James Ramsay, a former naval surgeon. Ramsay's first notable publication was *An Essay on the Duties and Qualifications of a Sea Officer* (1765) – it ran to three editions and was praised by officers for helping to 'introduce method, manners and religion into the royal navy'.[120] Having joined the navy in 1757, Ramsay served on ships in the West Indies, where he encountered the horrific conditions on British slave trading ships. After injuring his leg, he became an Anglican priest, married and settled on the island of Saint Kitts, where he ministered spiritually and medically to both Europeans and Africans. Hounded for criticising planters, he left the island, re-enlisted in the navy as a chaplain in 1778, and acted as a spy against the French. In 1781 Ramsay settled near his friend and patron, Charles Middleton, in the Kent village of Teston. Middleton encouraged him to publish *An Essay on the Treatment and Conversion of African Slaves in the British Sugar Colonies* (1784), which provoked a furious response from the West India interest and ignited widespread debate about the nature of British slavery.[121] After a young Cambridge scholar, Thomas Clarkson, published *An Essay on the Slavery and Commerce of the Human Species* (1786), Ramsay invited him to Teston where, in Middleton's house, his decision to 'devote myself to the cause' of abolition was applauded.[122] In 1787 Clarkson and some Quakers established an Abolition Committee in London, and a nation-wide movement soon developed. From a small beginning, the campaign against the slave trade rapidly became a large-scale pioneer of pressure group politics.[123]

In comparison to the role of various moral and economic arguments in the abolition debate, the issue of Britain's naval power has not been given its due weight.[124] As 'our seamen are the pillars of the state', Clarkson observed there was 'no one argument' the champions of the slave trade 'declaimed with greater exultation' than that it was 'a *nursery for our seamen*'.[125] While visiting ports to collect information, Clarkson gathered evidence that the opposite was true: the unhealthy and violent slave trade was destroying the lives of many seamen. And even worse, shipping thousands of slaves into the French and Spanish colonies, Clarkson argued, was doubly damaging: as some slaves become seamen in the West Indies, the trade was increasing the maritime manpower of Britain's Bourbon enemies.[126] Clarkson made this argument central to *An Essay on the Impolicy of the African Slave-Trade* (1788), thousands of which were circulated by the Abolition Society. Providing detailed statistics of seamen lost on individual ships, he argued that the slave trade was 'the *grave* of our seamen', with twice as many dying as 'in all the other trades of Great Britain' combined.[127] If the French expanded slave trading after British abolition, they would be taking on a '*losing* trade' and '*the grave of their marine*'. Abolitionists argued that, if the trade were stopped, planters would have to nurture their slaves rather than simply work them to death and buy more. Asserting that better treated slaves were less likely to revolt, Clarkson argued this would release some of Britain's garrison soldiers to 'act on the offensive: whereas the French...would have to defend their islands, in conjunction with a people who had been robbed of the natural rights of men, and who would seize the first opportunity that offered of gratifying their revenge'. Given this, he concluded, even if 'we could lay our hands on our hearts' and say the slave trade was 'humane or just', there are few things 'we could wish for more to the interest of this kingdom than that, when the English relinquished it, the French would take it up'.[128]

Turning the 'nursery of seamen' argument on its head struck hard at a pillar of slave trade defence. Charles Middleton gave Clarkson permission to board navy ships to interview seamen on his fact-finding tours, and sat on a parliamentary committee that confirmed Clarkson's account of mortality rates. In the May 1789 debate, Wilberforce referred MPs to Clarkson's *Impolicy* pamphlet as an answer to objections 'he had frequently heard stated' that abolition would lead to 'the total ruin of our navy', and that the French would be advantaged by taking over the slave trade.[129] In a few years the arguments and popular agitation for abolition saw the West India interest fall back on parliamentary tactics. Thus, when the House of Commons voted to abolish the slave trade in 1792 the bill was blocked in the Lords; but when the Foxite Whigs finally came to power they passed an act of abolition though both houses in 1807.[130]

Abolition of the slave trade became central to Britain's self-identity as a 'humane' imperial power. Abolition distracted attention from the fact that Britain had been the world's leading slave trader throughout the eighteenth century. Slavery persisted in its colonies until it was abolished in the 1830s, while much empire-building work continued to be done by convict and indentured 'unfree labour'. Considering the 'multifarious systems of bonding labour adopted in the growing European empires', Christopher Bayly has observed, 'the years 1760–1830 saw the highest peak of slave trade and slave exploitation in world history'.[131] Nevertheless, the global ramifications of the successful British popular campaign to abolish the slave trade were profound. The British navy switched from defending the slave trade to the difficult task of policing its abolition. Another mass campaign to abolish slavery in Britain's colonies achieved success in the 1830s. The British example and transatlantic organisational links aided the rise of abolitionism in the USA. Without the early success of British abolitionism, chattel slavery might have persisted in the Atlantic world into the twentieth century.[132] The spread of anti-slavery sentiment among the British population, and its achievements, played a key role in fostering positive attitudes toward empire. Widespread belief in the benign nature of British imperialism underpinned support for an empire that inevitably caused much suffering and destruction in various parts of the world.[133]

Revolutionary Ireland

War with France had a profound impact on Anglo-Irish relations and set in train events that led to the Great Reform Act of 1832. Ireland was both a hierarchical *ancien régime* European kingdom and England's first colony.[134] It was governed by a lord lieutenant, who was also a minister in the British government, and was only permanently resident in Dublin Castle after 1767. Unlike the case in Britain, the lord lieutenant and his administration stood separate from the Irish parliament, which was itself subordinate to the Westminster parliament. Compared to many parts of Europe, Ireland was not exceptional in the poverty of its peasants or its discriminatory religious laws. It was exceptional, however, in the depth of its ethnic and religious divide and the scale of land confiscated from Catholics in the seventeenth century by Cromwell's Puritan soldiers and William of Orange's Protestant Revolution. Enlightenment print culture and politeness tended to create a broad divide between elite and popular culture throughout Europe. In Ireland, folk-culture criticism of the elite had an edge hardened by religious and ethnic differences between the 80% of the population that were Catholic and 10% who were members of the ruling Protestant Church of Ireland. Between these two groups stood a remaining 10% who were Protestant Dissenters, mostly Presbyterian, who were also subject to civil disabilities – though far less severe than the Catholics. Among many disabilities, Catholics were not allowed to vote, purchase land, own guns or own a horse worth more than five pounds. Irish popular belief in a pre-modern 'Golden Age' was strong because the seventeenth-century changes had been particularly dramatic and violent. A sense of loss and injustice was cultivated and kept alive in popular culture by the descendants of the old Gaelic elite, priests and Gaelic poets.[135]

It appears, nevertheless, that many Catholics were adapting to the realities of life under the 'Protestant Ascendancy' in the eighteenth century. After years of stagnation and famine, from the late 1740s Ireland's highly commercialised economy boomed as it exported food and linen into Britain's expanding Atlantic empire. This saw the population double in the second half of the eighteenth century, and use of the English language spread. While this increased competition for resources among the poor, some Catholics were able to become prosperous as merchants and physicians, or by working around penal laws that were often unenforced. There was a degree of cultural convergence between Catholic and Protestant elites in a late-eighteenth-century 'gentrification of Ireland'.[136] The Protestant elite increasingly self-identified as 'Irish', displaying an interest in antiquities and identifying with Saint Patrick. For its part, the Catholic elite sent loyal addresses to British monarchs, and in 1760 offered to raise a 'Roman Legion' of six regiments of Irish Catholic soldiers to serve in the Portugal campaign.[137] By 1786 Charles O'Conor, founder of the Catholic Committee, could declare 'we are all become good Protestants in politics'.[138] Yet the leadership appears to have been out of step with many ordinary Catholics, who displayed hostility toward the British army during the American war and wished to see the Bourbon powers triumph.[139]

The British fiscal-naval state nevertheless provided some opportunities for Catholics. The port city of Cork, for example, became a key supply base for the Royal Navy and staging post for empire bound troop ships.[140] As outlined in Chapter 3, under the pressures of war and the influence of Enlightenment rationalism Catholics were increasingly recruited into the British army. In the early 1790s Catholics were granted the vote and allowed to bear arms in a state-regulated militia, and a Catholic college was established at Maynooth in 1795. In the context of war with Revolutionary France, the British state was keen to secure the loyalty of prosperous Catholics and tap the peasantry as a source of military manpower.

Ireland's revolutionary era troubles were started by Protestant Patriots, who championed a form of 'colonial nationalism'. A small French incursion in 1760 at Carrickfergus, near Belfast, spurred the spread of patriotic volunteer units. Not wishing to encourage the arming of Patriots, who were demanding independence for the Irish parliament, the government allowed the militia to lapse in the 1760s. Inspired by the American example, however, revival of the militia became a central demand of Irish Patriots in the 1770s. The legal right to bear arms was a key privilege that united Protestants and excluded Catholics from citizenship.[141] Thus, it was a profound political statement when liberal Protestants illegally encouraged some Catholics to join their volunteer corps, or when Catholic rebels stole guns, because carrying a gun was a symbol of citizenship.[142]

The American Revolution both provided ideological inspiration for champions of liberty and occasioned the widespread formation of volunteer corps to resist a French invasion. Patriots in the Irish parliament, led by Henry Grattan, and backed by the overwhelmingly Protestant Volunteers, demanded free trade and independence for the Dublin parliament. In response, under wartime pressures, Lord North's government made trade concessions. When the liberal-minded Rockingham Whigs gained government in 1782 they repealed the Declaratory Act. This 'Constitutional Revolution' saw the Irish parliament gain independence, but the administration in Dublin Castle continued to be appointed by the British government. It was a constitutionally unsatisfactory state of affairs.

During the nineteenth and twentieth centuries Irish nationalism became associated with Catholicism, but that was not the case at the end of the eighteenth century. Dublin Castle was particularly concerned by the enthusiasm for independence among Presbyterians in Ulster.[143] As in England, Protestant Dissenters in Ireland also suffered discrimination under laws that privileged the Anglican Church of Ireland. One lord lieutenant declared that 'the Presbyterians of the north...in their hearts are Americans'.[144] By the 1790s one Belfast Presbyterian minister,

Sinclare Kelburn, was reportedly beginning prayers with: 'O Lord, *if it be possible*, have mercy on the king.'[145]

The support many Protestants showed for the American rebels contrasted unfavourably with demonstrations of loyalty by leading Catholics. This encouraged the British government to sponsor partial repeal of the penal laws in 1778 and 1782; and, in the face of strong Protestant Ascendancy opposition, propertied Catholics were granted the vote and the right to bear arms in 1793. Yet when the newly appointed lord lieutenant, Earl Fitzwilliam, promised support for full emancipation in 1795, he outraged many Protestant loyalists and was recalled to London by an embarrassed government. With Pitt having drawn a wartime line in the sand on the issue, an increasing number of Catholics joined the radical United Irishmen that had been established in 1791.

Tom Paine's *Rights of Man* was very widely read in Ireland, and, according to a government spy, the ideals of the French Revolution helped to create 'a strong union between the better classes of Papists and Dissenters. They have been brought to think alike.'[146] Unsatisfied with the limited nature of government reforms, the United Irishmen began to work for a revolution that, with French support, would establish the rights of man and citizen in an independent Ireland. Among its leading lights were idealistic Anglicans such as Theobald Wolfe Tone and Lord Edward Fitzgerald, and it had solid support among Ulster Presbyterians. Wolfe Tone spent much time in France lobbying for an invasion of Ireland, and accompanied attempts in 1796 and 1798. Some historians share the United Irish belief that, with substantial French support, a successful revolution would have seen Ireland become a united and independent republic with a prosperous future.[147]

In the context of the French Revolutionary war, however, religious divisions flared and undermined the efforts of the United Irishmen. In *An Argument on Behalf of the Catholics of Ireland* (1791) Wolfe Tone had influentially urged national unity around the cause of independence. He took for granted that 'there existed in the breast of every Irish Catholic an inextirpable abhorrence of the English name and power'. Expecting little support from privileged members of the established Church of Ireland, he pitched his appeal to the Dissenters, 'whom I knew to be patriotic and enlightened', while 'all prejudice was not yet entirely removed from their minds'.[148] Though many Protestants supported the United Irishmen, their anti-Catholic prejudice was ultimately strengthened by the experience of rebellion.

In the early 1780s Protestant Volunteer agitation for broader voting rights had split on the question of enfranchising Catholics. Radical Protestants were confident that if Catholics were granted full citizenship they would gradually turn away from such an 'irrational' religion. When urging the Volunteers to support equal rights for Irish Catholics, John Jebb argued that 'the Roman Catholic religion, or at least the worst part of it, would decay', confidently asserting that 'persecution being removed, light, and learning, and industry would effect the rest'.[149] This radical Enlightenment view was widely held among radical Irish Protestants. Defenders of the Protestant Ascendancy, however, were sceptical, and condemned the limited rights granted by government and the increasing upward mobility of Catholics.

In this context, sectarian violence in County Armagh escalated and spread. Armagh was a densely populated county with a roughly equal number of Protestants and Catholics. Competition for work in linen-weaving had seen armed Protestant 'Peep o' Day Boys' attacking Catholics since the late 1770s. In response, a shadowy movement of 'Catholic Defenders' emerged in the early 1780s. As thousands of Catholics were forced to flee Armagh in the winter of 1795–96, Defenderism spread. By this time, the ideology of the Defenders had become a syncretic mix of traditional Catholic grievances and revolutionary ideals. Fragmentary evidence of Defender oaths include: 'The French Defenders will uphold the cause and Irish Defenders will pull down the British laws,' and the aim to 'dethrone all kings and plant the true religion that was lost since the Reformation'.[150] Links were forged between the Defenders and the United Irishmen, and by 1798 the government estimated that over 200,000 had taken the United Irish oath.[151] Despite the non-sectarian ideals of the United Irish leadership, various sources indicate that many of the Catholic rebels saw themselves as going to war with Protestant 'heretics'.[152]

Concerned by the uncontrolled violence of the Peep o' Day Boys, propertied loyalists sought to impose discipline on militant Protestantism by establishing an Orange Order. As sectarian conflict escalated, Ascendancy Protestants became paranoid about cooperation between the plebeian Catholic Defenders and the revolutionary United Irishmen. With the French endeavouring to invade in support of a revolution, the government reluctantly agreed to the formation of a volunteer yeoman cavalry that inevitably contained members of the Orange Order. In the words of General Thomas Knox: 'As for the Orangemen, we have rather a difficult card to play ... we must to a certain degree uphold them, for with all their licentiousness, on them we must rely for the preservation of our lives and properties should critical times occur.'[153]

When the revolution was finally launched in May 1798 it was short, bloody and unsuccessful. With Lord Castlereagh playing an important role as Chief Secretary of Ireland, Crown forces severely disrupted the United Irishmen through the widespread use of informers and military repression, and by early 1798 the whole of Ireland was under martial law. As a result, the rebellion was sporadic and uncoordinated, and the cities of Dublin and Belfast failed to rise. The necessary French invasion was too late, too small and landed on the remote west coast. The neglected south-eastern county of Wexford surprised everyone in producing the most successful uprising. A Protestant loyalist in the town of Wexford provided a vivid description of the rebels: 'They had no kind of uniform, but were most of them in the dress of labourers, white bands round their hats, and green cockades...their arms consisted chiefly of pikes of an enormous length...scythes, hay-knives, scrapers, currying knives, and old rusty bayonets fixed on poles; some carried rusty muskets.'[154] In the second week of June a small uprising of mostly Presbyterian United Irishmen was quickly crushed by Crown forces, including many Catholic militia. After bloody battles at New Ross and Vinegar Hill, Wexford had been brought under control by the time a small French force landed in late August in Killala Bay. In this final 'tragi-comic episode', battle hardened Jacobin soldiers, who had exterminated Catholic peasants in the French Vendée, found themselves hailed as liberators by Irish peasants falling to their knees clutching rosaries and invoking the 'Blessed Virgin'.[155] A much larger Crown force moved cautiously across Ireland to defeat this invasion force, after which they massacred those Irish who had fought alongside the French.[156]

The French officers were shocked by what they encountered in Ireland and bitterly complained that the envoys of the United Irishmen had misled them. Instead of finding a united nation ready to rise up and throw off British rule, they encountered a vicious civil war. Whatever existed in the breasts of Irish Catholics, many of them fought for the Crown. They were encouraged to do so by the hierarchy of the Catholic Church, for whom Britain was an ally in the European struggle against the anti-Christian French revolutionaries. And many Irish who supported the Crown, or at least declined to rebel, may have had an eye to the consequences of republican 'liberation' in rural France and other regions of Europe such as the Netherlands and Italy.[157]

The attempted revolution of 1798 was a complex and confusing conflict with profound consequences. As Brendan Simms has argued, it was 'both a revolution *and* a counter-revolution'.[158] While the United Irishmen looked to make an American or French style revolution, the Catholic Defenders who joined them were bent on enacting a long delayed counter-revolution against seventeenth-century Protestant conquests. The leading United Irishmen worked hard to politicise 'the people' with the ideals of liberty and equality.[159] Yet they took a big risk in starting a revolution in a country with deep sectarian prejudices. Study of popular ballads suggests that traditional Catholic and agrarian concerns remained more influential among the population than the Enlightenment ideals of the United Irish.[160] And the presence of Orangemen among the Crown forces, as they raped, flogged, pitch-capped, murdered and burned their way though counties, sparked panic among Catholics. Rebel Catholics in turn murdered 'heretics', with Protestant prisoners piked to death on Wexford Bridge and burned alive in a barn at Scullabogue.[161] As the revolution failed, and reports of sectarian violence circulated, many Presbyterian radicals in Ulster joined the Orangemen in order to cover their tracks. By mid-1799 one observer noted there had been an 'astonishing change in the public mind' in Ulster: 'The word "Protestant" which was becoming obsolete in the north has regained its influence and all of that description seem to be drawing closer.'[162]

In the years leading up to the Irish rebellion the British government and people were distracted by the war against France. In October 1797, the radical philosopher, William Godwin, declined a request to write a tract encouraging Britons to support Irish liberty, arguing that

> a very great part of the English public, are, at present, in a state of political apathy & torpor. The rest are engrossed by the great changes & events going on upon the continent, & cannot be prevailed upon to consider what is passing upon the comparatively inconsiderable stage of Ireland as the principal object of their attention.[163]

By the end of the year, however, reports of brutal repression by the Crown forces in Ireland had become a hot topic of debate in the British press.

Having lost patience with the Protestant Ascendancy, William Pitt proposed union as the only long-term solution to Irish instability. In light of the success of the Union with Scotland in 1707 the idea of an Anglo-Irish union had been discussed for many years, and the rebellion made it possible to encourage the Irish parliament to abolish itself. After vigorous debate in parliament and press, Westminster voted overwhelmingly for Union, but it required many publications, and lavish applications of oratory and bribes to gain a majority in the Irish parliament. With Britain and France locked in 'the most important and momentous conflict that ever occurred in the history of the world', Pitt argued that Ireland was a 'mighty limb of the Empire' and that union would strengthen it and Britain.[164] He warned defenders of the Ascendancy parliament that Catholics would eventually gain full political rights, and they would find themselves a minority in an independent republic. By uniting in the British parliament, Irish Protestants could ensure their future as part of a Protestant-dominated political system. Union would also allow the Irish greater access to opportunities in the rest of the British Empire. And along with Cornwallis and Castlereagh in Ireland, Pitt also hinted to Catholics that the granting of full citizenship rights might follow union. Regardless of this, Catholics had no reason to mourn the passing of the Protestant Ascendancy parliament. Their support for union, or at least neutrality on the question, left anti-unionist Protestants isolated and ensured its success. The Act of Union came into effect in 1801, adding 100 Irish MPs, 28 peers and four bishops to the Westminster parliament.

The pressures of war with France, however, led Pitt's ministry to rush the Act of Union without paying attention to detail. While the Irish parliament disappeared, the Dublin Castle administration remained largely untouched. Most damaging, George III declared unbending opposition to Catholic emancipation, which led Pitt to resign as prime minister. Union did act as a gateway to empire, and many Irish prospered in settler colonies. Thus, when anti-Union movements arose in the nineteenth century they tended to declare a desire to remain within the British Empire.[165] But in many ways, divisions between Ireland and Britain grew deeper following the Union. Ireland effectively remained a farm for a rapidly industrialising Britain. British, and particularly English, prejudices against the 'wild Irish' intensified, and Irish accents were mocked in parliament and press. Irish poverty and turbulence was the subject of numerous parliamentary inquiries, and was increasingly ascribed to ingrained cultural and racial characteristics.[166] The belief that a 'fanatical fury' existed in 'the mind of a people easily excited at all times' led to the passing of Insurrection Acts and other interventionist policies, which in turn created more resentment among Catholics.[167]

Some historians blame the British state for reigniting sectarianism in order to prevent the creation of a united Irish republic that was 'non-sectarian, democratic and inclusive'.[168] Yet while the Crown accepted the support of Orangemen during the rebellion, the latent sectarianism of both Protestants and Catholics needed little encouragement. It is also possible that a successful revolution might have involved even more bloodshed. Up to 30,000 people died in the Irish rebellion, but this was far fewer than the quarter of a million the French revolutionaries killed in the Vendée. While Crown forces behaved brutally, there was no state-directed policy of extermination as occurred in the Vendée, and there were commanders on both sides who tried to prevent atrocities.[169] Given its strategic importance, a republican Ireland would undoubtedly have become a major battleground in the Anglo-French war; and the Irish Jacobin regime would probably have used very harsh measures against any Catholics or Protestants who resisted the republican project. In short, as Brendan Simms has noted, a successful Irish Revolution would probably have resulted in 'a murderous bourgeois secular satellite state' that was 'subservient to the needs of French foreign policy'.[170]

On the other hand, if Britain and Ireland had experienced the genera-tion of peace that Pitt forecast in 1792, there is a chance Ireland may have evolved into a peaceful and prosperous 'West Britain', like Scotland's 'North Britain'. In the context of war and Enlightenment, late eight-eenth-century British ministers grew increasingly impatient with the Protestant Ascendancy and were gradually granting rights to Catholics. This was interrupted by the polarising impact of the French Revolution. Yet, even then, many Catholics supported the Crown during the rebel-lion and supported the Act of Union. And even in the wake of 1798, there was some cooperation between Catholics and liberal Protestants in the nineteenth century.[171] In light of this, George III's refusal to allow Catholic emancipation had a devastating impact on the future of Anglo-Irish relations. As Sean Connolly has observed, while 'the successful integration of Ireland into the British state' remained possible, the odds against it had lengthened.[172]

In the context of a global ideological war, the bloody chaos of 1798 revived and propelled Irish sectarianism into the age of nationalism.[173] Richard Musgrave's *Memoirs of the Different Rebellions in Ireland* (1801) detailed the sectarian violence committed against Protestants, and became a defining text of British conservatism in the early nineteenth century.[174] While Orangemen had been opponents of the Act of Union, they became committed Unionists with strong support among British

Tories – and Dublin beat Edinburgh and London in being the first to raise a monument to Admiral Nelson in 1809.[175] In the 1820s Dan O'Connell led a mass movement that forced Wellington's Tory government to grant Catholic emancipation rather than risk civil war. Along with Repeal of the Test and Corporation Acts, this breached the defences of the eighteenth-century constitution. Irish Catholic MPs proceeded to help the Whigs to pass the Great Reform Act of 1832. A successful alliance between Irish Catholics and liberal Protestants remained possible at least until Gladstone's efforts to enact Home Rule were defeated.[176] But Irish nationalism was increasingly associated with Catholicism. The Union of all Ireland with Britain remained in place until another civil war broke out during the First World War. Most of Ireland became a republic with strong ties to the Catholic Church, while Ulster remained a deeply divided part of the United Kingdom. The sectarianism that revived in 1798 has had a profoundly negative influence on the modern history of Ireland and Britain.

Conclusion

As Wellington and Napoleon prepared to do battle at Waterloo, Australia's first steam engine started work powering a flour mill in Sydney on 29 May 1815. Symbolic of the forces that enabled Britain to resist France, at the edge of the empire this piece of the industrial revolution was unveiled before Governor Lachlan Macquarie, a career soldier born on the western Scottish island of Ulva. Macquarie had served in America, Jamaica, India and Egypt, and was in the middle of his decade-long governorship, summarised thus by his biographer:

> Hard work typified his regime, as did a paternalism that verged on autocracy. The notion of regularity ruled his outlook, stamped his plans, and endorsed his deeds. He brought system and efficiency to the government and brooked no opposition, whether from clergyman or judge. Capable of doing things on a grand scale to implement his dreams, he appreciated that symmetry could be achieved only by orderly, pragmatic, and daily attention to detail. The antipodean outposts progressed materially under his governorship. The population grew from 11,590 to 38,778; sheep multiplied from 26,000 to 290,000, cattle from 12,500 to 103,000; the land under tillage increased from 7500 to 32,000 acres; roads, bridges, towns, churches, schools, hospitals, parks, and gardens were developed; improvements were effected in trade and manufacturing, in banking and currency, and in public morals; and attempts were made to befriend the Aborigines. Macquarie ruled New South Wales during a time of transition: he found a gaol, he left a burgeoning colony.[1]

Macquarie was the sort of Scot that Wilkite Whigs had denounced in the 1760s: a Tory on the make, rebuilding his family fortune while building the British Empire. An enemy of democracy, he nevertheless supported the social and economic rights of emancipated convicts in the face of hostile wealthy settlers. Macquarie's rule in Sydney reflected the moderate Enlightenment paternalism, ruling over a dynamic economy stimulated by public expenditure, that characterised British government during the Seventy Years War.

We should avoid reifying Jonathan Israel's concepts of 'Moderate' and 'Radical Enlightenments', but it is helpful to think in terms of the lower case: moderate Enlightenment values were deployed in opposition to more radical Enlightenment notions of religious or political equality.[2] Mid-century French Enlightenment thinkers, such as Voltaire, often admired Britain, with its parliament, religious toleration and relatively free press. For their part, the British elite drew on Enlightenment rationalism in order to defend the post-1688 *status quo*. The British constitution, it was argued, fostered 'rational liberty' under an established church and parliament of the propertied. In the late eighteenth century, radical Enlightenment voices, such as those of Joseph Priestley and Mary Wollstonecraft, became more numerous. Yet, moderate Enlightenment values remained dominant in Britain, in forms such as Whig constitutionalism and Pittite liberal Toryism. Evangelicalism rose and often clashed with Enlightenment, but they also worked together to discipline the 'unwashed masses', promote humanitarian reform and oppose revolutionary ideas. The rise of evangelicalism among naval officers has long been recognised. While neglected by historians, it is clear that the armed forces were broadly influenced by Enlightenment values and played a role in their further dissemination.

Enlightenment Britain adapted in many ways to fight France in a long struggle, especially when revolution transformed the war-making capacity of the French. The navy and army were expanded and reformed. The British public constantly complained about taxes, and the British American colonists launched a tax revolt that created the USA. The fiscal-naval state funded wars primarily through borrowing until, at breaking point, the younger Pitt took the radical step of introducing income tax. At the start of the twenty-first century many in the Anglosphere denounce 'debt and deficit' and 'big new taxes', little knowing that without them the British Empire that many conservatives admire would not have existed.[3] Not only did a ballooning public debt enable Britain to defend itself against the threat of invasion, it stimulated the economy and underwrote a global empire. In effect, prolonged and massive wartime borrowing helped build capacity within the domestic and imperial economy. In the more peaceful nineteenth century, that capacity enabled Britain to gradually pay off its public debt. In the words of Patrick O'Brien, 'Hanoverian governments knew some big things, namely that security, trade, empire and military power really mattered.' In the more peaceful late nineteenth century, liberals extolled the virtues of laissez-faire economics and criticised the 'corruption' of eighteenth-century mercantilism. 'By that time men of the pen, especially the pens of political economy, had forgotten, and did not wish to be reminded, what the first industrial nation owed to men of the sword.'[4]

The Seventy Years War was central to what Christopher Bayly has called the 'first age of global imperialism'. During this period the balance tipped rapidly as sophisticated civilisations in Asia and the Near East fell under European domination in 'a massive and historic redistribution of the world's resources'. This process was driven by contending fiscal-military states desperate to increase their revenue bases. There were similarities in the way Napoleon swept away traditional structures as he conquered Europe and the way men influenced by the British Enlightenment governed India.[5] It was something that provoked rage in Edmund Burke, who saw both French Jacobins and British East India Company officials as destroying organic traditional social elites and substituting a rule by 'sophisters, economists and calculators'.[6] While the fiscal-naval state shrank rapidly in Britain after the war, it lingered long in the empire. Indian peasants continued to fund a large standing army that could be deployed to trouble-spots, and garrisons remained scattered around the empire, forming the basis of the thin red lines of the Victorian era.

In Britain the immediate years of retrenchment following the war were hard. Liverpool's Tory government moved to appease the economic interests of its support base among the landowning elite – income tax was repealed and Corn Laws introduced. The navy was rapidly demobilised, with the number of active warships in 1818 only a sixth of what it had been in 1814. Since Trafalgar the navy had been doing the vital but unglamorous work of blockade, while the army finished the war bathing in public praise for its victories in the Peninsula and Waterloo. Economic recession ignited protest and large-scale agitation for parliamentary reform, and so the policing role of the army saw it demobilise slowly, with 44,000 troops still stationed in Britain in 1825.[7] Industry gradually re-tooled for a peacetime economy, and with a 'secondary ripple of inventions' after 1820 growth resumed.[8] Early British industrialisation was characterised by slow growth, low rates of private investment (which remained stable in times of war and peace) and very low rates of investment in housing and urban infrastructure. It took a long time before the 'fiscally emasculated state' that emerged from the Seventy Years War could do much to help with alleviating urban squalor.[9]

Linda Colley's *Britons: Forging the Nation, 1707–1837* has proved one of the most influential books published on eighteenth-century history. She rightly highlights the ways a modern British nationalism was constructed around Protestantism, profits, parliament and monarchy during this period. Her work has been criticised by those who argue that British nationalism was thin and superficial compared to deeper-rooted local and pre-modern national identities within the United Kingdom. Growth of the British state was often resisted, actively or passively, by both plebs and local patricians, and, ironically, the English were often the most resistant to thinking of themselves as British. Nevertheless, the increasing frequency with which the terms Britain and British were used, with all of their underlying tensions, is testament to the rise of British nationalism in the eighteenth century. English, Welsh, Scottish and even Irish identities could be worn along with a British identity, and military service appears to have fostered this among millions of men and their families. While the term 'England' was often conventionally and lazily used, especially by the English, the high number of soldiers and sailors from the Celtic regions made it a truly British war with France. Even the serious threats to the state posed by Jacobitism and Jacobinism, in their own ways, only aimed to unite Britons under a different political regime. War with France pressed on the lives and, through texts, on the minds, of millions. They discussed the causes and course of war, celebrated victories and lamented defeats. This fostered a sense of Britain being united as an embattled island, with an anxious question mark hanging over the strategically crucial island of Ireland.

Britain's fiscal-naval state operated in the glare of increasing parliamentary and public scrutiny. Country Whigs and radicals were constantly calling government to account. Doing this eloquently made Charles James Fox one of the most famous politicians in British history, despite the fact he spent very little time on the ministerial benches in a long parliamentary career.[10] Government was never unopposed, and even at the height of the struggle with Napoleon there were anti-war voices who called for a negotiated peace.[11] Even during Pitt's repression in the 1790s, Rational Dissenters and other radical Enlightenment intelligentsia continued to voice criticisms of the government's 'war system'. This was backed up by mass petitions for peace, many signed by the rapidly growing denomination of evangelical Methodists. The campaign for parliamentary reform that emerged among hard-pressed taxpayers in the late eighteenth century ebbed and flowed in the nineteenth century, gradually forcing reform of the British political system.

The critical eye of opposition MPs and taxpayers forced governments to implement utilitarian and liberal reforms. In the 1740s government positions were viewed primarily as pieces of patronage, to be granted for political favour and possessed for personal gain. By the end of the Seventy Years War a culture of civil service had evolved that underpinned the 'organisation of victory'. One of the leading architects of victory, Lord Castlereagh, worked himself to the point of mental breakdown and committed suicide by cutting his throat in 1822.[12] To wage war successfully against Napoleon, as John Cookson has argued, the Crown's Anglican aristocratic ministers had to accommodate the growing economic and religious diversity of Britain. When possible, concessions were made to industrial interests, and in 1813 toleration was extended to Unitarian Dissenters. The question of emancipation for Irish Catholics remained contentious, and liberal and ultra hard-line Tories divided over the issue. In all, 'high Toryism was submitting to liberal Toryism even while the war lasted'.[13] The roots of the Great Reform Act of 1832 lay in the growth of popular politics and the pressures that built on government during decades of war.

The nineteenth century witnessed many colonial and civil wars, but, under relatively peaceful international relations secured by its navy, Britain and its settler colonies developed into modern states characterised by a creative tension between Tory paternalism, Whig constitutionalism, utilitarian liberalism and Anglo-Irish radicalism. It was a culture forged in the experience of Seventy Years War with France.

Notes

Introduction

1. B. Harris, 'The Anglo-Scottish Treaty of Union, 1707 in 2007: Defending the Revolution, Defeating the Jacobites', *Journal of British Studies*, 49 (2010), pp. 28–46.
2. J.C.D. Clark, *English Society, 1688–1832: Ideology, Social Structure and Political Practice during the Ancien Régime* (2nd edn, Cambridge, 2000); R. Porter, *Enlightenment: Britain and the Creation of the Modern World* (Harmondsworth, 2000) builds on his influential essay 'Enlightenment in England', in R. Porter and M. Teich, eds., *The Enlightenment in National Context* (Cambridge, 1981), pp. 1–18.
3. A. Briggs, *The Age of Improvement, 1783–1867* (1979), p. 129.
4. In addition to his many articles, see S. Conway, *The British Isles and the War of American Independence* (Oxford, 2000); idem., *War, State and Society in Mid-Eighteenth-Century Britain and Ireland*.
5. The scholarship is vast, but a good place to start is D. Bell, *The First Total War: Napoleon's Europe and the Birth of Modern Warfare* (2007).
6. R. Knight, *Britain against Napoleon: The Organization of Victory, 1793–1815* (2013). This eagerly anticipated volume was published when I was in the last weeks of drafting this book.
7. J. Black, *Eighteenth-Century Britain* (2nd edn, Basingstoke, 2008), p. 242.
8. H.M. Scott, *The Birth of a Great Power System, 1740–1815* (Harlow, 2006), p. 74.
9. Something noted by Linda Colley, *Britons: Forging the Nation* (2nd edn, New Haven, CT, 2009), p. 86.
10. P.G.M Dickson, *The Financial Revolution in England: A Study in the Development of Public Credit 1688–1756* (London, 1967); J. Brewer, *The Sinews of Power: War, Money and the English State, 1688–1783* (Cambridge, MA, 1988), p. 124.
11. M.J. Daunton, *Progress and Poverty: An Economic and Social History of Britain 1700–1850* (Oxford, 1995), p. 391.
12. John Ashley cited in J.T. Adams, 'On the Term British Empire', *American Historical Review*, 27 (1922), p. 488; P.J. Marshall, ed., *The Eighteenth Century* (Oxford, 1998), p. 7.

13. T.H. Breen, 'An Empire of Goods: The Anglicization of Colonial America, 1690–1776', *Journal of British Studies*, 25 (1986), pp. 467–99.

14. K. Wilson, *The Sense of the People* (Oxford, 1995), pp. 140–65.

15. P.J. Marshall, 'Introduction', in Marshall, ed., *Eighteenth Century*, p. 7; D. Armitage, *The Ideological Origins of the British Empire* (Cambridge, 2000).

16. B. Harris, 'War, Empire, and the "National Interest" in Mid-Eighteenth-Century Britain', in J. Flavell and S. Conway, eds., *Britain and America Go to War* (Gainesville, FL, 2004), pp. 13–40.

17. F. McLynn, *Invasion: From the Armada to Hitler, 1588–1945* (London, 1987), pp. 39–112.

18. On the concept of the 'Atlantic Archipelago', see J.G.A. Pocock, *The Discovery of Islands: Essays in British History* (Cambridge, 2005), pp. 29–30, 77–79.

19. J. Black, *Natural and Necessary Enemies: Anglo-French Relations in the Eighteenth Century* (Athens, GA, 1986).

20. H. Smith, *Georgian Monarchy: Politics and Culture, 1714–1760* (Cambridge, 2006), p. 2.

21. J. Adamson, ed., *The Princely Courts of Europe: Rituals, Politics and Culture under the Ancien Régime, 1500–1750* (London, 1999).

22. C. Jones, *The Great Nation: France from Louis XV to Napoleon* (Harmondsworth, 2002), p. 589.

23. D. Baugh, 'Withdrawing from Europe: Anglo-French Maritime Geopolitics, 1750–1800', *International History Review*, 20 (1998), p. 14.

24. A. Wright, *Britain, France and the Gothic, 1764–1820: the Import of Terror* (Cambridge, 2013), p. 6.

25. Scott, *The Birth of a Great Power System, 1740–1815* (Harlow, 2006), pp. 8–12.

26. G. Parker, 'Military Revolutions, Past and Present', *Historically Speaking*, 4 (2003), pp. 2–6.

27. N.A.M. Rodger, 'From the "Military Revolution" to the "Fiscal-Naval State"', *Journal for Maritime Research*, 13 (2011), pp. 119–28.

28. D.A. Baugh, 'Naval Power: What Gave the British Naval Superiority?', in L.P. de la Escosura, ed., *Exceptionalism and Industrialisation: Britain and Its European Rivals, 1688–1815* (Cambridge, 2004), pp. 236, 249–51; M. Duffy, 'The Establishment of the Western Squadron as the Linchpin of British Naval Strategy', in M. Duffy, ed., *Parameters of British Naval Power, 1650–1850* (Exeter, 1992), pp. 60–81.

29. Porter and Teich, eds., *The Enlightenment in National Context*.

Chapter 1: The Seventy Years War

1. F. Crouzet, 'The Second Hundred Years War: Some Reflections', *French History*, 10 (1996), pp. 432–50.

2. T. Harris, *Revolution: The Great Crisis of the British Monarchy, 1685–1720* (2006); S. Pincus, *1688: The First Modern Revolution* (New Haven, CT, 2009).

3. D.A. Baugh, 'Withdrawing from Europe: Anglo-French Maritime Geopolitics, 1750–1800', *International History Review*, 20 (1998), p. 1.

4. J.R. Dull, *The Age of the Ship of the Line: The British and French Navies, 1650–1815* (Lincoln, NE, 2009), p. 38.

5. A. Smith, *An Inquiry into the Nature and Causes of the Wealth of Nations* (2 vols., 1776), vol. II, p. 310.

6. Brewer, *Sinews of Power*, p. 27.

7. S. Conway, *War, State and Society in Mid-Eighteenth-Century Britain and Ireland* (Oxford, 2006), p. 1.

8. In comparison, in the 'Second Hundred Years War' 1689–1815 Britain was at war for 65 out of 126 years, or 51% of the time. D. Hay and N. Rogers, *Eighteenth-Century English Society* (Oxford, 1997), p. 152.

9. R. Pares, 'American versus Continental Warfare, 1739–63', *English Historical Review*, 51 (1936), p. 441.

10. J. Black, *Debating Foreign Policy in Eighteenth-Century Britain* (Farnham, 2011).

11. Most notably K. Wilson, *The Sense of the People* (1995).

12. B. Simms, *Three Victories and a Defeat: The Rise and Fall of the First British Empire* (Harmondsworth, 2007), p. 358.

13. Black, *Debating Foreign Policy*, pp. 215–31.

14. N.A.M. Rodger, 'The Continental Commitment in the Eighteenth Century', in L. Freedman, P. Hayes and R. O'Neill, eds., *War, Strategy and International Politics* (Oxford, 1992), p. 55.

15. Thompson, *Britain, Hanover and the Protestant Interest, 1688–1756* (Woodbridge, 2006); H. Smith, 'The Idea of a Protestant Monarchy', *Past and Present*, 185 (2004), pp. 91–118.

16. Thompson, *Britain, Hanover and the Protestant Interest*, p. 40.

17. The sash was made blue in John Wootton's painting of the battle. Simms, *Three Victories*, p. 319.

18. Simms, *Three Victories and a Defeat*, p. 315.

19. R. Harris, *A Patriot Press: National Politics and the London Press in the 1740s* (Oxford, 1997), p. 166.

20. R. Browning, *The War of the Austrian Succession* (Basingstoke, 1995), p. 210.

21. *Universal Register*, 27 July 1745, cited in Black, *Natural and Necessary Enemies*, p. 50.

22. Simms, *Three Victories*, p. 350.

23. H. Walpole to H. Mann, 27 Sept. 1745, in B.L. Blakeley and J. Collins, *Documents in British History*, vol. 2, p. 37.

24. J. Black, *Culloden and the '45* (Stroud, 2010), p. 135.

25. Colley, *Britons*, p. 76; A.E. MacRobert, 'The Myths about the 1745 Jacobite Rebellion', *Historian*, 99 (2008), pp. 16–23.

26. J. Stephen, 'Scottish Nationalism and Stuart Unionism: The Edinburgh Council, 1745', *Journal of British Studies*, 49 (2010), pp. 47–72.

27. A.E. MacRobert, *The 1745 Rebellion and the Southern Scottish Lowlands* (Ely, 2006), pp. 96–7.

28. J. Black, *What If? Counterfactualism and the Problem of History* (2008), pp. 116–35.

29. A. Macinnes, *Clanship, Commerce and the House of Stuart, 1603–1788* (East Linton, 1996), pp. 211–13.

30. G. Plank, *Rebellion and Savagery: The Jacobite Rising of 1745 and the British Empire* (Philadelphia, 2006).

31. J.R. Dull, *The French Navy and the Seven Years War* (Lincoln, NE, 2005), p. 6.

32. Baugh, 'Withdrawing from Europe', p. 13.

33. Duffy, 'The Establishment of the Western Squadron as the Linchpin of British Naval Strategy', pp. 60–81; R. Harding, *The Emergence of Britain's Global Naval Supremacy: The War of 1739–1748* (Martlesham, 2010).

34. M. Duffy, 'Contested Empires, 1756–1815', in P. Langford, ed., The *Eighteenth Century* (Oxford, 2001), p. 216.

35. Black, *Natural and Necessary Enemies*, pp. 51–2.

36. Simms, *Three Victories and a Defeat*, p. 359.

37. Conway, *War, State and Society*, p. 5.

38. D. Baugh, *The Global Seven Years War 1754–1763* (London, 2011), p. 1.

39. S. Brumwell, *George Washington: Gentleman Warrior* (New York, 2012), p. 78.

40. H. Walpole to H. Mann, 9 Feb. 1758, *Letters of Horace Walpole* (Lord Dover, ed., 1833), vol. II, p. 358.

41. Jones, *Great Nation*, p. 240.

42. J.W. Fortescue, *History of the British Army*, vol. I (reprint, Uckfield, 2006), pp. 495–6.

43. F. McLynn, *1759: The Year Britain became Master of the World* (London, 2004).

44. Samuel Kenrick to James Wodrow, 30 June 1759, Dr Williams's Library mss. 24.157 f. 32a.

45. N.A.M. Rodger, *The Command of the Ocean: A Naval History of Britain, 1649–1815* (London, 2005), p. 277.

46. B. James, 'The Battle that Gave Birth to an Empire', *History Today*, 59:12 (2009).

47. H. Walpole to H. Mann, 23 July 1761, *The Yale Edition of Horace Walpole's Correspondence* (ed. W.S. Lewis, New Haven, 1937–83), XXI, p. 518.

48. J. Black, *George III: America's Last King* (New Haven, CT, 2006), p. 44.

49. Black, *George III*, pp. 55, 58.

50. F. Thackeray, *A History of the Right Honourable William Pitt, Earl of Chatham* (2 vols, 1827), vol. II, p. 19.

51. J. Black, *Pitt the Elder* (Cambridge, 1992), p. 215.

52. Hardwicke to Newcastle, 18 April 1761, *The Life and Correspondence of Philip Yorke, Earl of Hardwicke* (London, 1977), vol. III, p. 317.

53. I. Mauduit, *Considerations on the Present German War* (1760), pp. 78, 56.

54. H.D. Schmidt, 'The Idea and Slogan of "Perfidious Albion"', *Journal of the History of Ideas*, 14 (1953), p. 608.

55. F. Spencer, 'The Anglo-Prussian Breach of 1762', *History*, 41 (1956), pp. 100–112.

56. R. Hyam, 'Imperial Interests and the Peace of Paris (1763)', in R. Hyam and G. Martin, *Reappraisals in British Imperial History* (1975), p. 25.

57. Hyam and Martin, *Reappraisals in British Imperial History*, p. 26.

58. M. Peters, *Pitt and Popularity* (Oxford, 1980), pp. 195–96, 255–56.

59. R. Hyam, 'The Primacy of Geopolitics: the Dynamics of British Imperial Policy, 1763–1963', *Journal of Imperial and Commonwealth History*, 27 (1999), pp. 27–52.

60. Hyam, *Reappraisals in British Imperial History*, p. 35.

61. B. Williams, *The Life of William Pitt, Earl of Chatham* (2 vols., 1913), vol. II, p. 147.

62. H.M. Scott, 'The Importance of Bourbon Naval Reconstruction to the Strategy of Choiseul after the Seven Years' War', *International History Review*, 1 (1979), pp. 17–35.

63. G.W. Rice, 'Deceit and Distraction: Britain, France and the Corsican Crisis of 1768', *International History Review*, 28 (2006), pp. 287–315.

64. A. Frost, *The Global Reach of Empire* (Melbourne, 2003), pp. 43–85; G. Blainey, *Sea of Dangers: Captain Cook and his Rivals* (Melbourne, 2008).

65. Scott, 'Britain's Emergence as a European Power', in H.T. Dickinson, ed., *A Companion to Eighteenth-Century Britain* (Oxford, 2002), p. 442.

66. Black, *A System of Ambition? British Foreign Policy, 1660–1793* (Harlow, 1991), p. 204.

67. J.P. Greene, 'The Seven Years War and the American Revolution: the Causal Relationship Reconsidered', *Journal of Imperial and Commonwealth History*, 8 (1980), pp. 85–105.

68. D. French, *The British Way in Warfare* (London, 1990), p. 63.

69. J.P. Greene, 'The British Revolution in America', in W.R. Louis, ed., *More Adventures with Britannia: Personalities, Politics and Culture in Britain* (Austin, TX, 1998), pp. 31–44.

70. D.H. Fischer, *Paul Revere's Ride* (Oxford, 1994), pp. 109–10.

71. J.J. Ellis, *Passionate Sage: The Character and Legacy of John Adams* (New York, 2001), p. 104.

72. S. Conway, *The War of American Independence 1775–1783* (London, 1995).

73. French, *British Way in Warfare*, p. 68.

74. D. Armitage, *The Declaration of Independence: A Global History* (Cambridge, MA, 2007); E.H. Gould, *Among the Powers of the Earth: The American Revolution and the Making of a New World Empire* (Chapel Hill, NC, 2012), p. 111–44.

75. S. Conway, 'British Governments and the Conduct of the American War', in H.T. Dickinson, ed., *Britain and the American Revolution* (London, 1998), pp. 171–2.

76. R. Price to Lord Shelburne, 21 Aug. 1779, in *The Correspondence of Richard Price*, ed. W.B. Peach and D.O. Thomas, 3 vols., (Durham, NC, 1991), vol. II, p. 50.

77. M. Balderston and D. Syrett, eds., *The Lost War: Letters from British Officers during the American Revolution* (New York, 1975), p. 183.

78. A.J. O'Shaughnessy, *An Empire Divided: The American Revolution and the British Caribbean* (Philadelphia, 2000).

79. Conway, 'Conduct of the American War', in Dickinson, ed., *Britain and the American Revolution*, p. 167.

80. S. Conway, ' "A Joy Unknown for Years Past": the American War, Britishness and the Celebration of Rodney's Victory at the Saints', *History*, 86 (2001), pp. 180–99; E.H. Gould, *The Persistence of Empire* (Chapel Hill, NC, 2000).

81. J.H. Owen, 'Operations of the Western Squadron, 1781–82', *Naval Review*, 15 (1927), pp. 33–53.

82. Conway, 'A Joy Unknown for Years Past', p. 186.

83. T. Bickham, *Making Headlines* (DeKalb, IL, 2009), pp. 173–75; J. Bonehill, 'Exhibiting War: John Singleton Copley's *The Siege of Gibraltar* and the Staging of History', in J. Bonehill and G. Quilley, eds., *Conflicting Visions: War and Visual Culture in Britain and France, 1700–1830* (Aldershot, 2005), pp. 139–68.

84. A. Stockley, 'Shelburne, the European Powers, and the Peace of 1783', in N. Aston, and C. Campbell Orr, eds., *An Enlightenment Statesman in Whig Britain: Lord Shelburne in Context, 1737–1805* (Woodbridge, 2011), p. 177.

85. P. Langford, *The Eighteenth Century, 1688–1815* (London, 1976), p. 180.

86. Chatham had collapsed during his last speech in the House of Lords condemning a Rockinghamite call to recognise American independence, and died soon after.

87. J. Cannon, 'The Loss of America', in Dickinson, ed., *Britain and the American Revolution*, pp. 233–57; Bickham, *Making Headlines*, ch. 6; A. Stockley, *Britain and France at the Birth of America: The European Powers and the Peace Negotiations of 1782–1783* (Exeter, 2001).

88. M. Jasanoff, *Liberty's Exiles: American Loyalists in the Revolutionary World* (New York, 2011), p. 80.

89. G. Selwyn cited in L.G. Mitchell, *Charles James Fox* (Oxford, 1992), p. 46.

90. J. Black, *British Foreign Policy in an Age of Revolutions, 1783–1793* (Cambridge, 1994), p. 30.

91. W. Pitt to W. Eden, 14 Sept. 1787, cited in J. Ehrman, *Pitt the Younger: The Years of Acclaim* (Stanford, CA, 1969), p. 534.

92. Frost, *Global Reach of Empire*, p. 230.

93. *Cobbett's Parliamentary History*, vol. 29, p. 826.

94. C. Fox to R. Fitzpatrick, 30 July 1789, cited in Mitchell, *Charles James Fox*, p. 111.

95. Black, *British Foreign Policy in an Age of Revolutions*, pp. 413–71.

96. Ehrman, *Pitt the Younger*, vol. II, pp. 233–34.

97. L. and M. Frey, ' "The Reign of the Charlatans is Over": the French Revolutionary Attack on Diplomatic Practice', *Journal of Modern History*, 55 (1993), pp. 706–44.

98. M. Duffy, 'William Pitt and the Origins of the Loyalist Association Movement of 1792', *Historical Journal*, 39 (1996), pp. 943–62.

99. *Cobbett's Parliamentary History*, vol. 30, pp. 182, 188–9.

100. *Cobbett's Parliamentary History*, vol. 30, pp. 232, 236.

101. E.V. Macleod, *A War of Ideas: British Attitudes to the Wars Against Revolutionary France, 1792–1802* (Aldershot, 1998), ch. 2.

102. H.T. Dickinson, *Britain and the French Revolution, 1789–1815* (London, 1989), p. 150.

103. Rodger, *Command of the Ocean*, p. 427.

104. T.C.W. Blanning, *The French Revolutionary Wars, 1787–1802* (Sevenoaks, 1996), pp. 100–101.

105. P. Higonet, *Goodness beyond Virtue: Jacobins during the French Revolution* (Cambridge, MA, 1998).

106. Over quarter of a million died in the Vendée. D. Andress, *The Terror* (New York, 2005), pp. 244–51.

107. George III to W. Pitt, 14 Sept. 1793, cited in Macleod, *War of Ideas*, p. 48.

108. Lord Auckland to Lord Henry Spencer, 6 Oct. 1794, *The Journal and Correspondence of William, Lord Auckland*, vol. III, p. 247.

109. Rodger, *Command of the Ocean*, p. 430.

110. Rodger, *Command of the Ocean*, p. 436.

111. M. Duffy, *Soldiers, Sugar and Seapower: The British Expeditions to the West Indies and the War Against Revolutionary France* (Oxford, 1987).

112. *Evening Mail*, 3 March 1797.

113. R. Knight, *The Pursuit of Victory: The Life and Achievement of Horatio Nelson* (Harmondsworth, 2005), p. 232.

114. Rodger, *Command of the Ocean*, pp. 445–53, 456. After the mutinies discipline became stricter and relations between officers and men more strained.

115. E.P. Thompson, *The Making of the English Working Class* (London, 1963), p. 188.

116. C. Cornwallis to Major-General Ross, in *Correspondence of Charles, First Marquis Cornwallis* (ed. Charles Ross, 3 vols., 2nd edn, 1859), vol. II, p. 358.

117. Rodger, *Command of the Ocean*, p. 460; Knight, *Pursuit of Victory*, p. 303.

118. Blanning, *French Revolutionary Wars*, p. 260.

119. Frost, *Global Reach of Empire*, pp. 237–41.

120. B. Simms, 'Britain and Napoleon', in P. Dwyer, ed., *Napoleon and Europe* (Harlow, 2001), p. 190.

121. C. Esdaile, *Napoleon's Wars* (London, 2007), pp. 140–54, cited at p. 154.

122. M. Philp, *Resisting Napoleon: The British Response to the Threat of Invasion, 1797–1815* (Aldershot, 2006).

123. Rodger, *Command of the Ocean*, p. 543.

124. Collins, *War and Empire*, p. 241.

125. Ehrman, *Younger Pitt*, vol. III, p. 635.

126. Duffy, 'World-Wide War and British Expansion, 1793–1815', p. 192.

127. Collins, *War and Empire*, p. 218.

128. R. Hopton, *The Battle of Maida 1806* (London, 2002), pp. 160–64.

129. On the Tory party in this period see F. O'Gorman, *The Long Eighteenth Century: British Political and Social History, 1688–1832* (London, 1997), p. 284.

130. Esdaile, *Napoleon's Wars*, p. 312.

131. M. Duffy, 'British Diplomacy and the French Wars 1789–1815', in Dickinson, ed., *Britain and the French Revolution*, pp. 140–41.

132. Pitt's speech 21 June 1805, in Coupland, *War Speeches of William Pitt the Younger* (Oxford, 1915), p. 345; Near the end of the war Castlereagh reworked Pitt's proposal to the Russians in January 1805 as the basis for a 'Concert of Europe' committed to the defeat of Napoleon. Ehrman, *The Younger Pitt*, vol. III, pp. 726–35.

133. Cited in J. Bew, *Castlereagh* (London, 2011), p. 249.

134. Bew, *Castlereagh*, pp. 207–20.

135. R. Muir, *Wellington: The Path to Victory* (New Haven, CT, 2013).

136. P. Mackesy, 'Strategic Problems of the British War Effort', in Dickinson, ed., *Britain and the French Revolution*, pp. 163–4.

137. A. Zamoyski, *1812: Napoleon's Fatal March on Moscow* (New York, 2005) provides a riveting account of this campaign.

138. *Correspondence, Despatches and Other Papers of Viscount Castlereagh* (1853), vol. IX, p. 41.

139. Black, 'British Strategy and the Struggle with France 1793–1815', *Journal of Strategic Studies*, 31 (2008), p. 565.

140. Langford, *Eighteenth Century*, p. 232.

141. Bew, *Castlereagh*, p. 358.

142. Bew, *Castlereagh*, p. 408.

143. Earl of Harrowby to Earl Bathurst, 16 Jan. 1814, *H.M.C Report on the Manuscripts of Earl Bathurst* (1923), p. 261.

144. N. Gash, 'Wellesley , Arthur, first Duke of Wellington (1769–1852)', *Oxford Dictionary of National Biography* (Oxford, 2004; online edn, January 2011).

145. Duffy, 'Contested Empires', in Langford, ed., *Eighteenth Century*, p. 239.

146. J. Black, *Louis XIV to Napoleon: The Fate of a Great Power* (London, 1999).

Chapter 2: The Fiscal-Naval State

1. Cited in P.K. O'Brien and S.L. Engerman, 'Exports and the Growth of the British Economy from the Glorious Revolution to the Peace of Amiens', in B.L. Solow, ed., *Slavery and the Rise of the Atlantic system* (Cambridge, 1991), p. 177.
2. For a survey of scholarship see H. Zmora, *Monarchy, Aristocracy and the State in Europe, 1300–1800* (New York, 2001).
3. Key works include G. Parker, *The Military Revolution: Military Innovation and the Rise of the West, 1500–1800* (Cambridge, 1988); idem. 'Military Revolutions, Past and Present', *Historically Speaking*, 4 (2003), pp. 2–6; J. Black, *A Military Revolution? Military Change and European Society 1550–1800* (Basingstoke, 1990).
4. A. Starkey, *War in the Age of Enlightenment, 1700–1789* (Westport, CT, 2003), p. 35.
5. M. Mann, 'State and Society, 1130–1815: an Analysis of English State Finances', *Political Power and Social Theory*, 1 (1980), p. 196.
6. Brewer, *Sinews of Power*, p. 250.
7. P.K. O'Brien, 'Fiscal and Financial Preconditions for the Rise of British Naval Hegemony, 1485–1815', London School of Economics, Working Paper No. 91, 2005, p. 37; Rodger, 'From the "Military Revolution" to the "Fiscal-Naval State"', pp. 119–28.
8. See my detailed discussion in A. Page, 'The Seventy Years War, 1744–1815, and Britain's Fiscal-Naval State', *War and Society*, 34:3 (2015).
9. P.K. O'Brien and X. Duran, 'Total Factor Productivity for the Royal Navy from Victory at Texel (1653) to Triumph at Trafalgar (1805)', in R.W. Unger, ed., *Shipping and Economic Growth 1350–1850* (Leiden, 2011), pp. 280–83.
10. B. Yun-Casalilla and P.K. O'Brien, eds., *The Rise of Fiscal States: A Global History 1500–1914* (Cambridge, 2012), p. 453.
11. J.C. Riley, *The Seven Years War and the Old Regime in France* (Princeton, NJ, 1986), pp. 13–23; J. Horn, *The Path Not Taken: French Industrialisation in the Age of Revolution* (Cambridge, MA, 2006), pp. 60–63.
12. J. Macdonald, *A Free Nation Deep in Debt: The Financial Roots of Democracy* (New York, 2003), p. 239.
13. R. Bonney, 'Towards the Comparative Fiscal History of Britain and France during the "Long" Eighteenth Century', in Escosura, ed., *Exceptionalism and Industrialisation* (2004), p. 209.
14. P. Harling and P. Mandler, 'From "Fiscal Military" State to Laissez-faire State, 1760–1850', *British Journal of British Studies*, 32 (1993), p. 48.
15. R. Bonney, 'The Eighteenth Century. II. The Struggle for Great Power Status and the End of the Old Fiscal Regime', in R. Bonney, ed., *Economic Systems and State Finance* (Oxford, 1995), p. 382.
16. W. Prest, *Albion Ascendant: English History 1660–1815* (Oxford, 1998), p. 157.
17. P. Langford, *Public Life and the Propertied Englishman* (Oxford, 1991); J. Cookson, *The British Armed Nation, 1793–1815* (Oxford, 1997).
18. P.J. Marshall, 'The British State Overseas, 1750–1850', in B. More and H. van Nierop, eds., *Colonial Empires Compared: Britain and the Netherlands, 1750–1850* (Aldershot, 2003), pp. 171–84.
19. J. Innes, *Inferior Politics: Social Problems and Social Polities in Eighteenth-Century Britain* (Oxford, 2009), pp. 49–53, cited p. 51.

20. Conway, *War, State and Society*, ch. 2.
21. J. Hoppit, 'The Nation, the State and the First Industrial Revolution', *Journal of British Studies*, 50 (2011), pp. 315–16.
22. J. Innes, 'Parliament and the Shaping of Eighteenth-Century English Social Policy', in *Inferior Politics*, pp. 21–47.
23. D. Eastwood, '"Amplifying the Province of the Legislature": the Flow of Information and the English State in the Early Nineteenth Century', *Historical Research*, 62 (1989), pp. 276–94.
24. J. Innes, 'Legislating for Three Kingdoms: how the Westminster Parliament Legislated for England, Scotland and Ireland, 1707–1830', in J. Hoppit, ed., *Parliaments, Nations and Identities in Britain and Ireland, 1660–1850* (Manchester, 2003), p. 40.
25. P. Mathias and P.K. O'Brien, 'Taxation in England and France. 1715–1810', *Journal of European Economic History*, 5 (1976), pp. 608–13; P.K. O'Brien, 'Fiscal, Financial and Monetary Foundations for the Formation of Nation States in the West Compared to Imperial States in the East c.1415–c.1839', *Journal of Chinese Economic and Business Studies*, 11 (2013), pp. 161–68.
26. Macdonald, *Free Nation Deep in Debt*, pp. 253–54; for a discussion of the difficulties involved in comparative finance, see Bonney, 'Comparative Fiscal History', in Escosura, ed., *Exceptionalism and Industrialisation* (2004), pp. 191–215.
27. P.K. O'Brien, 'The Political Economy of British Taxation, 1660–1815', *Economic History Review*, 1 (1988), p. 3.
28. P.K. O'Brien, 'The Nature and Historical Evolution of an Exceptional Fiscal State and its Possible Significance for the Precocious Commercialization and Industrialization of the British Economy from Cromwell to Nelson', *Economic History Review*, 64 (2011), pp. 427–8.
29. P.K. O'Brien and P.A. Hunt, 'The Rise of a Fiscal State in England, 1485–1815', *Historical Research*, 66 (1993), pp. 87–8.
30. M. Daunton, 'The Politics of British Taxation, from the Glorious Revolution to the Great War', in Yun-Casalilla and O'Brien, eds., *The Rise of Fiscal States*, p. 119.
31. O'Brien, 'Britain's Exceptional Fiscal State', p. 429. In the 1790s import duties rose to nearly 40% of total tax and dropped back to near 30% following the introduction of income tax, while domestic indirect tax dropped to around 40% of total tax revenue.
32. Brewer, *Sinews of Power*, p. 66.
33. T. Paine, *The Thomas Paine Reader* (I. Kramnick, ed., 1987), p. 42.
34. Bonney, 'Comparative Fiscal History of Britain and France', in Escosura, ed., *Exceptionalism and Industrialisation* (2004), p. 196.
35. W.M. Ormrod, 'The West European Monarchies in the Later Middle Ages', in R. Bonney, ed., *Economic Systems and State Finance* (Oxford, 1995), p. 129.
36. O'Brien, 'Political Economy of British Taxation', pp. 12–13.
37. F. Capie, 'Money and Economic Development in Eighteenth-Century England', in Escosura, ed., *Exceptionalism and Industrialisation*, pp. 216–32.
38. O'Brien, 'Political Economy of British Taxation', p. 6.
39. Mathias and O'Brien, 'Taxation in Britain and France', pp. 610–50.
40. Daunton, 'Politics of British Taxation', in Yun-Casalilla and O'Brien, eds., *Rise of Fiscal States*, p. 112.

41. M. Sonenscher, *Before the Deluge: Public Debt, Inequality, and the Intellectual Origins of the French Revolution* (Princeton, NJ, 2007), pp. 6–7.

42. Macdonald, *Free Nation Deep in Debt*, p. 241.

43. Daunton, 'Politics of British Taxation', in Yun-Casalilla and O'Brien, eds., *Rise of Fiscal States*, p. 120.

44. Macdonald, *Free Nation Deep in Debt*, p. 252.

45. F.R. Velde and D.R. Weir, 'The Financial Market and Government Debt Policy in France, 1746–1793', *Journal of Economic History*, 52 (1992), pp. 1–39, cited p. 8.

46. J. Wells and D. Wills, 'Revolution, Restoration, and Debt Repudiation: the Jacobite threat to England's Institutions and Economic Growth', *Journal of Economic History*, 60 (2000), pp. 418–41, Defoe cited at p. 428.

47. Daunton, 'Politics of British Taxation', in Yun-Casalilla and O'Brien, eds., *Rise of Fiscal States*, p. 116.

48. J. Hoppit, 'Financial Crises in Eighteenth-Century England', *Historical Journal*, 39 (1986), p. 56.

49. L. Sutherland, 'The City of London in Eighteenth-Century Politics', in R. Pares and A.J.P. Taylor, eds., *Essays Presented to Sir Lewis Namier* (1956), pp. 50–53.

50. P.G.M. Dickson, *The Financial Revolution in England* (1967), pp. 229–45.

51. D. Hume, 'Of Public Credit', in *Essays Moral, Political and Literary* (Indianapolis, 1985), p. 362.

52. Richard Price to William Pitt, Earl of Chatham, 11 March 1773, in *Correspondence of Richard Price*, I, p. 157.

53. O'Brien, 'Political Economy of British Taxation', p. 4. Only during the Napoleonic War, following the introduction of income tax, did borrowing drop to 42% of additional wartime revenue.

54. In 1946 British public debt peaked at 252%, J.E. King, 'Four Theses on the Global Financial Crisis', in S. Kates, ed., *The Global Financial Crisis: What Have We Learnt?* (Cheltenham, 2011), p. 131; P.K. O'Brien, 'Contentions of the Purse between England and its European Rivals from Henry V to George IV', *Journal of Historical Sociology*, 19 (2006), p. 360.

55. F. Crouzet, 'The Sources of England's Wealth: Some French Views in the Eighteenth Century', in P.L. Cottrell and D.H. Aldcroft, eds., *Shipping, Trade and Commerce* (Leicester, 1981), p. 72.

56. Black, *Culloden*, pp. 123–4.

57. French, *British Way in Warfare*, p. 51.

58. Bonney, 'Struggle for Great Power Status', p. 386.

59. G. Daly, 'Napoleon and the "City of Smugglers", 1810–1814', *Historical Journal*, 50 (2007), pp. 333–52.

60. Bonney, 'Comparative Fiscal History of Britain and France', in Escosura (ed.), *Exceptionalism and Industrialisation* (2004), p. 196.

61. M.D. Bordo and E.N. White, 'A Tale of Two Currencies: British and French Finance During the Napoleonic Wars', *Journal of Economic History*, 51 (1991), p. 315.

62. J. Mokyr, *The Enlightened Economy: an Economic History of Britain, 1700–1850* (New Haven, CT, 2009), p. 435.

63. H. Dundas to W. Pitt, 9 July 1794, in A. Aspinall, ed., *English Historical Documents: 1783–1832* (1959), p. 124.

64. L. Stone, 'Introduction', in *An Imperial State at War: Britain from 1689 to 1815* (New York, 1993), p. 6.

65. S. Conway, 'Checking and Controlling British Military Expenditure, 1739–1783', in R.T. Sanchez, ed., *War, State and Development: Fiscal-Military States in the Eighteenth Century* (Pamplona, 2007), p. 45. For some fine examples see: R. Morriss, *The Foundations of British Maritime Ascendancy* (Cambridge, 2011); R. Knight and M. Wilcox, *Sustaining the Fleet, 1793–1815: War, the British Navy and the Contractor State* (Woodbridge, 2010); H.V. Bowen and A.G. Enciso, eds., *Mobilising Resources for War: Britain and Spain at Work during the Early Modern Period* (Pamplona, 2006).

66. E. Charters, 'The Caring Fiscal-Military State during the Seven Years War, 1756–1763', *Historical Journal*, 52 (2009), pp. 921–41.

67. T. Pennant cited in A. Page, 'The Dean of St Asaph's Trial: Libel and Politics in the 1780s', *Journal for Eighteenth-Century Studies*, 32 (2009), p. 28.

68. Charters, 'Caring Fiscal-Military State', p. 928.

69. R Lamb, *Journal of Occurrences during the Late American War* (Dublin, 1809), p. 135.

70. Captain J. Bowater to Lord Denbigh, 22 May 1777, in Balderstone, *Lost War*, p. 124.

71. Wellington to C. Stuart, *The Dispatches of Field Marshal the Duke of Wellington* (ed. J. Gurwood, 13 vols, 1837), VII, p. 394.

72. Charters, 'Caring Fiscal-Military State', p. 941.

73. D. Parrott, *The Business of War: Military Enterprise and Military Revolution in Early Modern Europe* (Cambridge, 2012).

74. Knight and Wilcox, *Sustaining the Fleet*, p. 5.

75. D. Hancock, *Citizens of the World: London Merchants and the Integration of the British Atlantic Community, 1735–1785* (Cambridge, 1997), pp. 226–7, 236–7.

76. G.E. Bannerman, 'The "Nabob of the North": Sir Lawrence Dundas as Government Contractor', *Historical Research*, 83 (2010), p. 102.

77. Knight and Wilcox, *Sustaining the Fleet*, p. 5.

78. Hancock, *Citizens of the World*, pp. 227, 238n.

79. Bannerman, 'Nabob of the North', pp. 120, 122.

80. G.E. Bannerman, *Merchants and the Military in Eighteenth-Century Britain: British Army Contracts and Domestic Supply, 1739–1763* (2007), p. 48; Knight and Wilcox, *Sustaining the Fleet*, pp. 212–13.

81. R.J.B. Knight, 'Civilians and the Navy, 1660–1832', in P.G.W. Annis, ed., *Sea Studies* (Greenwich, 1983), p. 63.

82. For example, R. Knight, *Britain Against Napoleon: the Organization of Victory, 1793–1815* (2013).

83. C. Buchet, *The British Navy, Economy and Society in the Seven Years War* (Woodbridge, 2013), pp. 253–5.

84. H.M. Little, 'The Emergence of a Commissariat during the Seven Years War in Germany', *Journal of the Society for Army Historical Research*, 61 (1983/84), p. 205.

85. Report cited in Little, 'Emergence of a Commissariat', p. 206.

86. Conway, *War, State and Society*, p. 123.

87. S. Foote, *The Commissary* (1765), p. 13.

88. R.A. Bowler, 'The American Revolution and British Army Reform', *Journal of the Society for Army Historical Research*, 58 (1980), pp. 66–77.

89. Knight and Wilcox, *Sustaining the Fleet*, p. 55.

90. D. Syrett, *Shipping and the American War, 1775–83* (1970), p. 78.

91. Morriss, *Foundations of British Maritime Ascendancy*, p. 77.

92. Morriss, *Foundations of British Maritime Ascendancy*, p. 397.
93. J. Torrance, 'Social Class and Bureaucratic Innovation: the Commissioners for Examining the Public Accounts, 1780–1787', *Past and Present*, 78 (1978), pp. 56–81.
94. Morriss, *Foundations of British Maritime Ascendancy*, pp. 12, 193–5.
95. J.R. Breihan, 'William Pitt and the Commission on Fees, 1785–1801', *Historical Journal*, 27 (1984), pp. 59–81.
96. The late eighteenth century rational reformer, William Godwin, praised Pitt for 'a considerable reform of the pay-office, which of all others is most liable to abuse'. W. Godwin, *The History of the Life of William Pitt, Earl of Chatham* (1783), p. 43.
97. L.S. Sutherland, 'Henry Fox as Paymaster General of the Forces', *English Historical Review*, 70 (1955), p. 254.
98. Williams, *Life of Pitt*, pp. 152–7.
99. Bartlett, 'Development of the British Army', pp. 71–4.
100. Harling and Mandler, ' "Fiscal-Military" State to Laissez-faire State', p. 54.
101. R. Morriss, *Naval Power and British Culture, 1760–1850* (Aldershot, 2004), pp. 3–5, 147–77.
102. P. Harling, 'Parliament, the State, and "Old Corruption": Conceptualizing Reform, c. 1790–1832', in A. Burns and J. Innes, *Rethinking the Age of Reform: Britain 1780–1850* (Oxford, 2003), pp. 98–113.
103. M. Daunton, 'The Wealth of the Nation', in Langford, ed., *The Eighteenth Century*, p. 143.
104. M.J. Daunton, *Progress and Poverty: an Economic and Social History of Britain 1700–1850* (Oxford, 1995), p. 34.
105. E.P. Thompson, 'The Moral Economy of the English Crowd in the Eighteenth Century', *Past and Present*, 50 (1971), pp. 76–136.
106. J. de Vries, 'Between Purchasing Power and the World of Goods: Understanding the Household Economy in Early Modern Europe', in J. Brewer and R. Porter, *Consumption and the World of Goods* (New York, 1993), p. 112.
107. Daunton, *Progress and Poverty*, p. 329.
108. T. Hayter, *The Army and the Crowd in Mid-Georgian England* (1978).
109. R. Wells, *Wretched Faces: Famine in Wartime England, 1793–1801* (Gloucester, 1988), p. 265.
110. D. Hay, 'War, Dearth and Theft in the Eighteenth Century: the Record of the English Courts', *Past and Present*, 45 (1982), pp. 139, 126.
111. N. Rogers, *Mayhem: Post-War Crime and Violence in Britain, 1748–1753* (New Haven, CT, 2012), p. 213.
112. J.M. Beattie, *Crime and the Courts in England, 1660–1800* (Oxford, 1986), p. 230.
113. J.M. Beattie, *The First English Detectives: the Bow Street Runners and the Policing of London, 1750–1840* (Oxford, 2012).
114. H. Maxwell-Stewart, 'Convict Transportation from Britain and Ireland, 1615–1870, *History Compass*, 8 (2011), p. 1230.
115. M. Ignatieff, *A Just Measure of Pain: The Penitentiary in the Industrial Revolution, 1750–1850* (New York, 1978), pp. 86–98.
116. Innes, *Inferior Politics*, p. 68.
117. R. Harris, 'Government and the Economy', in R. Floud and P. Johnson, eds., *The Cambridge Economic History of Modern Britain, volume 1, Industrialisation, 1700–1860* (Cambridge, 2004), p. 221.

118. E. Royle, *Revolutionary Britannia? Reflections on the Threat of Revolution in Britain, 1789–1848* (Manchester, 2000), p. 106.
119. P.M. Solar, 'Poor Relief and English Economic Development: a Renewed Plea for Comparative History', *Economic History Review*, 50 (1997), pp. 373, 370.
120. P.H. Lindert, 'Poor Relief before the Welfare State: Britain versus the Continent, 1780–1880', *European Review of Economic History*, 2 (1998), pp. 101–40.
121. P.M. Solar, 'Poor Relief and English Economic Development before the Industrial Revolution', *Economic History Review*, 48 (1995), pp. 8–9.
122. Hay and Rogers, *Eighteenth-Century English Society*, p. 79.
123. C. Emsley, *British Society and the French Wars, 1793–1815* (London, 1979), p. 158.
124. N.F.R. Crafts and Knick Harley, 'Output Growth and the British Industrial Revolution: A Restatement of the Crafts–Harley View', *Economic History Review*, 45 (1992), pp. 703–30.
125. E. Griffin, *A Short History of the British Industrial Revolution* (Basingstoke, 2010) is an excellent introduction to the subject.
126. H.V. Bowen, *War and British Society, 1688–1815* (Cambridge, 1998), pp. 74–5.
127. T.S. Ashton, *Economic Fluctuations in England, 1700–1800* (Oxford, 1959), p. 83.
128. J. Jurado-Sánchez and M. Jerez-Méndez, 'Warfare, Economic Performance and the Struggle for World Hegemony in the Early Modern Period: Guns versus Butter in Eighteenth-Century Britain and Spain', *Defence and Peace Economics*, 23 (2012), pp. 389–412.
129. P.K. O'Brien, 'The Impact of the Revolutionary and Napoleonic Wars, 1793–1815, on the Long-Run Growth of the British Economy', *Review*, 12 (1989), pp. 355–56.
130. L. Neal, *The Rise of Financial Capitalism: International Capital Markets in the Age of Reason* (Cambridge, 1990), p. 223.
131. Bonney, 'Comparative Fiscal History of Britain and France', in Escosura (ed.), *Exceptionalism and Industrialisation* (2004), p. 214.
132. A. Smith, *An Inquiry into the Nature and Causes of the Wealth of Nations* (2 vols., 1776), II, pp. 291, 310–13.
133. P.K. O'Brien, 'Deconstructing the British Industrial Revolution as a Conjuncture and Paradigm for Global Economic History', in M.R. Smith, L.N. Rosenband and J. Horn, eds., *Reconceptualizing the Industrial Revolution* (Cambridge, MA, 2010), p. 24.
134. E.A. Wrigley, *Energy and the Industrial Revolution* (Cambridge, 2010).
135. P.K. O'Brien, 'Provincializing the First Industrial Revolution', London School of Economics, Working Papers of the Global Economic History Network, No. 17/06, 2006, p. 11.
136. S. Pincus, *1688: the First Modern Revolution* (New Haven, CT, 2009).
137. N.S. Poser, *Lord Mansfield: Justice in the Age of Reason* (Montreal, 2013), ch. 13.
138. J. Hoppit, 'Patterns of Parliamentary Legislation, 1660–1800', *Historical Journal*, 39 (1996), p. 126.
139. R.C. Allen, *The British Industrial Revolution in Global Perspective* (Cambridge, 2009), p. 5.
140. S. Quinn, 'Money, Finance and Capital Markets', in Floud and Johnson, *Cambridge Economic History of Modern Britain*, pp. 149, 168–71.

141. L. Neal, 'How it All Began: the Monetary and Financial Architecture of Europe during the First Global Capital Markets, 1648–1815', *Financial History Review*, 7 (2000), pp. 123–28, 136.

142. P. Temin and H.J. Voth, 'Credit Rationing and Crowding out during the Industrial Revolution: Evidence from Hoare's Bank, 1702–1862', *Explorations in Economic History*, 42 (2005), pp. 345–46.

143. See, for example, Mokyr, *Enlightened Economy*, p. 392.

144. N.A.M. Rodger, 'War as an Economic Activity in the Long Eighteenth Century', *International Journal of Maritime History*, 22 (2010), p. 13.

145. O'Brien, 'Impact of the Revolutionary and Napoleonic Wars', p. 366.

146. S. Broadberry, B.M.S. Campbell and B. van Leeuwen, 'When did Britain Industrialise? The Sectoral Distribution of the Labour Force and Labour Productivity in Britain, 1381–1851', *Explorations in Economic History*, 50 (2013), p. 26.

147. Griffin, *Short History*, p. 65; R.C. Allen, 'Agriculture during the Industrial Revolution', in Floud and Johnson, *Cambridge Economic History of Modern Britain*, p. 116.

148. E.A. Wrigley, 'British Population during the "Long" Eighteenth Century', in Floud and Johnson, *Cambridge Economic History of Modern Britain*, p. 89.

149. Rodger, 'War as an Economic Activity', pp. 14–15.

150. R.C. Allen, 'Britain's Economic Ascendancy in a European Context', in Escosura, ed., *Exceptionalism and Industrialisation*, pp. 27–34.

151. M. Berg, *Luxury and Pleasure in Eighteenth-Century Britain* (Oxford, 2007)

152. J. Guldi, *Roads to Power: Britain Invents the Infrastructure State* (Cambridge, MA, 2012), p. 4.

153. D.S. Jacks, 'Foreign Wars, Domestic Markets: England, 1793–1815', *European Review of Economic History*, 15 (2011), p. 281.

154. E. Williams, *Capitalism and Slavery* (1944).

155. K. Morgan, *Slavery, Atlantic Trade and the British Economy, 1660–1800* (Cambridge, 2000), pp. 53–4, 70.

156. R.A. Austen and W.D. Smith, 'Private Tooth Decay as Public Economic Virtue: the Slave–Sugar Triangle, Consumerism, and European Industrialization', *Social Science History*, 14 (1990), pp. 95–115.

157. J.E. Inikori, *Africans and the Industrial Revolution in England* (Cambridge, 2002), pp. 362–472.

158. Conway, *British Isles and American Independence*, p. 70.

159. J.C. Esteban, 'Comparative Patters of Colonial Trade: Britain and its Rivals', in Escosura, ed., *Exceptionalism and Industrialisation*, pp. 51–2.

160. D.J. Starkey, 'War and the Market for Seafarers in Britain, 1736–1792', in L.R. Fischer and H.W. Nordvik, eds., *Shipping and Trade 1750–1950* (Pontefract, 1990), p. 39.

161. J. Uglow, *The Lunar Men: the Friends who Made the Future* (London, 2002).

162. Bowen, *War and British Society*, pp. 71–72.

163. A.H. John, 'War and the English Economy, 1700–1763', *Economic History Review*, 7 (1955), pp. 331–3.

164. J.L. Anderson, 'Aspects of the Effect on the British Economy of the Wars Against France, 1793–1815', *Australian Economic History Review* 12 (1972), p. 15.

165. Bowen, *War and British Society*, pp. 67–9.

166. Anderson, 'Effect on the British Economy of the Wars Against France', p. 16.

167. C. Trebilcock, '"Spin-Off" in British Economic History: Armaments and Industry, 1760–1914', *Economic History Review*, 22 (1969), pp. 476–8.

168. John, 'War and the English Economy', p. 334s.

169. R.A. Mott and P. Singer, *Henry Cort, the Great Finer: Creator of Puddled Iron* (London: 1983), p. 40.

170. P. Dean, *The First Industrial Revolution* (Cambridge, 1969), p. 130.

171. Allen, *British Industrial Revolution*, pp. 272–5.

172. M.C. Jacob and L. Stewart, *Practical Matter: Newton's Science in the Service of Industry and Empire, 1687–1851* (Cambridge, MA, 2004).

173. Mokyr, *The Enlightened Economy*, p. 10.

174. Rodger, 'War as an Economic Activity', p. 10.

175. E.A. Wrigley, *Energy and the English Industrial Revolution* (Cambridge, 2010).

176. Allen, *British Industrial Revolution*.

177. Allen, *British Industrial Revolution*, p. 34.

178. O'Brien, 'The Impact of the Revolutionary and Napoleonic Wars', pp. 354–5. O'Brien suggests that the failure of real wages to rise in the period 1793–1815, despite 11–14% of adult males aged 20–45 being absorbed into the military, suggests there was a significant amount of unemployment in the 1780s.

179. Harling and Mandler, '"Fiscal-Military" State to Laissez-faire State', p. 44.

180. M. Daunton, 'The Entrepreneurial State, 1700–1914', *History Today*, 44 (June 1994), pp. 11–16.

181. Morris, *Foundations of British Maritime Ascendancy*, p. 402.

Chapter 3: Britain's Armed Forces

1. J. Nicol, *The Life And Adventures of John Nicol, Mariner*, ed. T. Flannery (Melbourne, 2012), pp. 169–70.

2. Brewer, *Sinews of Power*, pp. 34–5.

3. The best short survey is D.A. Baugh, 'The Eighteenth-Century Navy as a National Institution, 1690–1815', in J.R. Hill, ed., *The Oxford Illustrated History of the Royal Navy* (Oxford, 1995), pp. 120–60.

4. N. Rogers, 'The Dynamic of News in Britain during the American War: the Case of Admiral Keppel', *Parliamentary History*, 25 (2006), pp. 49–67.

5. C. Wilkinson, *The British Navy and the State in the Eighteenth Century* (Woodbridge, 2004), p. 208.

6. N.A.M. Rodger, *The Insatiable Earl: a Life of John Montagu, 4th Earl of Sandwich* (1994).

7. Wilkinson, *British Navy and the State*, p. 211.

8. N.A.M. Rodger, *The Wooden World: An Anatomy of the Georgian Navy* (1987), p. 110; Greenwich Hospital had been established in 1694 as a home for disabled seamen.

9. Rodger, *Command of the Ocean*, pp. 412–18.

10. J. Glete, *Navies and Nations* (2 vols, Stockholm, 1993), I, p. 311.

11. Rodger, *Command of the Ocean*, pp. 606–8.

12. J. Dull, 'Why did the French Revolutionary Navy Fail?', *Consortium on Revolutionary Europe 1750–1850: Proceedings*, 18 (1989), pp. 121–37.

13. Rodger, *Command of the Ocean*, p. 606.

14. Baugh, 'Naval Power' in Escosura, *Exceptionalism and Industrialisation*, p. 240.

15. Baugh, 'Naval Power', in Escosura, *Exceptionalism and Industrialisation*, p. 235.

16. Wilkinson, *British Navy and the State*, pp. 71–94.

17. R. Knight, 'The Introduction of Copper Sheathing into the Royal Navy, 1779–1786', *Mariner's Mirror*, 59 (1973), pp. 299–309.

18. Brewer, *Sinews of Power*, p. 35.

19. J. Glete, 'Europe and the Sea', in P.H. Wilson, ed., *A Companion to Eighteenth-Century Europe* (Oxford, 2008), p. 422.

20. Rodger, *Wooden World*, pp. 83–85.

21. C. Buchet, *The British Navy, Economy and Society in the Seven Years War* (Woodbridge, 2013), p. 55.

22. R. Morriss, *The Foundations of British Maritime Ascendancy: Resources, Logistics and the State, 1755–1815* (Cambridge, 2011), p. 76n.

23. R. Morriss, 'Colonization, Conquest, and the supply of Food and Transport: the Reorganization of Logistics Management, 1780–1795', *War in History*, 14 (2007), pp. 310–24.

24. A. Frost, *The Global Reach of Empire* (Melbourne, 2003).

25. Rodger, *Command of the Ocean*, pp. 638–39.

26. Baugh, 'National Institution', in Hill, *History of the Royal Navy*, p. 138.

27. D.J. Starkey, 'War and the Market for Seafarers in Britain, 1736–1792', in L.R. Fischer and H.W. Nordvik, eds., *Shipping and Trade 1750–1950* (Pontefract, 1990), pp. 25–42.

28. N. Roger, *The Press Gang: Naval Impressment and its Opponents in Georgian Britain* (New York, 2008).

29. W. Spavens, *Memoirs of a Seafaring Life*, ed. N.A.M. Rodger (London, 2000), p. 46.

30. J. Dancy, 'British Naval Manpower in the French Revolutionary Wars, 1793–1802' (Oxford, DPhil, 2012), p. 83.

31. Roger, *Wooden World*, pp. 158–9; W.J. Bolster, *Black Jacks: African American Seamen in the Age of Sail* (Cambridge, MA, 1997), pp. 30–32, 70–73.

32. O. Equiano, *The Interesting Narrative and Other Writings*, ed. V. Carretta (Harmondsworth, 2003), pp. 65–8, 84–5, 91–2.

33. N.A.M. Rodger, 'Introduction', *Memoirs of a Seafaring Life*; J. Hirst, *Freedom on the Fatal Shore: Australia's first Colony* (Melbourne, 2008).

34. Anderson, *Lineages of the Absolutist State*, p. 134; I. Land, *War, Nationalism, and the British Sailor, 1750–1850* (Basingstoke, 2009).

35. N. Frykman, 'Seamen on Late Eighteenth-Century European Warships', *International Review of Social History*, 54 (2009), pp. 67–93.

36. N.A.M. Rodger, 'Honour and Duty at Sea, 1660–1815', *Historical Research*, 75 (2002), p. 446.

37. C. Collingwood to J.E. Blackett, 27 June 1797, in G.L.N. Collingwood, ed., *A Selection of the Public and Private Correspondence of Vice-Admiral Lord Collingwood* (1828), p. 49.

38. Rodger, *Command of the Ocean*, p. 499.

39. Nicol, *Life and Adventures*, p. 175; Rodger, *Command of the Ocean*, p. 506.

40. Dancy, 'British Naval Manpower', pp. 58–9, 67–8.

41. Spavens, *Memoirs*, p. 99.

42. French, *British Way in Warfare*, p. 34.
43. Dancy, 'British Naval Manpower', p. 153; Dancy provides an excellent discussion of the numerous motives for volunteering, pp. 144–65.
44. Nicol, *Life and Adventures*, p. 23.
45. M. Estensen, *The Life of Matthew Flinders* (Sydney, 2002), p. 5.
46. W. Cobbett, *Life of Peter Porcupine* (Port Washington, NY), pp. 24–7.
47. J. Boswell, *Life of Johnson* (1859), vol 3, pp. 178–9.
48. E. Costello, *Rifleman Costello: The Adventures of a Soldier of the 95th (Rifles) in the Peninsular & Waterloo Campaigns of the Napoleonic Wars* (2005 [1841]), p. 21.
49. Rodger, 'Honour and Duty at Sea', p. 428.
50. H. Nelson to the Duke of Clarence, 26 May 1797, in C. White, ed., *Nelson: the New Letters* (Woodbridge, 2005), p. 195.
51. Rodger, *Wooden World*, ch. 7; A.B. McLeod, *British Naval Captains of the Seven Years' War* (Woodbridge, 2012), pp. 9–42.
52. J. Glete, 'Europe and the Sea', p. 427.
53. P.W. Bamford, *Forests and French Sea Power* (Toronto, 1956).
54. Scott, 'Bourbon Naval Reconstruction', pp. 20–23.
55. Dull, *Age of the Ship of the Line*, p. 114.
56. Baugh, 'Withdrawing from Europe', p. 13n.
57. Glete, 'Europe and the Sea', p. 421.
58. R. Harding, 'Sailors and Gentlemen of Parade: Some Professional and Technical Problems Concerning the Conduct of Combined Operations in the Eighteenth Century', *Historical Journal*, 32 (1989), p. 54.
59. J. Gregory and J. Stevenson, *The Longman Companion to Britain in the Eighteenth Century, 1688–1820* (Harlow, 2000), p. 195.
60. T. Hayter, 'The Army and the First British Empire' 1714–1783', in D. Chandler and I. Beckett, *Oxford History of the British Army* (Oxford, 1996), p. 112.
61. P. Wilson, 'Warfare in the Old Regime, 1648–1789', in J. Black, ed., *European Warfare, 1453–1815* (1999), pp. 75, 80.
62. Esdaile, *Napoleon's Wars*, p. 123.
63. I. Woloch, 'Napoleonic Conscription: State Power and Civil Society', *Past and Present*, 111 (1986), p. 126.
64. K. Linch, *Britain and Wellington's Army: Recruitment, Society and Tradition, 1807–15* (Basingstoke, 2011), p. 34.
65. D. Gates, 'The Transformation of the Army, 1793–1815', in Chandler and Beckett, *History of the British Army*, p. 139.
66. J.A. Fortescue, *The County Lieutenancies and the Army, 1803–1814* (1909), p. 269.
67. J.A. Houlding, *Fit for Service: the Training of the British Army, 1715–1795* (Oxford, 1981), p. 153.
68. J. Wolfe to W. Rickson, 9 June 1751, in R. Wright, *The Life of Major-General James Wolfe* (1864), p. 168.
69. E.M. Charters, 'Disease, Wilderness Warfare, and Imperial Relations: the Battle for Quebec, 1759–1760', *War in History*, 16 (2009), p. 17.
70. Brigadier-General Charles Lawrence, cited in S. Brumwell, 'The Scottish Military Experience in North America, 1756–1783', in E. Spiers and J. Crang, eds., *A Military History of Scotland* (Edinburgh, 2012), p. 397.
71. S. Conway, 'Britain and the Impact of the American War 1775–1783', *War in History*, 2 (1995), p. 139.

72. Brumwell, 'The Scottish Military Experience in North America', p. 390.
73. Harding, *Fit for Service*, p. 10.
74. A.J. Guy, 'The Irish Military Establishment, 1660–1776', in T. Bartlett and K. Jeffery, eds., *A Military History of Ireland* (Cambridge, 1997) pp. 228–9.
75. See the judicious discussion of this in I. McBride, *Eighteenth-Century Ireland* (Dublin, 2010), pp. 37–50.
76. A. Wellesley to Lord Hawksbury, 7 May 1807, in A.R. Wellington, ed., *Civil Correspondence and Memoranda of Field Marshal Arthur Duke of Wellington* (1860), p. 30.
77. Cited in S. J. Connolly, 'Varieties of Britishness: Ireland, Scotland and Wales in the Hanoverian State', in A. Grant and K. Stringer, eds., *Uniting the Kingdom? The Making of British History* (London, 1995), p. 207.
78. M. Snape, *The Redcoat and Religion: The Forgotten History of the British Soldier from the Age of Marlborough to the Eve of the First World War* (London, 2005), p. 10.
79. R.K. Donovan, 'The Military Origins of the Roman Catholic Relief Programme of 1778', *Historical Journal*, 28 (1985), pp. 79–102.
80. Conway, *War, State and Society*, pp. 202–3.
81. A.J. Guy, 'The Army of the Georges 1714–1783', in Beckett, *Oxford History of the British Army*, p. 104.
82. S. Brumwell, 'Rank and File: A Profile of One of Wolfe's Regiments', *Journal of the Society for Army Historical Research*, 79 (2001), p. 10n.
83. Conway, *War, State and Society*, p. 210; S. Brumwell, *Redcoats: The British Soldier and War in the Americas* (Cambridge, 2002), pp. 74, 318.
84. E.J. Coss, *All for the King's Shilling: the British soldier under Wellington, 1808–1814* (Norman, OK, 2010), p. 246.
85. Cited in L. Winstock, *Songs and Music of the Redcoats: A History of the War Music of the British Army* (London, 1970), p. 111.
86. William Wheeler to —, 20 June 1809, W. Wheeler, *The Letters of Private Wheeler, 1809–1828*, ed. B.H. Liddell Hart (London, 1951), p. 21.
87. J.E. Cookson, 'Service Without Politics? Army Militia and Volunteers in Britain During the American and French Revolutionary Wars', *War in History*, 10 (2003), p. 384: 'There is good evidence that the regiments self-consciously felt and cultivated a British identity where the wider society displayed much greater ambivalence.'
88. P.J. Marshall, *The Making and Unmaking of Empires: Britain, India and America c. 1750–1783* (Oxford, 2005), p. 66; Duffy, 'World-Wide War', p. 202.
89. Brumwell, *Redcoats*, pp. 76–7.
90. G.F. Tyson, 'The Carolina Black Corps: Legacy of Revolution (1782–1798)', *Interamericana Review*, 5 (1975–6), pp. 648–64.
91. R.N. Buckley, *The British Army in the West Indies* (Gainsville, FL, 1998), pp. 116–24.
92. W.E. Lee, *Barbarians and Brothers* (Oxford, 2011), pp. 215–31.
93. M. McCormack, 'Masculinity, Nationhood and Citizenship in the Affair of the Hanoverian Soldier, 1756', *Historical Journal*, 49 (2006), pp. 971–93.
94. J.H. Leslie, ed., 'Letters of Captain Philip Brown – 1737 to 1746', *Journal of the Society for Army Historical Research*, 5 (1926), p. 150.
95. Simms, *Three Victories and a Defeat*, p. 442.
96. S. Conway, 'Continental European Soldiers in British Imperial Service, c. 1756–1792', *English Historical Review*, 129 (2014), p. 95.

97. G. Hanger, *The Life, Adventures, and Opinions of Col. George Hanger*, ed. W. Combe (1801), p. 20.

98. Fortescue, *County Lieutenancies*, p. 269.

99. E.H. Gould, 'To Strengthen the King's Hands: Dynastic Legitimacy, Militia Reform and Ideas of National Unity in England 1745–1760', *Historical Journal*, 34 (1991), pp. 329–48.

100. Cited in N. Rogers, *Crowds, Culture and Politics in Georgian Britain* (Oxford, 1998), p. 78.

101. I. Beckett, *The Amateur Military Tradition, 1558–1945* (Manchester, 1991), p. 68.

102. Beckett, *Amateur Military Tradition*, p. 72.

103. Linch, *Britain and Wellington's Army*, p. 150.

104. J. Robertson, *The Scottish Enlightenment and the Militia Issue* (Edinburgh, 1985).

105. Though some fensible regiments were raised in the American war – regular army regiments that were confined to home defence.

106. Connolly, 'Varieties of Britishness', p. 193.

107. D.W. Miller, 'Non-Professional Soldiery, c. 1600–1800', in Bartlett and Jeffery, *Military History of Ireland*, pp. 324–32.

108. Cited in M. Durey, ' "Black Bob" Craufurd and Ireland, 1798–1804', *War in History*, 16 (2009), pp. 141–2.

109. S. Conway, 'British Mobilization in the War of American Independence', *Historical Research*, 72 (1999), p. 63.

110. Conway, 'Britain and the Impact of the American War', p. 130.

111. Colley, *Britons*, p. 294.

112. J. Cookson, 'British Society and the French Wars, 1793–1815', *Australian Journal of Politics & History*, 31 (1985), p. 196.

113. A. Gee, *The British Volunteer Movement, 1794–1814* (Oxford, 2003), pp. 47–50.

114. Houlding, *Fit for Service*, pp. 1–98.

115. R. Muir, *Wellington: The Path to Victory, 1769–1814* (New Haven, CT, 2013), pp. 533–6.

116. D. Ogg, *Europe of the Ancien Regime* (1965), p. 154.

117. J. Shy, *Toward Lexington: the Role of the British Army in the Coming of the American Revolution* (Princeton, NJ, 1965), p. 277.

118. S. Nicholas, ed., *Convict Workers: Reinterpreting Australia's Past* (Cambridge, 1988).

119. G. Daly, 'Plunder on the Peninsula: British Soldiers and Local Civilians during the Peninsular War, 1808–1813', in E. Charters, E. Rosenhaft and H. Smith, eds., *Civilians and War in Europe, 1618–1815* (Liverpool, 2012), pp. 209–24.

120. R. Lamb, *Memoir of His Own Life* (Dublin, 1811), p. 66.

121. Cited in D.E. Leach, *Roots of Conflict: British Armed Forces and Colonial Americans, 1677–1763* (Chapel Hill, NC, 1986).

122. Duke of Wellington to W. Wellesley-Pole, 19 June 1815, in *Wellington at War, 1794–1815: A Selection of His Wartime Letters* (ed. E.A.B. James, 1961), p. 168.

123. Cited in I.D. Gruber, ' "On the Road to Poonamalle" an Irish Officer's View of the War for American Independence', *The American Magazine*, 4 (1988), pp. 6–7.

124. 8 Feb. 1782, J. Peebles, *John Peebles' American War: the Diary of a Scottish Grenadier, 1776–1782*, ed. I.D. Gruber (Stroud, 1998), p. 507.

125. J. Woodward, *The Soldier's Monitor: Being Serious Advice to Soldiers to Behave Themselves with a Just Regard to Religion and True Manhood* (7th edn, 1773), p. 7.

126. H. Smith, 'The Army, Provincial Urban Communities, and Loyalist Cultures in England, c. 1714–50', *Journal of Early Modern History*, 15 (2011), p. 156.
127. Brumwell, *Redcoats*; Linch, *Britain and Wellington's Army*.
128. Coss, *King's Shilling*, p. 253.
129. Frey, *The British Soldier in America*, pp. 12–16.
130. Hay, 'War, Dearth and Theft', p. 141.
131. M. Dziennik, 'Hierarchy, Authority, and Jurisdiction in the mid Eighteenth-Century Recruitment of the Highland Regiments', *Historical Research*, 85 (2012), pp. 89–104.
132. M.P. Dziennik, 'Through an Imperial Prism: Land, Liberty, and Highland Loyalism in the War of American Independence', *Journal of British Studies*, 50 (2011), pp. 332–58.
133. Linch, *Britain and Wellington's Army*, p. 93.
134. Costello, *Rifleman Costello*, pp. 11–12.
135. Cited in Guy, 'Army of the Georges', p. 103.
136. C. Storrs and H.M. Scott, 'The Military Revolution and the European Nobility, c. 1600–1800', *War in History*, 3 (1996), pp. 16–17.
137. M. Glover, *Wellington's Army in the Peninsula, 1808–1814* (Newton Abbot, 1977), p. 37.
138. C. James, *The Regimental Companion* (3 vols, 7th edn, 1811), pp. 66–7.
139. M. Glover, *Peninsular Preparation: the Reform of the British Army, 1795–1809* (Cambridge, 1963), pp. 145–6.
140. P.J. Marshall, 'Empire and Opportunity in Britain, 1763–75', *Transactions of the Royal Historical Society*, 5 (1995), pp. 124–6.
141. D. Lambert and A. Lester, eds., *Colonial Lives Across the British Empire: Imperial Careering in the Long Nineteenth Century* (Cambridge, 2006).
142. I.D. Gruber, ' "On the Road to Poonamalle" an Irish Officer's View of the War for American Independence', *The American Magazine*, 4 (1988), p. 3.
143. Cited in S. Conway, 'British Army Officers and the American War for Independence', *William and Mary Quarterly*, 3rd ser., 41 (1984), p. 274.
144. Ibid., p. 276.
145. Glover, *Wellington's Army in the Peninsula 1808–1814*, p. 44.
146. S. Brumwell, *Paths of Glory: the Life and Death of General James Wolfe* (Kingston, Ontario, 2006).
147. Houlding, *Fit for Service*, p. 390.
148. B. Williams, *The Life of William Pitt, Earl of Chatham* (1913), I, p. 171.
149. Cookson, 'Service Without Politics?'.
150. W. Cobbett, *The Soldier's Friend* (1792), p. 21; Cobbett was probably only a co-author of this pamphlet, M. Dury, 'William Cobbett, Military Corruption and London Radicalism in the Early 1790s', *Proceedings of the American Philosophical Society*, 131 (1987), pp. 348–66.
151. Frey, *British Soldier in America*, pp. 117–23.
152. Brumwell, 'Rank and File', pp. 14–15.
153. W. Wheeler to —, 5 August 1809, in Wheeler, *Letters*, p. 28.
154. Linch, *Britain and Wellington's Army*, pp. 103–5.
155. Glover, *Peninsular Preparation*, p. 118.
156. K. Bartlett, 'The Development of the British Army during the Wars with France, 1793–1815' (PhD, Durham, 1997), p. 258.

157. M. Duffy, 'The Foundations of British Naval Power," in M. Duffy, ed. *The Military Revolution and the State, 1500–1800* (Exeter, 1980), pp. 49–90.

158. Costello, *Rifleman Costello*, p. 115.

159. T. Simes, *A Military Course for the Government and Conduct of a Battalion* (2nd edn, 1777), pp. 238–9n.

160. Frey, *British Soldier in America*, pp. 125–6.

161. H. Hoock, *Empires of the Imagination: Politics, War and the Arts in the British World, 1750–1850* (2010), pp. 94–5.

162. Coss, *King's Shilling*, p. 126.

163. Coss, *King's Shilling*, p. 44.

164. Hayter, 'Army and the First British Empire', p. 125.

165. Guy, 'Army of the Georges', p. 106; Houlding, *Fit for Service*, pp. 358–9.

166. Anon., *Journal of a Soldier of the 71st* (Edinburgh, 1819), p. 133.

167. See for example, Anon., *Journal of a Soldier of the 71st*, p. 127.

168. Edmund Wheatley cited in R. Holmes, *Redcoat: The British Soldier in the Age of Horse and Musket* (London, 2002), p. 53.

169. Coss, *King's Shilling*, p. 45.

170. R. Ingrams, *The Life and Adventures of William Cobbett* (London, 2005), p. 84.

171. Snape, *Redcoat and Religion*, p. 35.

172. Cited in C. Kennedy, *Narratives of the Revolutionary and Napoleonic Wars* (Basingstoke, 2013), p. 194.

173. K. Linch and M. McCormack, 'Defining Soldiers: Britain's Military, c. 1740–1815', *War in History*, 20 (2013), p. 159.

174. Hay and Rogers, *Eighteenth-Century English Society*, p. 158.

175. S. Brumwell, 'Home from the Wars', *History Today*, 52 (2002), p. 42.

176. Costello, *Rifleman Costello*, pp. 28–9.

177. J. Innes, *Inferior Politics*, p. 66.

178. Brumwell, 'Home from the Wars', pp. 44–5.

179. Brumwell, 'Home from the Wars', p. 44.

180. A. Eccles, *Vagrancy in Law and Practice Under the Old Poor Law* (Aldershot, 2012), pp. 75–80.

181. J. White, *A Great and Monstrous Thing: London in the Eighteenth Century* (Cambridge, MA, 2013), pp. 133, 202.

182. R. Costello, *Black Salt: Seafarers of African Descent on British Ships* (Liverpool, 2012), p. 77.

183. M.J. Cardwell, *Arts and Arms: Literature, Politics and Patriotism During the Seven Years War* (Manchester, 2004), p. 7.

184. Conway, 'Britain and the Impact of the American War', p. 130.

185. Conway, 'British Mobilization', p. 66; L. Colley, 'Whose Nation? Class and National Consciousness in Britain 1750–1830', *Past and Present*, 113 (1986), p. 101.

Chapter 4: Enlightenment, Evangelicalism and War

1. Snape, *Redcoat and Religion*, p. 244.

2. P. Gay, *The Party of Humanity* (New York, 1963).

3. R. Darnton, 'An Early Information Society: News and the Media in Eighteenth-Century Paris', *American Historical Review*, 105 (2000), pp. 1–35.

4. K. O'Brien, *Women and Enlightenment in Eighteenth-Century Britain* (Cambridge, 2009).
5. R. Porter and M. Teich, eds., *The Enlightenment in National Context* (Cambridge, 1981).
6. J. Israel, *Radical Enlightenment* (Oxford, 2001); idem., *Enlightenment Contested* (Oxford, 2006); idem., *Democratic Enlightenment* (Oxford, 2011).
7. M. Fitzpatrick, 'Enlightenment, Dissent and Toleration', *Enlightenment and Dissent*, 28 (2012), pp. 42–72.
8. H.F. May, *The Enlightenment in America* (Oxford, 1976), p. xiv.
9. M. Fitzpatrick, 'Reforming the World', in Fitzpatrick, *Enlightenment World*, p. 424.
10. J. Sheehan, *The Enlightenment Bible* (Princeton, 2005).
11. J.G.A. Pocock, 'Conservative Enlightenment and Democratic Revolutions: the American and French cases in British perspective', *Government and Opposition*, 24 (1989), pp. 81–105.
12. J. Gascoigne, *Joseph Banks and the English Enlightenment* (Cambridge, 2002).
13. Cited in B.W. Young, *Religion and Enlightenment in Eighteenth-Century England* (Oxford, 1998), p. 1.
14. *The Writings and Speeches of Edmund Burke* (ed. P. Langford, Oxford, 1981), II, p. 230.
15. E. Burke, 'Letters on a Regicide Peace', in I. Kramnick, ed., *The Portable Edmund Burke* (1999), p. 520.
16. D. Spadafora, *The Idea of Progress in Eighteenth-Century Britain* (New Haven, 1990); L. Wolfe, 'Discovering Cultural Perspective: the Intellectual History of Anthropological Thought in the Age of Enlightenment', L. Wolfe and M. Cipolloni, eds., *The Anthropology of the Enlightenment* (Stanford, CA, 2007), p. 10.
17. A. Smith, *Lectures on Jurisprudence* (ed. R.L. Meek and D.D. Raphael, Oxford, 1978), p. 14.
18. Cited in C. Kidd, 'The Ideological Significance of Robertson's *History of Scotland*', in S.J. Brown, *William Robertson and the Expansion of Empire* (Cambridge, 1997), p. 122.
19. J.G.A. Pocock, *Virtue, Commerce and History* (Cambridge, 1985), p. 115.
20. J.G.A. Pocock, *Barbarism and Religion: Volume I, the Enlightenments of Edward Gibbon, 1736–1764* (Cambridge, 1999), p. 7.
21. Macleod, *War of Ideas*, p. 18.
22. Starkey, *War in the Age of Enlightenment*; N.A.M. Rodger, 'Navies and the Enlightenment', in *Essays in Naval History, from Medieval to Modern* (Aldershot, 2009), ch. XIV, pp. 5–23.
23. E. de Vattel, *The Law of Nations; or, Principles of the Law of Nature: Applied to the Conduct and Affairs of Nations and Sovereigns* (3 vols., 1759), II, p. 59.
24. J.A. Lynn, *Battle: a History of Combat and Culture* (2003), p. 114–15.
25. A. Gat, *A History of Military Thought: from the Enlightenment to the Cold War* (Oxford, 2001), p. 69.
26. P. Speelman, *Henry Lloyd and the Military Enlightenment of Eighteenth-Century Europe* (Westport, CT, 2002).
27. I.D. Gruber, *Books and the British Army in the Age of the American Revolution* (2010), p. 3.
28. Gruber, *Books and the British Army*, p. 106.
29. I.D. Gruber, 'Classical Influences on British Strategy in the War for American Independence', in J.W. Eadie, ed., *Classical Traditions in Early America* (Ann Arbor, MI, 1976), p. 179.

30. C. Boutflower, *Journal of an Army Surgeon in the Peninsular War* (Driffield, 2009), pp. 13–14.

31. Gruber, *Books and the British Army*, pp. 30–2.

32. Cited in N.A.M. Rodger, 'The Naval Chaplain in the Eighteenth Century', *Journal for Eighteenth Century Studies*, 18 (1995), p. 36.

33. C. Kennedy, 'John Bull into Battle: Military Masculinity and the British Army Officer during the Napoleonic Wars', in K. Hagemann, G. Mettele and J. Rendall, eds., *Gender, War and Politics* (Basingstoke, 2010), p. 138.

34. M. McCormack, 'Dance and Drill: Polite Accomplishments and Military Masculinities in Georgian Britain', *Cultural and Social History*, 8 (2011), pp. 315–30, quoted p. 317.

35. Conway, *War, State and Society*, p. 124.

36. A. Vickery, 'Golden Age to Separate Spheres? A Review of the Categories and Chronology of English Women's History', *Historical Journal*, 36 (1993), pp. 383–414; B. Taylor and S. Knott, eds., *Women, Gender and Enlightenment* (Basingstoke, 2005).

37. L. Carter, 'Scarlet Fever: Female Enthusiasm for Men in Uniform, 1780–1815', in K. Linch and M. McCormack, eds., *Britain's Soldiers: Rethinking War and Society, 1715–1815* (Liverpool, 2014), pp. pp. 158–67, 179.

38. Starkey, *War in the Age of Enlightenment*, pp. 60–63.

39. Glover, *Peninsular Preparation*, pp. 122–9.

40. H. Strachan, 'Review of D. Gates, The British Light Infantry Arm, c. 1790–1815', *English Historical Review*, 106 (1991), p. 213.

41. Fortescue, *History of the British Army*, VI, p. 410.

42. J. Epstein, 'Politics of Colonial Sensation: the Trial of Thomas Picton and the Cause of Louisa Calderon', *American Historical Review*, 112 (2007), pp. 712–41.

43. R. Havard, *Wellington's Welsh General: a life of Thomas Picton* (1996), p. 225.

44. G.A. Steppler, 'British Military Law, Discipline, and the Conduct of Regimental Courts Martial in the Later Eighteenth Century', *English Historical Review*, 102 (1987), pp. 859–86.

45. J.D. Bryn, *Crime and Punishment in the Royal Navy: Discipline on the Leeward Islands Station, 1784–1812* (Aldershot, 1989), p. 108.

46. V. Smith, *Clean: a History of Personal Hygiene and Purity* (Oxford, 2007), pp. 262–3.

47. Rodger, *Wooden World*, pp. 105–9.

48. W.D. Churchill, 'Efficient, Efficacious and Humane Responses to Non-European Bodies in British Military Medicine, 1780–1815', *Journal of Imperial and Commonwealth History*, 40 (2012), pp. 137–58.

49. M. Jacob and L. Stewart, *Practical Matter: Newton's Science in the Service of Industry and Empire, 1687–1851* (Cambridge, MA, 2004).

50. Glover, *Peninsular Preparation*, pp. 73–5.

51. S. Schaffer, 'Instruments, Surveys and Maritime Empire', in D. Cannadine, ed., *Empire, the Sea and Global History* (Basingstoke, 2007), p. 86.

52. D.A. Baugh, 'Seapower and Science: the Motives for Pacific Exploration', in D. Howse, ed., *Background to Discovery: Pacific Exploration from Dampier to Cook* (Berkley, 1990), p. 34.

53. J. Gascoigne, *Science in the Service of Empire: Joseph Banks, the British State and the Use of Science in the Age of Revolution* (Cambridge, 1998).

54. P.J. Marshall and G. Williams, *The Great Map of Mankind: Perceptions of New Worlds in the Age of Enlightenment* (Cambridge, MA, 1982); G. Daly, 'Liberators and Tourists: British Soldiers in Madrid during the Peninsular War', in C. Kennedy and M. McCormack, eds., *Soldiering in Britain and Ireland, 1750–1850: Men of Arms* (Basingstoke, 2013), pp. 117–35.

55. Cited in A. Page, 'Enlightenment, Empire and Lachlan Macquarie's Journey through Persia and Russia', *History Australia*, 6 (2009), p. 70.6.

56. C. Pybus, *Black Founders: the Unknown Story of Australia's First Black Settlers* (Sydney, 2006), pp. 165–7.

57. K. Wilson, ed., *A New Imperial History: Culture, Identity and Modernity in Britain and the Empire, 1660–1840* (Cambridge, 2004), pp. 3–5.

58. D. Ghosh, *Sex and the Family in Colonial India* (Cambridge, 2006); C.A. Bayly, *Indian Society and the Making of the British Empire* (Cambridge, 1988), p. 78.

59. Glover, *Peninsular Preparation*, pp. 112–13.

60. G. Hennell, *A Gentleman Volunteer: Letters of George Hennell from the Peninsular War, 1812–1813* (ed. M. Glover, 1979), p. 17.

61. G. Plank, *Rebellion and Savagery: the Jacobite Rising of 1745 and the British Empire* (Philadelphia, 2006).

62. Captain J. Bowater to Lord Denbigh, 5 June and 23 July 1777, in Balderstone, *Lost War*, pp. 131, 138.

63. Captain William Glanville Evelyn, cited in S. Conway, 'To Subdue America: British Army Officers and the Conduct of the Revolutionary War', *William and Mary Quarterly*, 3rd ser. 43 (1986), p. 396.

64. Cited in E. Hay, *History of the Irish Insurrection of 1798* (1847), p. 406.

65. Cornwallis to the Duke of Portland, 16 Sept. 1798, in *Correspondence of Charles, First Marquis Cornwallis* (ed. Charles Ross, 3 vols., 2nd ed., 1859), II, p. 407.

66. Simms, *Three Victories*, p. 446.

67. G. Daly, *The British Soldier in the Peninsular War* (Basingstoke, 2013), pp. 135–6, 168–71, 213.

68. See, for example, A. Starkey, 'War and Culture, a Case Study: the Enlightenment and the Conduct of the British Army in America, 1755–1781', *War & Society*, 8 (1990), pp. 1–28.

69. Starkey, 'War and Culture', p. 10.

70. A. Starkey, 'Paoli to Stony Point: Military Ethics and Weaponry during the American Revolution', *Journal of Military History*, 58 (1994), pp. 7–27.

71. I.D. Gruber, 'The Education of Sir Henry Clinton', *Bulletin of the John Rylands University Library*, 72 (1990), p. 141.

72. H. Clinton, *Observations on Mr. Stedman's History of the American War* (1794), p. 6.

73. Bell, *First Total War*, p. 17.

74. R. Mackay and M. Duffy, *Hawke, Nelson and British Naval Leadership, 1747–1805* (Woodbridge, 2009), pp. 5, 11.

75. Rodger, *Wooden World*, p. 50.

76. Lynn, *Battle*, pp. 180–1.

77. A. Page, ' "Probably the Most Indefatigable Prince that Ever Existed": a Rational Dissenting Perspective on Frederick the Great', *Enlightenment and Dissent*, 23 (2007), pp. 85–130.

78. M. Durey, M., ' "Black Bob" Craufurd and Ireland, 1798–1804', *War in History*, 16 (2009), pp. 134–5, 153, 155.

79. Cited in P.J. Haythornthwait, *Wellington: the Iron Duke* (2007), p. 3.

80. Cookson, 'Regimental Worlds', p. 26; Rodger, *Wooden World*, p. 45; Allen, *British Industrial Revolution*, p. 53.

81. Rodger, *Command of the Ocean*, p. 212; Rodger, *Wooden World*, p. 45.

82. R.M. Wilson, 'Remarks on Board His Majesty's Ship *Unité* of 40 Guns', in H.G. Thusfield, ed., *Five Naval Journals, 1789–1817* (1951), p. 257.

83. Lincoln, *Naval Wives and Mistresses*, p. 123.

84. R. Marks, *Nautical Essays: or, a Spiritual View of the Ocean and Maritime Affairs* (1818), p. 26.

85. Equiano, *Interesting Narrative*, pp. 68, 78–9, 84–5.

86. Wheeler, *Letters*, pp. 46–7.

87. H. Melville, *Moby Dick, or The Whale* (ed. A. Delbanco and T. Quirk, Harmondsworth, 1992), p. 169.

88. Spavens, *Memoirs*, p. 118.

89. J. Peebles, *John Peebles' American War: the Diary of a Scottish Grenadier, 1776–1782* (ed. I.D. Gruber, Stroud, 1998), p. 507.

90. Lt. W. Fielding to Lord Denbigh, 19 January 1776, in Balderstone, *Lost War*, p. 58.

91. Snape, *Redcoat and Religion*, p. 143.

92. 23 August 1812, *Letters of Private Wheeler*, p. 94.

93. Wheeler, *Letters*, pp. 108–9.

94. J.G. Seume, 'Memoirs of a Hessian Conscript: J.G. Seume's Reluctant Voyage to America', *William and Mary Quarterly*, 5 (1948), p. 559.

95. Daly, *British Soldier*, p. 33.

96. W. St Clair, *The Reading Nation in the Romantic Period* (Cambridge, 2004), pp. 355, 157.

97. The following owes much to Snape, *Redcoat and Religion*; R. Blake, *Evangelicals in the Royal Navy, 1775–1815: Blue Lights and Psalm Singers* (Woodbridge, 2008).

98. P.E. Kopperman, 'Religion and Religious Policy in the British Army, c. 1700–96', *Journal of Religious History*, 14 (1987), p. 400.

99. Blake, *Evangelicals in the Royal Navy*, p. 76.

100. Snape, *Redcoat and Religion*, p. 18.

101. J. Walsh, C. Haydon and S. Taylor, *The Church of England c. 1689–c. 1833* (Cambridge, 1993).

102. Kopperman, 'Religious Policy', pp. 402, 390.

103. Rodger, 'Naval Chaplain', p. 42.

104. While Scottish regiments were allowed to have Presbyterian ministers, they were expected to conform to the Anglican Communion when serving outside of Scotland. Kopperman, 'Religious Policy', p. 403n.

105. Rodger, 'Naval Chaplain', p. 33.

106. J. Knox, *The Siege of Quebec* (ed. B. Connell, 1976), p. 21.

107. Snape, *Redcoat and Religion*, p. 9.

108. R. Lamb, *Memoir of His Own Life* (Dublin, 1811), p. 70.

109. G. Hanger, *The Life, Adventures, and Opinions of Col. George Hanger* (ed. W. Combe, 1801), pp. 116–17.

110. Starkey, *War in the Age of Enlightenment*, p. 165.

111. Captain J. Bowater to Lord Denbigh, 4 April 1777, in Balderstone, *Lost War*, p. 122.

112. Major J. Bowater to Lord Denbigh, 31 July 1778, in Balderstone, *Lost War*, p. 167.
113. Blake, *Evangelicals in the Royal Navy*, pp. 69–104.
114. Knight, *Pursuit of Victory*, p. 460.
115. Henry D. Rack, 'Wesley, John (1703–1791)', *Oxford Dictionary of National Biography* (Oxford, 2004).
116. G.M. Ditchfield, *The Evangelical Revival* (1998), p. 78.
117. J. Haime, *A Short Account of God's Dealings with Mr. John Haime* (1799), p. 17.
118. Snape, *Redcoat and Religion*, pp. 56–7.
119. T. Jackson, *The Lives of Early Methodist Preachers, Chiefly Written by Themselves* (2 vols., 1802), II, p. 150.
120. Haime, *A Short Account of God's Dealings*, pp. 22, 20.
121. Jackson, *Lives of Early Methodist Preachers*, II, pp. 164–7.
122. Snape, *Redcoat and Religion*, pp. 36, 273n.
123. Sampson Staniforth noted that 'when off duty' he and fellow Methodists met 'twice a day' for prayer and Bible reading during the 1740 revival in Flanders. Jackson, *Lives of Early Methodist Preachers*, II, p. 160.
124. P. Doddridge, *Some Remarkable Passages in the Life of the Honourable Col. James Gardiner* (1747).
125. Snape, *Redcoat and Religion*, p. 147.
126. Snape, *Redcoat and Religion*, pp. 147–9.
127. Blake, *Evangelicals in the Royal Navy*, pp. 153–4.
128. Rodger, *Wooden World*, p. 11–12.
129. Blake, *Evangelicals in the Royal Navy*, 35n.
130. Richard Marks cited in Blake, *Evangelicals in the Royal Navy*, p. 236.
131. Blake, *Evangelicals in the Royal Navy*, p. 238.
132. Daly, *The British Soldier in the Peninsular War*, ch. 6.
133. Costello, *Rifleman Costello*, p. 86; a surgeon in the 40th Foot worried about the prospect of increased 'disease' caused by excessive drinking on St Patrick's Day in 1810: 'The regimental bands played through the streets, as is usual on this occasion, commencing at midnight'. Boutflower, *Journal of an Army Surgeon*, p. 48.
134. M. Cronin and D. Adair, *The Wearing of the Green: a History of St Patrick's Day* (2002), pp. 8–9.
135. Snape, *Redcoat and Religion*, p. 238.
136. Cited in P. Mack, *Heart Religion in the British Enlightenment* (Cambridge, 2008), p. 54.
137. Snape, *Redcoat and Religion*, p. 145.
138. C. Wesley, *Short Hymns on Select Passages of the Holy Scriptures* (1762), I, p. 312.
139. J. Priestley, *The Doctrine of Philosophical Necessity Illustrated* (1777), p. ix; he was echoing the King James Bible, Hebrews 2:10 – thanks to Emma Macleod for pointing this out.
140. Lincoln, *Naval Wives and Mistresses*, p. 29.
141. M.A., Favret, 'War and Everyday Life in Britain', in R. Chickering and S. Forster, eds., *War in an Age of Revolution, 1775–1815* (Cambridge, 2010), p. 395.
142. D. Hume, 'My Own Life', in *Essays, Moral, Political and Literary* (ed. E.F. Miller, Indianapolis, 1985), pp. xxxv, xxxix.
143. Cited in R. Porter, *Gibbon: Making History* (1988), pp. 58, 94.

144. J. Crowley, *Imperial Landscapes: Britain's Global Visual Culture, 1745–1820* (New Haven, 2011), p. 4.
145. D. Fordham, *British Art and the Seven Years War: Allegiance and Autonomy* (Philadelphia, 2010).
146. Lincoln, *Representing the Royal Navy*, p. 6.
147. D.H. Solkin, 'Portraiture in Motion: Edward Penny's Marquis of Granby and the Creation of a Public for English Art', *Huntington Library Quarterly*, 49 (1986), pp. 1–23.
148. J. Bonehill, 'Exhibiting War: John Singleton Copley's *The Siege of Gibraltar* and the Staging of History', in J. Bonehill and G. Quilley, eds., *Conflicting Visions: War and Visual Culture in Britain and France, 1700–1830* (Aldershot, 2005), pp. 139–68.
149. McBride, *Eighteenth-Century Ireland*, p. 46.
150. W. Tench, *A Complete Account of the Settlement at Port Jackson, in New South Wales* (1793), p. 25.
151. G. Russell, *The Theatres of War: Performance, Politics and Society, 1793–1815* (Oxford, 1995).
152. J. Black, *Culture in Eighteenth-Century England* (2005), p. 106.
153. S. Wollenberg and S. McVeigh, eds., *Concert Life in Eighteenth-Century Britain* (Aldershot, 2004), p. 4.
154. D.W. Jones, *The Life of Haydn* (Cambridge, 2009), pp. 165–6.
155. D. Thomas, *Henry Fielding: a Life* (1990), pp. 6, 20.
156. G. Russell, 'The Army, the Navy and the Napoleonic Wars', in C.L. Johnson and C. Tuite, eds., *A Companion to Jane Austen* (2009), p. 262.
157. H.C. Robinson, *Diary, Reminiscences and Correspondence* (ed. T. Sadler, 3 vols., 1869), I, pp. 274–5.
158. R. Holmes, *Coleridge: Early Visions* (1989), pp. 10, 56.
159. R. Southey to S.T. Coleridge, [1] May [1800] in I. Packer and L. Pratt, ed., *The Collected Letters of Robert Southey, Part Two: 1798–1803*, http://www.rc.umd.edu/editions/southey_letters/Part_Two/HTML/letterEEd.26.516.html.
160. D. Griffin, *Patriotism and Poetry in Eighteenth-Century Britain* (Cambridge, 2002), pp. 9–10.
161. Cardwell, *Arts and Arms*, pp. 280, 265.
162. A. Seward, 'Monody on Major Andre', in W. Scott, ed., *The Poetical Works of Anna Seward* (3 vols., Edinburgh, 1810), II, p. 84;
163. C.T. Kairoff, *Anna Seward and the End of the Eighteenth Century* (Baltimore, 2012), p. 96.
164. S. Bainbridge, *British Poetry and the Revolutionary and Napoleonic Wars: Visions of Conflict* (Oxford, 2003).
165. Leigh Hunt, 'Walcheren Expedition; Or, the Englishman's Lamentation for the Loss of His Countrymen' (January 1810).
166. J. Rendall, 'Women Writing War and Empire: Gender, Poetry and Politics in Britain during the Napoleonic Wars', in K. Hagemann, G. Mettle and J. Rendall, eds., *Gender, War and Politics: Transatlantic Perspectives, 1775–1830* (Basingstoke, 2010), pp. 265–83.
167. S. Bainbridge, *Napoleon and British Romanticism* (Cambridge, 1995).
168. B.T. Bennett, *British War Poetry in the Age of Romanticism, 1793–1815* (1976), para. 129.

169. Favret, 'War and Everyday Life in Britain', in Chickering and Forster, *War in an Age of Revolution*, p. 408.
170. Colley, *Britons*, p. 303.
171. K. Wilson, *Island Race: Englishness, Empire and Gender in the Eighteenth Century* (New York, 2003), p. 59.
172. A. Kippis, *The Life of Captain Cook* (1788), pp. 482–6, 503–4.

Chapter 5: War and Politics

1. P.K. O'Brien, 'State Formation and Economic Growth: The Case of Britain 1688–1846', in J.G. Backhouse, ed., *Navies and State Formation: The Schumpeter Hypothesis Revisited and Reflected* (Zurich, 2012), p. 235.
2. Smith, *Georgian Monarchy*, p. 108.
3. P. Mansel, 'Monarchy, Uniform and the Rise of the *Frac*, 1760–1830', *Past and Present*, 96 (1982), p. 112.
4. L. Colley, 'The Apotheosis of George III: Loyalty, Royalty and the British Nation, 1760–1820', *Past and Present*, 102 (1984), pp. 94–129.
5. W.A. Speck, *Stability and Strife: England 1714–1760* (1977), p. 212.
6. L. Namier and J. Brooke, *The House of Commons, 1754–1790* (3 vols., Oxford, 1964), I, p. 126.
7. J. Cannon, *Parliamentary Reform, 1640–1832* (1972), p. 42.
8. J.A. Phillips, 'Popular Politics in Unreformed England', *Journal of Modern History*, 52 (1980), pp. 599–625.
9. F. O'Gorman, 'The Unreformed Electorate of Hanoverian England: the Mid–Eighteenth Century to the Reform Act of 1832', *Social History*, 11 (1986), pp. 42, 48.
10. F. O'Gorman, *Voters, Patrons, and Parties: the Unreformed Electorate of Hanoverian England 1734–1832* (Oxford, 1989), p. 296.
11. P. Langford, 'Property and "Virtual Representation" in Eighteenth-Century England', *Historical Journal*, 31 (1988), p. 98.
12. Brewer, *Sinews*, p. 45. 'Of the thirty admirals serving during the mid-Century Seven Years War, twenty of them were also Members of Parliament', Buchet, *British Navy*, p. 263.
13. R.G. Thorne, *The House of Commons, 1790–1820* (5 vols., 1986), I, pp. 306–17.
14. Lincoln, *Representing the Royal Navy*, pp. 43–4.
15. Edmund Burke, *Thoughts on the Cause of the Present Discontents* (1770).
16. Page, *John Jebb*, p. 251.
17. Bew, *Castlereagh*, p. 444.
18. J. Priestley to W. Graham, [1774], in J.T. Rutt, ed., *The Theological and Miscellaneous Works of Joseph Priestley* (25 vols., 1832), I, pt. 1, p. 256.
19. E.P. Thompson, 'Patricians and Plebs', in *Customs in Common* (1991); Clark, *English Society*, pp. 186, 197–200.
20. D. Wahrman, *Imagining the Middle Class: the Political Representation of Class in Britain, c. 1780–1840* (Cambridge, 1995).
21. K. Wilson, 'Inventing Revolution: 1688 and Eighteenth-Century Popular Politics', *Journal of British Studies*, 28 (1989), pp. 349–86.

22. C. Robbins, *The Eighteenth-Century Commonwealthman* (Cambridge, MA, 1959); C. Hill, 'The Norman Yoke', in *Puritanism and Revolution* (New York, 1958).

23. N. Rogers, 'The Urban Opposition to Whig Oligarchy, 1720–1760', in M.C. and J.R. Jacob, ed., *The Origins of Anglo-American Radicalism* (1984), p. 166.

24. J.E. Bradley, *Religion, Revolution and English Radicalism: Nonconformity in Eighteenth-Century Politics and Society* (Cambridge, 1990).

25. Clark, *English Society*, pp. 318–422.

26. J. Hoppit, ed., *Parliaments, Nations and Identities in Britain and Ireland, 1660–1850* (Manchester, 2003).

27. K. Navickas, *Loyalism and Radicalism in Lancashire, 1798–1815* (Oxford, 2009), p. 3.

28. Pitt speech 10 Dec. 1742, *Cobbett*, XII, cols. 1033–6.

29. J. Brewer, 'English Radicalism in the Age of George III', in Pocock, *Three British Revolutions: 1641, 1688, 1776*, pp. 323–67.

30. Rogers, *Crowds, Culture and Politics*, pp. 103–5.

31. E. Burke to Lord Rockingham, 7 Sept. 1770, in J. Sainsbury, *Disaffected Patriots: London Supporters of Revolutionary America, 1769–1782* (Kingston and Montreal, 1987), p. 48.

32. P.D.G. Thomas, 'The Beginnings of Parliamentary Reporting in Newspapers, 1768–1774', *English Historical Review*, 74 (1959), pp. 624, 632–4; J. Brewer, 'The Wilkites and the Law, 1763–74: a Study of Radical Notions of Governance', in J. Brewer and J. Styles, eds., *An Ungovernable People* (1980), pp. 128–71.

33. P.D.G. Thomas, *John Wilkes: a Friend to Liberty* (Oxford, 1996), p. 218.

34. Conway, *War, State and Society*, p. 168.

35. Drescher, *Capitalism and Antislavery*, p. 68.

36. J. Shy, 'The American Revolution: the Military Conflict Considered as a Revolutionary War', in S.G. Kurtz and J.H. Hutson, eds., *Essays on the American Revolution* (Chapel Hill, NC, 1973), pp. 147–51.

37. T. Bickham, *Making Headlines: the American Revolution as Seen Through the British Press* (DeKalb, IL, 2009).

38. Major J. Bowater to Lord Denbigh, 4 January 1778, in Balderstone, *Lost War*, p. 156.

39. Cobbett, *Life of Peter Porcupine*, pp. 21–3.

40. J. Burgh, *Political Disquisitions* (1774); J. Cartwright, *Take Your Choice!* (1776).

41. Jebb, *Works*, II, pp. 456, 480, 469.

42. C. Wyvill, *A Defence of Dr. Price and the Reformers of England* (1792), p. 6.

43. Christie, *Wilkes, Wyvill and Reform*, p. 97.

44. H. Butterfield, *George III: Lord North, and the People, 1779–80* (1949), p. 315.

45. J. Cannon, *The Fox–North Coalition: Crisis of the Constitution, 1782–84* (Cambridge, 1969).

46. I.R. Christie, 'Great Britain after the American Revolution', in J.P. Green and J.R. Pole, *A Companion to the American Revolution* (Malden, MA, 2000), p. 501.

47. P. Kelly, 'Radicalism and Public Opinion in the General Election of 1784', *Bulletin of the Institute for Historical Research*, 45 (1972), pp. 73–88.

48. J.E. Cookson, 'Political Arithmetic and War in Britain, 1793–1815', *War and Society*, 1 (1983), p. 50.

49. M. Butler, ed., *Burke, Paine, Godwin, and the Revolution Controversy* (Cambridge, 1984), pp. 35, 108; R. Price, *Political Writings* (ed. D.O. Thomas, Cambridge, 1991), p. xv.

50. The scholarship is vast, but see, for example, J. Barrell, *Imagining the King's Death: Figurative Treason, Fantasies of Regicide, 1793–1796* (Oxford, 2000); M. Philp, ed., *The French Revolution and British Popular Politics* (Cambridge, 1991).

51. E. Baigent and J.E. Bradley, 'The Social Sources of Late Eighteenth-Century English Radicalism: Bristol in the 1770s and 1780s', *English Historical Review*, 124 (2009), pp. 1075–108.

52. A. Page, 'The Dean of St Asaph's Trial: Libel and Politics in the 1780s', *Journal for Eighteenth-Century Studies*, 32 (2009), p. 28.

53. Page, *John Jebb*, p. 188.

54. C. Wyvill to S. Shore, 28 May 1792, in Wyvill, *Political Papers*, V, p. 51.

55. F. O'Gorman, 'The Paine Burnings of 1792–1793', *Past and Present*, 193 (2006), pp. 111–55.

56. C. Emsley, 'Repression, "Terror" and the Rule of Law in England during the Decade of the French Revolution', *English Historical Review*, 100 (1985), p. 822.

57. K.R. Johnston, *Unusual Suspects: Pitt's Reign of Alarm and the Lost Generation of the 1790s* (Oxford, 2013).

58. E.V. Macleod, *A War of Ideas: British Attitudes to the Wars Against Revolutionary France, 1792–1802* (Aldershot, 1998).

59. J.E. Cookson, *The Friends of Peace: Anti–War Liberalism in England, 1793–1815* (Cambridge, 1982).

60. R. Dozier, *For King, Constitution, and Country: the English Loyalists and the French Revolution* (Lexington, KY, 1983).

61. M. Philp, 'Vulgar Conservatism, 1792–1793', *English Historical Review*, 110 (1995), p. 49.

62. Cookson, 'British Society and the French Wars', p. 194.

63. Cookson, *The British Armed Nation, 1793–1815* (Oxford, 1997), pp. 8–9.

64. Lamb, *Memoir of His Own Life*, p. 69.

65. S. Bamford, *Passages in the Life of a Radical* (1844), I, pp. 22–3.

66. Nicol, *Life and Adventures*, pp. 187–9.

67. G. Jordan and N. Rogers, 'Admirals as Heroes: Patriotism and Liberty in Hanoverian England', *Journal of British Studies*, 28 (1989), pp. 201–24.

68. K. Wilson, 'How Nelson became a Hero', *The Historian*, 87 (2005), pp. 6–17; T. Jenks, 'Contesting the Hero: the Funeral of Admiral Lord Nelson', *Journal of British Studies*, 39 (2000), pp. 422–53.

69. M. Lincoln, *Representing the Navy* (Aldershot, 2002), pp. 3–4.

70. K. Wilson, 'Empire, Trade and Popular Politics in Mid–Hanoverian Britain: the Case of Admiral Vernon', *Past and Present*, 121 (1988), pp. 74–109.

71. N. Rogers, 'The Dynamic of News in Britain During the American War: the Case of Admiral Keppel', *Parliamentary History*, 25 (2006), pp. 49–67.

72. F.D. Cartwright, *The Life and Correspondence of Major Cartwright* (1826), II, p. 159.

73. J.W. Osborne, *John Cartwright* (1972), p. 11.

74. S. Bamford, *Passages in the Life of a Radical* (1844), I, pp. 31–2.

75. W. Cobbett, *Advice to Young Men* (1862 [1829]), p.43.

76. J.R. Dinwiddy, 'The Early Nineteenth-Century Campaign against Flogging in the Army', *English Historical Review*, 97 (1982), p. 312.

77. Cited in R. Williams, *Cobbett* (Oxford, 1983), p. 5.

78. Colley, *Britons*, p. 92.

79. William Wilberforce diary entry 28 October 1787, cited in M.J.D. Roberts, *Making English Morals: Voluntary Association and Moral Reform in England, 1787–1886* (Cambridge, 2004), p. 17.

80. J. Innes, 'Politics and Morals: the Reformation of Manners Movement in Later Eighteenth-Century England', in *Inferior Politics*, pp. 179–226.

81. T.C.W. Blanning, *The Culture of Power and the Power of Culture: Old Regime Europe 1660–1789* (Oxford, 2002).

82. G. Newman, *The Rise of English Nationalism* (1987), pp. 14–18, 37.

83. J. Brown, *An Estimate of the Manners and Principles of the Times* (1757), pp. 140–1.

84. Conway, *War, State and Society*, p. 120.

85. Brown, *Estimate of the Manners and Principles*, pp. 181, 67, 221.

86 M. McCormack, *The Independent Man* (Manchester, 2005), p. 75.

87. M. McCormack, 'The New Militia: War, Politics and Gender in 1750s Britain', *Gender and History*, 19 (2007), pp. 483–500.

88. Price, *Political Writings*, p. 145.

89. Page, *John Jebb*, p. 255.

90. McCormack, *Independent Man*, p. 126.

91. J. Cartwright, *England's Aegis: or, the Military Energies of the Empire* (1804), pp. 22, v, 177–91, 63–4.

92. Osborne, *John Cartwright*, p. 73.

93. H. Guest, *Small Change: Women, Learning, Patriotism, 1750–1810* (Chicago, 2000), pp. 220–51.

94. M. Wollstonecraft, *A Vindication of the Rights of Men and A Vindication of the Rights of Woman* (ed. S. Tomaselli, Cambridge, 1995), pp. 236, 233.

95. A. Chernock, *Men and the Making of Modern British Feminism* (Stanford, 2010).

96. B. Taylor, *Mary Wollstonecraft and the Feminist Imagination* (Cambridge, 2003).

97. E. Chalus, *Elite Women in English Political Life, c. 1754–1790* (Oxford, 2005).

98. A. Page, ' "A Great Politicianess": Ann Jebb, Rational Dissent and Politics in Late Eighteenth-Century Britain', *Women's History Review*, 17 (2008), pp. 743–65.

99. J. Cartwright, *An Appeal, Civil and Military, on the Subject of the English Constitution* (2nd edn, 1799), p. 17.

100. Conway, *British Isles and American Independence*, pp. 88–9.

101. Colley, *Britons*, pp. 64–70.

102. A.K. Mellor, *Mothers of the Nation: Women's Political Writing in England, 1780–1830* (Bloomington, 2000), p. 11.

103. Thomas Coutts cited in Ruth M. Larsen, 'Pitt, Hester, countess of Chatham and suo jure Baroness Chatham (1720–1803)', *Oxford Dictionary of National Biography* (Oxford, 2005).

104. B. Hilton, *A Mad, Bad and Dangerous People? England 1783–1846* (Oxford, 2006), p. 370.

105. A.J. O'Shaughnessy, *An Empire Divided: the American Revolution and the British Caribbean* (Philadelphia, 2000), p. 251n.

106. S. Sen, 'Liberal Empire and Illiberal Trade: the Political Economy of "Responsible Government" in Early British India', in Wilson, *A New Imperial History*, p. 136.

107. P.J. Marshall, 'Hastings, Warren (1732–1818)', *Oxford Dictionary of National Biography* (Oxford, 2004).

108. T.W. Nechtman, *Nabobs: Empire and Identity in Eighteenth-Century Britain* (Cambridge, 2010).

109. P.J. Marshall, 'Hastings, Warren (1732–1818)', *Oxford Dictionary of National Biography*, (Oxford, 2004); online edn, Oct 2008 [http://www.oxforddnb.com/view/article/12587, accessed 29 Nov 2013].

110. A. Clark, *Scandal: the Sexual Politics of the British Constitution* (Princeton, 2004), pp. 84–112.

111. 'The Address of Warren Hastings in his Defence', 2 June 1791, in G. Carnall and C. Nicholson, eds., *The Impeachment of Warren Hastings* (Edinburgh, 1989), p. 24.

112. J. Pitts, *A Turn to Empire* (Princeton, 2005), pp. 80–1, 65.

113. C.A. Bayly, *Imperial Meridian: the British Empire and the World, 1780–1830* (1989), pp. 193–6.

114. C.L. Brown, *Moral Capital: Foundations of British Abolitionism* (Chapel Hill, NC, 2006).

115. A Christian belief in the unity of mankind as 'all God's children' was no barrier to various forms of racism. C. Kidd, *The Forging of Races: Race and Scripture in the Protestant Atlantic World, 1600–2000* (Cambridge, 2006).

116. K. Morgan, *Slavery, Atlantic Trade and the British Economy, 1660–1800* (Cambridge, 2000), p. 10.

117. N. Rogers, 'Archipelagic Encounters: War, Race, and Labor in American-Caribbean Waters', in F.A. Nussbaum, ed., *The Global Eighteenth Century* (Baltimore, 2003), p. 224.

118. W.J. Bolster, *Black Jacks: African American Seamen in the Age of Sail* (Cambridge, MA, 1997), p. 32.

119. J. Walvin, *The Zong: a Massacre, the Law and the End of Slavery* (New Haven, 2011), pp. 104–5.

120. Blake, *Evangelicals in the Navy*, pp. 59–60.

121. C.L. Brown, *Moral Capital: Foundations of British Abolitionism* (Chapel Hill, NC, 2006), pp. 364–6.

122. T. Clarkson, *The History of the Abolition of the Slave Trade* (2 vols., 1808), I, pp. 181–3.

123. The scholarship on abolition is vast and the best place to start is S. Drescher, 'Public Opinion and Parliament in the Abolition of the British Slave Trade', in S. Farrell, M. Unwin and J. Walvin, eds., *The British Slave Trade: Abolition, Parliament and People* (Edinburgh, 2007), pp. 42–65.

124. For example, there is only a passing reference in S. Swaminathan, *Debating the Slave Trade: Rhetoric of British National Identity, 1759–1815* (Farnham, 2009), p. 159.

125. T. Clarkson, *An Essay on the Impolicy of the African Slave-Trade* (1788), p. 31.

126. Clarkson, *Impolicy of the African Slave-Trade*, p. 78.

127. Clarkson, *Impolicy of the African Slave-Trade*, pp. 49–50. Clarkson provided data from ship muster rolls amounting to a sample of 20,000 seamen. R. Anstey, *The Atlantic Slave Trade and British Abolition, 1760–1810* (1975), p. 265.

128. Clarkson, *Impolicy of the African Slave-Trade*, pp. 130–2.

129. Clarkson, *History of Abolition*, II, p. 49.

130. S. Farrell, ' "Contrary to the Principles of Justice, Humanity and Sound Policy": the Slave Trade, Parliamentary Politics and the Abolition Act, 1807', in S. Farrell, M. Unwin and J. Walvin, eds., *The British Slave Trade: Abolition, Parliament and People* (Edinburgh, 2007), pp. 141–202.

131. C.A. Bayly, 'The First Age of Global Imperialism, c. 1760–1830', *Journal of Imperial and Commonwealth History*, 26 (1998), p. 40.

132. J. Walvin, *Black Ivory: a History of British Slavery* (1992); S. Drescher, *Abolition: a History of Slavery and Antislavery* (Cambridge, 2009).

133. See, for example, the excellent discussion of domestic attitudes compared to the reality of empire in southern Africa: R. Price, *Making Empire: Colonial Encounters and the Creation of Imperial Rule in Nineteenth-Century Africa* (Cambridge, 2008).

134. McBride, *Eighteenth-Century Ireland*, p. 14; S. Howe, 'Questioning the (Bad) Question: "Was Ireland a Colony?"', *Irish Historical Studies*, 36 (2008), pp. 138–52.

135. N. Canny, 'Early Modern Ireland', in Foster, *Illustrated History of Ireland*, pp. 154–60.

136. T.C. Barnard, 'The Gentrification of Eighteenth-Century Ireland', *Eighteenth-Century Ireland*, 12 (1997), pp. 137–55.

137. J. Hill, 'Convergence and Conflict in Eighteenth-Century Ireland', *Historical Journal*, 44 (2001), pp. 1039–63.

138. J. Smyth, *The Making of the United Kingdom, 1600–1800* (2001), p. 136.

139. V. Morely, *Irish Opinion and the American Revolution, 1760–1783* (Cambridge, 2002).

140. Knight and Wilcox, *Sustaining the Fleet*, pp. 81–2.

141. N. Garnham, *The Militia in Eighteenth-Century Ireland: in Defence of the Protestant Interest* (Woodbridge, 2012).

142. J. Smyth, 'The Men of No Popery: the Origins of the Orange Order', *History Ireland*, 3 (1995), pp. 48–53.

143. I. McBride, *Scripture Politics: Ulster Presbyterians and Irish Radicalism in the Late Eighteenth Century* (Oxford, 1998).

144. Marshall, *Making and Unmaking of Empire*, p. 340.

145. Foster, *Illustrated History of Ireland*, p. 180.

146. M. Elliott, 'Ireland and the French Revolution', in H.T. Dickinson, ed., *Britain and the French Revolution* (1989), p. 92.

147. Most notably K. Whelan, *The Tree of Liberty* (Cork, 1996); for a good assessment of recent representations of 1798, see I. McBride, 'Reclaiming the Rebellion: 1798 in 1998', *Irish Historical Studies*, 31 (1999), pp. 395–410.

148. T.W. Tone, *The Life of Theobald Wolfe Tone* (ed. T. Bartlett, Dublin, 1998), p. 46.

149. Page, *John Jebb*, p. 256.

150. T. Bartlett, 'Select Documents 38: Defenders and Defenderism in 1795' *Irish Historical Studies*, 24 (1985), pp. 389–90.

151. McBride, *Eighteenth-Century Ireland*, p. 407.

152. T. Dunne, 'Subaltern Voices? Poetry in Irish, Popular Insurgency and the 1798 Rebellion', *Eighteenth-Century Life*, 22 (1998), pp. 31–44.

153. Bartlett, *A Military History of Ireland*, p. 262.

154. *Narrative of the Sufferings and Escape of Charles Jackson, Late Resident at Wexford in Ireland* (4th ed., 1802), p. 14.

155. Elliott, 'Ireland', in Dickinson, *Britain and the French Revolution*, p. 99.

156. M. Elliott, *Partners in Revolution: the United Irishmen and France* (New Haven, CT, 1982), p. 229.

157. B. Simms, 'Continental Analogies with 1798: Revolution or Counter-Revolution?', in T. Bartlett, D. Dickson, D. Keogh and K. Whelan, eds., *1798: a Bicentenary Perspective* (Dublin, 2003), p. 595.

158. Simms, 'Continental Analogies with 1798', p. 588.

159. J. Smyth, *The Men of No Property: Irish Radicals and Popular Politics in the Late Eighteenth Century* (Basingstoke, 1992), pp. 157–70.

160. T. Dunne, 'Popular Ballads, Revolutionary Rhetoric and Politicisation', in H. Gough and D. Dickson, eds., *Ireland and the French Revolution* (Dublin, 1990); V. Morley, 'The Continuity of Disaffection in Eighteenth-Century Ireland', *Eighteenth-Century Ireland*, 22 (2007), pp. 189–205.

161. T. Dunne, *Rebellions: Memoir, Memory and 1798* (Dublin, 2010), pp. 247–64.

162. T. Bartlett, *Ireland: a History* (Cambridge, 2010), p. 226.

163. W. Godwin to [Hugh Skeys], 17 Oct. 1797, *The Letters of William Godwin* (ed. P. Clemit, Oxford, 2011), I, pp. 255–6.

164. T. Bartlett, 'Ireland, Empire and Union, 1690–1801', in K. Kenny, ed., *Ireland and the British Empire* (Oxford, 2004), p. 83.

165. T. Bartlett, 'Ireland, Empire and Union, 1690–1801', in Kenny, *Ireland and the British Empire*, p. 88.

166. K. Whelan, 'The Other Within: Ireland, Britain and the Act of Union', in D. Keogh and K. Whelan, eds., *Acts of Union: the Causes, Contexts and Consequences of the Act of Union* (Blackrock, Ireland, 2001), p. 24.

167. K.T. Hoppen, 'An Incorporating Union: British Politicians and Ireland, 1800–30', *English Historical Review*, 123 (2008), p. 349.

168. K. Whelan, *The Tree of Liberty* (Cork, 1996), pp. 129–30, ix.

169. McBride, *Eighteenth-Century Ireland*, pp. 366–7.

170. Simms, 'Continental Analogies with 1798', p. 592.

171. J. Ridden, 'Irish Reform between the 1798 Rebellion and the Great Famine', Burns and Innes, *Rethinking the Age of Reform*, pp. 271–94.

172. Connolly, 'Varieties of Britishness', in Grant and Stringer, *Uniting the Kingdom?*, p. 207.

173. J. Kelly, ' "We Were all to have been Massacred": Irish Protestants and the Experience of Rebellion', in Bartlett et al., *1798*, p. 330.

174. J.J. Sack, *From Jacobite to Conservative: Reaction and Orthodoxy in Britain, c. 1760–1832* (Cambridge, 1993), p. 241.

175. Cookson, *British Armed Nation*, p. 11.

176. S.J. Connolly, 'Reconsidering the Irish Act of Union', *Transactions of the Royal Historical Society*, 10 (2000), pp. 399–408.

Conclusion

1. J. Ritchie, 'Macquarie, Lachlan (1761–1824)', *Oxford Dictionary of National Biography* (Oxford, 2004).

2. J. Israel, *Enlightenment Contested: Philosophy, Modernity and the Emancipation of Man, 1670–1752* (Oxford, 2006).

3. In 2013 Australia had one of the lowest public debt to GDP ratios in the developed world, and yet the conservative Liberal Party were able to win government with a promise to end 'debt and deficit' and 'stop the big new taxes'.

4. P.K. O'Brien, *Power with Profit: the State and the Economy, 1688–1815* (1991), p. 33.

5. C.A. Bayly, 'The First Age of Global Imperialism, c. 1760–1830', *Journal of Imperial and Commonwealth History*, 26 (1998), pp. 29, 36–9; see also, J. Darwin, *After Tamerlane: the Rise and Fall of Global Empires, 1400–2000* (2008), pp. 157–218.

6. Pitts, *Turn to Empire*, p. 76; E. Burke, *Reflections on the Revolution in France* (1790), p. 113.

7. Knight, *Organization of Victory*, pp. 468–9.

8. J. Mokyr, 'Accounting for the Industrial Revolution', in Floud and Johnson, *Cambridge Economic History of Modern Britain*, p. 15.

9. O'Brien, 'Provincializing the First Industrial Revolution', p. 33.

10. L.G. Mitchell, *Charles James Fox* (1992).

11. M. Ceadel, *The Origins of War Prevention: the British Peace Movement and International Relations, 1730–1854* (Oxford, 1996), pp. 166–221.

12. Knight, *Organisation of Victory*, p. 473.

13. Cookson, *Friends of Peace*, p. 261.

Select Bibliography

Two electronic sources are invaluable in providing access to printed primary sources: *Eighteenth Century Collections Online* and the *17th and 18th Century Burney Collection Newspapers*. The scholarship is vast for many of the subjects discussed in this book. For reasons of space, what follows is a selective list of the most helpful and most recent publications. A more comprehensive bibliography is available on my University of Tasmania webpage:

http://www.utas.edu.au/humanities/people/h-and-c-profiles/Anthony-Page
Unless otherwise stated London is the place of publication.

Allen, R.C., *The British Industrial Revolution in Global Perspective* (Cambridge, 2009).

Armitage, D., *The Ideological Origins of the British Empire* (Cambridge, 2000).

Baigent, E. and J.E. Bradley, 'The Social Sources of Late Eighteenth-Century English Radicalism: Bristol in the 1770s and 1780s', *English Historical Review*, 124 (2009), pp. 1075–108.

Bartlett, T., D. Dickson, D. Keogh and K. Whelan, eds., *1798: A Bicentenary Perspective* (Dublin, 2003).

Bartlett, T. and K. Jeffery, eds., *A Military History of Ireland* (Cambridge, 1997).

Baugh, D.A., 'Great Britain's "Blue–Water" Policy', *International History Review*, 10 (1988), pp. 33–58.

Baugh, D.A., 'The Eighteenth-Century Navy as a National Institution, 1690–1815', in J.R. Hill, ed., *The Oxford Illustrated History of the Royal Navy* (Oxford, 1995), pp. 120–60.

Baugh, D.A., *The Global Seven Years War 1754–1763* (2011).

Bayly, C.A., *Imperial Meridian* (1989).

Bell, D., *The First Total War: Napoleon's Europe and the Birth of Modern Warfare* (2007).

Bickham, T., *Making Headlines: the American Revolution as seen through the British Press* (DeKalb, IL, 2009).

Black, J. and P. Woodfine, eds., *The British Navy and the use of Naval Power in the Eighteenth Century* (Leicester, 1988).

Black, J., *Britain as a Military Power, 1688–1815* (1999).

Black, J., *Debating Foreign Policy in Eighteenth–Century Britain* (Farnham, 2011).

Black, J., *Eighteenth–Century Britain, 1688–1783* (Basingstoke, 2008).

Black, J., *George III: America's Last King* (New Haven, CT, 2006).

Black, J., *Natural and Necessary Enemies: Anglo–French Relations in the Eighteenth Century* (Athens, GA, 1986).

Blanning, T., *The Pursuit of Glory: Europe 1648–1815* (2007).

Bonehill J. and G. Quilley, eds., *Conflicting Visions: War and Visual Culture in Britain and France, 1700–1830* (Aldershot, 2005).

Bonney, R., 'The Eighteenth Century. II. The Struggle for Great Power Status and the End of the Old Fiscal Regime', in R. Bonney, ed., *Economic Systems and State Finance* (Oxford, 1995), pp. 315–90.

Bowen, H., 'British Conceptions of Global Empire, 1756–1783', *Journal of Imperial and Commonwealth History*, 26 (1998), pp. 1–26.

Bowen, H.V. and A.G. Enciso, eds., *Mobilising Resources for War: Britain and Spain at Work during the Early Modern Period* (Pamplona, 2006).

Bowen, H.V., *War and British Society, 1688–1815* (Cambridge, 1998).

Bradley, J.E., *Religion, Revolution and English Radicalism: Nonconformity in Eighteenth–Century Politics and Society* (Cambridge, 1990).

Brewer, J., *The Sinews of Power: War, Money and the English State, 1688–1783* (New York, 1789).

Brown, C.L., *Moral Capital: Foundations of British Abolitionism* (Chapel Hill, NC, 2006).

Brown, S.J., *William Robertson and the Expansion of Empire* (Cambridge, 1997).

Brumwell, S., 'Rank and File: A Profile of One of Wolfe's Regiments', *Journal of the Society for Army Historical Research*, 79 (2001), pp. 3–24.

Brumwell, S., *Redcoats: The British Soldier and War in the Americas* (Cambridge, 2002).

Burns, A. and J. Innes, *Rethinking the Age of Reform: Britain 1780–1850* (Oxford, 2003).

Cannon, J., *Aristocratic Century* (Cambridge, 1984).

Carnall, G. and C. Nicholson, eds., *The Impeachment of Warren Hastings: Papers from a Bicentenary Commemoration* (Edinburgh, 1989).

Ceadel, M., *The Origins of War Prevention: the British Peace Movement and International Relations, 1730–1854* (Oxford, 1996).

Chandler, D.G. and I.F.W. Beckett, eds., *The Oxford History of the British Army* (Oxford, 1996).

Charters, E., 'The Caring Fiscal-Military State during the Seven Years War, 1756–1763', *Historical Journal*, 52 (2009), pp. 921–41.

Chernock, A., *Men and the Making of Modern British Feminism* (Stanford, CA, 2010).

Christie, I.R., *Stress and Stability in Late Eighteenth-Century Britain* (Oxford, 1984).

Clark, A., *Scandal: the Sexual Politics of the British Constitution* (Princeton, 2004).

Clark, J.C.D., *English Society, 1660–1832* (1985 & 2nd ed., 2000)

Colley, L., *Britons: Forging the Nation, 1707–1837* (2nd ed., New Haven, CT, 2009).

Collins, B., *War and Empire: the Expansion of Britain, 1790–1830* (Harlow, 2010).

Connolly, S.J., *Divided Kingdom: Ireland 1630–1800* (Oxford, 2008).

Conway, S., *Britain, Ireland, and Continental Europe in the Eighteenth Century* (Oxford, 2011).

Conway, S., *The British Isles and the War of American Independence* (Oxford, 2000).

Conway, S., *War, State, and Society in Mid-Eighteenth-Century Britain and Ireland* (Oxford, 2006).

Cookson, J., 'Service Without Politics? Army Militia and Volunteers in Britain during the American and French Revolutionary Wars', *War in History*, 10 (2003), pp. 381–97.

Cookson, J., 'British Society and the French Wars, 1793–1815', *Australian Journal of Politics & History*, 31 (1985), pp. 192–203.

Cookson, J., *The British Armed Nation, 1793–1815* (Oxford, 1997).

Cookson, J., *The Friends of Peace: Anti-War Liberalism in England, 1793–1815* (Cambridge, 1982).

Connolly, S.J., *Divided Kingdom: Ireland, 1630–1800* (Oxford, 2008).

Connolly, S.J., 'Varieties of Britishness: Ireland, Scotland and Wales in the Hanoverian State', in A. Grant and K. Stringer, eds., *Uniting the Kingdom? The Making of British History* (1995), pp. 193–207.

Cross, E.J., *All for the King's Shilling: the British Soldier under Wellington, 1808–1814* (Norman, OK, 2010).

Crouzet, F., 'The Second Hundred Years War: Some Reflections', *French History*, 10 (1996), pp. 432–50.

Cullen, L.M., *The Emergence of Modern Ireland, 1600–1900* (Dublin, 1983).

Curtin, N.J., *The United Irishmen: Popular Politics in Ulster and Dublin, 1791–1798* (Oxford, 1994).

Daly, G., *The British Soldier in the Peninsular War* (Basingstoke, 2013).

Dancy, J., 'British Naval Manpower in the French Revolutionary Wars, 1793–1802' (Oxford, DPhil., 2012).

Daunton, M.J., *Progress and Poverty: an Economic and Social History of Britain 1700–1850* (Oxford, 1995).

de la Escosura, L.P., ed., *Exceptionalism and Industrialism: Britain and its European Rivals, 1688–1815* (Cambridge, 2004).

Dickinson, H.T., ed., *Britain and the American Revolution* (1998).

Dickinson, H.T., *The Politics of the People in Eighteenth-Century Britain* (New York, 1994).

Dickson, D. and K. Whelan, eds., *The United Irishmen: A Bicentennial Perspective* (Dublin, 1993).

Duffy, M., 'The Establishment of the Western Squadron as the Linchpin of British Naval Strategy', in M. Duffy, ed., *Parameters of British Naval Power, 1650–1850* (Exeter, 1992), pp. 60–81.

Durey, M., ' "Black Bob" Craufurd and Ireland, 1798–1804', *War in History*, 16 (2009), pp. 133–56.

Dziennik, M.P., 'Hierarchy, Authority, and Jurisdiction in the Mid-Eighteenth-Century Recruitment of the Highland Regiments', *Historical Research*, 85 (2012), pp. 89–104.

Elliott, M., *Partners in Revolution: the United Irishmen and France* (1982).

Elliott, M., *When God Took Sides: Religion and Identity in Irish History: Unfinished History* (Oxford, 2009).

Emsley, C., *British Society and the French Wars, 1793–1815* (1979).

Esdaile, C., *Napoleon's Wars: an International History 1803–1815* (2007).

Farrell, S., M. Unwin and J. Walvin, eds., *The British Slave Trade: Abolition, Parliament and People* (Edinburgh, 2007).

Favret, M.A., *War at a Distance: Romanticism and the Making of Modern Wartime* (Princeton, 2009).

Fitzpatrick, M., 'Patriotism and Patriotisms: Richard Price and the Early Reception of the French Revolution in England', *Studies of Voltaire and the 18thc*, 335 (1995), pp. 211–29.

Fitzpatrick, M., et al., eds., *The Enlightenment World* (2004).

Fordham, D., *British Art and the Seven Years War: Allegiance and Autonomy* (Philadelphia, 2010).

French, D., *The British Way in Warfare* (London, 1990).

Frey, S., *The British Soldier in America: a Social History of Military Life in the Revolutionary Period* (Austin, TX, 1981).

Frost, A., *The Global Reach of Empire: Britain's Maritime Expansion in the Indian and Pacific Oceans, 1764–1815* (Melbourne, 2003).

Gascoigne, J., *Science in the Service of Empire: Joseph Banks, the British State and the Use of Science in the Age of Revolution* (Cambridge, 1998).

Glover, M., *Peninsular Preparation: the Reform of the British Army, 1795–1809* (Cambridge, 1963).

Gould, E.H., *The Persistence of Empire: British Political Culture in the Age of the American Revolution* (Chapel Hill, NC, 2000).

Greene, J.P., 'The British Revolution in America', in W.R. Louis, ed., *More Adventures with Britannia: Personalities, Politics and Culture in Britain* (Austin, TX, 1998), pp. 31–44.

Greene, J.P., 'The Seven Years War and the American Revolution: The Causal Relationship Reconsidered', *Journal of Imperial and Commonwealth History,* 8 (1980), pp. 85–105.

Griffin, E., *A Short History of the British Industrial Revolution* (Basingstoke, 2010).

Gruber, I.D., *Books and the British Army in the Age of the American Revolution* (Chapel Hill, NC, 2010).

Gruber, I.D., '"On the Road to Poonamalle" an Irish Officer's View of the War for American Independence', *The American Magazine*, 4 (1988), pp. 1–12.

Guest, H., *Small Change: Women, Learning, Patriotism, 1750–1810* (Chicago, 2000).

Hagemann, K., G. Mettle and J. Rendell, eds., *Gender, War and Politics: Transatlantic Perspectives, 1775–1830* (Basingstoke, 2010).

Hall, C.D., *British Strategy in the Napoleonic War, 1803–15* (Manchester, 1992).

Harding, R., ed., *Naval History 1680–1850* (Aldershot, 2006).

Harling, P., and P. Mandler, 'From "Fiscal-Military" State to Laissez-Faire State, 1760–1850', *Journal of British Studies*, 32 (1993), pp. 44–70.

Harling, P., 'The Perils of "French Philosophy": Enlightenment and Revolution in Tory Journalism, 1800–1832', *Studies on Voltaire and the Eighteenth Century*, 6 (2004), pp. 199–220.

Harling, P., *The Waning of 'Old Corruption': The Politics of Economical Reform in Britain, 1779–1846* (Oxford, 1996).

Harris, B., *Politics and the Nation: Britain in the Mid-Eighteenth Century* (Oxford, 2002).

Hilton, B., *A Mad, Bad and Dangerous People? England 1783–1846* (Oxford, 2006).

Hoppit, J., 'The Nation, the State, and the First Industrial Revolution', *Journal of British Studies*, 50 (2011), pp. 307–31.

Hoppit, J., ed., *Parliaments, Nations and Identities in Britain and Ireland, 1660–1850* (Manchester, 2003).

Houlding, J.A., *Fit for Service: the Training of the British Army, 1715–1795* (Oxford, 1981).

Hyam, R. and Martin, G., *Reappraisals in British Imperial History* (Basingstoke, 1975).

Innes, J., *Inferior Politics: Social Problems and Social Polities in Eighteenth-Century Britain* (Oxford, 2009).

Israel, J. *Enlightenment Contested: Philosophy, Modernity and the Emancipation of Man, 1670–1752* (Oxford, 2006).

Jasanoff, M., *Liberty's Exiles: American Loyalists in the Revolutionary World* (2011).

Jenks, T., 'Contesting the Hero: The Funeral of Admiral Lord Nelson', *Journal of British Studies*, 39 (2000), pp. 422–53.

Jordan, G., and N. Rogers, 'Admirals as Heroes: Patriotism and Liberty in Hanoverian England', *Journal of British Studies*, 28 (1989), pp. 201–24.

Kennedy, C., and M. McCormack, eds., *Soldiering in Britain and Ireland, 1750–1850: Men of Arms* (Basingstoke, 2013).

Knight, R., and M. Wilcox, *Sustaining the Fleet, 1793–1815: War, the British Navy and the Contractor State* (Woodbridge, 2010).

Knight, R., *Britain against Napoleon: the Organization of Victory, 1793–1815* (2013).

Knight, R., *The Pursuit of Victory: the Life and Achievement of Horatio Nelson* (2005).

Langford, P., *A Polite and Commercial People: England 1727–1783* (Oxford, 1989).

Langford, P., *Englishness Identified* (Oxford, 2000).

Lavery, B., *Nelson's Navy: the Ships, Men and Organisation, 1793–1815* (1990).

Lee, W.E., *Barbarians and Brothers: Anglo-American Warfare, 1500–1865* (Oxford, 2011).

Linch, K., *Britain and Wellington's Army: Recruitment, Society and Tradition, 1807–15* (2011).

Lincoln, M., *Representing the Navy* (Aldershot, 2002).

Lynn, J.A., *Battle: a History of Combat and Culture* (2003).

Macdonald, J., *A Free Nation Deep in Debt* (New York, 2003).

Macinnes, A.I., 'Jacobitism in Scotland: Episodic Cause or National Movement?', *The Scottish Historical Review*, 86 (2007), pp. 225–52.

Mackay, R., and M. Duffy, *Hawke, Nelson and British Naval Leadership, 1747–1805* (Woodbridge, 2009).

Mackillop, A., 'The Political Culture of the Scottish Highlands from Culloden to Waterloo', *Historical Journal*, 46 (2003), pp. 511–32.

Macleod, E.V., 'British Attitudes to the French Revolution', *Historical Journal*, 50 (2007), pp. 689–709.

Macleod, E.V., *A War of Ideas: British Attitudes to the War Against Revolutionary France, 1792–1802* (Aldershot, 1998).

MacRobert, A.E., *The 1745 Rebellion and the Southern Scottish Lowlands* (Ely, 2006).

Marshall, P.J., *Remaking the British Atlantic* (Oxford, 2012).

Marshall, P.J., *The Making and Unmaking of Empires: Britain, India and America c. 1750–1783* (Oxford, 2005).

Marshall, P.J., ed., *The Eighteenth Century* (Oxford, 1998).

Mathias, P., and P.K. O'Brien, 'Taxation in England and France. 1715–1810', *Journal of European Economic History*, 5 (1976), pp. 601–50.

McBride, I., *Eighteenth–Century Ireland: the Isle of Slaves* (Dublin, 2010).

McCormack, M., *The Independent Man: Citizenship and Gender Politics in Georgian England* (Manchester, 2006).

Mellor, A.K., *Mothers of the Nation: Women's Political Writing in England, 1780–1830* (Bloomington, 2000).

Morley, V., *Irish Opinion and the American Revolution, 1760–1783* (Cambridge, 2002).

Morriss, R., 'Colonization, Conquest, and the Supply of Food and Transport: the Reorganization of Logistics Management, 1780–1795', *War in History*, 14 (2007), pp. 310–24.

Morriss, R., *Naval Power and British Culture, 1760–1850: Public Trust and Government Ideology* (Aldershot, 2004).

Morriss, R., *The Foundations of British Maritime Ascendancy: Resources, Logistics and the State, 1755–1815* (Cambridge, 2011).

Muir, R., *Britain and the Defeat of Napoleon, 1807–1815* (New Haven, CT, 1996).

Muir, R., *Wellington: the Path to Victory* (New Haven, CT, 2013).

Murdoch, A., *British History, 1660–1832: National Identity and Local Culture* (Basingstoke, 1998).

Newman, G., *The Rise of English Nationalism: a Cultural History, 1740–1830* (1987).

O'Brien, K., *Women and Enlightenment in Eighteenth-Century Britain* (Cambridge, 2009).

O'Brien, P.K., 'The Political Economy of British Taxation, 1660–1815', *Economic History Review*, 1 (1988), pp. 1–32.

O'Brien, P.K., 'The Impact of the Revolutionary and Napoleonic Wars, 1793–1815, on the Long-Run Growth of the British Economy', *Review (Fernand Braudel Center)*, 12 (1989), pp. 335–95.

O'Brien, P.K., 'The Nature and Historical Evolution of an Exceptional Fiscal State and its Possible Significance for the Precocious Commercialization and Industrialization of the British Economy from Cromwell to Nelson', *Economic History Review*, 64 (2011), pp. 408–46.

O'Brien, P.K., 'Fiscal, Financial and Monetary Foundations for the Formation of Nation States in the West Compared to Imperial States in the East c.1415–c.1839', *Journal of Chinese Economic and Business Studies*, 11 (2013), pp. 161–8.

O'Brien, P.K., and X. Duran, 'Total Factor Productivity for the Royal Navy from Victory at Texal (1653) to Triumph at Trafalgar (1805)', in R.W. Unger, *Shipping and Economic Growth 1350–1850* (Leiden, 2011), pp. 279–307.

O'Gorman, F., *Voters, Patrons, and Parties: the Unreformed Electorate of Hanoverian England 1734–1832* (Oxford, 1989.)

O'Gorman, F., *The Long Eighteenth Century: British Political and Social History, 1688–1832* (1997).

O'Shaughnessy, A.J., *An Empire Divided: the American Revolution and the British Caribbean* (Philadelphia, 2000).

Page, A., *John Jebb and the Enlightenment Origins of British Radicalism* (2003).

Pares, R., 'American versus Continental Warfare, 1739–63', *English Historical Review*, 51 (1936), pp. 429–65.

Peters, M., *Pitt and Popularity* (Oxford, 1980).

Philp, M., ed., *The French Revolution and British Popular Politics* (Cambridge, 1991).

Philp, M., 'Vulgar Conservatism, 1792–1793', English Historical Review, 110 (1995), pp. 42–69.

Philp, M., ed., *Resisting Napoleon: the British Response to the Threat of Invasion, 1797–1815* (Aldershot, 2006).

Pincus, S., *1688: The First Modern Revolution* (New Haven, CT, 2009).

Pocock, J.G.A., 'Conservative Enlightenment and Democratic Revolutions: the American and French cases in British perspective', *Government and Opposition*, 24 (1989), pp. 81–105.

Pocock, J.G.A., *Barbarism and Religion: Volume I, the Enlightenments of Edward Gibbon, 1736–1764* (Cambridge, 1999).

Pocock, J.G.A., *The Discovery of Islands: Essays in British History* (Cambridge, 2005).

Porter, R., *Enlightenment: Britain and the Creation of the Modern World* (2000).

Powell, M.J., *Britain and Ireland in the Eighteenth-Century Crisis of Empire* (2003).

Prest, W., *Albion Ascendant: English History 1660–1815* (Oxford, 1998).

Ramsay, N., 'Romanticism and War', *Literature Compass*, 3 (2006), pp. 117–26.

Ramsay, N., *The Military Memoir and Romantic Literary Culture, 1780–1835* (2012).

Randall, A., *Riotous Assemblies: Popular Protest in Hanoverian England* (Oxford, 2006).

Robbins, C., *The Eighteenth-Century Commonwealthman* (Cambridge, MA, 1959).

Rodger, N.A.M., 'The Continental Commitment in the Eighteenth Century', in L. Freedman, P. Hayes and R. O'Neill, eds., *War, Strategy and International Politics* (Oxford, 1992), pp. 39–55.

Rodger, N.A.M., *The Command of the Ocean: a Naval History of Britain, 1649–1815* (2005).

Rodger, N.A.M., 'From the "Military Revolution" to the "Fiscal-Naval State"', *Journal for Maritime Research*, 13 (2011), pp. 119–28.

Rogers, N., *Crowds, Culture and Politics in Georgian Britain* (Oxford, 1998).

Rogers, N., 'The Dynamic of News in Britain During the American War: the Case of Admiral Keppel', *Parliamentary History*, 25 (2006), pp. 49–67.

Rule, J., *The Vital Century: England's Developing Economy, 1714–1815* (1992).

Russell, G., 'The Army, the Navy and the Napoleonic Wars', in C.L. Johnson and C. Tuite, eds., *A Companion to Jane Austen* (2009), pp. 261–71.

Russell, G., *The Theatres of War: Performance, Politics and Society, 1793–1815* (Oxford, 1995).

Sanchez, R.T., ed., *War, State and Development: Fiscal-Military States in the Eighteenth Century* (Pamplona, 2007).

Scott, H.M., 'The Second "Hundred Years War", 1689–1815', *Historical Journal*, 35 (1992), pp. 443–69.

Scott, H.M., *The Birth of a Great Power System, 1740–1815* (Harlow, 2006).

Scott, H.M., 'The Seven Years War and Europe's Ancien Regime', *War in History*, 18 (2011), pp. 419–55.

Shy, J., 'The American Revolution: the Military Conflict Considered as a Revolutionary War', in S.G. Kurtz and J.H. Hutson, *Essays on the American Revolution* (Chapel Hill, NC, 1973), pp. 121–56.

Simms, B., 'Britain and Napoleon', *The Historical Journal*, 41 (1998), pp. 885–94.

Simms, B., *Three Victories and a Defeat: the Rise and Fall of the First British Empire* (2007).

Smith, H., *Georgian Monarchy: Politics and Culture, 1714–1760* (Cambridge, 2006).

Smyth, J., ed., *Revolution, Counter-Revolution, and Union: Ireland in the 1790s* (Cambridge, 2000).

Snape, M., *The Redcoat and Religion* (2005).

Speelman, P., *Henry Lloyd and the Military Enlightenment of Eighteenth-Century Europe* (Westport, CT, 2002).

St Clair, W., *The Reading Nation in the Romantic Period* (Cambridge, 2004).

Starkey, A., 'Paoli to Stony Point: Military Ethics and Weaponry during the American Revolution', *Journal of Military History*, 58 (1994), pp. 7–27.

Starkey, A., *War in the Age of the Enlightenment, 1700–1789* (Westport, CT, 2003).

Steppler, G.A., 'British Military Law, Discipline, and the Conduct of Regimental Courts Martial in the Later Eighteenth Century', *English Historical Review*, 102 (1987), pp. 859–86.

Storrs, C., ed., *The Fiscal-Military State in Eighteenth-Century Europe* (Farnham, 2009).

Tatum, W.P., 'Challenging the New Military History: The Case of Eighteenth-Century British Army Studies', *History Compass*, 5 (2007), pp. 72–84.

Taylor, B., and S. Knott, eds., *Women, Gender and Enlightenment* (Basingstoke, 2005).

Thompson, A.C., *George II* (New Haven, 2011).

Vickery, A., 'Golden Age to Separate Spheres? A Review of the Categories and Chronology of English Women's History', *Historical Journal*, 36 (1993), pp. 383–414.

Wahrman, D., 'The English Problem of Identity in the American Revolution', *American Historical Review*, 106 (2001), pp. 1236–62.

Wahrman, D., *The Making of the Modern Self* (New Haven, 2004).

Wells, R., *Insurrection: the British Experience, 1795–1803* (Gloucester, 1983).

Wells, R., *Wretched Faces: Famine in Wartime England, 1793–1801* (Gloucester, 1988).

Western, J.R., *The English Militia in the Eighteenth Century* (1965).

Wilkinson, C., *The British Navy and the State in the Eighteenth Century* (Woodbridge, 2004).

Wilson, K., *The Sense of the People* (Oxford, 1995).

Wilson, K., *Island Race: Englishness, Empire and Gender in the Eighteenth Century* (New York, 2003).

Wilson, K., ed., *A New Imperial History: Culture, Identity and Modernity in Britain and the Empire, 1660–1840* (Cambridge, 2004).

Wilson, K., 'How Nelson became a Hero', *The Historian*, 87 (2005), pp. 6–17.

Wilson, P., 'Warfare in the Old Regime 1648–1789', in J. Black, ed., *European Warfare 1453–1815* (1999), pp. 69–95.

Wrigley, E.A., *Energy and the English Industrial Revolution* (Cambridge, 2010).

Index